JOACHIM JEREMIAS

THE PARABLES OF JESUS

JOACHIM JEREMIAS

THE PARABLES
OF JESUS

SECOND REVISED EDITION

CHARLES SCRIBNER'S SONS
NEW YORK

5 7 9 11 13 15 17 19 K/P 20 18 16 14 12 10 8 6 4

Printed in the United States of America
Library of Congress Catalog
Card Number 63–22114
ISBN 0-684-16244-X

CONTENTS

ABBREVIATIONS

Bill.	H. L. Strack–P. Billerbeck, *Kommentar zum N.T. aus Talmud und Midrasch*, I–VI, Munich, 1922–61
BZNW	*Beihefte zur Zeitschrift für die neutestamentliche Wissenschaft*
Dodd	C. H. Dodd, *The Parables of the Kingdom*, London, 1935; Revised Edition, 1936 (I used the reprint of 1938). The Revised Edition, London, 1961 (also Fontana Books, 571 R, Glasgow, 1961), has been retouched in a few places, but not materially altered.
Hawkins	J. C. Hawkins, *Horae Synopticae₂*, Oxford, 1909
JThSt	*Journal of Theological Studies*
Jülicher I, II	A. Jülicher, *Die Gleichnisreden Jesu*, I, Tübingen, 1888; ₂1899 (= 1910); II, 1899 (= 1910)
Manson, Sayings	T. W. Manson, *The Sayings of Jesus*, London, 1937 (= 1949, 1950; the last-mentioned reprint is quoted)
Manson, Teaching	T. W. Manson, *The Teaching of Jesus₂*, Cambridge, 1935 (= 1948, the reprint is quoted)
NTS	*New Testament Studies*
RAC	*Reallexikon für Antike und Christentum*, Stuttgart, 1950 ff.
RB	*Revue Biblique*
B. T. D. Smith	B. T. D. Smith, *The Parables of the Synoptic Gospels*, Cambridge, 1937
ThLZ	*Theologische Literaturzeitung*
ThWBNT	G. Kittel, *Theologisches Wörterbuch zum Neuen Testament*, Stuttgart, 1933 ff. (English Translation, *Theological Dictionary of the New Testament*, Grand Rapids, 1964 ff., has virtually the same pagination)
ZDPV	*Zeitschrift des Deutschen Palästina-Vereins*
ZNW	*Zeitschrift für die neutestamentliche Wissenschaft*

FOREWORD

THIS TRANSLATION IS based on the eighth German edition (1970). As compared with the first English edition (1954) which was based on the third German edition (1954) the book has been thoroughly revised and considerably enlarged and the text has again been revised and updated in many places since the second English edition of 1963. More room has been allowed to the exegesis of the individual parables, particular attention being paid to interpreting them against their local Palestinian background. Besides, a discussion of the parables in the Gospel of Thomas, translated into German by O. Hofius, is included. It was an unexpected encouragement to me to find that they confirmed the results reached in the second section of my book to a considerable extent. I wish to express my gratitude to Professor S. H. Hooke who devoted his great skill as a translator to both English editions of this book, to Miss K. Downham, Assistant Editor of SCM Press, to Professor B. Gerrish of McCormick Theological Seminary, Chicago, Ill., and to my assistant, Dr. C. Burchard, who helped with the manuscript and the proofs.

How much the work is indebted for stimulus and instruction to C. H. Dodd's fundamentally important book *The Parables of the Kingdom₂*, London, 1936, is indicated at many points. Professor Dodd's book has opened a new era in the study of the parables; although differences of opinion with regard to some details may exist, yet it is unthinkable that there should ever be any retreat from the essential lines laid down by Dodd for the interpretation of the parables of Jesus. My own contribution is the attempt to arrive at the earliest attainable form of Jesus' parabolic teaching. It is to be hoped that the reader will perceive that the aim of the critical analysis contained in the second part of this book is nothing less than a return, as well grounded as possible, to the very words of Jesus himself. Only the Son of Man and his word can invest our message with full authority.

Göttingen
February 1962
February 1972

JOACHIM JEREMIAS

I

THE PROBLEM

THE STUDENT OF the parables of Jesus, as they have been
transmitted to us in the first three Gospels, may be confident
that he stands upon a particularly firm historical foundation.
The parables are a fragment of the original rock of tradition. It is a
generally accepted fact that pictures leave a deeper impress on the
mind than abstractions. Among the special characteristics of the
parables of Jesus is the fact that everywhere they reflect with peculiar
clarity the character of his good news, the eschatological nature of
his preaching, the intensity of his summons to repentance, and his
conflict with Pharisaism.[1] Everywhere behind the Greek text we get
glimpses of Jesus' mother tongue.[2] Also the pictorial element of the
parables is drawn from the daily life of Palestine. It is noteworthy,
for instance, that the sower in Mark 4.3–8 sows so clumsily that much
of the seed is wasted; one might have expected a description of the
regular method of sowing, and that, in fact, is what we have here.
This is easily understood when we remember that in Palestine sowing
precedes ploughing.[3] Hence, in the parable the sower is depicted as

[1] H. D. Wendland, 'Von den Gleichnissen Jesu und ihrer Botschaft', in *Die
Theologin*, 11 (1941), pp. 17–29.

[2] From the great number of examples one may be selected, namely, the frequency, especially in the parables and similitudes, with which the definite article
is used where we translate by the indefinite (Mark 4.3, 4, 5, 7, 8, 15, 16, 18, 20,
21, 26; Matt. 5.15; 7.6, 24–27 and elsewhere). The usage is characteristic of
Semitic imagery. Already we find in the O.T. the use of the definite article with
an indefinite meaning often in parables and pictorial narratives. In such cases
the Semite thinks pictorially and has an image in his mind of a concrete instance,
though he may be speaking of a general phenomenon.

[3] G. Dalman, 'Viererlei Acker', in *Palästina-Jahrbuch*, 22 (1926), pp. 120–32.
b. Shab. 73b: 'In Palestine ploughing comes after sowing'; this is still done today
(G. Dalman, *Arbeit und Sitte in Palästina*, II, Gütersloh, 1932, pp. 179 ff.). Tos.
Ber. 7.2 mentions eleven successive processes leading up to the finished product:
'he sows, ploughs, reaps, binds the sheaves, threshes . . .'; Shab. 7.2, *'Sowing,*

striding over the unploughed stubble, and this enables us to understand why he sows 'on[4] the path': he sows intentionally on the path
which the villagers have trodden over the stubble,[5] since he intends
to plough the seed in when he ploughs up the path. He sows intentionally among the thorns standing withered in the fallow because
they, too, will be ploughed up. Nor need it surprise us that some
grains should fall upon rocky ground; the underlying limestone,
thinly covered with soil, barely shows above the surface until the
ploughshare jars against it. What appears to the western mind as
bad farming is simply customary usage in Palestinian conditions.

Further, Jesus' parables are something entirely new. In all the
rabbinic literature, not one single parable has come down to us from
the period before Jesus; only two similes from Rabbi Hillel (c. 20 BC),
who jokingly compared the body with a statue, and the soul with a
guest (Lev. r. 34 on 25.35). It is among the sayings of Rabban
Jochanan ben Zakkai (d.c. AD 80) that we first meet with a parable
(see p. 188 below). As its imagery resembles one of Jesus' parables, we
may well ask whether Jesus' model (together with other factors, such
as Greek animal fables) did not have an important influence on the
rabbi's adopting parables as a narrative form.

The uniqueness of Jesus' parables comes out clearly when they are
compared with analogous productions from the same period and
cultural context, such as the Pauline similitudes or the rabbinic
parables. Comparison reveals a definite personal style, a singular
clarity and simplicity, a matchless mastery of construction. The conclusion is inevitable that we are dealing with particularly trustworthy
tradition. We stand right before Jesus when reading his parables.

Not only do the parables of Jesus regarded as a whole represent a
specially reliable tradition, but they also present the appearance of
being entirely free from problematic elements. The hearers find
themselves in a familiar scene where everything is so simple and

---

ploughing . . .' (yet these are also given in reverse order in some rabbinical texts
cf. Dalman, op. cit., p. 195). A relevant example is quoted by W. G. Essame in
'Sowing and Ploughing', in *Exp. T.*, 72 (1960–1), p. 54b, 'Prince Mastema sent
ravens and birds to devour the seed which was sown in the earth . . . before they
could *plough in the seed* the ravens plucked it from the surface of the ground' (Jub.
11.11). Cf. most recently, J. Jeremias, *NTS*, 13 (1966–7), pp. 48–53.

[4] παρὰ τὴν ὁδόν (Mark 4.4; Matt. 13.4; Luke 8.5) is, like the Aramaic *'al
'orḥa*, ambiguous and may mean (a) 'on the path', or (b) 'beside the path'. The
context makes it quite clear that (a) was the meaning intended, particularly
κατεπατήθη (Luke 8.5); cf. C. C. Torrey, *The Four Gospels*, London, 1933, p. 98.
The Gospel of Thomas 9 understands it in the same sense: 'some seeds fell *on* the
path'. [5] G. Dalman, in *Palästina-Jahrbuch*, 22 (1926), pp. 121–3.

clear that a child can understand, so plain that those who hear can say, 'Yes, that's how it is.' Nevertheless, the parables confront us with the difficult problem of recovering their original meaning.

Already in the earliest period of all, during the first decades after the death of Jesus, the parables had undergone a certain amount of reinterpretation. At a very early stage the process of treating the parables as allegories had begun, a process which for centuries concealed the meaning of the parables under a thick layer of dust. Many circumstances contributed to this result. At first there may have been an unconscious desire to discover a deeper meaning in the simple words of Jesus. In the Hellenistic world it was usual to interpret the myths as vehicles of esoteric knowledge, and in Hellenistic Judaism allegorical exegesis was highly esteemed; hence it was to be expected that Christian teachers would resort to the same method.[6] In the succeeding period a stimulus was given to the tendency by the fact that there were four Gospel parables which had received a detailed allegorical interpretation of individual features (Mark 4.14–20 par.; Matt. 13.37–43, 49–50; John 10.7–18). But above all, the 'hardening' theory which regarded the parables as intended to conceal the mystery of the Kingdom of God from outsiders, led to the predominance of the allegorical method of interpretation.

We shall discuss the allegorizing interpretation of the parables on p. 77 ff., 81 ff., but here, in view of the fundamental importance of the passage, something must be said about Mark 4.10–12 par., the 'hardening' theory.

In order to understand the passage it is necessary first of all to recognize that the grouping of the parables in Mark 4.1–34 is an artificial one. This is shown (1) by the contradictory details in the description of the situation: according to v. 1 Jesus is teaching the crowd out of the boat, and v. 36 resumes this detail: the disciples row him over the lake 'even as he was, in the boat'. But in v. 10 this detail has been long since forgotten. (2) Parallel with this break in the situation goes a change of audience: in vv. 1 f. Jesus is addressing the crowd, as also in v. 33, cf. v. 36; but this is incompatible with v. 10, where we find Jesus replying to the questions of a narrower circle (οἱ περὶ αὐτὸν σὺν τοῖς δώδεκα). Hence v. 10 reveals a join in the narrative. (3) This join in v. 10 is explained by the recognition of the fact that on decisive linguistic grounds (see pp. 77 f.) the interpretation of the parable of the Sower (4.14–20) must be assigned to a later stage of the tradition than the parable itself. (4) But the recognition that Mark 4.10–20 does not belong to the oldest layer

[6] C. H. Dodd, *The Parables of the Kingdom*, London, 1935, Revised edition, 1936=1938, p. 15 (henceforward cited as Dodd).

of tradition fails to exhaust the literary-critical problems with which
Mark 4.10–12 presents us. It must further be observed that the question which is put to Jesus in v. 10 ('they asked him about the
parables'[7]) receives a double answer with two different introductory
formulae: in vv. 11 f. Jesus says why he is speaking in parables, and in
vv. 13 ff. he interprets the parable of the Sower. Nothing in v. 10
suggests that Jesus was asked why he usually spoke in parables;
rather does the reproach in v. 13 with which the interpretation is
rightly connected suggest that the question in v. 10 originally related
to the meaning of the parable of the Sower. Thus vv. 11 f. break the
connection between v. 10 and vv. 13 ff.

The view that vv. 11 f. is actually an insertion into an older context is confirmed by the introductory phrase καὶ ἔλεγεν αὐτοῖς (v. 11),
which is one of Mark's typical link-phrases (2.27; 4.2, 21, 24; 6.10;
7.9; 8.21; 9.1).[8] This also explains the unusual [9] detailed description
of the audience οἱ περὶ αὐτὸν σὺν τοῖς δώδεκα: it may be an inci-
dental adaptation of vv. 11 f. arising from the addition of two
different groups of hearers.[10] From this it results that vv. 11 f. is a
logion belonging to a wholly independent tradition, which was
adapted by Mark to the word παραβολή (vv. 10–11), and must
therefore be interpreted without reference to its present context.[11]

[7] The plural τὰς παραβολάς (v. 10) is probably neither a reference to v. 2
(καὶ ἐδίδασκεν αὐτοὺς ἐν παραβολαῖς πολλά), nor one of the generalizing plurals
common in the Gospels (for this Semitism, cf. p. 68, n. 75), but it should be
regarded as a Marcan alteration due to the insertion of vv. 11 f.

[8] The Marcan link-phrase καὶ ἔλεγεν αὐτοῖς must be distinguished from the
simple καὶ ἔλεγεν which occurs in the Gospel of Mark only in 4.9, 26, 30 and may
be pre-Marcan; a parallel is to be found in the common introduction to rabbinical
sayings by the words hu haya 'omer (e.g. in Pirqe 'Abhoth).

[9] The only analogy (though of a different kind) is to be found in Mark 8.34.

[10] Ch. Masson, Les Paraboles de Marc IV, Neuchâtel-Paris, 1945, p. 29, n. 1. οἱ
δώδεκα is characteristic of Mark himself.

[11] In view of what has been said above, it may be conjectured that there were
three stages in the growth of the material of Mark 4.1 ff.: (1) The tradition
brought together the three parables of Jesus known as the Sower, the Seed growing by itself, and the Mustard-seed; they are linked by καὶ ἔλεγεν. (2) Marked by
the altered situation already mentioned (v. 10) a question was inserted, and as its
answer the interpretation of the parable of the Sower (vv. 10, 13–20); v. 33 also
belongs to this stage of the tradition, as the absolute use of ὁ λόγος shows (cf. p. 77).
(3) With the formula καὶ ἔλεγεν αὐτοῖς (vv. 11, 21, 24), Mark has introduced in
vv. 11 f. by means of the term παραβολαί a second answer to the question in v. 10, and
has also added two more parables (the one about Light in vv. 21–23, and about
Measure in vv. 24 f., see p. 91, below). Moreover, he has worked over the framework: πάλιν, ἤρξατο, συνάγεται (historic present), καὶ ἔλεγεν αὐτοῖς, διδαχή (vv. 1 f.)
are linguistic characteristics of Mark; he has expanded the details about the
audience in v. 10 by the addition of vv. 11 f. and has at the same time provided the
plural τὰς παραβολάς; v. 34, too, must come from him, since the phrase χωρὶς δὲ
παραβολῆς is a reference to v. 11b. The three stages of the tradition (Jesus . . . the
primitive Church . . . Mark) are recognizable throughout the whole of Mark's
Gospel, but nowhere so clearly as in ch. 4.

We may assume, therefore, that Mark 4.11–12 is a very early logion. It is earlier than Mark,[12] and comes from a Palestinian tradition. The antithetic parallelism (v. 11),[13] the redundant demonstrative ἐκείνοις (v. 11b),[14] and the circumlocution thrice used to indicate the divine activity,[15] are typically Palestinian. But above all we must observe that the free quotation from Isa. 6.9 f. in Mark 4.12 varies widely from the Hebrew text and from the LXX, while it agrees with the Targum. (1) Whereas in the Hebrew text and the LXX Isa. 6.9b is couched in the 2nd person, i.e. in oratio recta, Mark 4.12a (ἵνα βλέποντες βλέπωσιν, etc.) and the Targum have the 3rd person.[16] Moreover, only in the Targum have the participles βλέποντες and ἀκούοντες (Mark 4.12a) a participial equivalent (ḥazan, šam‛in). (2) Still more striking is the fact, pointed out by Manson, but calling for further discussion, of the agreement between Mark 4.12b and the Targum of Isa. 6.10. The text of Mark καὶ ἀφεθῇ αὐτοῖς departs completely from the Hebrew text (w‛rapha' lo), as also from the LXX (καὶ ἰάσομαι αὐτούς) and Symmachus (καὶ ἰαθῇ), but on the other hand it agrees with the Peshitta (w‛nešt‛bheq leh), and even more closely with the Targum (w‛yišt‛bheq l‛hon). This agreement between Mark and the Targum extends to details: (a) instead of the verb 'heal' (Isa. 6.10 Heb., LXX, Sym.) Mark and Targum have 'forgive'; [17] (b) instead of the sing. lo (Isa. 6.10 Heb.) both have the pl.; [18] (c) both avoid the use of the divine name by means of the passive. Hence Mark follows the paraphrase of Isa. 6.9 f. commonly used in the synagogue and known to us through the Peshitta and the written Targum. The recognition of this agreement 'creates a strong presumption in favour of the authenticity' of our logion [19] and is of fundamental importance for the exegesis of Mark 4.11 f.

[12] The concordance readily shows that. μυστήριον, δέδοται as a circumlocution of the divine action, οἱ ἔξω, τὰ πάντα, ἐπιστρέφειν used for conversion, all that appears in Mark only at 4.11 f. Furthermore, our passage limits the application of Isa. 6.9 f. to οἱ ἔξω, whereas Mark himself extends it to the disciples, as 8.14–21 shows.
[13] C. F. Burney, The Poetry of Our Lord, Oxford, 1925, pp. 20 f., 71 ff.
[14] J. Jeremias, The Eucharistic Words of Jesus, London, 1966, p. 184, nn. 1–3.
[15] v. 11: δέδοται, γίνεται; v. 12: ἀφεθῇ.
[16] T. W. Manson, The Teaching of Jesus₂, Cambridge, 1948 (1935₁), p. 77 (in future cited as T. W. Manson, Teaching).
[17] Targ. derives rapha' (Isa. 6.10 with final aleph means 'to heal') from raphah (with final hē means 'to remit'), as do the Pesh. and Mark.
[18] So previously: Mark ἐπιστρέψωσιν, Targ. withubhun (Isa. 6.10 Heb. has the sing.).
[19] T. W. Manson, Teaching, p. 77.

In v. 11 we find an antithesis between the disciples of Jesus ('to you') and those who are 'outside' (ἔξω). 'And he said to them: "To you has God [20] given the secret of the Kingdom of God".' This is surely nothing less than a cry of exultation! God's gift is for the disciples. Moreover, 'the secret of the Kingdom of God' which constitutes God's gift must not be understood as implying general information about the coming Kingdom of God, but, as the singular shows, a particular piece of information, the recognition of its dawn in the present.[21] This recognition is wholly the result of God's grace. In v. 11 a sharp contrast is drawn between the disciples and those who are without: ἐκείνοις δὲ τοῖς ἔξω ἐν παραβολαῖς τὰ πάντα γίνεται. Here two linguistic points must be noticed. (1) The contrasting parallelism of the two clauses v. 11a and v. 11b requires that μυστήριον and παραβολή should correspond. But this does not happen if παραβολή is translated by 'parable', but only if παραβολή is given the usual meaning of its Hebrew equivalent mašal and Aramaic mathla, viz. 'riddle'.[22] This gives us the required antithesis: to you the secret is revealed; those outside are confronted by riddles! There is an antithesis with similar content in John 16.25, where there is a contrast, in reverse order, between παροιμίαις λαλεῖν and παρρησίᾳ ἀπαγγέλλειν = speak in veiled discourse (not: in parables!) and proclaim openly. (2) γίνεσθαι 'to happen', used as an impersonal verb with the person in the dative and the thing in the nominative, is not idiomatic Greek but a semitism. It renders an Aramaic hᵃwa lᵉ 'to belong to someone, to happen to someone, to be assigned to someone'. It is followed by bᵉ (ἐν Mark 4.11), e.g., Gen. 15.1, 'The word of the Lord came unto Abraham in a vision'. Hence Mark 4.11b must be translated: 'But to those who are without all

[20] The passive δέδοται is used as a circumlocution for the divine name.

[21] A. Jülicher, *Die Gleichnisreden Jesu*, I₂, Tübingen, 1899 (=1910), pp. 123 f. (in future cited as Jülicher, I); J. Schniewind in *Das Neue Testament Deutsch*, I, on Mark 4.11; G. Bornkamm, *ThWBNT*, IV, pp. 824 f.; M. Hermaniuk, *La parabole évangélique*, Bruges-Paris-Louvain, 1947, p. 282.

[22] Examples: *Mašal* is synonymous (as already in the O.T.: Ezek. 17.2; Hab. 2.6; Ps. 49.5; 78.2; Prov. 1.6) in Sirach (47.17, possibly also in 39.2, 3) and in IV Ezra (4.3) with *ḥidha* (riddle, dark saying); in Eth. Enoch the Ethiopic *mesal* has the meaning of an apocalyptic secret (37.5; 38.1; 45.1; 57.3; 58.1; 68.1; 69.29), similarly Num. r. 14 on 7.89: 'With Moses God spoke face to face, but with Balaam only in mᵉšalim (oracles)'; Targ. on II Chron. 9.1 renders the Heb. *ḥidhoth* by *mithlawan dᵉḥidhin*. The same holds good for παραβολή. Sir. 47.17 renders *ḥidha* by παραβολή, 47.15 has παραβολαὶ αἰνιγμάτων, and 39.3 has αἰνίγματα παραβολῶν. In Mark 7.17 παραβολή has the meaning 'dark saying, riddle', so too Barn. 6.10; 17.2 and occasionally in the Shep. of Herm. (cf. O. Eissfeldt, *Der Maschal im Alten Testament*, Giessen, 1913, pp. 17–19; Jülicher, I, pp. 40, 204 f.). In John 16.25, 29 παροιμία, as opposed to παρρησία, also means 'dark saying' (cf. J. A. T. Robinson, 'The Parable of the Shepherd (John 10.1–5)', *Twelve New Testament Studies*, London, 1962, pp. 67 ff.

things are imparted in riddles,'[23] i.e. they remain obscure for them. In order to understand the ἵνα-clause of Mark 4.12 which follows it is imperative that the words coming after ἵνα should be regarded as a free quotation from Isa. 6.9 f., and as if in inverted commas. Hence the ἵνα is not expressing the purpose of Jesus but that of God; in fact it almost amounts to an abbreviation of ἵνα πληρωθῇ, and is therefore to be translated 'in order that': 'in the case of divine decisions purpose and fulfilment are identical.'[24] The verse therefore reads: 'in order that (as it is written) they "may see and yet not see, may hear and yet not understand".' Finally, so far as the μήποτε-clause of Mark 4.12 (μήποτε ἐπιστρέψωσιν καὶ ἀφεθῇ αὐτοῖς) is concerned, the μήποτε, like the Aramaic dilᵉma underlying it, is ambiguous; both words can mean (1) 'in order that not', and (2) 'lest perhaps',[25] while dilᵉma in addition can mean (3) 'unless'. The μήποτε from the LXX of Isa. 6.10, as a rendering of the Hebrew pen, is better understood in the first sense ('in order that not'); the meaning of the dilᵉma of the Targum on Isa. 6.10b is different. In whatever way the Targumist himself may have understood it, rabbinical exegesis took it to mean 'unless', as may be gathered from the fact that it regarded the conclusion of Isa. 6.10 absolutely as a promise that God would forgive his people if they repented.[26] This contemporary interpretation of Isa. 6.10b as a promise of forgiveness must also be presupposed for Mark 4.12b, since the wording of the end of Mark 4.12, as we saw on p. 15, shows a detailed agreement with the Targum translation of Isa. 6.10b. The μήποτε of Mark 4.12 is therefore a rendering of the Targumic dilᵉma, and must be rendered 'unless'. Hence we must translate Mark 4.11 f.: 'To you has God given the secret of the Kingdom of God; but to those who are without everything is obscure, in order that they (as it is written) may "see and yet not see, may hear and yet not understand, unless they turn and God [27] will forgive them".' Hence we conclude that the logion is not concerned with the parables of Jesus,

[23] Similarly, Ch. Masson, *Les Paraboles de Marc IV*, Neuchâtel-Paris, 1945, p. 28: 'But for those who are without, everything takes place in symbols.'

[24] W. Bauer, *Wörterbuch zum N.T.₅*, Berlin, 1958, col. 747. It is also possible that the Aram. dᵉ underlying the ἵνα as in the Targ. on Isa. 6.9, had the force of a relative pronoun: 'For those who are without everything remains obscure, who "see and yet do not see"' (T. W. Manson, *Teaching*, pp. 76 ff.). The meaning is the same. [25] μήποτε frequently has both meanings in the LXX.

[26] H. L. Strack–P. Billerbeck, *Kommentar zum Neuen Testament aus Talmud und Midrasch*, 6 vols., Munich 1922–61 (in future cited as Bill.), in I, pp. 662 f. gives four examples of the rabbinical exegesis of Isa. 6.10b; they all agree in understanding Isa. 6.10b, not as a threat of final hardening, but as a promise.

[27] The passive ἀφεθῇ is another case (like δέδοται in Mark 4.11) of avoidance of the use of the divine name by means of the passive.

but with his preaching in general.[28] The secret of the present Kingdom is disclosed to the disciples, but to the outsiders the words of
Jesus remain obscure because they do not recognize his mission nor
repent. Thus for them the terrible oracle of Isa. 6.9 f. is fulfilled. Yet
a hope still remains: 'if they repent God will forgive them'. The last
words afford a glimpse of God's forgiving mercy.

On account of the sharp contrast between the disciples and the
outsiders [29] which it presents, the logion, of whose antiquity mention
was made on p. 15, may not be earlier than the confession of Peter,
the period of the secret teaching of Jesus. It describes the perpetual
twofold issue of all preaching of the gospel: the offer of mercy and
the threat of judgement inseparable from it (Isa. 6.9 f.), deliverance
and offence, salvation and destruction, life and death.[30] But Mark,
misled by the catchword παραβολή, which he erroneously understood as 'parable', inserted our logion into the parable-chapter.[31] If,
however, Mark 4.11 f. has no reference whatever to the parables of
Jesus, then the passage affords no criterion for the interpretation of
the parables, nor any warrant for seeking to find in them by means
of an allegorical interpretation some secret meaning hidden from
the outsiders. On the contrary, Mark 4.11 f. asserts that the parables
too, like all the words of Jesus, announce no special 'secrets', but only
the one 'secret of the Kingdom of God', to wit, the secret of its
present dawning in the words and work of Jesus.[32]

It is well known that we owe to A. Jülicher the final discarding of
the allegorical method of interpretation. It is positively alarming to
read in his *History of the Interpretation of the Parables of Jesus* [33] the
story of the centuries of distortion and ill-usage which the parables
have suffered through allegorical interpretation. Only against such
a background is it possible to estimate the extent of the liberation achieved when Jülicher not merely proved incontestably by
hundreds of cases that allegorizing leads to error, but also maintained
the fundamental position that it is utterly alien to the parables of
Jesus. Although the emphasis may have been one-sided (current
apocalyptic from Daniel onwards uses allegory in order to present

[28] Cf. John 16.25a, where the whole of Jesus' preaching is designated as speaking ἐν παροιμίαις (cf. Mark 4.11b: ἐν παραβολαῖς).
[29] For the same contrast in another metaphor cf. Matt. 11.25 f. par.
[30] J. Schniewind in *Das Neue Testament Deutsch*, I, on Mark 4.12.
[31] Mark 4.10 was originally followed by v. 13 (see above, pp. 13 f.).
[32] See p. 16 and J. Horst in *ThWBNT*, V, p. 553, n. 102.
[33] Jülicher, I, pp. 203–322.

its revelations in a veiled form to avoid political attack; to a lesser degree, rabbinical literature does the same),[34] nevertheless his work remains fundamental; isolated reversions to the allegorical method in recent studies can only serve to confirm this judgement.

But, as none has better shown than C. H. Dodd, Jülicher left the work half done.[35] His struggle to free the parables from the fantastic and arbitrary allegorical interpretations of every detail caused Jülicher to fall into a fatal error. In his view the surest safeguard against such arbitrary treatment lay in regarding the parables as a piece of real life and in drawing from each of them a single idea and (here lay the error) of the widest possible generality. The broadest application will prove to be the true one. 'The story of the rich man and poor Lazarus was intended to induce joy in a life of suffering, and fear of the life of pleasure' (Luke 16.19–31).[36] That 'even the richest of men is at every moment wholly dependent upon the power and mercy of God' is the lesson of the parable of the Rich Fool (Luke 12.16 ff.).[37] 'Wise use of the present as the condition of a happy future' is the lesson of the parable of the Unjust Steward (Luke 16.1–8).[38] The original form of Matt. 24.45–51 was intended to stir up the disciples to 'the most earnest fulfilment of their duty toward God'.[39] 'A reward is only earned by performance' is the fundamental idea of the parable of the Talents (Matt. 25.14 ff.).[40] We are told that the parables announce a genuine religious humanity; they are stripped of their eschatological import. Imperceptibly Jesus is transformed into an 'apostle of progress' (II, p. 483), a teacher of wisdom who inculcates moral precepts and a simplified theology by means of striking metaphors and stories. But nothing could be less like him. Unfortunately Jülicher stopped half-way. He cleansed the parables from the thick layer of dust with which the allegorical interpretation had covered them, but after achieving this preliminary task he did not move forward. The main task still remains to be done: the attempt must be made to recover the original meaning of the parables. How can this be done?

[34] I. Heinemann, *Altjüd. Allegoristik*, Breslau, 1936; Bill. III, pp. 388–99.
[35] Dodd, pp. 24 ff.
[36] A. Jülicher, *Die Gleichnisreden Jesu*, II, Tübingen, 1899 (=1910), p. 638 (in future cited as Jülicher, II).
[37] Jülicher, II, p. 616.
[38] Op. cit., p. 511.
[39] Op. cit., p. 161.
[40] Op. cit., p. 495.

The effect of Jülicher's work was so overwhelming that for a long time no special studies on the parables of any significance appeared. At last the Form-criticism school essayed an advance along the lines of a classification of the parables according to categories. A distinction was drawn between metaphor, simile, parable, similitude, allegory, illustration, and so forth—a fruitless labour in the end, since the Hebrew *mašal* and the Aramaic *mathla* embraced all these categories and many more without distinction. This word may mean in the common speech of post-biblical Judaism, without resorting to a formal classification, figurative forms of speech of every kind: parable,[41] similitude,[42] allegory,[43] fable,[44] proverb,[45] apocalyptic revelation,[46] riddle,[47] symbol,[48] pseudonym,[49] fictitious person,[50] example,[51] theme,[52] argument,[53] apology,[54] refutation,[55] jest.[56] Similarly παραβολή in the New Testament has not only the meaning 'parable', but also 'comparison' (Luke 5.36; Mark 3.23) and 'symbol' (Heb. 9.9; 11.19; cf. Mark 13.28); in Luke 4.23 it should be rendered 'proverb' or 'commonplace', in 6.39 'proverb'; in Mark 7.17 it means 'riddle'[57] and in Luke 14.7 simply 'rule'. Similarly, the meaning of παροιμία varies between 'parable' (John 10.6), 'proverb' (II Peter 2.22), and 'riddle' (John 16.25, 29). The word 'parable' is used in this study, as I should like to emphasize, in the broad sense of *mašal* or *mathla*. To force the parables of Jesus into the categories of Greek rhetoric is to impose upon them an alien law.[58] Indeed no progress was achieved along this line. The fundamentally important insights which we owe to the Form-criticism school have so far received no

[41] Numerous examples.
[42] b. Pes. 49a.
[43] Mech. Ex. 21.19 par. cf. Bill., III, p. 391.
[44] IV Ezra 4.13 (Armenian); b. Ber. 61b; b. Sukka 28a; b. Sanh. 38b.
[45] Midr. Lam. Prooemium 24, cf. W. Bacher, *Die exegetische Terminologie der jüdischen Traditionsliteratur*, II, Leipzig, 1905, p. 121.
[46] See above, p. 16, n. 22.
[47] Ibid.
[48] b. Sanh. 92b.
[49] Nidda 2.5.
[50] b. B.B. 15a; b. 'Er. 63a.
[51] Ex. r. 40 on 31.1 f.
[52] b. Keth. 22ab.
[53] j. Yoma 3.41d.
[54] j. Keth. 2.26c.
[55] Giṭ. 9.9; b. Giṭ. 88b, 89ab.
[56] b. Pes. 114a.
[57] See above, p. 16, n. 22.
[58] J. Wellhausen, *Das Evangelium Marci₂*, Berlin, 1909, p. 29.

fruitful application in the field of the study of the parables.[59]

The point of view which decisively opened the way to further advance was, if I mistake not, first put forward by A. T. Cadoux,[60] who laid down the principle that the parables must be placed in the setting of the life of Jesus. Unfortunately, the way in which Cadoux attempted to develop this correct perception in his book was open to objections, so that the value of his work was limited to acute comments on details. B. T. D. Smith[61] followed more cautiously along this line, and in many passages succeeded in illuminating the historical background of the parables; it is the more to be regretted that he confined himself to the factual details of the parables, and did not deal with their theological interpretation. But it was C. H. Dodd's book [62] which achieved a break-through in the direction first indicated by Cadoux. In this extraordinarily significant book for the first time a really successful attempt was made to place the parables in the setting of the life of Jesus, thereby introducing a new era in the interpretation of the parables. Nevertheless Dodd limited his attention to the parables of the Kingdom of Heaven, and the one-sided nature of his conception of the Kingdom (Dodd's whole emphasis being laid on the view that in the works of Jesus the Kingdom had now finally broken through), resulted in a contraction of the eschatology which has continued to exercise an influence upon his otherwise masterly interpretation.

What we have to deal with is a conception which is essentially simple but involves far-reaching consequences. It is that the parables of Jesus are not—at any rate primarily—literary productions, nor is it their object to lay down general maxims ('no one would crucify a teacher who told pleasant stories to enforce prudential morality'[63]), but each of them was uttered in an actual situation of the life of Jesus, at a particular and often unforeseen point. Moreover, as we shall see, they were mostly concerned with a situation of conflict— with justification, defence, attack, and even challenge. For the most part, though not exclusively, they are weapons of controversy. Every one of them calls for an answer on the spot.

[59] For the form-critical analysis of the parables, see below, pp. 25 ff., esp. pp. 90 ff.
[60] *The Parables of Jesus. Their Art and Use*, New York, 1931.
[61] *The Parables of the Synoptic Gospels*, Cambridge, 1937 (in future cited as B. T. D. Smith).
[62] *The Parables of the Kingdom*, London, 1935, Revised Edition, 1936. I have used the reprint of 1938.
[63] C. W. F. Smith, *The Jesus of the Parables*, Philadelphia, 1948, p. 17.

The recognition of this fact indicates the nature of our task. Jesus spoke to men of flesh and blood; he addressed himself to the situation of the moment. Each of his parables has a definite historical setting. Hence to recover this is the task before us.[64] What did Jesus intend to say at this or that particular moment? What must have been the effect of his word upon his hearers? These are the questions we must ask in order, so far as may be possible, to recover the original meaning of the parables of Jesus, to hear again his authentic voice.

[64] 'It is perhaps possible by glancing at the collection of parables in Matt. 13 to explain the problem thus: it is as though all that remained to us of the preaching of a celebrated preacher of our time were a collection of illustrative stories' (F. C. Grant, 'A New Book on the Parables', *Anglican Theological Review*, 30 (1948), p. 119). Such a collection could give us an idea of their full value only if we knew in every case what ideas of the preacher were intended to be illustrated by each individual example. Similarly we shall understand rightly each individual parable in the collection of Matt. 13 only if we can reconstruct for ourselves the precise situation in which Jesus uttered it.

II

THE RETURN TO JESUS FROM
THE PRIMITIVE CHURCH

As they have come down to us, the parables of Jesus have a double historical setting.[1] (1) The original historical setting of the parables, as of all his utterances, is some specific situation in the pattern of the activity of Jesus. Many of the parables are so vividly told that it is natural to assume that they arise out of some actual occurrence.[2] (2) But subsequently, before they assumed a written form, they 'lived' in the primitive Church, of whose proclamations, preaching, and teaching, the words of Jesus were the content, in its missionary activities, in its assemblies, or in its catechetical instruction. It collected and arranged the sayings of Jesus according to their subject-matter, created a setting for them, sometimes modifying their form, expanding here, allegorizing there, always in relation to its own situation between the Cross and the *Parousia*. In our study of the parables of Jesus it is important to bear in mind the difference between the situation of Jesus and that of the primitive Church. In many cases it will be necessary to remove sayings and parables of Jesus from their setting in the life and thought of the primitive Church, in the attempt to recover their original setting in the life of Jesus,[3] if we are to hear once more the original tones of the utterances of Jesus, and to experience anew the vital qualities of force, conflict, and authority in the historical events. As soon as we attempt to ascertain the original historical setting of the parables, we meet with certain definite principles of transformation.

[1] Dodd, p. 111.
[2] The Unjust Steward (Luke 16.1 ff., cf. p. 182), the Tares among the Wheat (Matt. 13.24 ff., cf. p. 224), the Burglar (Matt. 24.43 f., cf. p. 49), perhaps, too, the Rich Fool (Luke 12.16 ff.) and the Good Samaritan (Luke 10.30 ff.), cf. M. Meinertz, *Die Gleichnisse Jesu*₄, Münster, 1948, p. 64.
[3] Dodd, p. 111.

The fact that the Gospel of Thomas[4] provides us with its own version[5] of eleven of the synoptic parables is a great help in making this attempt.

They are as follows:

Logion   9   The Sower (cf. p. 28).
 ,,   20   The Mustard Seed (cf. p. 146).
 ,,   21b and 103   The Burglar (cf. pp. 87, 95).
 ,,   57   The Tares among the Wheat (cf. p. 224).
 ,,   63   The Rich Fool (cf. p. 164, n. 62).
 ,,   64   The Great Supper (cf. p. 176).
 ,,   65   The Wicked Husbandmen (cf. pp. 70–72).
 ,,   76   The Pearl (cf. p. 199).
 ,,   96   The Leaven (cf. p. 146).
 ,,   107   The Lost Sheep (cf. p. 133).
 ,,   109   The Treasure (cf. p. 32).[6]

	Synoptic	Gospel of Thomas
Mark	6	3
Material common to Matt.–Luke	10	4
Special Matt.	10	3
Special Luke	15	1

[4] The numbering of the logia follows that given in *The Gospel according to Thomas*, Coptic Text edited and translated by A. Guillaumont, H.-Ch. Puech, G. Quispel, W. Till and †Yassah 'Abd al Masīh, Leiden, 1959.

[5] Literature relating to the parables in the Gospel of Thomas: L. Cerfaux-G. Garitte, 'Les Paraboles du Royaume dans l'Évangile de Thomas', in *Le Muséon*, 70 (1957), pp. 307–27; A. J. B. Higgins, 'Non-Gnostic Sayings in the Gospel of Thomas', in *Novum Testamentum*, 4 (1960), pp. 292–306; C.-H. Hunzinger, 'Unbekannte Gleichnisse Jesu aus dem Thomas-Evangelium', in *Judentum, Urchristentum, Kirche* (BZNW 26), Berlin, 1960, pp. 209–20; H. Montefiore, 'A Comparison of the Parables of the Gospel according to Thomas and of the Synoptic Gospels', in *NTS*, 7 (1960–61), pp. 220–48.

[6] The Gospel of Thomas also contains four more parables not found in the N.T.:

Logion   8   The Great Fish (cf. p. 201).
 ,,   21a   The Little Children in the Field.
 ,,   97   The Careless Woman.
 ,,   98   The Slayer (cf. pp. 196 f.).

I. THE TRANSLATION OF THE PARABLES INTO GREEK

Jesus spoke Galilean Aramaic.[7] The task of translating his sayings into Greek, which was undertaken at an early date, necessarily involved, sometimes to a considerable, but generally only to a slight degree, innumerable alterations in their meaning. Hence the re-translation of the parables into the mother-tongue of Jesus is perhaps the most important aid to the recovery of their original meaning.[8] It is to be hoped that the numerous examples given in this book will establish the truth of this statement better than theoretical conjectures.

Every intelligent person will realize the tentative nature of such retranslations. Nevertheless it cannot be denied that they rest upon a firm foundation. In a special degree the numerous variations in translation which occur in the gospel tradition provide reliable information concerning the underlying Aramaic vocabulary. Unfortunately the significance of this valuable aid is hardly yet recognized, much less systematically employed. The parable of the Places at the Banquet may serve as an example showing how two widely differing Greek versions lead us back to one and the same Aramaic tradition. The variants are underlined.

Luke 14.8–10	Matt. 20.28 D it syᶜ
Ὅταν κληθῇς ὑπό τινος εἰς γάμους,	Εἰσερχόμενοι δὲ καὶ παρακλη-θέντες δειπνῆσαι
μὴ κατακλιθῇς εἰς τὴν πρωτο-κλισίαν,	μὴ ἀνακλίνεσθε εἰς τοὺς ἐξέχοντας τόπους,
μήποτε ἐντιμότερός σου ᾖ κεκλη-μένος ὑπ' αὐτοῦ,	μήποτε ἐνδοξότερός σου ἐπέλθῃ
καὶ ἐλθὼν ὁ σὲ καὶ αὐτὸν καλέσας ἐρεῖ σοι·	καὶ προσελθὼν ὁ δειπνοκλήτωρ εἴπῃ σοι·
δὸς τούτῳ τόπον,	ἔτι κάτω χώρει,
καὶ τότε ἄρξῃ μετὰ αἰσχύνης τὸν ἔσχατον τόπον κατέχειν.	καὶ καταισχυνθήσῃ.

---

[7] This has been established above all by the works of G. Dalman. H. Birkeland, in *The Language of Jesus*, Oslo, 1954, has recently claimed that Jesus spoke Hebrew, since this was the language of the lower classes; only the educated classes spoke Aramaic. Such a view is the exact opposite of the truth.

[8] For the studies which have laid the foundations we are indebted to Dalman, Wellhausen, Burney, Joüon, Torrey, Odeberg and, most recently, Black.

Luke 14.8-10

'Αλλ' ὅταν κληθῇς,
  πορευθεὶς ἀνάπεσε εἰς τὸν
    ἔσχατον τόπον,
  ἵνα ὅταν ἔλθῃ ὁ κεκληκώς σε
    ἐρεῖ σοι·
  φίλε, προσανάβηθι ἀνώτερον·
  τότε ἔσται σοι δόξα ἐνώπιον πάν-
    των τῶν συνανακειμένων σοι.

Matt. 20.28 D it sy

'Εὰν δὲ
  ἀναπέσῃς εἰς τὸν ἥττονα
  τόπον καὶ ἐπέλθῃ σου ἥττων,
  ἐρεῖ σοι ὁ δειπνοκλήτωρ·

  σύναγε ἔτι ἄνω,
  καὶ ἔσται σοι τοῦτο χρήσιμον.

The following points must be observed: (a) Aramaic *mištutha* has the double meaning, (1) 'banquet', (2) 'wedding'. The variants γάμοι, δειπνῆσαι (l.1) thus go back to *mištutha*, which has here the meaning 'banquet'. (b) The remarkable variants δόξα, χρήσιμον (l.18) are due to the ambiguity of the Aramaic *šibhḥa* which means (1) 'praise', 'honour', 'fame', (2) 'gain', 'share'. In our passage the meaning is 'honoured'. (c) We find variant compound forms (l.1 καλεῖν, παρακαλεῖν, l.3 κατακλίνεσθαι, ἀνακλίνεσθαι, l.7 ἔρχεσθαι, προσέρχεσθαι, l.17 προσαναβαίνειν, συνάγειν). These variants are due to the fact that Aramaic does not form compounds; hence in all these examples the underlying Aramaic form is uncompounded. (d) If M. Black's work *An Aramaic Approach to the Gospels and Acts*, Oxford, 1967₃, pp. 171-5, is taken into account, where it is established that, when retranslated into Aramaic, our parable reveals several examples of alliteration and paranomasia, and (e) if it is remembered that, in the translations of the gospels into Syriac and Christian-Palestinian (where, however, the dialectal differences must be reckoned with), we possess an additional means of controlling the process of retranslation—the impression created by all this must be that there is now a greatly increased probability of getting back to the original text by the aid of translation variants.

2. REPRESENTATIONAL CHANGES

It was inevitable that in the process of translation into Greek, not only the vocabulary, but also the presentation of the material, should undergo a 'translation' into terms of the Hellenistic environment. Thus in the Lukan parables changes appear, such as the substitution of Hellenistic building technique,[9] Roman lawcourt procedure,[10] non-Palestinian horticulture[11] and scenery[12]; in Luke 7.32 ἐκλαύσατε may be used with the intention of avoiding the passionate Palestinian gesture of smiting the breast (par. Matt. 11.17, ἐκόψατε) as a sign of mourning. In Mark we meet with the Roman division of the night into four watches (Mark 13.35, cf. 6.48), based on the requirements of Roman military service (cf. Acts 12.4), instead of the Palestinian [13] division into three (Luke 12.38)—one of the numerous indications that the second gospel was written in Rome. In such cases it is the Palestinian description of the situation which calls for preference.

Nevertheless we must proceed with caution. We shall see, for example, that Jesus repeatedly and intentionally uses by way of illustration Levantine methods of punishment, regarded by the Jews as particularly merciless.[14] Hence non-Palestinian modes of representation do not always indicate editorial activity or lack of authenticity. We can only reach a judgement with some degree of confidence in those cases where the tradition is divided.

3. EMBELLISHMENT

In the parable of the servants to whom money was entrusted, the Matthaean form tells of three servants, of whom the first received five talents, the second two, and the third one, that is to say, 50,000, 20,000 and 10,000 denarii respectively (Matt. 25.15);[15] in the Lucan form we have ten servants who only receive 100 denarii each (Luke 19.13). The continuation of the story in Luke (Luke 19.16–21, especially the article before ἕτερος, 19.20) shows that the number

[9] Luke 6.47 f.; 11.33: houses with cellars (not usual in Palestine); 8.16; 11.33: a house with an entrance passage from which the light shines out upon those who enter.

[10] Luke 12.58: πράκτωρ='bailiff' (otherwise in Matt. 5.25, ὑπηρέτης='synagogue official').

[11] Luke 13.19: in Luke the mustard-seed is sown εἰς κῆπον; this agrees with Theophrastus, *Historia plantarum*, VII, 1.1 f., where mustard is included among garden-herbs (κηπευόμενα). In Palestine, on the other hand, sowing mustard in garden-beds was forbidden (Kil. 3.2; Tos. Kil. 2.8, cf. Bill. I, p. 669). Luke 14.35: there is no Palestinian evidence for the use of salt as manure.

[12] Luke 6.48: the river overflowing its bank (otherwise in Matt. 7.25: 'cloudburst').

[13] Judg. 7.19; Jub. 49.10, 12.

[14] See pp. 180, 212 f.

[15] See below, p. 210, n. 6.

of the servants (three) in Matthew is original; similarly with regard
to the amounts, the lesser sum (as in Luke) must be original, since in
both evangelists the amount is expressly stated to be small (Matt.
25.21, 23, ὀλίγα, par. Luke 19.17, ἐλάχιστον); 10,000–50,000 denarii
hardly agrees with this. Luke, then, has increased the number of
the servants, while Matthew has immensely magnified the amounts
involved. The delight of the oriental storyteller in large numbers has
thus led to embellishment in both versions of the story.[16] Pleasure in
embellishment will also have played a part in the secondary expansion of details which the parable of the Great Supper has undergone in Matthew. In Luke (14.16) and in the Gospel of Thomas (64)
the host is a private individual, but in Matt. 22.2 he is a king, which
ill agrees with the course of the story (see p. 176). The change of the
'host' to a 'king' must be regarded as the same kind of shift in the
tradition as we meet with in rabbinical literature where parables of
daily life are changed into parables in which a king figures (see
p. 102, n. 59) in truly oriental fashion.[17] Finally, in the version of this
parable in the Gospel of Thomas the excuses are much more vividly
related, and the rural setting is changed into an urban one.[18] The
parable of the Sower as it appears in the Gospel of Thomas (9)
provides another example of embellishment: 'Jesus said: See, the
sower went out, he filled his hand and threw. Some (seeds) fell on the
road; the birds came and gathered them. Others fell on the rock
and did not strike root in the earth and sent up no ears to heaven.
And others fell on the thorns; they choked the seed and the worm ate
them. And others fell on the good earth; and it brought forth good
fruit going up to heaven; it bore sixty per measure and one hundred
and twenty per measure.' Here, as additions to the synoptic form of
the parable, we have the antithesis '(did not strike root in the earth
and sent up no ears to heaven)', the mention of the worm and the
increase in the number, 120. Sometimes the embellishments are quite

[16] Even insignificant numbers may increase. The Gospel of Thomas presents us
in the parable of the Great Supper with four guests who decline the invitation (64),
and in the parable of the Sower the good earth bears fruit sixtyfold and a hundred
and twentyfold.
[17] In the parable of the Wicked Servant (Matt. 18.23–35) the title 'king' only
occurs in the introduction (v. 23), while in the rest of the parable we only hear of
a 'lord' and his servants. It might therefore be inferred that the title 'king' is
secondary, having been introduced because of the identification of the 'lord' with
the heavenly Father in v. 35. Nevertheless, this conclusion is uncertain, since the
content of the story is only suitable to a king (see pp. 210 f.).
[18] See p. 176.

trivial; for example, the metaphor relating to divided service (Matt. 6.24; Luke 16.13) appears in the Gospel of Thomas (47a) as: 'It is impossible for a man to mount two horses (at once), and to stretch two bows (at once), and it is impossible for a servant to serve two masters.'

Included in cases of embellishment, we have to deal with the use of stylistic expedients which help to increase the realism of the narrative. An example is the insertion of the two words λέγουσιν αὐτῷ in Matt. 21.41, which are wanting in Mark 12.9, and Luke 20.16. Through their introduction Jesus' hearers are made to pronounce judgement on themselves without being aware of it—a feature which is both to be found in the Old Testament (e.g. the prophet Nathan's parable, II Sam. 12.5 f.; the parable of the woman of Tekoa, II Sam. 14.8 ff.; the parable of one of the sons of the prophets, I Kings 20.40) and in other parables of Jesus (Matt. 21.31; Luke 7.43).[19]

Even very slight additions can cause a shift in the emphasis. In the introduction to the parable of the fig-tree in Luke, when we are told to observe the fig-tree 'and all the trees' (Luke 21.29), the words 'and all the trees', wanting in Mark 13.28 and Matt. 24.32, though true to nature, nevertheless distract our attention from the peculiarly bare appearance of the fig-tree in winter (p. 120) which makes it a specially apt symbol of the mystery of Death and Life. A comparison of Luke 5.36 with Mark 2.21, exhibits a similar shift of emphasis caused by embellishment. In both passages it is a question of repairing an old garment, but the development of the illustration is different. Mark says: 'No one sews a piece of new cloth upon an old garment; if he does, the patch takes something from it—the new from the old—and the rent is made worse'; the emphasis is laid on the worsening of the rent caused by the repair. Luke says: 'No one cuts a piece from a new garment and puts it on an old one; if he does the new is spoilt, and the piece from the new cloth does not match the old.' Here, while the picturesqueness of the story is increased by introducing the grotesque destruction of the new garment, the point that the rent is made worse by the repair is lost.

Nevertheless our quest calls for great caution. It is a special characteristic of Jesus' use of parables that they are drawn from life, but in a number of cases they exhibit unusual features, intended to arouse the attention of the hearers, and on which generally a special

[19] M. Meinertz (see p. 23, n. 2), p. 38.

emphasis is laid.[20] It is a wholly unusual occurrence that all the guests should rudely refuse an invitation,[21] and that the master of the house (or the king) should be obliged to call in to his table the best he can find from the streets (Matt. 22.9; Luke 14.21–23); and that the virgins awaiting the bridegroom should one and all fall asleep (Matt. 25.5), and that the bridegroom should refuse entrance to late-comers to the wedding (Matt. 25.12, cf. Luke 13.25); and that a guest should present himself at the marriage of the king's son in a filthy garment (Matt. 22.11 ff.); again it is unusual for a grain of corn to yield a hundredfold (Mark 4.8, cf. Gen. 26.12).[22] Such extravagant exaggerations are still characteristic of the oriental way of telling a story,[23] and the frequency with which they occur in the parables shows that Jesus intentionally adopted this style. The element of unexpectedness which they display was intended to indicate where the meaning was to be found. This appears most strikingly in the parable of the Wicked Servant. When the 'servant' [24] in the parable of the Unfaithful Servant is represented as owing the amount of 10,000 talents (i.e. 100 million denarii),[25] the monstrous nature of this fantastic sum becomes apparent when it is remembered that the yearly tribute of Galilee and Peraea in 4 BC amounted to 200 talents (Josephus, *Ant.*, 17. 318), i.e. a fiftieth of that sum! But the vastness of the amount is intentional. It is meant to impress upon the hearers by 'shock tactics' [26] that man cannot pay his debt to God, and it throws into strong relief the sharp contrast with the fellow servant's trivial debt of 100 denarii. Hence it by no means follows that a mass rejection of all the uncommon features in the parables of Jesus is called for; on the contrary, such introduction of the interpretation into the parable may be quite original. However, comparison of the parallel forms in which the parables have come down to us shows the correctness of the view that in many cases parables

[20] I. K. Madsen has made special reference to these characteristic features in his book, *Die Parabeln der Evangelien und die heutige Psychologie*, Copenhagen, 1936; he is followed by M. Brouwer, *De Gelijkenissen*, Leiden, 1946, pp. 71–79.

[21] See pp. 178 ff.

[22] See p. 150, n. 84.

[23] Cf. also M. Meinertz, op. cit., p. 46, n. 6: 'With reference to this it may be pointed out that oriental stories are not characterized by a high sense of probability —quite apart from the occurrence of marvels—a trait which is, nevertheless, not resented by the audience.'

[24] See p. 210.

[25] See p. 210. n. 6.

[26] J. J. Vincent, 'The Parables of Jesus as Self-Revelation', in *Studia Evangelica* (Texte und Untersuchungen 73), Berlin, 1959, p. 80.

have undergone elaboration, and that the simpler version represents the original.

4. INFLUENCE OF THE OLD TESTAMENT AND OF FOLK-STORY THEMES

In some passages references to Scripture occur in the parables (Mark 4.29, 32; 12.1, 9a, 10 f. par; Matt. 25.31, 46; cf. Luke 13.27, 29). The remarkably small number of examples is reduced by the recognition that of the four just referred to from Matthew and Luke, at least three, if not all four, are secondary.[27] Furthermore, in view of variants in the Gospel of Thomas, the rest of the occurrences call for careful examination. The version of the parable of the Vineyard in the Gospel of Thomas (65), like the Lukan form (20.9), does not contain the detailed description of the construction of the vineyard drawn from Isa. 5.1 (Mark 12.1 par. Matt. 21.33), nor does it give the closing question based on Isa. 5.5 (Mark 12.9 par.), and the final quotation from Ps. 118.22 f. appears as an independent logion (66). Since, then, as this logion shows, the Gospel of Thomas displays no objection on principle to quotations from Scripture, and above all since in the synoptic gospels Isa. 5.1 f., 5; Ps. 118.22 f. are not quoted from the Hebrew but from the Greek text,[28] these scripture references should not be regarded as belonging to the original form of the tradition. The conclusion of the parable of the Mustard Seed in the Gospel of Thomas (20) runs as follows: '. . . it produces a large branch and becomes shelter (σκέπη) for the birds of heaven'. This is possibly a passing allusion to Dan. 4.9, 18; Ezek. 17.23; 31.6; in Mark (4.32) the reference is to Ezek. 17.23 and Dan. 4.9, 18 Th. is clearer, while in Matthew (13.32) and Luke (13.19) it has become a free quotation from Dan. 4.18 Th. The unrealistic description of the mustard-plant as a tree, which only occurs in Matthew and Luke, but not in Mark or the Gospel of Thomas, is also derived from Dan. 4.17. Finally, in the parable of the Leaven, the immense quantity of three measures (se'a) of meal (Matt. 13.33; Luke 13.21; see p. 147) is absent from the Gospel of Thomas (96); it

---

[27] Luke 13.27, 29 are originally independent logia, not parts of a parable, see pp. 95 f. The reference in Matt. 25.31 is editorial (see p. 206); the same may also hold good for Matt. 25.46 (see p. 84, n. 83).

[28] See pp. 70, 73 f.

may come from Gen. 18.6 MT. Thus it appears that a strong tendency prevails to elucidate by or introduce references to Scripture. This does not, however, exclude the possibility that Jesus himself occasionally referred to Scripture in a parable. In at least two cases this is extremely probable: at the end of the parable of the Mustard Seed (see above), and at the end of the parable of the Seed growing of itself (Mark 4.29 cit. Joel 3.13, following the Hebrew text).

Side by side with such references to Scripture, occasional *folk-story themes* appear to have found their way into the parables. We shall see repeatedly that Jesus himself made use of such themes; but in two cases at least it can be shown that these are secondary.

The version of the parable of the Treasure hid in the Field as given in the Gospel of Thomas (109) is utterly degenerated. It tells of a man who bought a field, and subsequently discovered by chance in his property a treasure which made him a rich man. This has hardly anything in common with the Matthaean version, which is certainly original. On the other hand, the new version corresponds with a rabbinic story:[29]

G. of Th. 109	*Midr. Cant.*, 4.12
The kingdom is like a man who had a treasure hidden in his field, of which he knew nothing. And after he died he left it to his son. The son (also) knew nothing (about it). He took that field and sold it.	It (i.e. the situation described in Cant. 4.12) is like a man who inherited a place full of rubbish. The inheritor was lazy and he sold it for a ridiculously small sum.
And the purchaser went to plough and found the treasure.	The purchaser dug therein industriously and found in it a treasure.
He began to lend money on interest to whomsoever he wished.	He built therewith a great palace and passed through the bazaar with a train of slaves whom he had bought with the treasure. When the seller saw it he could have choked himself (with vexation).

---

[29] First noticed by L. Cerfaux, 'Les Paraboles du Royaume dans l'Évangile de Thomas', in *Le Muséon*, 70 (1957), p. 314.

Whereas in Matthew the parable of the Treasure in the Field describes the overwhelming joy of the finder (see pp. 200 f.), in the Gospel of Thomas, under the influence of the rabbinic story, the point is entirely lost: the parable now describes the rage of a man who has failed to seize a unique opportunity.

The second instance, in which a folk-story theme has been introduced as a secondary element into a parable, occurs in Matthew. Into the parable of the Great Supper he has inserted the description of a punitive expedition: the king, enraged by the abuse and slaughter of his servants, sends out his bodyguard [30] with orders to kill the murderers and burn up their city (Matt. 22.7). This episode, which breaks the connection (see pp. 68 f.) and is absent from Luke and the Gospel of Thomas, makes use of a theme [31] drawn from the Ancient East and current in late Judaism, which in Matt. 22.7 reflects the destruction of Jerusalem.

5. THE CHANGE OF AUDIENCE

The *parable of the Labourers in the Vineyard* affords a good example of the frequently occurring change of audience (Matt. 20.1–16). In order to realize the various interpretations which came to be attached to this parable we must transport ourselves backward in time.

(a) The Roman Church, and the Lutheran Church following the Roman tradition, reads this Gospel on Septuagesima Sunday,[32] at the beginning of the fast of the clergy,[33] i.e. at the beginning of the penitential period before the Passion. The Epistle is 1 Cor. 9.24–27, the summons to run the Christian race. What does the Church preach at the beginning of this period? The call to God's Vineyard. From the earliest times this was the source of much allegorizing: already from the time of Irenaeus [34] the hours of the fivefold summons were taken

---

[30] See p. 68, n. 75.

[31] K. H. Rengstorf, 'Die Stadt der Mörder (Mt 22, 7)', in *Judentum, Urchristentum, Kirche* (BZNW 26), Berlin, 1960, pp. 106–29, has provided a comprehensive collection of the material.

[32] Before the introduction of Septuagesima in Rome in the 6th or 7th cent., our pericope was already attached to this Sunday; it thus belonged originally to the cycle of Epiphany Sundays; cf. J. Dupont, 'La parabole des ouvriers de la vigne (Matthieu, xx, 1–16)', in *Nouvelle Revue Théologique*, 79 (1957), pp. 786 f.

[33] The fast of the community begins on Ash Wednesday.

[34] *Adv. haer.*, IV, 36.7 (ed. A. Stieren (1853), I, pp. 690 f.); Origen, *Comment. on Mt.*, tomos XV, 32 (Klostermann, pp. 446 f.).

to symbolize the periods in the history of redemption from Adam
onwards; from Origen's time they symbolized the different stages of
human life at which men become Christians.[35] Both these interpretations, from the periods of history and from the periods of human life,
are often linked together. But, leaving entirely out of account these
allegorical interpretations, the parable does not bear the meaning
of a summons to the divine vineyard. Such an interpretation misses
the point of the conclusion of the parable, which shows that the
emphasis does not lie on a call to the vineyard, but on the distribution of wages at the end of the day (vv. 8 ff.).

(b) Retracing our steps in time, we find that all the MSS. of the
New Testament, with the exception of ℵ BLZ 085 sa bo, read as the
concluding sentence of the parable, v. 16b: πολλοὶ γάρ εἰσιν κλητοί,
ὀλίγοι δὲ ἐκλεκτοί. How does the parable illustrate the truth that
many [36] are called but few chosen, that is, that only a few obtain salvation? The first, those who were summoned early in the morning,
are here presented as a warning: they were called. But they, since
they murmur, boast of their deserts, rebel against God's decision, in
short reject God's gift (a favourite interpretation),[37] cut themselves
off from salvation. To them the word ὕπαγε is addressed (v. 14). Here
the parable is represented as a parable of judgement: do not forfeit
salvation by murmuring, self-justification, or rejection. But this interpretation, too, misses the point of the parable. What the first receives
is not condemnation, but the agreed wage. It is not by accident that
v. 16b is wanting in the early Egyptian MSS. and versions (see
above). What we have here is one of those common generalizing
conclusions, in this case taken from Matt. 22.14 and added, at the
latest, in the second century.

(c) Hence, if we go back farther still, we come to the evangelist
Matthew himself. He has inserted into a Marcan context the parable
about the 'first' (Matt. 20.8, 10) and the 'last' (Matt. 20.8, 12, 14),
in order to illustrate the saying in Mark 10.31 (par. Matt. 19.30),
πολλοὶ δὲ ἔσονται πρῶτοι ἔσχατοι καὶ οἱ ἔσχατοι πρῶτοι, with which
Mark ends the previous address to Peter. Transposing the order of
'first' and 'last', he has used the saying as the conclusion of the par-

[35] Origen, op. cit., XV, 36 (Klostermann, pp. 456 f.).
[36] Πολλοί has here an inclusive meaning 'all', cf. IV Ezra 8.3: 'multi quidem
creati sunt, pauci autem salvabuntur' (J. Jeremias, *ZNW*, 42, 1949, p. 193, n. 64
and art. πολλοί in *ThWBNT*, VI, pp. 539–42).
[37] E.g. G. de Raucourt, 'Les ouvriers de la onzième heure', in *Rech. de sc. rel.*, 15
(1925), pp. 492 ff.

able (Matt. 20.16), and doubly, by the word γάρ (20.1) and by the
word οὕτως (20.16), has expressly brought it into relation with 19.30.[38]
In its Marcan context what this saying asserts is that in the age to
come all earthly gradations of rank will be reversed, and it is uncertain whether it is intended to confirm the promises which Jesus
has just made to the disciples, or as a warning to them against presumption. In either case, for Matthew our parable represented the
reversal of rank which would take place on the Last Day. He will
have drawn this conclusion from the instruction given to the steward,
v. 8b:

κάλεσον τοὺς ἐργάτας καὶ ἀπόδος τὸν μισθόν,
ἀρξάμενος ἀπὸ τῶν ἐσχάτων ἕως τῶν πρώτων.

The last become the first; with them the payment of wages begins.
Against the view that the parable is intended to illustrate the way in
which at the Last Day the first will become last and the last first, it is
not a valid objection that not merely two, but five groups are concerned, since from v. 8 onward only the first- and last-mentioned
groups occupy the stage; the three intermediate groups are forgotten; they were only introduced to illustrate the circumstances
leading up to the engagement of labourers, especially the urgent
need of workers. But it may be possible to raise another objection to
the view that the parable is intended to illustrate the final reversal
of order at the Last Day. It is based, as we have said, on v. 8b:
ἀρξάμενος ἀπὸ τῶν ἐσχάτων ἕως τῶν πρώτων. But that is clearly an
unimportant detail in the course of the parable. There can be no
great significance in the order of payment; a couple of minutes
earlier or later can hardly be said to assign precedence to any one
or deprive him of it.[39] In fact, no complaint is made later on about the
order of payment which, taken in its context, should merely emphasize the equality of the last with the first. Perhaps it is simply
intended to indicate how 'the first were made to witness the payment
of their companions'.[40] But it may be simpler to take ἀρξάμενος ἀπό
to mean, as it often does, 'not omitting', 'including',[41] so that v. 8
was not originally concerned with the order of payment at all,

[38] Οὕτως is absent from Mark 10.31; Matt. 19.30; Luke 13.30. It will have been
added by Matthew since οὕτως ἔσονται is one of Matthew's characteristic locu-
tions (see p. 84, n. 74).
[39] Jülicher, II, p. 462.
[40] Ibid.
[41] F. Passow, Handbuch der griechischen Sprache₅, I, Leipzig, 1841, p. 409a; Liddell
and Scott, A Greek-English Lexicon, I, New ed. Oxford, 1925, p. 254a. In the N.T.
this meaning may also be found in John 8.9, and perhaps also in Luke 23.5. Cf.

but meant, rather—'Pay them all their wages, including the last'. In any case the parable certainly conveys no lesson about the reversal of rank at the end since all receive exactly the same wage.

(d) Now, as Mark shows, the present Matthaean context is not original. We must therefore go behind Matthew and study the parable without reference to its context. It is possible that the concluding sentence in v. 16 may bear an entirely different meaning from that which its present Matthaean setting demands. The seer of IV Ezra is perplexed by the question whether the preceding generations will be at a disadvantage in comparison with those who survive to the End. He receives the answer: 'He said to me: I will make my judgement like a round dance;[42] the last therein shall not be behind, nor the first in front' (IV Ezra 5.42).[43] First and last, last and first—there is no difference, all are equal. This interpretation of the parable is generally accepted today, namely, that it is intended to teach the equality of reward in the Kingdom of God; some would add that it is intended to teach that reward is wholly of grace, but this is erroneous, since the first received their pay, as Paul would say, κατὰ ὀφείλημα, and not κατὰ χάριν (Rom. 4.4). But, leaving this out of consideration, the point of the story, intended to startle the audience, was surely not, 'Equal pay for all', but 'So much more pay for the last'.[44]

(e) Light begins to break if we disregard v. 16 (οὕτως ἔσονται οἱ ἔσχατοι πρῶτοι καὶ οἱ πρῶτοι ἔσχατοι). As we can see from Mark 10. 31; Luke 13.30 (cf. Mark 9.35),[45] this verse was originally an independent logion,[46] perhaps nothing more than a catchword,[47] which

Jos., *Ant.*, 7.255: ἀπὸ σοῦ καὶ τῶν σῶν ἀρξάμενοι τέκνων, 'including you and your children'; 6.133: ἀρξάμενος ἀπὸ γυναικῶν καὶ νηπίων, 'including women and young children'. With μέχρι: Plato, *Leg.*, 771c, all numbers μέχρι τῶν δώδεκα ἀπὸ μιᾶς ἀρξάμενος, 'from 1 to 12'. (In German also 'beginning with' can mean 'including' without any emphasis on the order.)

[42] Lat. *corona*; Syr., Arab. (ed. Ewald), Armen., 'wreath', 'crown', Eth. 'ring'. Derived by Violet from Heb. *ḥugh*, 'circle', and by Gunkel plausibly explained as a round dance.

[43] Cf. also Syr. Bar. 30.2 (of the general resurrection of the righteous): 'And the first shall rejoice and the last shall not be sad.'

[44] W. Pesch, *Der Lohngedanke in der Lehre Jesu* (Münchener Theologische Studien I, 7), Munich, 1955, pp. 11 f.

[45] Mark 9.35 is an exact parallel to Mark 10.31, if ἔσται is taken as a future (not as a jussive).

[46] R. Bultmann, *The History of the Synoptic Tradition*₂, Oxford, 1968, p. 186.

[47] Something like, 'How easily fortune changes overnight'; cf. J. Schniewind in *Das Neue Testament Deutsch*, I, on Mark 10.31. That the logion is early is shown (a) by the twofold repetition of the definite article, although the sense is general, and (b) by the antithetic parallelism obtained by inversion.

has been added to our parable as a generalizing conclusion, but
does not tally with its meaning.[48] Numerous examples of the insertion
of such generalizing conclusions can be adduced.[49] But if the parable
originally ended with the question in v. 15, without offering an
explanation, its shocking character was forced upon the attention.
Here is a story of bare-faced injustice. The double grievance (v. 12,
see p. 137) is indeed only too well-founded, and each hearer must
have been compelled to ask himself the question, 'Why does the
master of the house give the unusual order that all are to receive the
same pay? Why especially does he allow the last to receive a full
day's pay for only an hour's work? Is this a piece of purely arbitrary
injustice? a caprice? a generous whim?' Far from it! There is no
question here of a limitless generosity, since all receive only an
amount sufficient to sustain life, a bare subsistence wage. No one
receives more.[50] Even if, in the case of the last labourers to be hired,
it is their own fault that, in a time when the vineyard needs workers,
they sit about in the market-place gossiping till late afternoon;[51] even
if their excuse that no one has hired them (v. 7) is an idle evasion
(like that of the servant in Matt. 25.24 f.), a cover for their typical
oriental indifference,[52] yet they touch the owner's heart. He sees that
they will have practically nothing to take home; the pay for an hour's
work will not keep a family; their children will go hungry if the
father comes home empty-handed. It is because of his pity for their
poverty that the owner allows them to be paid a full day's wages. In
this case the parable does not depict an arbitrary action, but the
behaviour of a large-hearted man who is compassionate and full of
sympathy for the poor.[53] This, says Jesus, is how God deals with men.
This is what God is like, merciful. Even to tax-farmers and sinners
he grants an unmerited place in his Kingdom, such is the measure
of his goodness. The whole emphasis lies on the final words: ὅτι ἐγὼ
ἀγαθός εἰμι (v. 15)!

Why did Jesus tell the parable? Was it his object to extol God's
mercy to the poor? If that were so he might have omitted the second
part of the parable (vv. 11 ff.). But it is precisely upon the second part
that the main stress lies, for our parable is one of the double-edged

[48] R. Bultmann, ibid.
[49] See pp. 110 ff.
[50] A. T. Cadoux, *The Parables of Jesus*, New York, 1931, p. 101.
[51] See below, pp. 136 f.
[52] M. Meinertz, *Theol. Revue*, 46 (1950), col. 92.
[53] Dodd, p. 122.

parables. It describes two episodes: (1) the hiring of the labourers and the liberal instructions about their payment (vv. 1–8), (2) the indignation of the injured recipients (vv. 9–15). Now, in all the double-edged parables the emphasis lies on the second point (see pp. 131 f. on Luke 15.11 ff.; pp. 186 f. on Luke 16.19 ff.; p. 65 on Matt. 22.1–14). What, then, is the purpose of the second part, the episode in which the other labourers are indignant, rebel and protest, and receive the humiliating reply: 'Are you jealous because I am good?' (v. 15). The parable is clearly addressed to those who resembled the murmurers, those who criticized and opposed the good news, Pharisees for example. Jesus was minded to show them how unjustified, hateful, loveless and unmerciful was their criticism. Such, said he, is God's goodness, and since God is so good, so too am I. He vindicates the gospel against its critics.[54] Here, clearly, we have recovered the original historical setting. We are suddenly transported into a concrete situation in the life of Jesus such as the Gospels frequently depict. Over and over again we hear the charge brought against Jesus that he is a companion of the despised and outcast, and are told of men to whom the gospel is an offence. Repeatedly is Jesus compelled to justify his conduct and to vindicate the good news. So too here he is saying, This is what God is like, so good, so full of compassion for the poor, how dare you revile him?

As the context in Matthew (the question of Peter in 19.27) shows, the primitive Church related the parable to the disciples of Jesus, and thus applied it to the Christian community. That is easy to understand, since they were in the same position as the Church today when it preaches about the Pharisee-stories of the Gospels: it has to apply to the community words which were addressed to opponents. Thus we have gained a method of approach to the parables which is of far-reaching significance, an additional principle of transformation, namely: the tradition underwent an alteration or restriction of the audience. Many parables which were originally addressed to a different audience, namely, to the Pharisees, the scribes, or the crowd, were related by the primitive Church to the disciples of Jesus.

One more example out of a great number of similar cases may be mentioned: Luke 15.3–7 par. Matt. 18.12–14. According to Luke the *parable of the Lost Sheep* was occasioned by the Pharisees' indignant question: 'Why (ὅτι = τί ὅτι) does he receive these sinners (into

[54] Dodd, p. 123.

his house), and admit them to his table-fellowship?' (Luke 15.2), and it closes, in Luke, with the words, 'Thus God (at the Last Judgement[55]) will have more joy over one sinner who repents, than over ninety-nine just (δίκαιοι) persons who have no need of repentance' (15.7). It was with the object of justifying the gospel against its critics that Jesus asserted by means of a parable that, just as a shepherd, gathering his flock into the fold, rejoices over the lost sheep that he has found, so God rejoices over the repentant sinner. He rejoices because he can forgive. That, says Jesus, is why I receive sinners.[56]

The parable has an entirely different audience in Matthew. It is not addressed, as in Luke, to Jesus' opponents, but to his disciples, according to Matt. 18.1. Hence the concluding sentence in Matthew has a correspondingly different emphasis. It runs: 'Thus it is not the will [57] of God [58] that even [59] one [60] of the [61] very least [62] should be lost' (18.14). When it is brought into the context of the admonition not to despise one of the least (v. 10), and of the instruction concerning the discipline of an erring brother (vv. 15–17), the concluding sentence clearly means: It is God's will that you should go after your apostate brother as persistently as the shepherd of the parable seeks

---

[55] The fact is usually overlooked that the statement refers to the future: χαρὰ ἐν οὐρανῷ ἔσται.

[56] See pp. 132 f.

[57] Ἔστιν θέλημα ἔμπροσθεν, the equivalent of the Targumic ra⁽ᵃ⁾wa min qᵒdham (e.g. Targ. Isa. 53.6, 10), cf. Matt. 11.26 par.; I Cor. 16.12.

[58] A double circumlocution for the divine name: (1) ἔμπροσθεν=the angels standing before God, (2) 'your heavenly Father'. The anthropomorphic ascription of an act of will to God was avoided.

[59] It is a characteristic of Semitic speech that the word 'only', which must be expressed in English, is very often omitted (an example of frequent occurrence is the dayyenu-hymn of the Passover-Haggadah): Matt. 5.18 f., 28, 43, 46; 10.6; 11.13; 17.1; 18.6, 20, 28; 20.12; 24.8; Mark 1.8; 9.2, 41, 42; 10.5; 13.8; 14.51; Luke 6.32, 33, 34; 7.7; 9.28; 12.41; 13.23; 15.16; 16.16, 17, 21, 24; 17.10, 22; John 10.33; 12.35 et al. Hence the addition of μόνῳ in Matt. 4.10 and Luke 4.8 to the quotation from Deut. 6.13 LXX is actually correct. The observation is important for Rom. 3.28 (sola fide is what is meant) and Gal. 5.6b.

[60] The unusual neuter (ἕν) is to be explained by the fact that it represents the Aram. ḥadh, which should have been rendered by εἷς; the use of the neuter is due to πρόβατον (18.12) and αὐτό (18.13).

[61] Τούτων is a superfluous demonstrative which in English remains untranslated, cf. p. 207 on Matt. 25.40. On this Semitism, cf. J. Jeremias, The Eucharistic Words of Jesus, London, 1966, p. 184, nn. 1–3.

[62] Semitic has no superlative; μικροί=ἐλάχιστοι (Matt. 25.40, 45).

the lost sheep. Thus, in Matthew the parable is addressed to the disciples, a call to the leader of the community to exercise faithful pastorship toward apostates; [63] the emphasis does not lie, as in Luke, on the joy of the shepherd, but on the example of his persistent search. But the great instruction to the leader of the Christian community contained in Matt. 18 (for this is the intention of the chapter; the usual interpretation of it as an instruction to the community is incorrect[64]), in the context of which the Matthaean parable stands, is a secondary, wholly artificial composition, built up out of a collection of isolated sayings, an expansion of the corresponding Marcan collection in Mark 9.33-50. Hence the Matthaean context does not help us to determine the original situation in the life of Jesus which produced the parable of the Lost Sheep. There can be no doubt that Luke has preserved the original situation.[65] As in so many other instances, we have Jesus vindicating the good news against its critics and declaring God's character, God's delight in forgiveness, as the reason why he himself received sinners. We may accept this view with all the greater confidence, since in Aramaic the concluding sentence in Matthew (18.14) strikes the same note as the corresponding sentence in Luke (15.7): This rejoices the heart of God! For in Matt. 18.14, (1) the negative actually governs the second half of the sentence,[66] and (2) the word *ra'ᵃwa* (see p. 39, n. 57) has the meaning 'pleasure'.[67] Hence the original meaning of Matt. 18.14 is, 'There is joy in the heart of God when even one of the very least escapes destruction.' This agrees exactly with Luke 15.7a, which has, equally positively, 'So God will rejoice over a sinner who repents.'

Thus we are faced with the same issue as in Matt. 20.1-16, a parable originally directed against the opponents of Jesus (in Luke) has become one addressed to the disciples (in Matthew). The change of audience has resulted in a shift of emphasis; an apologetic parable has assumed a hortatory character.

Details about the audience belong to the setting of the parables, and were therefore liable to be more freely handled than the parables

[63] K. Stendahl, *The School of St. Matthew and its Use of the Old Testament* (Acta Seminarii Neotestamentici Upsaliensis 20), Uppsala, 1954, p. 27.

[64] Cf. *ThWBNT*, III, p. 751. 29-31.

[65] It should also be noticed that the Johannine Shepherd parable is addressed to opponents (John 10.6, cf. 9.40; 10.19 ff.), a fact which is generally overlooked.

[66] P. Joüon, *L'Évangile de Notre-Seigneur Jésus-Christ*, Paris, 1930, pp. 114 f.

[67] T. W. Manson, *The Sayings of Jesus*, London, 1950, p. 208 (cited as T. W. Manson, *Sayings*). *Ra'ᵃwa* may mean (1) 'will', (2) 'good pleasure' (Heb. *raṣon*). The Matthaean tradition has altered the meaning somewhat by the rendering θέλημα; the correct rendering should be εὐδοκία.

themselves. Hence they require a specially careful analysis, a view which is borne out by the fact that the Gospels are occasionally inconsistent with one another in such details. Perhaps too much stress should not be laid on the fact that in Mark (3.22) the parable about Beelzebub is addressed to the scribes, in Matthew (12.24) to the Pharisees, and in Luke to the crowd (11.14). Nor, again, when Mark (11.27) presents the parable of the Vine-dressers as addressed to the chief priests, scribes, and elders, Matthew to the chief priests and elders (21.23), or to the chief priests and Pharisees (21.45), and Luke, on the other hand, to the crowd (20.9) or to the scribes and chief priests (20.19). Of a little more importance is the instance of the proverb concerning the blind leading the blind, which in Matthew (15.14) is intended as a gibe at the Pharisees, but in Luke (6.39), on the other hand, is addressed as a warning to the audience.[68] But when in Matthew the parable of the Lost Sheep (18.12-14), and in Mark the proverb about Salt (9.50), are addressed to the disciples, while Luke, on the other hand, addresses the former to the opponents of Jesus (15.2), and the latter to the crowd (14.25), we are faced with a contradiction which can hardly be resolved by harmonizing methods. An extreme case occurs when the same Evangelist contradicts himself, for instance, when Matthew represents the saying about the Tree and its Fruit in one place as addressed to the crowd or to the disciples (7.16-20), and in another to the Pharisees (12.33-37); similarly Luke gives the parable of the Lamp on the Lampstand in 8.16 as addressed to the disciples, and in 11.33 to the crowd. While it may be possible to explain these two instances by the assumption that Jesus spoke these parables twice and to different audiences, this explanation is invalid in the case of Mark 4 where Mark in 4.10 makes the parables [69] of 4.21-32 addressed to the narrower circle of 'those who were about him together with the Twelve' (Matt. 13.10 to the disciples), while, on the other hand, in 4.33-34 (par. Matt. 13.34 f.), they are addressed to the crowd.

The detailed analysis of the two parables which we have made on

[68] In neither of the two Evangelists is the context original: Matt. 15.12-14 is an insertion by Matthew into the controversial discourse in Mark 7.1-23, and Luke 6.39 f. is a pre-Lucan(?) insertion into the Sermon on the Plain, as is shown by a comparison of Luke 6.37-42 with Matt. 7.1-5. In the Gospel of Thomas (34) the Logion stands alone, without indication of audience.

[69] Mark seems to have placed the logia of 4.21-25 in his parable-chapter because he regarded them as two parables (viz. of the Lamp, vv. 21-23, and of the Measure, vv. 24 f.).

pp. 33–40 shows that, in the transmission of the material of the Gospels, a strong tendency was at work to transform parables which Jesus addressed to the crowd or to opponents, into parables for the disciples: a tendency which is characteristic of all three Gospels. The following is a list of examples of this process: Mark 9.50a (see p. 168); 13.33 ff. (see pp. 53 ff.); Matt. 5.25 f. (see pp. 43 f.); 6.22 f. (see pp. 162 f.); 27 (see p. 171); 7.3–5 (see p. 167); 9–11 (see pp. 144 f.); 13 f. (see p. 195, n. 9); 16–18 (see p. 167); 13.47 f. (see pp. 224 ff.); 18.12–14 (see pp. 38 ff.); 20.1 ff. (see pp. 37 f.); 24.43 f. (see pp. 48 ff.); 24.45 ff. (see pp. 55 ff.); 25.1 ff. (see pp. 51 ff.); Luke 6.39 (see p. 41); 41 f. (see p. 167); 11.11–13 (see pp. 144 f.); 12.25 (see p. 171); 35 ff. (see pp. 53 ff.); 12.39 f. (see pp. 48 ff.); 12.41 ff. (see pp. 55 ff.); 13.23 f. (see p. 195, n. 9); 16.1 ff. (see pp. 45 ff.); 17.7 ff. (see p. 193); Gospel of Thomas 20. An examination of the above examples will show that the tendency to alter parables addressed to the crowd into parables addressed to the disciples is present in all layers of the synoptic tradition, and must have been operative at a very early period.[70] This process reached its conclusion in the Gospel of Thomas; here the entire collection of reported parables has come to be regarded as instruction for the true gnostics.[71] So far as I know there is no demonstrable case of the reverse process, by which a parable originally spoken to the disciples was converted into one addressed to the crowd.

Hence we must always ask who were the original hearers, and what a parable would mean if we take it as addressed to opponents or the crowd.

6. THE HORTATORY USE OF THE PARABLES BY THE CHURCH

In studying the parable of the Lost Sheep we saw that its original use

[70] T. W. Manson in: *Göttg. Gel. Anzeigen*, 207 (1953), pp. 143 f. A comparison between the Sermon on the Plain and the Sermon on the Mount shows the same process at work. The Sermon on the Plain is regarded as addressed to the crowd described in Luke 6.17–19, as may be seen from 6.24 ff. and 7.1 (6.20a is merely an introduction to the Beatitudes, 6.20b–23). Matthew, on the other hand, regards the disciples as the audience to whom the Sermon on the Mount is addressed; since Matt. 5.1a ((ἰδὼν δὲ τοὺς ὄχλους ἀνέβη εἰς τὸ ὄρος) states—as 8.18 (ἰδὼν δὲ ὁ Ἰησοῦς ὄχλον περὶ αὐτὸν ἐκέλευσεν ἀπελθεῖν εἰς τὸ πέραν) shows—that Jesus himself withdrew from the crowd. When 7.28, in contradiction to this, represents the crowd as the audience, it is due to the influence of Mark 1.22 (cf. H.-W. Bartsch, 'Feldrede und Bergpredigt', *ThZ*, 16, 1960, pp. 6–8). Here, then, we have a further instance of the process by which a discourse which was addressed in the first place to the crowd (Luke), is transferred to the disciples (Matthew).

[71] H. Montefiore, 'A Comparison of the Parables of the Gospel according to Thomas and of the Synoptic Gospels', in *NTS*, 7 (1960–61), pp. 229 f.

by Jesus was as a defence of the gospel against his opponents, but
that it had been placed by Matthew in the setting of the disciplinary
order of the community as an exhortation to the leaders of the community to exercise faithful pastorship. In other words, the parable
had lost its original historical setting, and had been taken over by the
Church completely as hortatory material. This process happened
frequently.

The little *parable concerning Going before the Judge*[72] has been
handed down to us in Matthew (5.25 f.) and in Luke (12.58 f.), with
essential agreement in content, in spite of minor verbal differences.[73]
But the Evangelists have each placed the parable in a widely different
setting. In Matthew it is connected with the first antithesis of the
Sermon on the Mount, the prohibition of hate (5.21 f.). It is better
to be reconciled, is the advice of 5.23 f., otherwise your worship is a
sham; not until you have been reconciled will God accept your offering and your prayer for forgiveness.[74] But if the dispute has reached
the stage of legal proceedings, possibly involving the amount due
to a creditor, in that case, the Matthaean form of the parable
continues, you should go to all lengths to come to an agreement
with the opposite party. You should yield, take the first step, meet
him; if not, there is danger ahead of you. He who trusts in the
presumed justice of his position and remains unreconciled, may
suffer at the hands of Justice. Hence in Matthew our parable is
construed as a direction for the conduct of life, and there is no
denying that the reason for such a direction sounds perilously near
triviality.

In Luke our parable has been placed in a very different context.
It is preceded (from 12.35 on) by a series of sayings which speak with
profound seriousness of the present crisis and the signs of the times.
Jesus severely rebukes the populace for its failure to grasp the gravity
of the present moment (12.56, 57). In this connection the parable of
the Debtor bears a different emphasis from that which it bears in
Matthew. In Luke the whole stress lies on the threatening situation

[72] Cf. Dodd, pp. 136–39.

[73] They are principally determined by the fact that Matthew is thinking of
Jewish (ὑπηρέτης) legal procedure, and Luke of Roman (ἄρχων, πράκτωρ). (See
p. 27, n. 10, cf. p. 180.)

[74] On this interpretation of Matt. 5.23 f., cf. *ZNW*, 36 (1937), pp. 150–4. The
saying has no intention of depreciating the value of the cultus (reconciliation is
more important than sacrifice), on the contrary, its purpose is to take it seriously
(reconciliation is an essential condition for the acceptance of the sacrifice).

of the defendant. It says to him, 'You are shortly to appear before the judge, in danger of condemnation and imprisonment. At any moment you may be arrested: act at once while you are still at liberty, and settle the matter while it is still possible.' There can be no doubt that Luke is right: the parable is an eschatological one, a parable of crisis. The crisis is imminent, the final crisis of history. The opportunity must be seized before it is too late.

The divergence between the two Evangelists reveals a characteristic shift of emphasis, namely, a movement from the eschatological to the hortatory point of view.[75] Luke emphasizes God's eschatological action, Matthew, the disciples' conduct. Jesus lives in the expectation of the great catastrophe, the final πειρασμός (Mark 14.38), the last crisis of history which his death will introduce.[76] The primitive Church saw itself, and increasingly with the passage of time, standing midway between two crises, of which one belonged to the past, the other to the future. Standing thus between the Cross and the *Parousia*, the Church, looking for the guidance of Jesus, found itself forced by the altered conditions to interpret those parables of Jesus which were intended to arouse the crowd to a sense of the gravity of the moment, as directions for the conduct of the Christian community, thus shifting the emphasis from the eschatological to the hortatory interpretation.[77] Nevertheless this did not bring about the complete elimination of the eschatological content of the sayings of Jesus, but 'actualized' it by stressing the necessity of reconciliation.[78]

The *parable of the Great Supper* in the Gospel of Thomas 64 ends with the sentence, 'Tradesmen and merchants shall not enter the places of my Father.' Even if the reference is, in the first place, to the prosperous who decline the invitation, its generalized terms convey the idea of a sharp attack on the rich. This attitude of class-consciousness is to some extent in line with that of Luke in this parable (14.16–24) which he introduces as a sequel to the warning not to invite the rich and prosperous, but the poor, lame, halt, and blind (14.12–14). By his repetition of this list in 14.21 he indicates that the parable is

---

[75] The strongly imperative tone of the parable (p. 180) effectively enforces the shift of emphasis (cf. R. Bultmann, *The History of the Synoptic Tradition*₂, Oxford, 1968₂, p. 96).

[76] Dodd, pp. 67 ff.; J. Jeremias, 'Eine neue Schau der Zukunftsaussagen Jesu', in *Theol. Blätter*, 20 (1941), col. 216–222.

[77] Dodd, pp. 134 f. On p. 135, Dodd describes this shift of emphasis as the 'homiletic' or 'paraenetic' motive.

[78] This suggestion was put forward by A. Vögtle, Freiburg. See p. 48, n. 96.

THE HORTATORY USE OF THE PARABLES

intended to be a hortatory illustration of 14.12–14: one should behave like the host in the parable who symbolically invites to his
table the poor, the lame, the blind and the halt. But that is surely
not the original intention of the parable: in it, as we shall see,[79] Jesus
should rather be regarded as vindicating before his critics his preaching of the good news to the poor: he is saying, in effect, 'Because you
are refusing salvation, God is calling the despised to share the
salvation of the people of God.' In Luke the story has been transformed
from a vindication into a warning. Once again the emphasis has been
shifted from the eschatological to the hortatory. Examples of this
shift of emphasis are numerous: a typical case presents itself in the
parable of the Unjust Steward (Luke 16.1 ff.) which, for reasons
which may be readily understood, has undergone considerable
expansion. It is a debatable question who is meant by the κύριος in
v. 8 (καὶ ἐπῄνεσεν ὁ κύριος τὸν οἰκονόμον τῆς ἀδικίας). The change of
subject (καὶ ἐγὼ ὑμῖν λέγω) at the beginning of v. 9 seems to point
decisively to the conclusion that the lord in the parable is intended.
According to this view v. 8 is still part of the parable; the short story
ends, quite surprisingly, with the approval that the employer gives to
his steward. The point of the parable only comes in v. 9: just as the
unjust steward cancelled debts in order that the debtors 'might receive him into their houses' (v. 4), the disciples of Jesus should so
make use of the unrighteous mammon that the angels[80] may 'receive
them into everlasting habitations'. But it is doubtful whether this is
the original meaning of the parable. It is hard to believe that the
κύριος of v. 8 refers to the lord of the parable: how could he have
praised his deceitful steward? Above all, the analogy of 18.6 suggests
that the κύριος in 16.8 is Jesus; since it is clear that in 16.8 with
the words εἶπεν δὲ ὁ κύριος the judgement of Jesus is inserted into a
parable (where the principal figure[81] is likewise indicated by the
genitive of quality τῆς ἀδικίας) and yet there occurs here, too, in
18.8 a λέγω ὑμῖν of Jesus. But if the κύριος in 16.8 originally referred
to Jesus,[82] the abrupt transition from the third person (v. 8) to the

[79] See pp. 176 ff.
[80] See p. 46, n. 85.
[81] That is, the Judge, not the Widow, see p. 156.
[82] The designation of Jesus as ὁ κύριος in the narrative, which occurs a further
seventeen times in Luke, is almost a characteristic feature of the Third Gospel.
All instances derive from the pre-Lucan tradition.

first (v. 9) indicates that there is a join between the two verses; this is explained by the fact that several sayings (vv. 9–13), marked by the term μαμωνᾶς (vv. 9, 11, 13), have been added to the parable.

The recognition of this fact enables us to make the following analysis of the section in Luke 16.1–13: (1) The parable (vv. 1–7) describes a criminal who, threatened with exposure, adopts unscrupulous but resolute measures to ensure his future security. In v. 8a we get the application of the parable by Jesus: he 'praised the deceitful steward for his prudent action.' The clever, resolute behaviour of the man when threatened by imminent catastrophe should be an example to Jesus' hearers.[83] (In v. 8b this surprising commendation by Jesus is explained: rightly understood, it is limited to the prudence of the children of this world in their dealings with one another,[84] and does not refer to their relations with God.) (2) In v. 9 we have an entirely different application of the parable from that which is given in v. 8a: 'Make to yourselves friends[85] of the unrighteous mammon,[86] that when it passes away,[87] God may receive you into eternal dwellings[88] (to share in the heavenly banquet).' This second application of the parable looks like an appeal to a sacrificial, sociable attitude. Even on this interpretation, the steward is presented as an example, not because of his prudent resolution, when

[83] Φρόνιμος is the same as Matt. 7.24; 24.45=Luke 12.42; Matt. 25.2, 4, 8, 9, he who 'has grasped the eschatological situation' (H. Preisker in *ThLZ*, 74 (1949), col. 89).

[84] The words εἰς τὴν γενεὰν τὴν ἑαυτῶν are emphatic by their very position. The reflexive shows that they relate to the subject (οἱ υἱοὶ τοῦ αἰῶνος τούτου). The expression 'children of light' has now been abundantly confirmed by the Qumran texts, and its Palestinian character established.

[85] The 'friends' are the angels, i.e. God (a conjecture which is supported by v. 9b, where the 3rd person pl. alludes to the angels as a circumlocution for God); less probably it means 'good works' (supported by such passages as Pirqe Abh. 4.11: 'He who fulfils a command gains for himself an intercessor', Tos. Pea 4.21: 'Where (does it say) that almsgiving and works of charity are a powerful intercessor?'). Still, in either case God (not 'the friends') is the natural subject of δέξωνται in v. 9b: 'Gain for yourselves an intercessor, so that God may receive you'; such changes of subject are typically semitic.

[86] It is incorrect to follow Bill. II, p. 220, in comparing *mamon dišᵉqar*='money obtained illegally' with μαμωνᾶς τῆς ἀδικίας. The correct comparison is rather *hon (ha)rišʻa* (CD 6.15; 8.5; 19.17)='Mammon who belongs to this evil world', cf. H. Kosmala, 'The Parable of the Unjust Steward in the Light of Qumran', *Annual of the Swedish Theological Institute*, III, Leiden, 1964, p. 116.

[87] Probably to be understood eschatologically, cf. Zeph. 1.18: 'Neither their

[88] Dwelling in tents (as of old in the wilderness) is a feature of the eschatological consummation: Mark 9.5; Acts 15.16; Apoc. 7.15; 21.3. Cf. E. Lohmeyer, in *ZNW*, 21 (1922), pp. 191 ff.; H. Bornhäuser, *Sukka*, Berlin, 1935, pp. 126–8; H. Riesenfeld, *Jésus transfiguré*, Copenhagen, 1947, pp. 181 ff.

threatened with disaster, to make a fresh start for himself, but on account of his wise use of money: he used it to help others. The observation that v. 9 is formed on the model of v. 4 suggests that in v. 9 we hear the voice of a primitive Christian preacher who is concerned to derive a lesson for his congregation from the parable. (Though it is questionable whether this is really the meaning of the parable.) (3) But it is doubtful whether the man was really presented as an example at all. In vv. 10–12 (linked up with v. 9 through the catch-words ἄδικος (v. 10) and ἄδικος μαμωνᾶς (v. 11)), we have a third interpretation of the parable in the form of a proverb composed of two antithetic members (v. 10), which deals with faithfulness and unfaithfulness in unimportant things, and in vv. 11–12 is applied to mammon and the everlasting riches. On this third interpretation the steward is not an example, but a dreadful warning —the parable being understood by contraries. (4) An originally isolated logion (v. 13), as Matt. 6.24 shows, attached to the word μαμωνᾶς, closed the section with a sharp contrast between the service of God and the service of mammon, and summoned men to decide between God and mammon. F. C. Grant makes the apposite remark that these sentences 'read like the notes of an early church preacher or teacher, who used the parables for Christian indoctrination and exhortation'.[89]

Thus the interpretation of the parable has simply to be developed out of v. 8a. If, as v. 8a suggests, it is a summons to resolute action in a crisis, it would hardly have been addressed to the disciples, but rather to the 'unconverted',[90] the hesitant, the waverers, the crowd.[93] They must be told of the imminent crisis: they must be urged to deal with it courageously, wisely, and resolutely, to stake all on the future. The primitive Church applied the parable to the Christian community (Luke 16.1: πρὸς τοὺς μαθητάς, v. 9: ὑμῖν)[92] and drew from it a direction for the right use of wealth, and a warning against unfaithfulness; that is, it shifted the

---

[89] *Anglican Theological Review*, 30 (1948), p. 120. It is not, however, maintained that the inserted logia are secondary compositions.

[90] B. T. D. Smith, p. 110. Cf. Dodd, p. 30; H. Preisker in *ThLZ*, 74 (1949), col. 89.

[91] Cf. Luke 16.14, where the Pharisees are expressly mentioned as part of the audience of the parables. It is, however, possible that ἤκουον may be rendered, 'it came to their ears'.

[92] In Luke 16.1 ἔλεγεν δὲ καὶ πρός is a Lucan usage; in v. 9 ὑμῖν λέγω (with ὑμῖν preceding) is characteristic of the Lucan source, see p. 45, n. 80.

emphasis from the eschatological to the hortatory application.[93]

It would, however, be erroneous to assume that by its hortatory application the primitive Church introduced an entirely foreign element into the parable. Exhortation is already implicit in the original form of the parable, for Jesus' command to be resolute and make a new start embraces the generosity of v. 9, the faithfulness of vv. 10–12, and the rejection of mammon in v. 13. Thus, by the hortatory application the parable is not misinterpreted, but 'actualized'.[94] But it would also be erroneous to conclude that the primitive Church had completely excised the eschatological element from the parable, since it was the eschatological situation of the Church which lent weight to its exhortations. It is not a question of adding or taking away, but of a shift of emphasis resulting from a change of audience.

7. THE INFLUENCE OF THE CHURCH'S SITUATION

(a) *The Delay of the Parousia.* The recognition of the fact that the primitive Church related the parables to its own concrete situation, and by doing so produced a shift of emphasis, is, as Dodd has so aptly pointed out,[95] of fundamental importance for the understanding of the five *Parousia* parables. Let us first examine the little *parable of the Nocturnal Burglar* (Matt. 24.43 f.;[96] Luke 12.39 f.). 'But know this: if the master of the house had known in what watch of the night (Luke "hour")[97] the thief would come, he would (Matthew adds "have watched and" (not have allowed[98] his house to be broken into. Be you also ready,[99] for the Son of Man will come at a moment[1] when you do not expect him.' In itself the meaning of the

[93] A similar case is Luke 12.21, see below, p. 106.
[94] A. Vögtle, 'Das Gleichnis vom ungetreuen Verwalter', in *Oberrheinisches Pastoralblatt*, 53 (1952), offprint, pp. 14 f.
[95] For what follows, cf. Dodd, pp. 154–74.
[96] V. 42 which is absent from Luke, belongs originally to the parable of the Doorkeeper, cf. Mark 13.35.
[97] "Ωρα=ša'atha, meaning 'a point of time', 'the twinkling of an eye', cf. Matt. 26.45; Mark 14.41; I Cor. 4.11; Gal. 2.5.
[98] With regard to οὐκ ἂν εἴασεν διορυχθῆναι τὴν οἰκίαν αὐτοῦ Matt. 24.43, and οὐκ ἂν ἀφῆκεν διορυχθῆναι τὸν οἶκον αὐτοῦ Luke 12.39, the following points should be noted: 1. οὐκ ἐᾶν is a variant translation of οὐκ ἀφιέναι, and both mean 'to prevent'; 2. διορύσσειν ('to dig through') need not lead us to assume that the thief, avoiding the door from superstitious motives (T. W. Manson, *Sayings*, p. 117), broke through the wall of the house. It is rather an instance of a slavishly literal translation of the Aramaic *ḥathar* which means (a) 'to break through', and (b) 'to break in' (Bill., I, p. 967). Similarly in Matt. 6.19 διορύσσειν should be rendered 'break in'.
[99] See note 97.
[1] Matt. 24.44, with the addition of διὰ τοῦτο (a stylistic peculiarity of Matthew).

parable is clear: as the aorists (Luke ἀφῆκεν, Matthew ἐγρηγόρησεν, εἴασεν) surely show, Jesus draws the parable from an actual happening,[2] some recently effected burglary, about which the whole village is talking; he uses the alarming occurrence as a warning of the imminent calamity which he sees approaching. Guard yourselves, says he, that you may not be caught unawares like this householder who has just had his house broken into. But the application of the parable to the return of the Son of Man is strange;[3] for if the subject of discourse is a nocturnal burglary, it refers to a disastrous and alarming event, whereas the *Parousia*, at least for the disciples of Jesus, is the great day of joy. In fact the christological application is missing from the Gospel of Thomas. Here the parable of the night-burglar has been preserved in two versions. The one contained in logion 21b resembles the Matthaean version,[4] while the one which appears as logion 103 seems to be a very free repetition in the form of a beatitude and exhibits some affinity with Luke 12.35 ff.[5] Both versions agree in the fact that neither of them compares the breaking in of the burglar to the return of the Son of Man. If we disregard the reference to the Son of Man, the nearest parallels are to be found in the parable of the Flood (Matt. 24.37–39; Luke 17.26 f.),[6] and the destruction of Sodom (Luke 17.28–32). Here, too, events, although of extreme antiquity, which overwhelmed men unprepared, are used by Jesus as a warning of terrors to come. He sees the approaching Fate, the disaster at the door; with his coming it has indeed already broken in; but those around him are as heedless as that householder, living in the shadow of doom like those before the Flood and the Rain of Fire, as though there was no danger. Jesus wishes to arouse them, io open their eyes to the peril of their position. Terror draws near, as unexpected as the housebreaker, as fearful as the Deluge. Prepare yourselves! Soon it will be too late. Thus would Jesus' hearers have understood the parable of the House-breaker: as a rousing cry to the crowd in view of the oncoming eschatological catastrophe.[7]

---

[2] Dodd, pp. 168 f.

[3] 'The application is, in my opinion, inconsistent (with the parable itself)'; so, too, E. Fuchs, *Hermeneutik*, Bad Cannstatt, 1954, p. 223.

[4] For the text see below, p. 87.

[5] See below, p. 95.

[6] Dodd, p. 169. Comparison should also be made with the second Flood-parable (Matt. 7.24–27; Luke 6.47–49).

[7] Dodd, pp. 169 f.

The primitive Church applied the parable to its members (Luke 12.22, πρὸς τοὺς μαθητάς; Matt. 24.3). Further, Luke expressly emphasizes the fact that it only concerns the apostles, the responsible leaders of the community; since, to the appended question of Peter, 'Are you speaking this parable only[8] to us, or also to all?' (Luke 12.41), the answer is given in the former sense by the parable of the steward who is put to the test by the delay of his lord's return (Luke 12.42–48): It is spoken to you, upon whom a special responsibility rests. Thus the parable becomes a summons to the leaders of the Church, in view of the delayed *Parousia*, not to sleep, and the burglar, by means of christological allegorizing, becomes a figure of the Son of Man.

We are fortunately able to establish the probable correctness of our interpretation. The symbol of the thief is frequently employed in early Christian literature, and, since it is foreign to the eschatological imagery of late Jewish literature, we may infer that the passages in which it is found are based on the parable of Jesus.[9] Now, two points arise in these passages: (1) In I Thess. 5.2, 4; II Pet. 3.10 the thief is a figure of the sudden irruption of the Last Day (ἡμέρα κυρίου, I Thess. 5.2; II Pet. 3.10; ἡ ἡμέρα, I Thess. 5.4). The anarthrous genitival phrase ἡμέρα κυρίου (I Thess. 5.2; II Pet. 3.10), which is only to be explained as a Semitism, is clearly an allusion to the *yom Yahweh* of Amos.[10] Indeed, both passages contain the threat that the Day of the Lord will come as a 'thief'. The first occurrence of the comparison of Christ himself to a thief is in the Apocalypse (3.3; 16.15). (2) In all these passages without exception, especially I Thess. 5.4 and Apoc. 3.3, the Last Day is represented as coming like a thief for the unbelievers and unrepentant; the children of light are prepared and will not be taken unawares. Thus the earliest interpretation confirms the view that this parable of Jesus was originally addressed to the crowd, and that the house-breaking was a figure of the imminent catastrophe. Our parable is therefore nothing else but one of the numerous crisis-parables.

To sum up, then, we may say that the parable of the Burglar was applied by the Church to its own altered situation, which· was characterized by the delay of the *Parousia*, and that a somewhat changed

---

[8] See p. 39, n. 59.
[9] This confirms the conjecture on p. 49 that Jesus was thinking of an actual occurrence.
[10] Amos 5.18; Isa. 2.12 *et al.*

emphasis resulted. Doubtless its eschatological character was preserved, but the warning to the crowd became an admonition to the Christian community and its leaders; the proclamation of the coming catastrophe became a direction concerning conduct in view of the delayed *Parousia*, and by means of an allegorical interpretation the parable received a christological twist.

At this point it is necessary to guard carefully against a misunderstanding. The fact that Jesus related the parable of the Burglar to the impending catastrophe does not mean that the *Parousia* lay outside his field of vision. On the other hand, the fact that the early Church related the parable to the *Parousia* does not imply that they were not aware of the catastrophe that must precede it. On the contrary, in the matter of the eschatological expectation there is no difference between Jesus and the early Church; they both expected that the first stage of the eschatological crisis would be marked by the sudden irruption of the time of tribulation and the revelation of satanic power over the whole earth, and they both—Jesus and the early Church—were certain that this last tribulation would end with the triumph of God, the *Parousia*. The difference lay simply in the fact that Jesus, addressing the crowd, emphasized the sudden irruption of the tribulation (Be ready, the tribulation will overtake you as unexpectedly as the thief's invasion), while the attention of the early Church was directed to the end of the tribulation (Let there be no relaxation of watchfulness, for the Lord's return will be as unexpected as the breaking-in of the thief).

Matthew's understanding of the *parable of the Ten Virgins* (25. 1–13), belonging to his special material, is shown by the context (24.32–25.46 are clearly *Parousia* parables), as well as by vv. 1 and 13. In v. 1 the τότε refers back to the *Parousia* mentioned in 24.44 and 50, of which v. 13 also speaks, 'Watch, for ye know not the day nor the hour.' Hence Matthew saw in the parable an allegory of the *Parousia* of Christ, the heavenly bridegroom: the Ten Virgins are the expectant Christian community, the 'tarrying' of the bridegroom (v. 5) is the postponement of the *Parousia*, his sudden coming (v. 6) is the unexpected incidence of the *Parousia*, the stern rejection of the foolish virgins (v. 11) is the final Judgement. Moreover, it would appear that at a very early date the foolish Virgins were interpreted as referring to Israel, and the wise Virgins as the Gentiles; the Lukan tradition apparently depicted the condemnation of Israel at the Last Judgement as the refusal of admittance to those who knocked too late at the door (Luke 13.25). But was all this the original meaning of the parable? In answering this question we shall have to disregard the Matthaean context, as well as the τότε in v. 1, which is one of Matthew's favourite and characteristic transition particles (see p. 82, n. 52). We must also disregard v. 13. For this concluding admonition to watch misses the meaning of the parable. All slept, the wise as well as the foolish! What is blamed is not the sleeping, but the failure of the foolish virgins to provide oil for their lamps. Thus the exhortation to watchfulness in v. 13 is one of those admonitions which people liked to add to the parables;[12] it repeats Matt. 24.42 and belonged originally to the parable of the Doorkeeper (Mark 13.35). Hence the references to the *Parousia* do not belong to the original form of the parable. This makes it doubtful whether Matt. 25.1–12 was originally an allegory, for the allegorical representation of the Messiah as a bridegroom is completely foreign to the whole of the Old Testament and to the literature of late Judaism,[13] and first makes its appearance in the Pauline writings (II Cor. 11.2). Jesus' audience could hardly have applied the figure of the bridegroom in Matt. 25.1 ff. to the Messiah. Since the allegory in question is also not found in the rest of the preaching of Jesus,[14] we must conclude that Matt. 25.1–13 is not an allegory of Christ the heavenly bridegroom, but that Jesus was telling a story about an actual wedding, or rather what immediately preceded the beginning of an actual wedding feast.[15] At the most the parable conceals a Messianic

---

[11] See pp. 110 ff.

[12] I gave the evidence in *ThWBNT*, IV, pp. 1094 f., s.v. νύμφη/νυμφίος. Cf. also J. Gnilka, 'Bräutigam—spätjüdisches Messiaspradikat?', in *Trierer Theol. Z.*, 69 (1960), pp. 298–301 (on 1Q Isa.ᵃ 61.10). Since then I have found an example in rabbinic literature: 'The garment in which God will one day clothe the Messiah, will shine ever more brightly from one end of the world to the other, cf. Isa. 61.10: "Like a bridegroom who puts on the priestly mitre" ' (Pesiq. 149a). This isolated and very late example does not affect the general picture.

[13] Neither is the allegory of the bridegroom as the Messiah to be found in Mark 2.19a (Matt. 9.15a; Luke 5.34). For the subordinate clause ἐν ᾧ ὁ νυμφίος μετ' αὐτῶν ἐστιν may have originally been merely a circumlocution for 'during the wedding'. To the question why his disciples did not fast, Jesus replied with the question: 'Can the wedding-guests fast during the wedding?' Just as meaningless would it be for the disciples to fast who are already in full enjoyment of the New Age! The allegory of the bridegroom as the Messiah first appears in Mark 2.20 (Matt. 9.15b; Luke 5.35). But this verse, which, in contradiction to Mark 2.19a, declares that a time will come for the disciples to fast, is (on other grounds as well, cf. *ThWBNT*, IV, p. 1096.19 ff.) a product of the early Church.

[14] The question whether the parable is an allegory or the account of a real wedding is dealt with more fully below, p. 171 ff.

utterance of Jesus which only his disciples could understand. How then must his audience have understood the parable, especially if we regard the audience as consisting of the crowd, as Luke 13.22–30 would suggest? The sudden coming of the bridegroom (v. 6) has its parallels in the sudden downpour of the Flood, in the unexpected entry of the thief, or in the unlooked-for return of the master of the house from the feast or the journey.[16] The common element of suddenness is a figure of the unexpected incidence of catastrophe. The crisis is at the door. It will come as unexpectedly as the midnight cry in the parable, 'Behold the bridegroom cometh!' And it brings the inexorable severance, even where mortal eyes see no distinction (cf. Matt. 24.40 f.; Luke 17.34 f.; Gospel of Thomas 61a). Woe to those whom that hour finds unprepared! Hence it was as a cry of warning in view of the imminent eschatological crisis that Jesus uttered the parable, and as such the crowd understood it.

The early Church interpreted the bridegroom as Christ and his midnight coming as the *Parousia*. It did not deviate from the original meaning, since, as we have already seen,[15] the eschatological catastrophe and the Messianic *Parousia* are simply two aspects of the same event; the christological interpretation of the bridegroom notwithstanding, the coming separation of the wise and foolish virgins continued to be the aim and central point of the text. In spite of this, an essential change of emphasis took place: the warning cry intended to awake the crowd from sleep became an exhortation to the band of disciples, and the parable became an allegory of Christ the heavenly bridegroom and the expectant Church.

The third of the *Parousia*-parables to be discussed is the *parable of the Doorkeeper* (Mark 13.33–37; Luke 12.35–38, cf. Matt. 24.42). It exhibits unusually wide variations in the three Synoptics; it has been very much used and, under the influence of the *Parousia*-motive, worked over and expanded—showing how important to the primitive Church was the exhortation to watchfulness. Starting with Luke 12.35–38, we have first the rewarding of the watchful servants: 'Verily, I say unto you, he (the master of the house) will gird himself and make them sit down to meat and will come forth and serve them' (12.37b). No earthly master would act thus (cf. Luke 17.7), but Jesus has done so (Luke 22.27; John 13.4–5). And he will again do so on his return. Hence v. 37b is an allegorizing detail,[17] which

---

[15] See p. 51.   [16] Cf. Dodd, p. 172.
[17] Dodd, p. 161, n. 1; B. T. D. Smith, p. 107.

disturbs the setting of the parable, breaking the connection between v. 37a and v. 38, and refers to the Messianic banquet at the *Parousia*.[18] A second detail in Luke is noteworthy: while in Mark it is only the doorkeeper, as befits his office, who receives the command to watch until the master returns, in Luke it is a number, evidently the whole staff of servants, who are to watch;[19] undoubtedly the application of the parable to the whole Christian community has here made its imprint on the text. The Marcan version of the parable (13.33–37) is so far original in that the command to watch is only addressed to the doorkeeper (v. 34b). But it exhibits secondary features in two places as the result of the influence of related parables. The words ὡς ἄνθρωπος ἀπόδημος (v. 34) must come from the parable of the Talents (Matt. 25.14), since the order to the doorkeeper to keep watch during the night, while it comports with an invitation for the master of the house to attend a banquet[20] (Luke 12.36) which may last far into the night, does not, on the other hand, suit a longer journey whose date of return is undetermined, and from which, in view of the oriental avoidance of night journeys, a nocturnal return is improbable. As in the case of ἄνθρωπος ἀπόδημος, so, in the second place, the transfer of authority to the servants (δοὺς τοῖς δούλοις αὐτοῦ τὴν ἐξουσίαν, Mark 13.34) is out of place in the parable of the Doorkeeper. It is derived from the parable of the Servant entrusted with Supervision (Matt. 24.45; Luke 12.42), which is concerned with the scrupulous administration of what is entrusted to him during the prolonged absence of the master; it is hardly necessary for a householder, who has merely accepted an invitation, to assign special powers to his servants.[21] Finally, in Matthew the parable has disappeared, and only the application remains: 'Watch therefore, for ye know not what day your lord cometh' (24.42, cf. 25.13). If we compare Mark 13.35: 'Watch therefore, for ye know not what hour the master of the house cometh, in the evening, at midnight, at cockcrow, or in the morning', we see that 'the master of the house' has become 'your lord' and

[18] V. 37b is probably secondary, although pre-Lucan, as is shown by the word ἀμήν, rarely used by Luke (6 occurrences), and by the semitizing redundant word παρελθών.
[19] Dodd, p. 163.
[20] For γάμοι = banquet, see p. 26.
[21] The 2nd pers. in vv. 35–36 may also be secondary in Mark (Luke 12.37a, 38 has the 3rd pers.); here the application of the parable has forced its way into the parable. It has often been suggested, perhaps rightly, that Mark 13.33, 37 are hortatory verses introduced to form a setting for the parable.

'the night-watch' has become 'the Day'—the christological interpretation is obvious. It occurs not only in Matt. 24.42 and Luke
12.37b, but also in Rev. 3.20, and had thus spread rapidly throughout the whole Church.

We are then left with a core which consists of the parable of the
Doorkeeper, who had received the command to keep watch (Mark
13.34b), and to open immediately as soon as his master, on his
return from the banquet, should knock (Luke 12.36). It would be
well for him if his master should find him watching, at whatever
watch of the night he might return (Luke 12.37a, 38; Mark 13.35 f.).
What had Jesus in mind, and to what audience was his exhortation
to watchfulness addressed? If Jesus spoke the parable to his disciples,
then we may compare the appeal to watch in Gethsemane: 'Watch
and pray, lest ye enter into temptation' (Mark 14.38), where he was
thinking of the final *peirasmos*, the beginning of the eschatological
tribulation, the attack of Satan upon the saints of God, whose
incidence he expected would be ushered in by his passion.[22] If Jesus
was speaking to the crowd, then we might compare the parable
about the Flood: calamity is impending, as unpredictable as the
return of the householder! Be watchful! It seems to me most probable
that the parable of the Doorkeeper was addressed to those who
claimed to possess the keys of the Kingdom of Heaven (Matt. 23.13;
Luke 11.52), that is, to the scribes: take heed that you be not found
sleeping when the moment of crisis arrives! Whoever may have been
the original hearers, it is plain that we have here a crisis-parable; if it
contains a Messianic utterance of Jesus about himself, it is, at the
most, a concealed one. The primitive Church applied the parable to
its own situation, lying between two crises, awaiting the delayed
Parousia. Hence the Church expanded the parable by the addition of
a series of new, allegorizing features: now the master of the house is
going on a long journey (Mark), he gives all his servants the command to watch (Luke), he gives authority to his servants before his
departure (Mark), the day (not the night-watch) of his return is
uncertain (Matthew), the reward which he gives is selfless service to
his own at the Messianic banquet (Luke).

A completely similar fate has befallen the closely related *parable
of the Servant entrusted with Supervision*, for so we must describe it—
the parable speaks of one, not of two servants[23] (Matt. 24.45-51;

---

[22] Dodd, p. 166, n. 1 (in the context of a discussion with M. Dibelius).
[23] This is shown by the word ἐκεῖνος in Luke 12.45. The well-attested ἐκεῖνος is

Luke 12.41–46). A position of trust was committed to this servant, and the unexpected return of his master from his journey would show whether he was worthy of the trust, or whether he had been tempted by his master's delayed return to abuse his power by terrorizing his fellow-servants and by self-indulgence. In Matthew and Luke, as is shown by the context (Matt. 24.44; Luke 12.40), and by the mention of the punishment of hell in Matt. 24.51bc; Luke 12.46c, the κύριος of the parable has been interpreted as the Son of Man returning to judge the world, and the parable has been understood as an admonition addressed to the disciples of Jesus not to fail in their trust because of the delay of the *Parousia*. The tradition underlying Luke [24] has gone a step further: influenced by the position of authority assigned to the servant over his fellow servants,[25] it has interpreted this of the apostles (Luke 12.41) and has limited the application of the parable to them. The passage in 12.47, peculiar to Luke, adds that a great responsibility has been entrusted to them; they know the master's will better than others, and more has been given to them than to others; hence a sterner reckoning will be demanded from them if they allow the delay of the *Parousia* to cause them to abuse their office. We can, however, hardly discern the original intention of the parable in these applications of it by Matthew and Luke.

First of all, we must entirely disregard the context, for in both Matthew and Luke the parable stands in a group of *Parousia*-parables (Matt. 24.32–25.46; Luke 12.35–59), and in both gospels the setting of the parable shows the formative influence of the tradition. The introductory question (Luke 12.41), which is missing in Matthew, exhibits quite a number of the literary peculiarities of the Lucan source,[26] and in Luke the conclusion is made up of two originally

---

also to be read in Matt. 24.48; ὁ κακὸς δοῦλος ἐκεῖνος in Matt. 24.48 means, 'that servant, since he is wicked' (W. Michaelis, *Die Gleichnisse Jesu*, Hamburg, 1956, pp. 71, 76).
[24] See p. 99, n. 39.
[25] In Luke this position of authority is emphasized by the use of the word οἰκονόμος (12.42); but it is not original, as is shown by the Matthaean parallel (24.45: δοῦλος) and by Luke vv. 43, 45, 46, 47 (where δοῦλος is used in each case). Moreover, it does not agree with the content of the parables: the servant's commission would not entail anything new or special if he was already in possession of the stewardship. The reason for the change from δοῦλος to οἰκονόμος was that Luke, as is shown by 12.41, limited the application of the parable to the apostles (W. Michaelis, ibid., p. 72, 74).
[26] See p. 99, n. 39.

independent logia (12.47 f.); [27] in Matthew the parable ends with one of his characteristic expressions (24.51c), [28] and the next parable is linked up with it by τότε, which is one of his favourite particles. [29] Moreover, the mention of the punishment of hell, introducing an element which transcends the limits of the parable, must, as has been independently recognized by various scholars, [30] go back to an erroneous translation of the original Aramaic form of the parable. [31] Originally the ending preserved its earthly setting. Above all, in the story no emphasis was laid on the delay of the master's return; [32] the words χρονίζει μου ὁ κύριος (Matt. 24.48; Luke 12.45) originally simply served to bring out the trying circumstances in which the servant found himself ('My Lord delayeth his coming'). Their object was rather to stress the sudden test to which his conduct was exposed.

If we wish to ascertain the original meaning of the parable, we must again ask how the picture of the servant, distinguished by a special position of trust and special responsibility, suddenly tested by the unexpected return of his master, would have affected Jesus' audience. From the Old Testament they were familiar with the

[27] In Luke 12.42–46 it is a question of a legitimate and misused trust; in vv. 47–48a (an antithetic pair of sentences), on the other hand, we are shown the differing degrees of severity with which one who knew God's will and one who did not, would be punished respectively; v. 48b, a synonymous pair of sentences, shows how the greater the divine gift, the greater is the responsibility.

[28] See p. 60, n. 44.

[29] See p. 82, n. 52.

[30] By A. Mingana, C. C. Torrey, T. W. Manson, K. A. Offermann (with varying suggestions for the Aramaic equivalent of διχοτομήσει, none of which is entirely satisfactory).

[31] Luke 12.46: καὶ διχοτομήσει αὐτὸν καὶ τὸ μέρος αὐτοῦ μετὰ τῶν ἀπίστων (Matt. 24.51: ὑποκριτῶν) θήσει· (Matt. 24.51: + ἐκεῖ ἔσται ὁ κλαυθμὸς καὶ ὁ βρυγμὸς τῶν ὀδόντων). With regard to this it should be noticed: (a) that the strange transition from natural to supernatural punishment may be explained by Aramaic. All the Syriac versions render διχοτομεῖν (to divide) by pallegh (divide, share, distribute). It may be assumed that the original Aramaic text read yᵉphallegh leh (for the construction with lᵉ cf. J. Levy, Chaldäisches Wörterbuch über die Targumim, Leipzig, 1881, II, 265b). That is ambiguous, since leh can be either accusative or dative. The translator understood it as accusative: 'he will divide him', while the original meaning was dative: 'he will give him (blows)' (so K. A. Offermann, Aramaic Origin of the New Testament, n.d., Downers Grove, Illinois, privately printed, pp. 22 f.), or: 'he will assign to him (his portion)'. (b) The enigmatic mention of the 'hypocrites' (τῶν ὑποκριτῶν) in Matthew (24.51) probably is due to Matthew himself, since ὑποκριτής belongs to his special vocabulary (Matt. 14 times, Mark once, Luke 3 times). (c) Τὸ μέρος τινὸς τιθέναι μετά . . . is a Semitism meaning 'to treat anyone as'. Hence, we should render 'he will give him blows and treat him as a profligate'.

[32] Dodd, p. 159.

designation of leaders, rulers, prophets, and sacred persons, as 'servants of God';[33] for them the scribes were overseers appointed by God, to whom the keys of the Kingdom of Heaven had been entrusted (Matt. 23.13; Luke 11.52).[34] Hence they would have seen in the responsible servant of the parable the religious leaders of their time. When this is recognized the parable falls into close relationship with the situation of the life of Jesus. It is seen to be one of his many stern words of warning to the leaders of the people, above all the scribes, that the day of reckoning was at hand, when God would reveal whether they had been faithful to the trust committed to them or had abused it.

It is comprehensible that the primitive Church should have interpreted the tarrying of the master of the house as the delay of the *Parousia*; for them the householder became the Son of Man who had departed to heaven and would suddenly return to judge the world; the servant was interpreted as the members, or (in Luke) the leaders, of the Christian community, who were exhorted not to allow themselves to fall into temptation during the period of waiting for the *Parousia*.

A more detailed counterpart to the parable of the servant entrusted with supervision, discussed above, is to be found in the *parable of the Talents*. It has come down to us in three versions: Matt. 25.14–30; Luke 19.12–27; and in the Gospel of the Nazarenes.[35] Let us work backwards from that version which has diverged most widely from the original. In the Gospel of the Nazarenes, in addition to the servant who had multiplied the money entrusted to him, and the one who hid his talent, there appears a third servant who squandered the money on harlots and flute-players; the first is commended, the second blamed, and the third is thrown into prison. This version, which substitutes extravagance for unfaithfulness (cf. Luke 15.30; 12.45), is a moralistic perversion which the parable has undergone in the Jewish-Christian Church. In Luke as compared with Matthew the parable wears a very different aspect. Matthew's merchant is replaced by Luke's nobleman who goes on a journey to claim a kingdom (v. 12); his fellow citizens attempt to frustrate his purpose by sending a deputation after him (v. 14); but he returns

[33] Dodd, p. 160.
[34] Bill., I, p. 741c; *ThWBNT*, III, p. 747, n. 42; p. 749 under b.
[35] E. Klostermann, *Apocrypha*, II₃ (Kleine Texte für Vorlesungen und Übungen, herausgegeben von H. Lietzmann, 8), Bonn-Berlin, 1929, p. 9, Fragm. 15.

as king (v. 15a, cf. also the 'cities' in vv. 17 and 19) and has his enemies slaughtered before his eyes (v. 27). In these features we may possibly have a second, originally independent, parable about a claimant for the throne, reflecting the historical situation of 4 BC. At that time Archelaus journeyed to Rome to get his kingship over Judaea confirmed; at the same time a Jewish embassy of fifty persons also went to Rome in order to resist his appointment.[36] The sanguinary revenge inflicted upon the people by Archelaus after his return had never been forgotten; Jesus appears to have used this incident in a crisis-parable as a warning to his audience against a false sense of security. Just as unexpectedly as the return and vengeance of Archelaus overtook his opponents, so unexpectedly will destruction overtake you. The pre-Lucan tradition would have already fused this parable with our parable.[37] The join is particularly obvious in vv. 24 f.; the additional rewarding of the first servant with 1 mina (=100 denarii), and the objection of the bystanders that the first servant has already 10 minas (=1,000 denarii), are meaningless,[38] after he has been appointed ruler over ten cities. To provide a setting for the conflated parable an introductory saying (19.11) has been prefixed which exhibits a number of Luke's literary characteristics (although it need not have come from Luke himself)[39]; it states that the parable was related in order to refute false expectations that the Kingdom was to appear immediately. Hence we can see how Luke interpreted our parable: Jesus, perceiving the existence of an eager expectation of the *Parousia*, announces the delay of that event, and for that reason instructs his disciples that the intervening period is to be a time of testing for them. Luke, then, would seem to have interpreted the nobleman who received a kingdom and demanded a reckoning from his servants on his return, as the Son of Man departing to heaven and returning to judgement. But Luke is certainly wrong. For it is hardly conceivable that Jesus would have compared himself, either with a man 'who drew out where he had not paid in,'[40]

[36] Josephus, *Bell. Jud.*, 2.80; *Ant.*, 17.299 f.
[37] For the fusion of parables, cf. pp. 94 ff. Since v. 11 is Lucan, the fusion must be early, especially as Luke is not accustomed to produce such fusions.
[38] W. Foerster, 'Das Gleichnis von den anvertrauten Pfunden', in *Verbum Dei manet in aeternum* (Festschrift für O. Schmitz), Witten, 1953, p. 39.
[39] See p. 99, n. 40.
[40] Αἴρεις ὃ οὐκ ἔθηκας belongs to the vocabulary of banking; the expression is a popular designation for a grasping person (cf. Brightman, *Journ. of Th. St.*, 29 (1928), p. 158).

and reaped where he had not sown' (Luke 19.21), that is, a rapacious man, heedlessly intent on his own profit: or with a brutal oriental despot, gloating over the sight of his enemies slaughtered before his eyes (v. 27: ἔμπροσθέν μου). It is clear, from the comparison of details, that Matthew has preserved the earliest version, although even here secondary features are to be observed.[41] Matthew, too, has interpreted our parable as a *Parousia*-parable (as we saw above that Luke has done—incorrectly!), since he has placed it among the *Parousia*-parables, 24.32–25.13 and 25.31–46. It must have been, as the γάρ of the introduction shows (25.14), intended to reinforce the exhortation to watchfulness in view of the unknown hour of the *Parousia* (25.13). Matthew has been influenced by the christological interpretation in two places in the parable: in the expression, 'Enter into the banquet[42] of thy lord' (25.21, 23) and in the command to cast the unprofitable servant 'into outer darkness' (25.30). In both utterances it is not an earthly merchant who is speaking, but the Christ of the *Parousia*, who awards a share in the New Age, and assigns men to eternal damnation.[43] Neither of these features comports with the original situation: this is established for 25.21, 23 by the comparison with Luke, where the reward remains in an earthly setting and the minatory words in Matt. 25.30 (absent from Luke), which break through the bounds of the earthly setting of the parable, reveal themselves as the product of editorial activity by the fact that they exhibit the stylistic peculiarities of Matthew,[44] and by the fact that they double the penalty by adding to the earthly penalty (v. 28) the punishment of hell.

If we discard these ethical and allegorizing expansions, there lies before us the story of a rich man, feared by his servants as an inconsiderate and rapacious employer, who, before setting out on a long

[41] In Matthew the servants are entrusted with very large amounts, and must therefore be thought of as governors of some kind; in Luke, they are so appointed after the accounting. It is evident that the more modest sum of 100 *denarii*, mentioned by Luke, is original (see p. 28).

[42] Χαρά=*hedhw*ᵉ*tha*= (1) 'joy', (2) 'a feast' (G. Dalman, *Die Worte Jesu*, I₂, Leipzig, 1930, p. 96; Bill., I, pp. 972 f.); in our two passages the second meaning is to be preferred because of the symbolic εἰσέρχεσθαι, meaning 'to enter' into the Kingdom of God, cf. J. Schneider in *ThWNBT*, II, pp. 674 f. The two servants were invited to a meal. Eating together implies equality of status.

[43] Cf. B. T. D. Smith, p. 166.

[44] Εἰς τὸ σκότος τὸ ἐξώτερον in v. 30a (cf. Matt. 8.12; 22.13) and ἐκεῖ ἔσται ὁ κλαυθμὸς καὶ ὁ βρυγμὸς τῶν ὀδόντων in v. 30b (cf. Matt. 8.12; 13.42,50; 22.13; 24.51) are expressions which Matthew likes to use as conclusions, cf. especially the similar combination of both expressions in 8.12 and 22.13.

journey, entrusts to each of three [45] of his servants the sum of 100 denarii [46] to be traded with, either merely not to leave his capital unemployed, during his absence,[47] or with the intention of testing the servants,[48] and requiring an account from them on his return. The two faithful servants are rewarded with increased responsibility.[49] The emphasis lies on the reckoning with the third servant,[50] who makes the unconvincing excuse that from an excess of caution he has made no use of the money entrusted to him, because he knew his master's rapacity and feared lest, through the failure of his business transactions, he might incur his master's extreme anger at the loss of his money. According to Luke the third servant had behaved with an inexcusable irresponsibility. While, according to Matt. 25.18, he had at least taken the precaution of burying the money entrusted to him, according to Luke 19.20 he had wrapped it in a napkin, thereby neglecting the most elementary safety measure.[51] How would Jesus' audience have understood the parable? What, in particular, would they have thought about the servant who buried his talent? Would they have applied the figure to the Jewish people to whom so much had been entrusted, but who had not made use of their trust?[52] Would they have thought of the Pharisees, who sought to secure their personal salvation by a scrupulous observance of the Law, but who by their selfish exclusiveness rendered their religion nugatory? [53] We have already seen that Jesus' hearers would have thought, in the first place, of their religious leaders, especially of the scribes. Since Jesus in Luke 11.52 had reproached them for withholding from their fellow

---

[45] In 19.13 Luke would seem to have ten servants, but the continuation (cf. especially ὁ ἕτερος in 19.20) betrays that three was the original number.

[46] See p. 60, n. 41.

[47] W. Michaelis, Die Gleichnisse Jesu, Hamburg, 1956, pp. 107 f.

[48] Thus, T. W. Manson, Sayings, p. 315, with reference to the kind of reward bestowed upon the servants (cf. next note).

[49] T. W. Manson, ibid., p. 247, refers to the fine saying in Pirqe Abh. 4.2: 'The reward of duty (done) is a duty (to be done).' According to Luke 19.17, 19 one was made governor of a Decapolis, and the other of a Pentapolis.

[50] Dodd, p. 150.

[51] Burying (Matt. 25.18), according to rabbinical law, was regarded as the best security against theft. Anyone who buried a pledge or a deposit immediately upon receipt of it, was free from liability (b.B.M. 42a). On the other hand, if anyone tied up entrusted money in a cloth, he was responsible to make good any loss incurred through inadequate care of the entrusted deposit (B.M. 3.10 f.). It should be observed that both Matthew and Luke presuppose Palestinian conditions. The napkin is a woven head-covering, about a yard square.

[52] M. Dibelius, Jesus, London, 1963, p. 116.

[53] Dodd, pp. 151 f.

men a due share in God's gift,[54] we may assume that Jesus originally
addressed the parable of the Talents to the scribes.[55] Much had been
entrusted to them: the Word of God; [56] but like the servants in the
parable, they would shortly have to render account of how they had
used that which had been committed to them: it would be seen whether
they had used it in accordance with the will of God, or whether, like
the third servant, they had frustrated the operation of the divine word
by self-seeking and careless neglect of God's gift.

Again we find that the primitive Church applied this parable in
various ways[57] to its own actual situation. The beginning of this
development can be seen in the fact that the command, 'Take from
him his pound, and give it to him that hath ten pounds' (Luke 19.24,
cf. Matt. 25.28) is confirmed by the generalizing explanatory comment: 'For to every one who has, God [58] will give; [59] but from him
who has not, he will take [58] even what he has'.[60] The saying is an
entirely relevant explanation of the command: actually the reward
of the industrious servant is increased, while what the unprofitable
servant has is taken away from him. Nevertheless, the addition of the
explanatory comment changes the outlook of the whole parable,
since the insertion of the comment immediately before the final
sentence makes it an interpretation of the whole parable, instead of
that of a single verse (Matt. 25.28 par.). The main emphasis is now
transferred to a secondary feature (v. 28), and the whole parable
consequently assumes the character of an exposition of the nature
and manner of divine retribution. It seems unjust to make the rich
man still richer and to deprive the poor man of his last penny. Luke
makes the audience openly express astonishment at such treatment.
'Lord, he hath ten pounds' (Luke 19.25). But the primitive Christian
teaching affirms that this is what God's justice is like, hence all the

[54] Cf. *ThWBNT*, III, pp. 746 f.
[55] B. T. D. Smith, p. 168.
[56] For the comparison of the divine Word with a deposit entrusted by God cf.
also I Tim. 6.20; II Tim. 1.12, 14.
[57] Dodd, pp. 152 f.
[58] The passives δοθήσεται/ἀρθήσεται are circumlocutions for the divine name.
[59] Matthew alone has added to both 25.29 and to 13.12 the words καὶ περισσευθήσεται; the tradition loves such additions.
[60] V. 29 (par. Luke 19.26) breaks the connection between vv. 28 and 30; the
verse is an originally isolated Logion (Mark 4.25; Matt. 13.12; Luke 8.18; Gospel
of Thomas 41), which was added to the parable as a generalizing conclusion, and
perhaps, as the agreement between Matthew and Luke shows, was already to be
found in the tradition underlying both gospels. The logion was perhaps originally
a proverb—That's what life is like, unjust.

more urgent is the need to avoid failure! In the Gospel of the
Nazarenes the emphasis is laid even more obviously on the hortatory
element; the parable has become a warning to the community against
riotous living.

With the hortatory application of the parable, however, another
tendency early made its appearance: the application to the delay of
the *Parousia*, and the accompanying allegorization. The journey of the
merchant, originally mentioned only to explain why the servants
were in charge of their master's money, becomes more and more the
central point of the story. In Matthew the merchant has become an
allegory of Christ, his journey has become the ascension, his subsequent return μετὰ πολὺν χρόνον (Matt. 25.19) has become the
Parousia, which ushers some into the Messianic banquet and casts
the others into outer darkness. Luke carries the process of allegorization still further: the merchant becomes a king, and the whole
parable an announcement and confirmation of the delay of the
Parousia.

The five *Parousia*-parables which we have discussed were originally a group of crisis-parables. They were intended to arouse a
deluded people and their leaders to a realization of the awful gravity
of the moment. The catastrophe will come as unexpectedly as the
nocturnal house-breaker, as the bridegroom arriving at midnight,
the master of the house returning late from the wedding-feast, the
nobleman returning from his far journey. See that you be not taken
unawares! It was the primitive Church which first interpreted the
five parables in a christological sense [61] and as addressed to the community, warning them not to become slack because of the delayed
Parousia.

(b) *The Missionary Church.* The *parable of the Great Supper* has
come down to us in a double tradition from Matthew and Luke
respectively (Matt. 22.1–14; Luke 14.16–24). It also occurs in the
Gospel of Thomas as logion 64 of which the version is given on
p. 176. A common feature of all three versions is the refusal of the
invitation by the invited guests and their replacement by the next
best. We have here one of the numerous parables which, like the
parables of the Labourers in the Vineyard and the Lost Sheep previously discussed, were applied by Jesus to his critics and opponents
in order to vindicate the good news against them. You, he says, are

[61] Jesus himself in public only once explicitly designated himself as Messiah:
Mark 14.62 par.

like the guests who slighted the invitation; you would not receive it: hence God has called the publicans and sinners and has offered them the salvation which you have spurned.

When we observe the divergences of the two versions, we find that in Matthew the parable has received a strongly allegorical treatment (see pp. 67 ff.), and a second parable (22.11–13) has been added, together with a generalizing conclusion (22.14, see p. 106). In Luke the parable serves as a story illustrating the warning in 14.12–14 to invite the poorest (see pp. 44 f.); it has further been expanded to contain a second invitation to the uninvited (14.22 f.); [62] Let us turn our attention first to the expansion in Luke 14.22 f. After the servant has called in from the streets and lanes of the city the poor, the maimed, the blind, and the lame (v. 21), there is still room in the dining-hall (v. 22). He is then ordered to summon more guests from the '(country) roads and the (vineyard) hedges' (v. 23); [63] i.e., he must go outside the city gates and call in the tramps in addition to the city poor (v. 21). Since Matthew (22.9 f.) and the Gospel of Thomas (64) refer to only *one* invitation to the uninvited, the double invitation will be an expansion of the parable. This development in the Lucan source is surely only intended to depict the host's purpose to have every place in his house filled at all costs. On the other hand, Luke may have read more into the double invitation. He may have understood the first invitation to the uninvited, which was confined to those in the city, to signify the publicans and sinners in Israel, while the invitation to those outside the city might indicate the Gentiles. For, as comparison with Matt. 21.43 (the immediately preceding parable) shows, Matthew had already apparently understood the uninvited to refer to the Gentiles. But in Luke the doubling has heightened the picture; to him the introduction of the Gentiles into the Kingdom of God was of the first importance. It was the Church in a situation demanding missionary activity, which interpreted the parable as a missionary command; the agreement of Matthew and Luke shows that this happened very early, but it could hardly have been the original meaning (see above, p. 63). This is not to suggest that the admission of the Gentiles to a share in the Kingdom of God lay beyond the horizon of Jesus' vision, but he envisaged the participation of the Gentiles in a different way, not in the form of the Christian mission, but as the inrush of the Gentiles in the eschatological hour,

[62] The final sentence v. 24, too, may be secondary (see pp. 177 f.).
[63] W. Michaelis in *ThWBNT*, V, p. 69.

now so imminent (Matt. 8.11 f.).[64] Hence we conclude that the primitive Church interpreted and expanded this parable of Jesus in accordance with its own missionary situation.

The Matthaean version of our parable provides us with a very similar observation. Its conclusion (22.11–13) has long troubled the expositors as they found themselves confronted by the puzzling question why a man called in from the streets should be expected to have a wedding-garment. The favourite explanation that it was customary to provide invited guests with a festal garment (cf. II Kings 10.22) breaks down here, since there is no example of the existence of such a custom in the time of Jesus.[65] On the contrary the absence of the verses from Luke and from the Gospel of Thomas, as well as the striking change from δοῦλοι (vv. 3, 4, 6, 8, 10) to διάκονοι (v. 13), shows that vv. 11–13 are an expansion, and the comparison with an analogous rabbinical parable,[66] leads to the conclusion that the episode of the man without a wedding garment is a wholly independent parable; the beginning of this second parable may be found in 22.2, and may have been the cause of the transformation of what was originally a parable concerning the supper of a private individual (Luke 14.16) into one about a king (Matt. 22.2). Why did Matthew (or his source) insert the second parable? Clearly care needed to be taken to avoid a misunderstanding which might arise from the indiscriminate[67] invitation of the uninvited (vv. 8 ff.), to wit, that the conduct of the men who were called was of no significance. Jesus was not afraid of this misunderstanding, as is shown by the other parables about the good news (see pp. 120 ff.), for instance, the parable of the Prodigal Son; this is not surprising if we remember that the parables about the good news, as we shall presently see, were addressed without exception to opponents and critics. Nevertheless the above-mentioned misunderstanding was bound to appear as soon as the parable was applied to the community; since v. 10 thereupon became a saying about baptism: it opened the door into the festal hall to both 'bad and good'. But was not this saying about baptism very unguarded and incomplete? In the course of its missionary activity the Church was continually confronted by the danger

---

[64] J. Jeremias, *Jesus' Promise to the Nations*₂, London, 1967, pp. 58 ff.

[65] The ceremonial garment mentioned on p. 130 is not an instance of a common custom, but denotes a special mark of honour.

[66] b. Shab. 153a (par. Midr. Qoh. 9.8; Midr. Prov. 16.11); see below, p. 188.

[67] Πονηροὺς τε καὶ ἀγαθούς (v. 10) emphasizes, as Matt. 5.45 shows, the indiscriminateness.

that the gospel of the free grace of God might be interpreted as freeing the baptized from their moral responsibilities (Rom. 3.8; 6.1, 15; Jude 4). In order to remove any ground for such a misunderstanding, the parable of the Wedding Garment was inserted into the parable of the Great Supper, introducing the principle of merit, and emphasizing the necessity for repentance as the condition of acquittal at the Last Judgement. Thus we see again how the Church related the parable to its own actual situation, and expanded it to meet a need arising out of its missionary experience.

In the Matthaean form of the simile of the lamp it is said that it gives light 'to all who are in the house' (5.15). In Luke, on the other hand, it says 'that all who enter may see the light' (11.33). The Lucan version reflects Hellenistic architecture (see p. 27) and also the missionary situation of the Church.[68] Also in Matt. 13.38 (ὁ δὲ ἀγρός ἐστιν ὁ κόσμος)[69] we find the mission expressed.

(c) *Regulations for the Leadership of the Church.* In the course of what has so far been said, we have repeatedly had occasion to observe the process whereby parables which were originally addressed to the religious leaders of Israel,[70] or to the opponents of Jesus,[71] were applied by editorial activity to the leaders of the Church. These transferences were facilitated by the symbols used (servant, shepherd), but they were also due in the first place to the need for finding some directions in the sayings of Jesus to the leaders of the Church. The discourse in Matt. 18 which has been compiled with this need in view shows how keenly the need was felt.[72] This factor also influenced the interpretation of individual parables.

8. ALLEGORIZATION

In the previous section (see pp. 48 ff.) we have seen that the primitive Church had applied many parables to its own situation, characterized by the delay of the *Parousia* and the Gentile mission. One of the expedients made use of by the Church in the process of reinterpreting the parables was the allegorical method of interpretation. In the foremost place we find christological allegorizing: the thief, the bridegroom, the master of the house, the merchant, the king, were

[68] T. W. Manson, *Sayings,* p. 93.
[69] Cf. p. 81.
[70] P. 55 (the parable of the Doorkeeper); p. 58 (the parable of the Servant entrusted with Supervision); pp. 61 f. (the parable of the Talents).
[71] See p. 39 (the parable of the Lost Sheep).
[72] See p. 40.

interpreted of Christ, where originally the self-revelation of Christ was for the most part veiled, and only hinted at in a few of the parables. But also, where reward and punishment were in question, there was a readiness, as we have seen, to seize on the allegorical interpretation (the supper of the time of salvation: Matt. 25.21, 23; Luke 12.37b; the outer darkness: Matt. 22.13; 25.30). The number of secondary allegorical interpretations is, however, much greater. All three Synoptics agree in finding in the parables obscure sayings which are unintelligible to the outsiders (Mark 4.10–12 and par. in their present setting). Since, however, the various branches of tradition differ in their use of allegorical interpretation, it would seem desirable to deal with each of them separately. We shall begin with the study of the material common to Matthew and Luke (A), passing on to the Marcan material (B), the special material of Matthew (C), the Gospel of John (D), the special material of Luke (E), and the Gospel of Thomas (F).

A. First of all, so far as the material common to Matthew and Luke is concerned, it has already been established that Matthew and Luke agree in applying the parables of the House-breaker (Matt. 24.43 f.; Luke 12.39 f.; see pp. 48 ff.), of the Servant entrusted with Supervision (Matt. 24.45–51; Luke 12.41–46, see pp. 55 ff.), and of the Talents (Matt. 25.14–30; Luke 19.12–27, see pp. 58 ff.), to Christ and his *Parousia*, in divergence from the original meaning of the parables. The agreement between Matthew and Luke in all three cases confirms us in the conclusion that these allegorical interpretations are not due to the two evangelists, but belonged to the tradition which already lay behind them.

A further example of allegorical interpretation is furnished from the material common to Matthew and Luke by the *parable of the Great Supper* (Matt. 22.1–14; Luke 14.16–24; Gospel of Thomas 64[73]). The Matthaean form of this parable, as compared with the Lucan and the version in the Gospel of Thomas, in addition to the expansion (22.11–14) already discussed on pp. 63 ff., and to several merely narrative variants, exhibits a series of divergences which spring from the allegorizing tendency. The fact that in Matthew the 'man' (Luke 14.16; Gospel of Thomas 64) has become a 'king' (Matt. 22.2), and the δεῖπνον (Gospel of Thomas) or the δεῖπνον μέγα (Luke 14.16) has become a marriage-feast for the king's son (Matt.

[73] For the text of the Gospel of Thomas see p. 176.

22.2), may possibly be explained by the supposition that this was the introduction to the second, inserted, parable (Matt. 22.11–13) dealing with a marriage-feast arranged by a king. But this leaves much to be explained. As is shown by v. 6 f., we cannot attribute to mere embellishment the fact that the single servant of Luke (14.17, 21, 22 f.) and of the Gospel of Thomas is in Matthew replaced by a number of servants, of whom the first merely deliver the invitation to the feast (22.3),[74] while the second group (22.4, ἄλλους δούλους) bring the message that the feast is ready, nor the additional feature that already in Matthew the first group has been rejected. For it is clear that both these verses (22.6–7), except the words ὁ δὲ βασιλεὺς ὠργίσθη (cf. Luke 14.21), are an expansion, since they are missing from Luke and from the Gospel of Thomas, break the original connection between v. 5 and v. 8, and entirely destroy the setting of the story. We are told, for instance, in v. 6, that the second group of servants were not only rejected, but were quite undeservedly ill-treated by the λοιποί (whoever they were) of the invited guests, and even killed. Even more surprising is the anticipatory description of the wrath of the king who, before the marriage-feast, already prepared, has been partaken of, sends out his bodyguard,[75] has those murderers (who are all inhabitants of one city) put to death, and 'their city' burnt (v. 7). Evidently v. 7, using an ancient folk-theme describing a punitive expedition,[76] refers to the destruction of Jerusalem, from which we are to infer that Matthew intends to represent by the first group of servants (v. 3) the prophets and the rejection of their message; by the second group (v. 4) the apostles and missionaries sent to Israel, i.e. Jerusalem, and the sufferings and

[74] About this first group we are told καὶ ἀπέστειλεν τοὺς δούλους αὐτοῦ καλέσαι τοὺς κεκλημένους εἰς τοὺς γάμους (22.3). The pf. ptcp. τοὺς κεκλημένους seems to imply that the actual invitation had already been sent out, hence in vv. 3–4 we would have to do with three invitations in all (Jülicher, II, p. 419; E. Klostermann, Das Matthäusevangelium₂, Tübingen, 1927, p. 175 on Matt. 22.4). In reality, we have here an underlying Semitism. In Semitic speech the pass. ptcp. has often a gerundive force (Gesenius-Kautzsch-Bergsträsser, Hebräische Grammatik₂₉, Leipzig, 1926, § 13d, p. 69; K. Albrecht, Neuhebräische Grammatik, München, 1913, §107m, p. 120), i.e. οἱ κεκλημένοι=those who are to be invited. It is otherwise in Matt. 22.4, 8; Luke 14.17, 24.

[75] Τὰ στρατεύματα αὐτοῦ is a generalizing plural 'his army', cf. for this Semitism, P. Joüon, L'Évangile de Notre-Seigneur Jésus-Christ, Paris, 1930, p. 135; J. Jeremias, 'Beobachtungen zu neutestamentlichen Stellen an Hand des neugefundenen griechischen Henoch-Textes', in ZNW, 38 (1939), pp. 115 f., and designates, as in IV Macc. 5.1; Mech. Ex. 15.2; Luke 23.11, the body-guard (cf. K. H. Rengstorf, 'Die Stadt der Mörder (Mt 22, 7)', in BZNW, 26, Berlin, 1960, p. 108).

[76] See p. 33, n. 31.

martyrdom (v. 6) undergone by some of them; the sending out into the streets (vv. 9 ff.) indicates the Gentile mission; the entry into the wedding hall (v. 10b) is baptism. In his picture of the feast to which the prophets bring the invitation, whose preparedness is heralded by the apostles, which is spurned by the invited guests, and filled by the uninvited, and which may only be partaken of by those who are clothed in a wedding garment, he depicts the feast of salvation; the inspection of the guests (v. 11) is the Last Judgement, the 'outer darkness' (v. 13) is hell (cf. Matt. 8.12; 25.30). Thus, by his allegorical interpretation, Matthew has transformed our parable into an outline of the plan of redemption from the appearance of the prophets, embracing the fall of Jerusalem, up to the Last Judgement.[77] This outline of the history of the plan of redemption is intended to vindicate the transference of the mission to the Gentiles: Israel had rejected it.

Luke is more restrained in his use of allegory. In his version of the parable there are certainly some allegorical features, although they are not carried to such length as in Matthew. It is clear, however, from the introduction in 14.15, and from the expression 'my supper' in v. 24,[78] that he too regarded the supper as the feast of the time of salvation. Moreover, we have already seen (p. 64) that for him the πόλις is Israel and that the parable symbolizes the call to the Gentiles.[79] But the question arises here whether Luke himself could have been responsible for these allegorical interpretations. At any rate the allegorical representation of the πόλις as Israel and the supper as the feast of the time of salvation is not his work, but, as is shown by the agreement with Matthew, is older than either. The earthly setting of the story forbids the supposition that Jesus himself could have uttered it as an allegory of this feast, but he may well have had it in mind, as well as the rejection of the invitation by the leaders of Israel.

Occasionally Matthew alone (not Luke) allegorizes parables of

[77] There may, perhaps, be some literal dependence on Matt. 21.33 ff.; ἀπέστειλεν τοὺς δούλους αὐτοῦ (22.3) is literally identical with 21.34; πάλιν ἀπέστειλεν ἄλλους δούλους (22.4) is literally identical with 21.36; the killing of the servants in 22.6 has its counterpart in 21.35 f.; with ἀπώλεσεν τοὺς φονεῖς ἐκείνους, cf. 21.41 ἀπολέσει αὐτούς. The motiveless ill-treatment of the servants in Matt. 22.6 (they are actually the bearers of an invitation), has a motive in 21.35 f., where they are the bearers of a demand.

[78] On Luke 14.24 see below, p. 177.

[79] That Luke could have interpreted the servant (vv. 17, 21, 22 f.) as referring to Jesus (Jülicher, II, p. 416; E. Klostermann, *Das Lukasevangelium*₂, Tübingen, 1929, p. 151), is an assumption which is not warranted by the use of the singular, and which is refuted by vv. 22 f.: can Luke have thought of Jesus as carrying out a mission to the Gentiles?

the logion material. Thus, in Luke, the parable of the Lost Sheep depicts an activity drawn from life (15.4–7), while in Matthew, on the other hand, it has become an ecclesiological allegory (18.12–14); the shepherd represents the leader of the Christian community, and the lost sheep an erring member.

B. We turn next to the Marcan material, with respect to which it may first of all be recalled that we have already found a secondary application of the bridegroom in Mark 2.19b–20 (see p. 52, n. 14), and of the master of the house in Mark 13.33–37 (pp. 53 ff.), to Christ. Since the latter instance is also found in Luke (12.35–38) and in Matthew (24.42), although Luke and probably Matthew as well are following their own special source, it must be inferred that it springs from the tradition already underlying Mark.

A further example of allegorical interpretation is the *parable of the Wicked Husbandmen* (Mark 12.1–11; par. Matt. 21.33–44; Luke 20.9–18; Gospel of Thomas 65). This parable, linked up as it is with the Song of the Vineyard in Isa 5.1–7, exhibits an allegorical character which is unique among the parables of Jesus. The vineyard is clearly Israel, the tenants are Israel's rulers and leaders, the owner of the vineyard is God, the messengers are the prophets, the son is Christ, the punishment of the husbandmen symbolizes the ruin of Israel, the 'other people' (Matt. 21.43) are the Gentile Church. The whole parable is evidently pure allegory. Nevertheless this impression undergoes radical modification when the different versions are compared. In the earlier editions the comparison has already led to the conclusion that the allegorical features which already occur in Mark, but especially in Matthew, are secondary. This result has now been amply confirmed by the Gospel of Thomas. (1) With regard to *the introduction to the parable* it is to be observed that the description in Mark 12.1 and Matt. 21.33 of the careful construction of the vineyard is in close agreement with the Song of the Vineyard in Isa. 5.1–7. The hedge, the wine-press, and the tower are derived from Isa 5.1 f. It is immediately apparent from these scriptural allusions in the first sentences that the reference is not to an earthly owner of a vineyard and to his vineyard, but to God and Israel, and that we are therefore confronted with an allegory. This allusion to Isa. 5 is, however, omitted by Luke (20.9). More significant is the fact that it is absent from the Gospel of Thomas, where the beginning of the parable runs: 'A good man had a vineyard. He gave it to husbandmen so that they would work it and that he would receive its fruit from

them.' Most significant is the fact that the LXX has been used.[80]
The connection with Isa. 5 must therefore be due to secondary
editorial activity.

(2) In *the sending of the servants* the secondary character of the
allegorical features may be recognized with even greater clarity. In the
Gospel of Thomas the introduction cited above continues: 'He sent his
servant so that the husbandmen would give him the fruit of the vineyard. They seized his servant, they beat him; a little longer and they
would have killed him. The servant came and told it to his master.
His master said: "Perhaps he was unknown to them."[81] He sent
another servant; the husbandmen beat him as well.' This description
does not transgress the limits of a straightforward story; there is no
indication of a deeper allegorical meaning. It is specially noticeable
that in the Gospel of Thomas only *one* servant at a time is sent. This
feature also reappears in Mark—at least at first (12.2–5a)—although
there the number of sendings is increased to three. Three times is a
servant sent; the first is soundly beaten, the second is shamefully
handled with blows in the face, the third is killed. Thus Mark
arranges the sequence of insults in an ascending order to end in a
climax; in arranging that order so that the third servant should
be killed, he is following a popular love of climax which, in this case,
is unfortunate, since, by anticipating the fate which the son was to
suffer, he weakens the course of the story.[82] This feature has no
allegorical significance. Nevertheless, by adding v. 5b the Marcan
form has abandoned the popular triple formula, since there follows
a summary account of a multitude of servants, some of whom are
beaten and some killed. It cannot be doubted that we have here a
reference to the prophets and their fate. This allegory, obscuring
the original picture, can hardly be other than an expansion.[83] It is

[80] The use of the LXX is most clearly observable in the phrase περιέθηκεν φραγμόν
(Mark 12.1); the Hebrew text of Isa. 5.2 has 'he dug it up', which is incorrectly
translated by the LXX as φραγμὸν περιέθηκα, 'I fenced it round'.
[81] Literally: Perhaps he did not know them.
[82] The Gospel of Thomas is much more restrained when it says of the first servant who was sent: 'a little longer and they would have killed him'. In Luke 20.12
the third servant is only wounded.
[83] V. 5b destroys the construction of the sentence; since a verb (perhaps
ἐκάκωσαν, Jülicher, II, p. 389) should follow πολλοὺς ἄλλους, while δέροντες dis-
agrees with the main verb ἀπέκτειναν in v. 5a (pointed out by Ernst Haenchen).
However, in all probability Mark may have found v. 5b in his source, since the
μέν-δέ construction, which he rarely uses, has evidently been taken over by him
in the other passages where it occurs (14.21, 38) (W. G. Kümmel in *Aux sources de la
tradition chrétienne*, Goguel Festschrift, Neuchâtel-Paris, 1950, p. 122, n. 12).

characteristic of Luke (12.10–12) that he has not taken over the
killing of the third servant, nor the allegorical conclusion of Mark.
He confined himself to the triple sending and ill-treatment of each
servant, trimming the three incidents to perfect symmetry.[84] We are no
longer in a position to say whether his sober restraint is merely due to
his sense of style, or to oral tradition. Matthew's treatment is wholly
different (21.34–36). He has pursued the allegorizing method con-
sistently to the end. The climax, as we find it in Mark and Luke, is
completely spoilt. He starts with the sending out of a number of
servants, some of whom are ill-treated, some killed, and some stoned.
Then follows a further mission, more numerous than the first, whose
fate is the same. In these two missions Matthew sees the earlier and
the later prophets, and the mention of stoning has special reference
to the fate of the prophets (II Chron. 24.21; Heb. 11.37; Matt. 23.
37; Luke 13.34). Nothing remains of the original simple story as we
read it in the Gospel of Thomas and in Luke, and may infer it from
Mark, a story which only tells of a single messenger repeatedly
dismissed by the tenants empty-handed, and driven out with con-
tumely and injury.

(3) With regard to *the sending of the son*, it must first be noticed
that the actual story of the son's fate closes abruptly with his murder.
Similarly in the Gospel of Thomas which continues as follows: 'Then
the owner sent his son. He said: perhaps they will respect my son.
Since those husbandmen knew that he was the heir of the vineyard,
they seized him and killed him. Whoever has ears let him hear.' This
conclusion makes it difficult to see in the parable an allegory which
the primitive Church would have put in the mouth of Jesus, since the
resurrection of Jesus had such a central importance for the primitive
Church that it must have been mentioned in the story.[85] But in the
situation of Jesus, to which we are thus referred, the murder of the
son formed an appropriate climax for the audience. They will have
understood that Jesus saw himself as being the son, the last messenger,

---

[84] According to the evidence furnished by linguistic and stylistic studies, the
faultless symmetry of Luke 20.10–12 is Luke's work, for in these verses Lucan
stylistic characteristics (cf. the list in J. C. Hawkins, *Horae Synopticae*₂, Oxford,
1909, pp. 16 ff.) are of frequent occurrence: v. 10 (ἐξαποστέλλειν), v. 11 (προστιθέναι
for πάλιν Mark 12.4, ἕτερος, δὲ καί, ἐξαποστέλλειν), v. 12 (προστιθέναι, δὲ καί,
τοῦτον=him). It is not a coincidence that we have a completely similar case in
the parable of the Great Supper (Luke 14.15–24), where vv. 18–20, with their
symmetrically constructed excuses, show the marks of the Lucan style.
[85] V. Taylor, *Jesus and his Sacrifice*, London, 1937, p. 107; A. M. Brouwer, *De
Gelijkenissen*, Leiden, 1946, p. 68. First noted by F. C. Burkitt.

though it could not be taken for granted that the son had messianic significance, since no evidence is forthcoming for the application of the title 'Son of God' to the Messiah in pre-Christian Palestinian Judaism.[86] 'No Jew, hearing in our parable the story of the mission and slaying of the "son", could have dreamed of applying it to the sending of the Messiah.'[87] It is significant that in the rabbinical parable of the Wicked Tenants[88] the son is interpreted to be the patriarch Jacob (as representing the people of Israel). From which it follows that the christological point of the parable would have been hidden from the audience.

The primitive Church did not wait long to bring this point out. According to the Marcan form of the story, the son is killed inside the vineyard, and his body is then thrown out of it (v. 8). This feature of the story simply emphasizes the full extent of the husbandmen's iniquity: they go on to wreak upon the corpse the final indignity of throwing it over the wall and denying to the slain so much as a grave; nothing here recalls the incidents of the passion of Jesus. Not so Matthew (21.39) and Luke (20.15): on the contrary, they represent the son as being first cast out of the vineyard, and then slain outside it—a reference to the slaying of Jesus outside the city (John 19.17; Heb. 13.12 f.). Thus, in Matthew and Luke, we meet with a christological colouring of the parable, whose first traces are, however, to be found in Mark: first in the words υἱὸν ἀγαπητόν (12.6), an echo of the voice from heaven in 1.11 and 9.7,[89] and then in vv. 10–11, where in the form of the Old Testament symbol of the rejected stone which God[90] made the key-stone[91] (Ps. 118.22 f.) there is introduced one of

---

[86] The evidence of the Chester-Beatty Papyrus (ed. C. Bonner, *The Last Chapters of Enoch in Greek*, London, 1937, pp. 76 f.), has shown that Eth. En. 105.2 is an interpolation; in IV Ezra 7.28 f.; 13.32, 37, 52; 14.9, the *filius meus* of the Latin version goes back to the Greek παῖς μου='my servant' (*ThWBNT*, V, p. 680, n. 196). A few infrequent occurrences of the designation of the Messiah as Son of God are first found in later rabbinical literature in agreement with Ps. 2.7 (Bill., III, pp. 19 f.).

[87] W. G. Kümmel (see above, p. 71, n. 83), p. 130.

[88] Sifre Dt. 32.9, § 312 (Bill., I, p. 874).

[89] Kümmel, ibid., p. 123.

[90] Ἐγενήθη (Mark 12.10): the passive is used as a circumlocution for the divine name.

[91] Κεφαλὴ γωνίας (Luther: 'corner-stone') is the keystone of the porch, cf. J. Jeremias, 'Der Eckstein', in *Angelos*, I (1925), pp. 65 ff.; *ZNW*, 29 (1930), pp. 264 ff.; *ThWBNT*, I, pp. 792 f.; K. H. Schelkle, 'Akrogoniaios', in *RAC*, I (1950), col. 233 f. The most important instance is in Test. Sol. 22.7 ff. (ed. McCown, pp. 66 f.).

the primitive Church's favourite proof-texts for the resurrection and exaltation of the rejected Christ.[92] This scriptural proof which is a literal rendering of the LXX, was probably inserted when the parable was allegorically applied to Christ, with the intention of finding scriptural grounds for the fate of the Son, and to add the missing mention of the resurrection.[93] But all these christological interpretations are absent from the Gospel of Thomas.[94]

(4) With regard to *the final question* which occurs in all three Synoptists (Mark 12.9 par.), but is missing from the Gospel of Thomas, it refers back (see pp. 70 f.) to Isa. 5.5, again not to its Hebrew text (which is not in the form of a question), but following the LXX. If the final question is secondary (the Gospel of Thomas has instead the call to hear, see p. 72), then so is the answer to the question. Neither of them is part of the original parable.

But even if it is true to say that the connection of the beginning and the end of the parable with Isa. 5 is secondary, and that neither the sending of the three servants nor that of the son had originally any allegorical significance, yet the question arises whether the parable as a whole so far transcends the setting of everyday life, that it must have been intended as an allegory. Taking into consideration the amazing long-suffering of the owner of the vineyard, the absurd expectation of the tenants that by killing the son they would obtain the title to the property (Mark 12.7), the slaying of the son, the question is bound to arise, Could things happen like this? Strange as it may seem, this question must be answered in the affirmative. As Dodd has recognized,[95] the parable is a realistic description of the revolutionary attitude of the Galilean peasants towards the foreign landlords, an attitude which had been aroused by the Zealot movement which had its headquarters in Galilee. It is necessary to realize that not only the whole of the upper Jordan valley, and probably the north and north-west shores of the Lake of Gennesaret as well,[96]

---

[92] Acts 4.11; I Pet. 2.7.

[93] B. T. D. Smith, p. 224. The insertion of the O.T. quotation, implying the allegorical application of the son to Christ, is earlier than Mark, since the absence of proof-texts is characteristic of Mark; in the few cases where he does use them, he is following an earlier tradition.

[94] It is interesting to observe that the Gospel of Thomas merely furnishes a starting-point to the process of interpretation described above to the extent that it allows the saying about the Cornerstone to be attached as an independent logion (66) to the completed parable (65).

[95] Pp. 124 ff.

[96] A. Alt, 'Die Stätten des Wirkens Jesu in Galiläa', in *ZDPV*, 68 (1949), pp. 67 f.

but also a large part of the Galilean uplands, at that time bore the character of latifundia, and were in the hands of foreign landlords.[97] In order to understand the parable it is essential to realize that the landlord is evidently living abroad (Mark 12.1: καὶ ἀπεδήμησεν), perhaps, indeed, regarded as a foreigner. The tenants can take such liberties with the messengers only if their master is living abroad. If that is the case, he must, after his messengers have been driven out with insults, look out for a messenger whom the rebels will respect. If he is living in a distant foreign country we have, then, the simplest explanation of the otherwise incredibly foolish assumption of the tenants that, after the removal of the sole heir,[98] they will be able to take unhindered possession of the property (Mark 12.7); they evidently have in mind the law that under specified circumstances an inheritance may be regarded as ownerless property, which may be claimed by any one,[99] with the proviso that the prior right belongs to the claimant who comes first.[1] The arrival of the son allows them to

[97] Thus, in the time of the great revolt (AD 66), we hear of corn belonging to the imperial revenues, from the villages of upper Galilee, stored in Gishala (ed-Dshish) (Josephus, Vita, §71); hence these villages belonged to the imperial domains. At the same period Princess Berenice had stored large quantities of corn in Besara, on the boundaries of Ptolemais (Akko) (§119). At an earlier date, one of the Zeno papyri gives evidence of the fact that Apollonius, who was finance minister for the Ptolemaic kingdom from 261 to 246 BC, possessed a property (κτῆμα) in Baitianata in Galilee, from which wine was sent to him in Egypt (Pubblicazioni della Società Italiana, Papiri Greci e Latini, 6, 1920, no. 594); the same place is mentioned in the Zeno papyri as a commissariat station which supplied Egyptian officials with meal on their journeys through the country (Catalogue général du Musée du Caire, 79, no. 59004, 59011); also in Talmudic times Beth-'ana was regarded as a 'lost city', i.e. as a non-Jewish city on Jewish territory (Tos. Kil.2.16; j. 'Orla 3.63b), cf. A. Alt in Palästina-Jahrbuch, 22 (1926), p. 56; J. Herz, ibid., 24 (1928), p. 109. The latifundial character of a large part of the Galilean hill country is explained by the fact that it was originally royal territory (A. Alt, ibid., 33, 1937, pp. 87 f.); Ned. 5.5 treating of the assignment of property to princes, says: 'The people of Galilee need not assign their share, since their fathers have done so for them already' (H. Danby, Mishnah (1933), p. 271).

[98] Ἀγαπητός (Mark 12.6) has here the meaning 'only' (and hence especially beloved), cf. C. H. Turner, J.Th.St., 27 (1926), pp. 120 f.; Dodd, p. 130, n. 1. He is thus the sole heir.

[99] Such a case arises, for example, when an inheritance is not claimed within a specified period of time. Cf. E. Bammel, 'Das Gleichnis von den bösen Winzern (Mk. 12.1–9) und das jüdische Erbrecht', in Revue Internationale des Droits de l'Antiquité, 3ᵐᵉ série, 6 (1959), pp. 11–17, here pp. 14 f.

[1] J. Jeremias, Jerusalem in the Time of Jesus, London, 1969, p. 328. A piece of land could be considered as lawfully taken possession of, if no matter how small a portion of it had been 'marked out, fenced, or provided with an entrance' (B.B. 3.3); we hear of a concrete case in which a garden which belonged to a proselyte who died intestate was successfully claimed by 'drawing a picture', i.e. by marking it with a sign (b.B.B. 54a).

assume that the owner is dead, and that the son has come to take up his inheritance.[2] If they kill him, the vineyard becomes ownerless property which they can claim as being first on the spot. It may, however, be asked whether the slaying of the son is not too crude a feature for a story taken from real life? We have to consider that the impression which the story was intended to produce made it necessary to intensify the wickedness of the tenants to such an extent that no hearer could miss it. Their depravity must be as starkly emphasized as possible. The introduction of the figure of the only son is the result, not of theological reflection on the Messiah as Son of God, but of the logic of the story.[3] This does not rule out, but requires that by the slaying of the owner's son the parable may point to the actual situation, the rejection of God's definite and final message. Hence we are left with the conclusion that Mark 12.1 ff. is not an allegory, but a parable drawing upon a definite situation.

We are now in a position to answer the question concerning the original meaning of the parable. Like so many other parables of Jesus, it vindicates the offer of the gospel to the poor. You, it says, you tenants of the vineyard, you leaders of the people! you have opposed, have multiplied rebellion against God. Your cup is full! Therefore shall the vineyard of God be given to 'others' (Mark 12.9). Since neither Mark nor Luke give any further indication who the 'others' may be, we must, following the analogy of the related parables (pp. 127 f.), interpret them as the πτωχοί.[4]

We may sum up the result of our examination as follows: The mention of the vineyard is a potential allegorical element. 'The vineyard of the Lord of Hosts is the house of Israel' (Isa. 5.7), a verse with which the audience was familiar. This implied that the tenants must represent the leaders of Israel (Mark 12.12b; Luke 20.19b). The pre-Marcan tradition has carried the process of allegorization further by inserting the interpretation of the servants as the prophets (Mark 12.5b), and by inserting the prediction of the resurrection it has sharpened the christological point of the parable (12.10 f.).[5] Matthew

---

[2] Bammel, op. cit., p. 13, offers the alternative supposition that the son had already become the owner of the property as a gift from his father during the latter's lifetime (see pp. 128 f. on Luke 15.12), and had died childless, his father thus becoming his heir. But in this case the son would not be the heir, but the father.

[3] Dodd, p. 130.

[4] Cf. Matt. 5.5; πραεῖς κληρονομήσουσιν τὴν γῆν.

[5] Cf. p. 74, n. 93.

has gone much further along the same road; in his version the parable as, for example, the parable of the Great Supper (see pp. 67 ff.) has become an exact outline of the story of redemption, from the covenant at Sinai (for so he may have understood ἐξέδοτο in 21.33), embracing the destruction of Jerusalem (21.41, cf. 22.7), the founding of the Gentile Church (21.43),[6] and passing on to the Last Judgement (21.44).[7] Luke shows great hesitation with regard to allegorization, but does not entirely avoid it (20.13, 15, 17 f.). The Gospel of Thomas is free from allegorical traits (except for one hint in the context, see p. 74, n. 94). C. H. Dodd (p. 129) had already conjectured that the parable, far from being an allegory, followed a common folk-tale pattern, and originally told of a climactic series of three messengers, that is, two servants and the son. That is precisely what we now read in the Gospel of Thomas.

Lastly, in connection with Marcan material, we must discuss the *interpretation of the parable of the Sower* in Mark 4.13–20 (the parallels in Matt. 13.18–23; Luke 8.11–15 are dependent on Mark, as is shown by the context). I have long held out against the conclusion that this interpretation must be ascribed to the primitive Church; but on linguistic grounds alone it is unavoidable: (1) The use of ὁ λόγος absolutely is a technical term for the gospel coined and constantly used by the primitive Church;[8] this absolute use of ὁ λόγος by Jesus only occurs in the interpretation of the parable of the Sower (8 times in Mark, 5 times in Matthew, and 3 times in Luke), and nowhere else. This tallies with the fact that in this short passage a number of sayings about 'the Word' occur, which are not found elsewhere in the teaching of Jesus, but on the other hand are common in the apostolic age:[9] the preacher preaches the word;[10] the word is

[6] The interpretation of ἄλλοι as Gentiles (only in Matt. 21.43) is earlier than Matthew, since ἡ βασιλεία τοῦ θεοῦ (only 4 times in Matthew) is not one of his characteristic expressions; his own usage is ἡ βασιλεία τῶν οὐρανῶν (32 times, only found elsewhere in the N.T. as a variant to John 3.5).

[7] V. 44 is very well attested, and therefore not to be omitted, see p. 108, n. 71.

[8] Mark 1.45 (a Marcan summary); 2.2 (a redactional introduction to the story of the paralytic, linked with 1.45 by verbal similarity); 4.33 (a summary); 8.32 (?); Ps.–Mark 16.20; Luke 1.2; Acts 4.4; 6.4; 8.4; 10.36, 44; 11.19; 14.25; 16.6; 17.11; 18.5; Gal. 6.6; Col. 4.3; I Thess. 1.6; II Tim. 4.2; Jas. 1.21; I Pet. 2.8; 3.1; I John 2.7.

[9] J. Schniewind in *Das Neue Testament Deutsch*, I, on Mark 4.14 ff.

[10] Mark 1.45, διαφημίζειν τὸν λόγον (Jesus is the subject in v. 45a, as in v. 45b, since ἤρξατο is an Aramaizing redundancy which should be left untranslated), cf. Acts 8.4; II Tim. 4.2 *et al.*

received,[11] and that with joy;[12] persecution arises on account of the word,[13] the word is a cause of stumbling,[14] the word 'grows',[15] the word brings forth fruit.[16] (2) In Mark 4.13–20 there are a number of words which do not occur elsewhere in the Synoptists, but, on the other hand, are common in the rest of the New Testament literature, especially in Paul;[17] σπείρειν with the meaning 'preach';[18] ῥίζα meaning inward stability;[19] πρόσκαιρος (a Hellenism, for which there is no corresponding adjective in Aramaic);[20] ἀπάτη;[21] πλοῦτος;[22] ἄκαρπος;[23] παραδέχεσθαι;[24] καρποφορεῖν in a metaphorical sense.[25] In Luke ἐπιθυμία occurs once more, but with a different meaning and use.[26] Other words which are only found once more in the Synoptists are διωγμός;[27] μέριμνα.[28] The expression αἱ μέριμναι τοῦ αἰῶνος[29] only occurs once. (3) The interpretation of 'sowing' as preaching (Mark 4.14) is not characteristic of Jesus' way of speaking;[30] he prefers to compare preaching with the gathering in of the harvest.[31] (4) We must add to these linguistic results the important observation that the interpretation of the parable of the Sower misses the eschato-

---

[11] I Thess. 1.6; 2.13; Acts 17.11; II Cor. 11.4; Jas. 1.21.

[12] I Thess. 1.6 et al.

[13] I Thess. 1.6; II Tim. 1.8; 2.9.

[14] I Pet. 2.8.

[15] Acts 6.7; 12.24; 19.20; Col. 1.6.

[16] Col. 1.6, 10.

[17] Dodd, pp. 13 f.

[18] In the N.T. elsewhere only in I Cor. 9.11, cf. John 4.36 f. On Matt. 13.37, see below, pp. 81 ff.

[19] In the N.T. elsewhere only in Col. 2.7 and Eph. 3.17: ἐρριζωμένοι.

[20] P. Joüon, L'Évangile de Notre-Seigneur Jésus-Christ, Paris, 1930, p. 87; G. Dalman, Palästina-Jahrbuch, 22 (1926), pp. 125 f. In the N.T. elsewhere only in II Cor. 4.18; Heb. 11.25.

[21] In the N.T. elsewhere only in Eph. 4.22; Col. 2.8; II Pet. 2.13, and with the genitive (as in Mark 4.19) II Thess. 2.10; Heb. 3.13. With the meaning 'desire, pleasure' (which must be the sense of Mark 4.19), only in II Pet. 2.13.

[22] Not found elsewhere in the Gospels. In the rest of the N.T. 19 times, 15 of which are in the Pauline literature.

[23] Elsewhere only in I Cor. 14.14; Eph. 5.11; Tit. 3.14; II Pet. 1.8; Jude 12.

[24] Elsewhere only in Acts 15.4; 16.21; 22.18; I Tim. 5.19; Heb. 12.6.

[25] Elsewhere only in Rom. 7.4 f.; Col. 1.6, 10.

[26] Luke 22.15, in a positive sense and in the singular.

[27] Mark 10.30 (wanting in Matt. 19.29 and Luke 18.30, perhaps secondary).

[28] Luke 21.34 (in Luke 21.34–36, a late composition, which is, however, made up of early material worked over).

[29] The striking absolute use of ὁ αἰών for ὁ αἰὼν οὗτος is found in the N.T. only in the expression (ἡ) συντέλεια (τοῦ) αἰῶνος which is peculiar to Matthew (see p. 84, n. 71).

[30] On Matt. 13.37, see below, pp. 81 ff.

[31] Matt. 9.37 f.; Luke 10.2; John 4.35, 38, cf. Dodd, p. 287; below, pp. 118 ff.

logical point of the parable (see pp. 149 ff.). The emphasis has been transferred from the eschatological to the psychological aspect of the parable.[32] In the interpretation the parable has become an exhortation to converts to examine themselves and test the sincerity of their conversion.[33] (5) The fact that the Gospel of Thomas leaves the parable (9) without interpretation confirms these critical conjectures.

We must conclude, then, that the interpretation of the parable of the Sower is a product of the primitive Church which regarded the parable as an allegory, and interpreted each detail in it allegorically. First the seed is interpreted as the Word, then in a kind of table, the fourfold description of the field is interpreted as four classes of persons. This resulted from the fusion of two entirely different conceptions, both of which are also to be met with in IV Ezra: on the one hand the comparison of the divine Word with God's seed,[34] and on the other hand the comparison of men with God's planting.[35] The interpretation is older than Mark, since the linguistic evidence (see pp. 77 ff.) and the literary analysis (see p. 14, n. 11) show that it is not his work.

Taking everything into consideration it would appear that, having regard to the relatively small amount of parable material in Mark, the allegorical method of interpretation had already gained considerable ground there. There can be no doubt as to the extent of its predominance in the tradition underlying Mark.[36]

C. We turn now to our third stratum of tradition, the special Matthaean material. In the light of the preceding results it will be no cause for surprise, as we study the parabolic element in this

[32] F. Hauck, *Das Evangelium des Markus*, Leipzig, 1931, p. 51.

[33] B. T. D. Smith, p. 59.

[34] IV Ezra 9.31: 'Today I am sowing my law in your heart, which will bring forth fruit in you', cf. 8.6. The comparison of the divine message with seed is unknown in the Old Testament. It may have been formed under the influence of the Hellenistic conception of the λόγος σπερματικός (cf. K. H. Rengstorf, *Das Evangelium nach Lukas* (NTD 3)₉, Göttingen, 1962, p. 106).

[35] IV Ezra 8.41: 'For as the husbandman soweth much seed upon the ground, and planteth many trees, and yet not all that is sown shall come up in due season, neither shall all that is planted take root; even so they that are sown in this world shall not all be saved.' The comparison of the community to God's planting is already to be found in the O.T., Isa. 61.3, *et al.*, cf. Ph. Vielhauer, *Oikodome*, Diss. Heidelberg, 1939, pp. 12 f. Intertestamental, Eth. En. 62.8: 'The community of the saints and the elect will be sown'; Ps. Sol. 14.3 ff.; Jub. 1.16; 21.24; 36.6; often in the Dead Sea Scrolls. Rabbinical, Num. r. 16 (Bill., I, p. 666; cf. also 721; III, p. 290). N.T., Matt. 15.13; I Cor. 3.6 f.; Heb. 12.15.

[36] On Mark 13.33, see p. 70; on 12.1–12, see p. 74, n. 93; on 4.13–20, see above.

material,[37] to find there an extensive amount of allegorical interpretation. We have already seen [38] that the parable of the Ten Virgins had come to be interpreted—wrongly—as an allegory of the heavenly Bridegroom, Christ. Similarly, at the end of the little parable of the Man without a Wedding-garment (Matt. 22.11–13),[39] which also belongs to the special Matthaean material, we find a secondary allegorical interpretation, characteristic of Matthew and breaking the pattern of the story, in the casting of the intruder into 'outer darkness', where there is 'wailing and gnashing of teeth',[40] i.e. hell.

The *parable of the Two Sons* (Matt. 21.28–32) receives, in v. 32, a surprising application to the Baptist. We learn that he had undergone a similar experience to that which had befallen the householder in the parable. He had found disobedience in those who by profession were the servants of God, and obedience from those whose way of life was ungodly. This application, however, is not original. For while the threat in v. 31 fits the parable well, v. 32 does not fit with it. It depicts a change of mind in the two sons, and nothing is known of any change of mind in either of the two different groups of people contrasted in v. 32 in relation to the Baptist. Weightier proof is to be found in the recognition of the fact that in Luke [41] v. 32 occurs as an independent logion; the verse has evidently become attached to Matt. 21.31 through verbal association (the link is οἱ τελῶναι καὶ αἱ πόρναι); moreover, the original conclusion of the parable betrays itself in v. 31b by the formula ἀμὴν λέγω ὑμῖν which in more than one instance marks the end of a parable.[42] Again we are confronted by the fact that a parable whose original purpose was to vindicate the good news (God's invitation, rejected by you, has been accepted by the despised ones, hence the promise for them!), has in Matthew, through its relation to the Baptist, received a soteriological application which is utterly foreign to it, and is akin to the soteriological interpretation of the parable of the Wicked Husbandmen [43] and of the Great Supper [44] in Matthew. Nevertheless, the application to the Baptist is not due to

---

[37] 13.24–30 (with 36–43), 44, 45 f., 47–50; 18.23–35; 20.1–15; 21.28–32; 22.11–14; 25.1–13, 31–46.
[38] See pp. 51 ff.
[39] See pp. 65 f.
[40] On this characteristic Matthaean expression see pp. 60, n. 44; 104 f.
[41] 7.29 f.
[42] Matt. 5.26; cf. Luke 14.24; 15.7, 10; 18.14.
[43] See pp. 76 f.
[44] See pp. 67 ff.

Matthew, but must have been already effected in the earlier tradition. Since Matthew has inserted the parable in his Gospel in connection with the word Ἰωάννης (21.25/21.32), he probably found the parable already possessing v. 32 as its conclusion.

An examination of the *interpretation of the parable of the Tares* (Matt. 13.36–43), which also belongs to the special Matthaean material, is of considerable importance for our subject. This interpretation consists of two widely differing parts: in vv. 37–39 the seven most important categories in the parable are interpreted allegorically seriatim, giving us a little 'lexicon' of allegorical interpretations; on the other hand, vv. 40–43 are confined to interpreting the contrasted fate of the tares and the wheat described in v. 30, as the destiny of the sinners and the righteous at the Last Judgement, thus providing us with a little apocalypse.[45] The following points are to be observed in this interpretation: (1) It passes over in silence the obvious motive of the parable, namely, the exhortation to patience, thus missing the point of the parable.[46] (2) It contains certain expressions, which, on linguistic grounds, Jesus can hardly have used, e.g. ὁ κόσμος with the meaning 'the world' (v. 38), since Dalman's careful studies of linguistic usage have thrown doubt on the occurence of *'al*ma with the meaning 'world' in pre-Christian times;[47] ὁ πονηρός with the meaning 'the Devil' (v. 38; cf. v. 19), since *biša* in Aramaic (the same holds good for *hara*ʿ in Hebrew and neo-Hebrew) is unknown as a designation of the Devil; ἡ βασιλεία without qualification, with the meaning 'the Kingdom of God' (v. 38), since *malkuth* without qualification always indicates the contemporary worldly government.[48] This agrees with the fact that ὁ διάβολος (v. 39) belongs to a later stratum of tradition in the Gospels; the earlier layer of tradition calls the Devil σατανᾶς, i.e. *saṭana*.[49] (3) Furthermore, the inter-

[45] M. de Goedt, 'L'explication de la parabole de l'ivraie (Mt. xiii, 36–43)', in *RB*, 66 (1959), pp. 32–54. Further, J. Jeremias, 'Die Deutung des Gleichnisses vom Unkraut unter dem Weizen (Mt. xiii, 36–43)', in *Neotestamentica et Patristica* (O. Cullmann-Festschrift), Leiden, 1962, pp. 59–63.
[46] R. Bultmann, *The History of the Synoptic Tradition*₂, 1968, p. 199.
[47] G. Dalman, *Die Worte Jesu*, I₂, Leipzig, 1930, pp. 132–6.
[48] Ibid., pp. 78 f.
[49] In the Gospels the term διάβολος occurs in the narratives of the Temptation (Matt. 4.1, 5, 8, 11; Luke 4.2, 3, 6, 13) and in Matt. 13.39; 25.41; Luke 8.12; John 6.70; 8.44; 13.2. It is completely absent from Mark, who has σατανᾶς in the narrative of the Temptation (1.13). In the interpretation of the parable of the Sower he also has σατανᾶς (4.15). Luke translates the Aramaic word by διάβολος (8.12). Likewise σατανᾶς in Mark 8.33 and Luke 22.3 is more original than διάβολος in John 6.70; 13.2.

pretation of the parable of the Tares exhibits certain peculiarities which are out of place in the setting of the preaching of Jesus. First of all, the expression οἱ υἱοὶ τῆς βασιλείας (v. 38) is unusual as a designation of the true citizens of the Kingdom of God, since the only New Testament example of it is in Matt. 8.12, where it has an entirely different meaning and refers to those Jews who have forfeited their title to the Kingdom of God; hence we have in 13.38 a Christian application of the expression. Next, it is remarkable that in v. 41 we hear of the angels of the Son of Man, since this expression occurs nowhere else in the New Testament except in two passages in Matthew's Gospel (16.27; 24.31). Most unusual of all is the statement that the angels will gather 'out of his (i.e. the Son of Man's) kingdom' all the false guides and their followers (v. 41) since the expression ἡ βασιλεία τοῦ υἱοῦ τοῦ ἀνθρώπου is peculiar to Matthew (in the New Testament it only occurs in Matt. 13.41; 16.28), and the conception of the Kingdom of Christ is foreign to the oldest stratum of tradition;[50] in our passages the 'Kingdom of the Son of Man' (v. 41), which at the *Parousia* (v. 40) is replaced by the Kingdom of God (v. 43), is simply a designation of the Church,[51] an isolated expression in the Gospels. (4) The explanation of the above peculiarities of language and content lies in the fact that Matt. 13.36–43 exhibits a simply unique collection of the linguistic characteristics of the Evangelist Matthew: v. 36, τότε,[52] ἀφείς,[53] οἱ ὄχλοι,[54] ἦλθεν,[55] εἰς τὴν οἰκίαν,[56] προσῆλθον [57] αὐτῷ οἱ μαθηταὶ αὐτοῦ,[58]

[50] Cf. Matt. 16.28 with Mark 9.1 and Luke 9.27; also Luke 22.30 with Matt. 19.28; and finally Matt. 20.21 with Mark 10.37. Chiliasm is not to be found in the earliest Synoptic tradition.

[51] E. Klostermann, *Das Matthäusevangelium*₂, Tübingen, 1927, in loc.; Dodd, p. 183.

[52] It occurs 90 times in Matthew, and is one of his chief characteristics. In the narratives (as in our passage) it occurs 60 times in Matthew, never in Mark, and twice in Luke. The use of the word as a particle of transition (τότε = 'thereafter') is an Aramaism, and a departure from the classical usage (τότε = 'then').

[53] The use of an introductory participial construction to link up with the preceding sentence is a typical Matthaean usage (E. Klostermann, ibid., p. 10).

[54] In the N.T. the plural occurs in Matthew 32 times, in Mark once, in Luke 15 times, in John once, in Acts 7 times, and in the Apocalypse once.

[55] The aorist ind. following an aor. ptcp. to describe an action following a preceding one is a Matthaean stylistic peculiarity (A. Schlatter, *Der Evangelist Matthäus*, Stuttgart 1929, p. 23).

[56] Εἰς τὴν οἰκίαν with the meaning 'into the house' only occurs in the N.T. in Matt. (9.28; 13.36; 17.25).

[57] A favourite word of Matthew (in Matthew 52 times, Mark 5 times, Luke 10 times).

[58] The expression is a peculiarity of Matthew (5.1; 13.36; 14.15; 24.3; cf. 24.1; 26.17).

λέγων,[59] φράσον[60] ἡμῖν τὴν παραβολήν,[61] ἡ παραβολὴ τῶν ζιζανίων τοῦ ἀγροῦ,[62] τοῦ ἀγροῦ;[63] v. 37, ὁ δὲ ἀποκριθεὶς εἶπεν;[64] v. 38, ὁ κόσμος,[65] οὗτοι (casus pendens),[66] ἡ βασιλεία (without qualifications),[67] οἱ υἱοὶ τῆς βασιλείας,[68] ὁ πονηρός (meaning 'the Devil'),[69] οἱ υἱοὶ τοῦ πονηροῦ;[70]

[59] A stylistic peculiarity of Matthew (A. Schlatter, *Der Evangelist Matthäus,* Stuttgart, 1929, pp. 16 f.), which he uses 112 times. In further agreement with Matthew's style is the fact that the interpretation of the parable is asked for in direct speech; since in the other two passages where Jesus is questioned about a parable, Mark's indirect speech (4.10: ἠρώτων αὐτὸν . . . τὰς παραβολάς, 7.17: ἐπηρώτων αὐτὸν . . . κτλ.) has each time been changed by Matthew into direct speech (Matt. 13.10; 15.15).

[60] In the N.T. the word only occurs in Matt. (13.36; 15.15). The *v.l.* διασάφησον, in spite of its good attestation (B ℵ* Θpc it sy as against φράσον CDWλφ lat) must be regarded as an early redactional alteration, since it replaces the indeterminate φράζειν by a verb of more definite meaning (cf. Jülicher, I, p. 47: 'in my opinion due to emendation'). Elsewhere διασαφεῖν only occurs in Matt. (13.36, *v.l.*; 18.31) and in Acts 10.25 D.

[61] The expression φράσον ἡμῖν τὴν παραβολήν recurs word for word in Matt. 15.15, and comparison with Mark 7.17 establishes it here as characteristically Matthaean.

[62] The designation of parables by name only occurs in Matthew (13.18, 36).

[63] ὁ ἀγρός in the singular occurs in Matthew, 15 times, Mark twice, and Luke 6 times, but this by itself is not significant, since ὁ ἀγρός in this case is a datum of the parable (Matt. 13.24, 27). It is, however, noteworthy (1) that Matthew has altered the words ἐπὶ τῆς γῆς (Mark 4.31) into ἐν τῷ ἀγρῷ (Matt. 13.31) and (2) that he is the only N.T. writer to use the adjectival genitive τοῦ ἀγροῦ: in 6.28 he has τὰ κρίνα τοῦ ἀγροῦ (Luke 12.27: τὰ κρίνα); in 6.30 he has τὸν χόρτον τοῦ ἀγροῦ (Luke 12.28: ἐν ἀγρῷ τὸν χόρτον); in 13.36 he has τῶν ζιζανίων τοῦ ἀγροῦ.

[64] Ἀποκριθεὶς εἶπεν is a Hebraism, or more precisely a Septuagintism, typical of Matthew (44 times) and Luke (30 times); Mark, who prefers other forms of expression, has only 10 examples; John has none. The expression ὁ δὲ ἀποκριθεὶς εἶπεν occurs in the N.T. only in the Synoptists: Matthew 17 times, Mark twice, Luke three times.

[65] A favourite word of Matthew (Matthew 9 times, Mark twice, and Luke 3 times), more frequently used later in the Gospel of John.

[66] The *casus pendens* occurs in Matthew 13 times, in Mark 4 times, in Luke 8–9 times. Matthew has inserted it into Mark's text in five passages, and in all five cases he has used οὗτος (even in Matt. 13.38).

[67] This striking usage (see p. 81) occurs in Matthew 6 times, elsewhere in the N.T. only in Luke 12.32.

[68] Only in Matt. 8.12; 13.38. The meaning differs in both passages (see p. 82), for in 8.12 we have the traditional interpretation as referring to Israel (cf. the Lucan parallel in 13.28), while the Christian application of the idea which appears in Matt. 13.38 is to be regarded as a characteristic usage of Matthew.

[69] τοῦ πονηροῦ in the expression οἱ υἱοὶ τοῦ πονηροῦ must be understood as masc. (='the Devil'), since there is no example of *bar, ben*, υἱός, τέκνον followed by a substantival adj. in the neuter, while we do find υἱὸς διαβόλου (Acts 13.10), τέκνα τοῦ διαβόλου (I John 3.10). Ὁ πονηρός = the Devil only occurs in the synoptic gospels in Matt. 13.19 (for ὁ σατανᾶς Mark 4.15).

[70] Only here in the N.T. Also there is no example outside the N.T. It is apparently an analogous form to οἱ υἱοὶ τῆς βασιλείας, coined by Matthew himself.

v. 39, συντέλεια αἰῶνος;[71] v. 40, ὥσπερ,[72] οὖν,[73] οὕτως ἔσται,[74] ἡ συντέλεια τοῦ αἰῶνος;[75] v. 41, οἱ ἄγγελοι αὐτοῦ (sc. τοῦ υἱοῦ τοῦ ἀνθρώπου),[76] ἡ βασιλεία αὐτοῦ (sc. τοῦ υἱοῦ τοῦ ἀνθρώπου),[77] τὸ σκάνδαλον,[78] ἡ ἀνομία;[79] v. 42, ἡ κάμινος τοῦ πυρός,[80] ἐκεῖ ἔσται ὁ κλαυθμὸς καὶ ὁ βρυγμὸς τῶν ὀδόντων;[81] v. 43, τότε,[82] οἱ δίκαιοι,[83] ἐκλάμπειν,[84] ὡς ὁ ἥλιος,[85] ἡ βασιλεία τοῦ πατρός,[86] ὁ πατὴρ αὐτῶν,[87] ὁ ἔχων ὦτα ἀκουέτω.[88]

In view of this impressive number of 37 examples it is impossible to avoid the conclusion that the interpretation of the parable of the

[71] An expression only occurring in Matthew (5 times). With the genitive pl. τῶν αἰώνων also in Heb. 9.26. The omission of the article on the analogy of the construct state is a Semitism common in Matthew.

[72] A favourite word of Matthew (Matthew 10 times, Mark 0, and Luke twice) cf. J. C. Hawkins, *Horae Synopticae*₂, Oxford, 1909, p. 8 (hereafter cited as Hawkins).

[73] οὖν in connection with other particles: Matthew 11 times, Mark 0, Luke 5 times.

[74] Οὕτως ἐστίν, ἦν, ἔσται: Matthew 12 times, Mark twice, Luke 3 times. Cf. p. 35, n. 38.

[75] See n. 71.

[76] See p. 82.

[77] See p. 82.

[78] Matt. 5 times, Mark 0, Luke once. Σκάνδαλον used of those who play the part of a σκάνδαλον only occurs in Matthew (13.41 and 16.23). Since σκάνδαλον εἶ ἐμοῦ in Matt. 16.23 is a Matthaean addition to Mark 8.33, it may be regarded as a characteristic Matthaean expression.

[79] In the Gospels only in Matthew (7.23; 13.41; 23.28; 24.12).

[80] In the N.T. this combination is only found in Matthew (13.42, 50); the redundant genitive τοῦ πυρός is a Semitism.

[81] A characteristic expression in Matthew. In the N.T. Matthew 6 times, Mark 0, Luke once.

[82] See p. 82, n. 52.

[83] Δίκαιος in relation to the Last Judgement and with an allusion to Dan. 12.2 f. only occurs in Matthew (13.43, echoed in v. 49; 25.46).

[84] A word only found in Matthew (a hapaxlegomenon in the N.T.), an allusion to Dan. 12.3. The circumstance that οἱ δίκαιοι and ἐκλάμψουσιν do not come from the Hebrew text, but follow a forerunner of Theodotion's version, suggests its attribution to Matthew.

[85] The comparison with the sun in the Gospels only occurs in Matthew (13.43; 17.2).

[86] The 'Kingdom of the Father' in the N.T. only occurs in Matthew (13.43; 26.29), and 7 times in the Gospel of Thomas (57; 76; 96; 97; 98; 99 ['of my Father']; 113). Elsewhere in N.T. only with a pronoun: Matt. 6.10 par. with the same words Luke 11.2 ('thy kingdom') and Luke 12.31 ('his Kingdom').

[87] Πατήρ σου, ἡμῶν, ὑμῶν, αὐτῶν is a characteristic Matthaean circumlocution for the divine name (Matthew 20 times, Mark once, Luke 3 times, John only in 20.17), cf. Hawkins, pp. 7, 31. With the 3rd person pro. only here in the N.T.

[88] The call to hear occurs 7 times in the Synoptics, but the form ὁ ἔχων ὦτα ἀκουέτω without the infinitive ἀκούειν (after ὦτα) and with the plural ὦτα is found only in Matthew (11.15; 13.9, 43).

Tares is the work of Matthew himself.[89] This conclusion is confirmed by the Gospel of Thomas which has preserved the parable
(57), but not the allegorizing interpretation. The same conclusion
also holds good for the *interpretation of the parable of the Seine-net*
(Matt. 13.49 f.) which is simply a shortened replica of 13.40b–43:
v. 49, οὕτως ἔσται (see p. 84, n. 74), ἡ συντέλεια τοῦ αἰῶνος (see p. 84,
n. 71), ἀφορίζειν,[90] οἱ δίκαιοι (see p. 84, n. 83); v. 50, ἡ κάμινος τοῦ
πυρός (see p. 84, n. 80), ἐκεῖ ἔσται κτλ. (see p. 84, n. 81). In transfer-
ring the interpretation of the Tares to the Seine-net it has been overlooked that ἐξελεύσονται (v. 49) is applicable to the reapers but not
to the fishermen, and that ἡ κάμινος τοῦ πυρός may describe the fate
of weeds and straw, but hardly that of fishes.[91]

We have thus in Matt. 13.36–43 and 49–50 two allegorical interpretations of parables from the hand of Matthew.[92] This pair of
parables, whose original purpose was to impress upon the impatient
the need of patience, insisting that the time for separation has not
yet come, but that God will bring it in his own time, has been turned
in Matthew to parenetic use as an allegorical description of the Last
Judgement, a warning against false security.

These two interpretations of parables bring out with special
clearness Matthew's decided tendency to allegorical interpretation.
That the traditional material already offered him occasion for this is
clear from the juxtaposition of πονηρός (13.38) and διάβολος (v. 39)
as designations of the devil (πονηρός is Matthaean usage, see p. 83,
n. 69, and διάβολος comes from the tradition), and the fact that both
the application of the parable of the Two Sons to the Baptist and his
activity (Matt. 21.32, see pp. 80 f.), and the reference of the ἄλλοι
(Matt. 21.43) to the Gentiles in the parable of the Wicked Husbandmen (see p. 77, n. 6) will be older than Matthew.

D. Before we turn to the Lucan material and the Gospel of
Thomas, it is advisable in the interests of comprehensiveness to turn
our attention to the Gospel of John. In the Fourth Gospel we meet

[89] The overwhelming number of linguistic peculiarities listed on pp. 82 ff. is not
confined to Matthew's special material, but is characteristic of the whole of the
first Gospel. The recognition of this fact invalidates the usual reference of Matthew
13.36–43 to a special Matthaean source.
[90] With reference to the separation at the Last Judgement in the N.T. only in
Matthew and there in all three places (13.49; 25.32 twice).
[91] A. T. Cadoux, *The Parables of Jesus*, New York, 1931, p.28 (acc. to McNeile).
[92] The interpretation of the parable of the Sower, which he found in Mark
4.14–20, may have served him as a pattern (C. W. F. Smith, *The Jesus of the
Parables*, Philadelphia, 1948, p. 89).

with two parables: the parable of the Good Shepherd (10.1–30) and the parable of the Vine and its Branches (15.1–10). The parable of the Good Shepherd has exactly the same pattern as the three synoptic parables to which a detailed interpretation has been attached, viz. the Sower (Mark 4.1–9, 14–20 par.), the Tares in the midst of the Wheat (Matt. 13.24–30, 36–43), and the Seine-net (Matt. 13.47–50): sharply distinguished from the parable (John 10.1–6) follows a much more extensive allegorical interpretation vv. 7–18).[93] The metaphor of the Vine and its Branches, on the other hand, introduces at once an allegorical interpretation (ἐγώ εἰμι ἡ ἄμπελος ἡ ἀληθινή, καὶ ὁ πατήρ μου ὁ γεωργός ἐστιν) which has completely absorbed the interpreted parable or metaphor into itself. From this it may be seen how great a prominence the Fourth Gospel has given to the allegorical interpretation. Nevertheless John also employs metaphors without an allegorical significance: John 3.8 (the wind); 8.35 (the slave and the son, where εἰς τὸν αἰῶνα does not mean 'eternally', but 'for ever'[94]); 11.9 f. and 12.35 f. (the wanderer in the dark); 12.24 (the corn of wheat); 13.16 (slaves and messengers); 16.21 (the woman in travail). Closer to allegory is the metaphor of the friend of the bridegroom (3.29), the group of sayings about the harvest (4.35–38), so, too, the numerous metaphorical expressions which the hearers misunderstood (3.3; 4.32; 6.27; 7.33; 8.21, 32; 13.33; 14.4, et al.).

E. When we turn to Luke and his special material, we meet with a surprisingly different picture. It must be admitted that in those parables which he has in common with Mark and Matthew, or only with Matthew, he presents a series of allegorical interpretations, less extensive, however, than those in Mark, and still less so than those in Matthew. As we have seen, he offers allegorical interpretations of the parable of the Sower (Luke 8.11–15, see pp. 77 ff.), of the Servants whom their Master finds Waiting and Serves (12.35–38, pp. 53 ff.), of the House-breaker (12.39 f., pp. 48 ff.), the parable of the Servant placed in a Position of Responsibility (12.41–46, pp. 55 ff.), of the Great Supper, with its double invitation to uninvited guests (14.16–24, pp. 63 ff.), the parable of the Talents (19.11–27, pp. 58 ff.), and the parable of the Wicked Husbandmen (20.9–18, pp. 70 ff.). But these allegorizations are probably without exception not the work

[93] J. A. T. Robinson, 'The Parable of the Shepherd (John 10.1–5)', *Twelve New Testament Studies*, London, 1962, pp. 67 ff; J. Jeremias, Art. ποιμήν, in *ThWBNT*, VI, pp. 484–98, esp. 493 ff.
[94] Cf. M. Meinertz, *Die Gleichnisse Jesu*₄, Münster, 1948, p. 47.

of Luke, but spring from the tradition lying behind him, since they are almost all to be found in the other Synoptists. Moreover, the allegorizing expressions and verses exhibit very few of the linguistic peculiarities of Luke. But above all, the Lucan special material in its rich collection of parables [95] shows, as far as I can see, no examples of allegorical interpretation.[96] On the contrary, the special parabolic material in Luke, in so far as it has been worked over, has rather been expanded and interpreted with a different purpose, namely a direct hortatory application.[97] Luke has thus taken over allegorical interpretations from an earlier tradition, but has not himself worked over his material with this end in view.

F. A final examination of the form in which the synoptic parables have been preserved in the Gospel of Thomas makes it clear that here allegorical features only occur in the first of the two versions of the parable of the Burglar (21b). 'Therefore I say: If the lord of the house knows that the thief is coming, he will stay awake before he comes and will not let him dig through into his house of his kingdom to carry away his goods. You then must watch for the world.' Here the two expressions 'his kingdom' and 'for the world' are Gnostic allegorical interpretations which interpret 'the goods' as the γνῶσις bestowed on the gnostic and identified with the βασιλεία, and appeal to him not to allow himself to be robbed of this knowledge by the world. With the exception of these two additions the parable of the Burglar is also free from all allegorical elements. The absence of allegorical features from the Gospel of Thomas [98] is extremely surprising, since the gnostic editor (or compiler) of the collection of logia understood the parables in a wholly allegorical sense, and intended them to be so understood. This is clear, for instance, from

[95] Luke 7.41–43; 10.30–37; 11.5–8; 12.16–21; 13.6–9; 14.7–11, 28–32; 15.8–10, 11–32; 16.1–8, 19–31; 17.7–10; 18.1–8, 9–14. Linguistic evidence enables us to assign all these parables to a pre-Lucan tradition, compare, for example, the remark on the historic present in the Lucan parables, pp. 182 f.

[96] J. A. T. Robinson has pointed out an exception: the parable of the Closed Door (Luke 13.24–30) is, in fact, allegorical. Yet this secondary compilation (see p. 96), which can only be called a parable in a limited sense, may be left out of account.

[97] Luke 11.5 ff., see pp. 157 ff.; 12.21, see p. 106; 14.28 ff., see p. 112, n. 91; 16.1 ff., see pp. 45 ff.; 18.1 ff., see p. 156 f.; 18.9 ff., see pp. 93, 156 f.

[98] Cf. C.-H. Hunzinger, 'Aussersynoptisches Traditionsgut im Thomas-Evangelium', in ThLZ, 85 (1960), col. 843–6, here col. 844 f.; H. Montefiore, 'A Comparison of the Parables of the Gospel According to Thomas and of the Synoptic Gospels', in NTS, 7 (1960–61), pp. 220–48, here pp. 235 ff.

the admonition, 'He that hath ears (to hear) let him hear',[99] five times attached editorially to a parable, with the object of appealing to the reader to grasp the secret meaning of these parables.[1] Thus would the gnostics, for example, have understood the pearl in the parable of the Pearl (76) as a metaphor for the γνῶσις, just as they understood the 'goods' which the burglar sought to steal in the parable of the Burglar (21b). Since the wording of the parables has not been transformed in the interests of allegorization (with the exception of the two additions to the parable of the Burglar), but remains intact, the parabolic tradition preserved in the Gospel of Thomas possesses great value. The parables in the Gospel of Thomas are just as free from allegorization as the special material of Luke.

We arrive thus at a strange result: the discourse-material in Matthew and Luke, the Marcan material, the special Matthaean material, the gospel as we have it in Matthew, Mark, Luke, and John, all contain allegorical interpretations, but the Lucan special material and the Gospel of Thomas have none. From the fact that the allegorical interpretations can be recognized as almost entirely secondary, it would seem to follow that the whole parabolic material was originally as free from allegorizing interpretations as were the special Lucan material and the Gospel of Thomas. In his preaching Jesus confined himself to the common metaphors, almost exclusively taken from the Old Testament and at that time in common use: father, king, judge, householder, owner of a vineyard, host, are metaphors for God; for men in relation to him, children, servants, debtors, guests; for God's people we have the vineyard, the flock; good and evil are white and black (cf. Matt. 25.32); the Last Judgement is the harvest; hell is fire and darkness; the marriage-feast and the great supper represent salvation, and so on. Sometimes he added new metaphors, such as a second Deluge for the end of the world.[2] It may repeatedly be noticed how such a comparison is the metaphor from which a parable starts on.

As we have already seen (pp. 20 f.), it is certain that the sharply defined distinction between parable, metaphor, and allegory is not Palestinian, and in particular the transition from metaphor to

[99] See p. 110.
[1] Cf. the Prologue and logion 1 of the Gospel of Thomas, 'These are the secret words which the Living Jesus spoke. . . . Whoever finds the explanation (ἑρμηνεία) of these words will not taste death.'
[2] Matt. 24.37–39 (Luke 17.26 f.); Matt. 7.24–27 (Luke 6.47–49). Cf., however, already Isa. 28.15.

allegory is easily made. But it is only necessary to compare the un-doubtedly pre-Christian animal allegories of Ethiopic Enoch, 85–90, which at wearisome length depict world-history from the creation under the symbols of bulls, sheep, and shepherds, with the vivid parables of Jesus, to realize how far removed he was from this kind of allegorizing. Our conclusions are strongly supported by the fact that in the rabbinic use of the *mašal*, by far the most common form is that of the parable which contains traditional metaphorical elements.[3]

Some indication of the early appearance of the allegorical inter-pretation of isolated features of the parables may be found in the fact that, as we have seen from the study of the discourse-material in Matthew and Luke, the Marcan material, and the special material of Matthew, it is older than the Synoptic Gospels; its origin is evidently to be found in the first place on Palestinian soil.[4] Of the evangelists, Matthew is the most addicted to the use of allegory; in Matt. 13.37–39 he actually provides a 'lexicon' of allegorical inter-pretations with seven items (see p. 81). The most reserved is the Gospel of Thomas. Next to the desire to reach a deeper meaning, the hortatory motive plays the largest part. Clear evidence of this is to be found in the reinterpretation of the parable of the Sower as an exhortation to the converted to examine themselves, in the reference of the crisis parables to the delay of the *Parousia*, and in the application of the parable of the Unjust Steward as an exhortation to the right use of wealth. Moreover, the soteriological interpreta-tions which we find in Matt. 21.28 ff., 33 ff.; 22.2 ff., must have been intended to serve the purposes of hortatory preaching; the instruc-tion to the messenger in Luke 14.22 f. would aim at intensifying missionary zeal. We have already spoken (pp. 12 f.) of the influence of Hellenistic allegory which would operate as a further motive in Hellenistic circles.

The result of this section of our study is that most of the allegorical traits which figure so prominently in the present form of the parables are not original.[5] In other words, only by discarding these secondary interpretations and features can we once more arrive at an under-standing of the original meaning of the parables of Jesus.

[3] That is the finding of the first main part of the extensive study by M. Her-maniuk, *La Parabole Evangélique*, Bruges-Paris-Louvain, 1947, p. 169.
[4] T. W. Manson, *Göttg. Gel. Anzeigen*, 207 (1953), p. 145.
[5] T. W. Manson, *Sayings*, p. 35, arrives at the same result by another way: the parables of the Synoptic Gospels are 'for the most part genuine parables'; the few allegories are later interpretations 'of what was originally a parable'.

9. COLLECTION AND CONFLATION OF PARABLES

(a) *Double Parables.* Let us begin with the observation that we find in the first three gospels a great number of paired parables and similes where the same ideas are expressed in different symbols.[6] We find associated, patches and wine-skins (Mark 2.21 f.; Matt. 9.16 f.; Luke 5.36–38; Gospel of Thomas 47b in inverted order); a divided kingdom and a divided family (Mark 3.24 f.; Matt. 12.25); lamp and measure (Mark 4.21–25, see p. 91); salt and light (Matt. 5.13–14a); a city set on a hill and a lamp (Matt. 5.14b–16; Gospel of Thomas 32, 33b, here however separated by the logion about Preaching from the Housetops); birds and flowers (Matt 6.26–30; Luke 12.24–28); dogs and swine (Matt. 7.6; Gospel of Thomas 93); stone and serpent (Matt. 7.9 f. cf. Luke 11.11 f.); grapes and figs (Matt. 7.16; Luke 6.44; Gospel of Thomas 45a); foxes and birds (Matt. 8.20; Luke 9.58; Gospel of Thomas 86); serpents and doves (Matt. 10.16; Gospel of Thomas 39b); disciple and slave (Matt. 10.24 f.); boys and girls (Matt. 11.17; Luke 7.32, see pp. 160 ff.); two kinds of tree and two kinds of treasure (Matt. 12.33–35; Luke 6.43–45); the tares among the wheat, and the seine-net (Matt. 13.24–30, 47 f.); mustard-seed and leaven (Matt. 13.31–33; Luke 13.18–21);[7] the treasure and the pearl (Matt. 13.44–46); lightning and vulture (Matt. 24.27 f.); burglar and suddenly returning householder (Matt. 24.43–51; Luke 12.39–46); tower-builder and king (Luke 14.28–32); the lost sheep and the lost piece of money (Luke 15.4–10); slave and messenger (John 13.16); prophet and physician (Ox. pap. 1, no. 6 = Gospel of Thomas 31). Whether in these cases the doubling is original is a question which must be examined for each case individually.

In the two parables of the Treasure in the Field and the Pearl (Matt. 13.44–46) the change of tense raises the question whether they originally belonged together; the Gospel of Thomas actually gives both parables, but separated (Treasure in the Field: logion 109; the Pearl: logion 76). This is not an isolated case; on the contrary, there is evidence that most of the double parables and double

---

[6] What is essential is the difference in symbols. Matt. 7.24–27 par. Luke 6.47–49 (house built on rock and sand), Matt. 7.13 f. (broad and narrow gate), Matt. 7.16–18 par. Luke 6.43 f. (good and bad tree), Matt. 12.35 par. Luke 6.45 (good and evil treasure), Matt. 24.45–51 par. Luke 12.42–46 (faithfulness and unfaithfulness of the servant), are therefore not double parables, but single parables arranged in the form of antithetic parallelism, and hence not belonging here. Cf. W. Salm, *Beiträge zur Gleichnisforschung,* Diss., Göttingen, 1953, p. 97.

[7] Cf. Rom. 11.16: bough and twig.

metaphors enumerated above were either transmitted alone without the other member of the pair, or separated from it by other material. The following have been preserved independently: the lamp (Luke 11.33); the measure (Matt. 7.2; Luke 6.38); salt (Mark 9.50; Luke 14.37); the disciple (Luke 6.40); the two kinds of tree (Matt. 7.17 f.); the two kinds of treasure (Gospel of Thomas 45b); the tares among the wheat (Gospel of Thomas 57); the mustard seed (Mark 4.30–32; Gospel of Thomas 20); the leaven (Gospel of Thomas 96); the treasure (Gospel of Thomas 109); the pearl (Gospel of Thomas 76); lightning (Luke 17.24); vulture (Luke 17.34); the burglar (Gospel of Thomas 21b; 103); the lost sheep (Matt. 18.12–14; Gospel of Thomas 107); the prophet (Luke 4.24). It would, however, be over-hasty to regard the pairing in all these cases as secondary; the falling out of one member of a pair may have taken place in an earlier strand of the tradition. There is, for instance, no reason to divorce the two parables of the Lost Sheep and the Lost Drachma (Luke 15.4–10), although the first of these has also been preserved independently.

Mark 4.21–25 may be cited as an example of *the secondary combination* of two metaphors to make a double parable. From the analysis of these verses we find (a) that, as is shown by Matt. 5.15 and Luke 11.33, the originally independently transmitted metaphor of the lamp that is not placed under a bushel but on a lamp-stand (Mark 4.21), attracted to itself as an explanatory comment the similarly independently transmitted logion in Mark 4.22 (cf. Matt. 10.26; Luke 12.2); (b) that a similar process was repeated in the case of the word about the measure (Mark 4.24, cf. Matt. 7.2; Luke 6.38), which, as a result of the verbal association προστεθήσεται/δοθήσεται attracted to itself by way of explanatory comment Mark 4.25 (cf. Matt. 25.29; Luke 19.26); (c) that the catch-word 'measure' (4.21 μόδιος/4.24 μέτρον) caused the two metaphors of the lamp and the measure, thus expanded, to combine as a double parable; (d) and finally that Mark inserted the combination 4.21–25 into his parable-chapter as an actual double parable, and not as a collection of sayings,[8] as is shown by the twice repeated warning to take heed in v. 23 (cf. with v. 9) and v. 24a (cf. with v. 3a).

We also meet the case in which *one and the same* metaphor is

[8] Thus, e.g., A. Huck-H. Lietzmann-F. L. Cross, *Synopsis of the First Three Gospels*, Oxford, 1935, p. 74; E. Lohmeyer, *Das Evangelium des Markus*, Göttingen, 1937, p. 85.

combined with *different* partners: for example, the metaphor of the two kinds of tree and their fruit is linked at one time with the saying about weeds which cannot yield good fruit (Matt. 7.16–18), and another time with the metaphor about the two kinds of treasure (Matt. 12.33–35), while the Gospel of Thomas combines the metaphor of the treasure with the saying about the weeds (45b); finally, in Luke 6.43–45 all three metaphors are combined. The metaphor of the lamp is treated similarly; in Mark 4.21–25 it is combined with the saying about the measure, while in Matt. 5.14b–16 it is linked with the saying about the city on a hill, and in Luke 11.33–36 with the saying about the eye as the light of the body. In Matt. 13.31–33; Luke 13.18–21 the parable of the leaven is partnered with the mustard seed, while in the Gospel of Thomas it is linked with the parable of the careless woman (96–97).

The only similes and parables which have exclusively been transmitted as pairs are: the patch and the wineskin; kingdom and family; birds and flowers; dogs and swine; stone and serpent; grapes and figs; foxes and birds; serpents and doves; tower-builder and king; slave and messenger.

From this collection it will appear that Jesus himself favoured the reduplication of *similes* as a means of illustration, choosing his pairs of related ideas from nature, especially from the animal world. On the other hand, there is only a single pair of *parables* in our collection, the tower-builder and the king. Hence, familiar as most twin parables may be to us, in view of this fact it must in every case be proved whether they originally served to express the same ideas. Even when this question can be answered in the affirmative, as in the case of the two parables of the Lost Sheep and the Lost Drachma, the possibility must at least be taken into account, considering the general picture, that the double parables may have been spoken independently on different occasions, and have been linked secondarily.

(b) *Collections of Parables*. The primitive Church commenced at an early date to make collections of parables. In Mark we find, besides the parable-chapter 4.1–34, a group of three eschatological [9] metaphors in 2.18–22 (wedding, garment, wine). In his parable-chapter 13 Matthew has brought together seven parables: he has taken over from Mark the parable of the Sower with its interpretation (vv. 1–23) and has added to it a group of three parables introduced by ἄλλην παραβολήν (vv. 24–33), then another group of three introduced by (πάλιν)

[9] See pp. 117 f.

ὁμοία ἐστίν (vv. 44-48).[10] Moreover he has also the following collections: ch. 18 with two parables relating to brotherly duties; chs. 21.28-22.14 with three threatening parables; chs. 24.32-25.46 containing seven *Parousia*-parables. In Luke we have ch. 6.39-49 with a group of parables forming the third part of the discourse on the plain;[11] ch. 12.35-59 with a series of *Parousia*-parables; ch. 14.7-24 with two supper-parables; ch. 15 containing three parables concerning what has been lost; ch. 16 with two parables dealing with the true and false use of wealth; ch. 18.1-14 with two parables about the right way to pray: prayer should be persistent and humble.[12]

We may pause for a moment over the last-mentioned example to remark that neither 18.9-14, nor, probably, 18.1-8, was originally intended as an instruction about the right way to pray; both parables seem rather intended to show, to the opponents of Jesus, God's pity for the humble and despised (see below pp. 139 ff., pp. 153 ff.)[13]. In endeavouring, then, to discover the meaning of the parables, we shall be well advised not to be guided by the meaning of the adjacent parables. How careful it is necessary to be in this respect appears from the fact that all the seven parables excluding the last which have been brought together in Matt. 13, recur in the Gospel of Thomas, but independently and distributed over the whole book (9, 57, 20, 96, 109, 76).[14]

Occasionally we can observe a collection of parables in the process of growth. The collection of the three seed-parables (Mark 4.3-9,

[10] At the end of each group Matthew has added an interpretation (vv. 36-43, 49 f.). Cf. J. W. Doeve, *Jewish Hermeneutics in the Synoptic Gospels and Acts*, Assen, 1954, pp. 101 f.

[11] The Discourse on the Plain falls into three sections: a prophetic (6.20-26), a hortatory (6.27-38), and a parabolic (6.39-49) (G. Heinrici, *Beiträge zur Geschichte und Erklärung des N.T.*, II, 1900, p. 43).

[12] The Gospel of Thomas has linked parables on four occasions: the parable of the Great Fish (8) is linked with the parable of the Sower (9); the parable of Mustard-seed (20) with the parable of the Little Children in the Field (21a) and that of the Burglar (21b); in logia 63-65 three parables beginning 'a man had', (the Rich Fool, the Great Supper, the Wicked Husbandmen) have been combined; in logia 96-98 the parables of the Leaven, the Careless Woman, and the Attacker are brought together.

[13] The introductions to both parables show characteristic features of Luke's style (18.1 f. πρὸς τό with infin., λέγων; 18.9 εἶπεν πρός, δὲ καί, probably also ἐξουθενοῦντας); yet their connection will be earlier than Luke, since in v. 1 πάντοτε is non-Lucan and λέγειν/εἶπεῖν παραβολήν (18.1, 9), although also Lucan (Luke 5.36; 20.9; 21.29), often goes back to the Lucan source, e.g. 12.41, cf. p. 99, n. 39.

[14] Cf. R. McL. Wilson, *Studies in the Gospel of Thomas*, London, 1960, pp. 53 f.

26–29, 30–32), is pre-Marcan, see p. 14, nn. 8, 11. It has been expanded both by Mark and by Matthew: the former has added the twin parables of the Lamp and the Bushel (4.21–25), while the latter has added five other parables, but has omitted the parable of the Seed growing of itself. Moreover, Matthew has retained the conclusion of the Marcan collection, which now stands in the middle of his own parable chapter (Matt. 13.34 f.) where it duplicates his own conclusion (13.51 f.)—a particularly significant example of the expansion of an earlier body of material. The two parables of the House-breaker and the Servant placed in Authority (Matt. 24. 42–51; Luke 12.39–46) afford a further example. They had already been linked together before Matthew and Luke, and both evangelists have inserted them in a larger collection of *Parousia*-parables (Matt. 24.32–25.46; Luke 12.35–59).

(c) *Fusion of Parables.* The tendency of the tradition to form collections of parables occasionally resulted in the fusion of two parables into one; the clearest example of such a fusion is provided by the Matthaean form of the parable of the Great Supper (22.1–14). We have already seen [15] that in this case two originally separate parables about a marriage feast (the parable about the invitation extended to the uninvited guests 22.1–10, and the parable about the guest without a wedding-garment 22.11–13), have been linked together as a pair of parables, and then, through the omission of the introduction of the second parable, have been fused into a single parable.[16] A second example of such a fusion is to be found in the similes of the two kinds of tree and two kinds of treasure. The simile of the two kinds of tree, which Matthew uses twice, occurs in the Sermon on the Mount (Matt. 7.17 f.; 12.33) as an independent simile, expanded by the saying about the cutting down of the tree (Matt. 7.19=3.10). It has then been linked with the simile of the two kinds of treasure to form a double parable (Luke 6.43–45). Lastly, in Matt. 12.33–37, by the insertion of v. 34, the two similes have been fused into a unity in such a way as to deprive the simile of the two kinds of treasure of its independence and to transform it into an interpretation of the simile of the two kinds of tree.[17] A last example

[15] See pp. 65 f.
[16] J. Sickenberger, 'Die Zusammenarbeit verschiedener Parabeln im Matthäus-Evangelium (22.1–14)', in *Byzantinische Zeitschrift*, 30 (1930), pp. 253–61; D. Buzy, 'Y a-t-il fusion de paraboles évangéliques?', in *Revue biblique*, 41 (1932), pp. 31–49; M. Meinertz, *Die Gleichnisse Jesu₄*, Münster, 1948, p. 52.
[17] Cf. M. Albertz, *Die Botschaft des N.T.*, I, 1, Zürich, 1947, pp. 89 f.

occurs in Luke 11.33–36: the metaphor, originally independent (cf. Matt. 6.22 f.), of the eye as the light of the body (vv. 34–36) seems to have become an interpretation of the metaphor of the lamp (v. 33).[18]

Frequently a fusion of parables takes place in such a way that only one or more features of a parable are transferred to another. We find, for instance, in the Marcan form of the parable of the Door-keeper (13.33–37), two features from another parable: the master's journey to a far country (ὡς ἄνθρωπος ἀπόδημος, 13.34) comes from the parable of the Talents, and the handing over of authority to the servants (13.34) comes from the parable of the Servant entrusted with Oversight.[19] Moreover, in the Lucan form of the same parable (12.35–38) the feature of the master waiting on the watchful servants at table (12.37) is derived from the simile of the serving Saviour (Luke 22.27), or perhaps from the symbolic action in John 13.1 ff.[20] Finally, in the Gospel of Thomas the parable of the Watching Servants (cf. Luke 12.35–38) has been interwoven with the parable of the Burglar. In the second version (103) of the latter it says: 'Jesus said: Blessed is the man (cf. Luke 12.37) who knows in which part (sc. of the night) (cf. Luke 12.38) [21] the robbers will come in, so that he will rise and collect his (....) and gird up his loins (cf. Luke 12.35) before they come in.' It is surely not accidental that the two parables, thus interwoven, are placed side by side in Luke (Luke 12.35–40). It is only a conjecture, though a well-founded one, that the form which the parable of the Pounds assumes in Luke (Luke 19.12–27), differing so widely from the Matthaean form, may be explained as the result of a fusion with a second parable;[22] this will have dealt with a claimant to the throne, who, after the recognition of his claim, returns as king, and metes out rewards to his friends and punishment to his enemies.

In one case we can actually watch the process by which a new parable has arisen out of the fusion of the conclusion of a parable

---

[18] Cf. J. Dupont, *Les Béatitudes*, Louvain, 1954, p. 52. J. A. T. Robinson, 'The Parable of the Shepherd (John 10.1–5)', *Twelve New Testament Studies*, London, 1962, pp. 67 ff., also finds a fusion of two parables in John 10: the first deals with the Doorkeeper (vv. 1–3a ἀνοίγει), the second with the Shepherd (vv. 3b–5).

[19] See above, p. 54.

[20] There are two further examples from Matt. 22.2 ff.: with ἄλλους (Matt. 22.4), cf. 21.36; with ὕβρισαν καὶ ἀπέκτειναν (Matt. 22.6), cf. 21.35 (see above, p. 69, n. 77).

[21] I follow Till in this addition; Quecke: 'in what place'.

[22] See above, p. 59.

with certain similes. This is to be found in Luke 13.24–30, a passage which, as ἐχεῖ in v. 28 shows, is intended to be taken as a unity. Jesus is urging men to strive to enter the narrow door (v. 24), before the master of the house rises (from his couch) and shuts it (v. 25a). He rejects the late-comers, since he will have nothing to do with the wicked (vv. 25b–27). Shut out, they must wail and gnash their teeth as they behold the patriarchs and prophets seated at the feast of salvation, and the Gentiles seated at table with them (vv. 28 f.). The interpretative conclusion is furnished by the saying about the last who become first, and the first who become last (v. 30). From a glance at the Matthaean parallels it appears that we have to do with a mosaic: through the fusion of the conclusion of one parable (Matt. 25.10–12) with three similes which are related to it in illustrative content (Matt. 7.13 f., 22 f.; 8.11 f.), a new parable has come into existence: the parable of the Closed Door.

If the attempt to discover the original meaning of the parables is to succeed, we must discard all these secondary connections.

10. THE SETTING

We are indebted to the results of form-criticism for the recognition of the fact that the framework of the gospel narrative is largely secondary, and this is equally true for the parables. Synoptic comparison shows that the parabolic element has been transmitted with greater fidelity than the introduction, interpretation and context.[23] This is of great importance for the right understanding of the parables of Jesus.

(a) *Secondary Context.* The parable of the litigant on the way to the judge (Matt. 5.25 f.; Luke 12.58 f.) belongs, as we have seen,[24] to the crisis-parables; its message is, 'Your situation is desperate! Come to terms with your brother before it is too late.' Hence it is one of the eschatological parables, envisaging the imminence of catastrophe. In Matthew the emphasis is diverted from an eschatological to a hortatory purpose; there it serves, together with the simile of the offering (Matt. 5.23 f.), as an illustration of the necessity of reconciliation, 'Give way, or it may be the worse for you!' Thus in Matthew the parable has been inserted into an apparently appro-

---

[23] Cf. N. A. Dahl, *RGG₃*, II, 1958, col. 1618 (art. 'Gleichnis und Parabel').
[24] See pp. 43 f.

priate secondary setting. The same process may be frequently observed.

In Luke, but not in Matthew, the parable of the Great Supper (Luke 14.16–24) has been placed in the setting of table-sayings in which Jesus addresses, first, those invited (14.7), then the host (14.12), and finally one of the guests (14.15 f.); it would seem appropriate to place a parable about a feast in a setting of table-sayings. Hence the parable in its present Lucan setting illustrates the advice to invite the poor, the lame, the halt, and the blind (14.12–14, cf. v. 21),[25] while originally it was one of the numerous parables intended to vindicate the gospel message.[26] This also was the original purpose of the parable of the Lost Sheep (Matt. 18.12–14), which in its present Matthaean setting illustrates the warning not to despise one of the little ones.[27] The parable of the Wicked Servant now illustrates the preceding exhortation to unlimited forgiveness (18.21 f.), which can hardly have been its original purpose, since in the parable itself nothing is said about repeated forgiveness.[28] The question will be dealt with later whether Luke 11.5–8 is really an exhortation to unwearied prayer (cf. 11.9 ff.).[29] All these examples, which might be multiplied, enforce the necessity of always examining critically the context in which a parable has reached us, in order to see whether it agrees with the original meaning of the parable in so far as it is possible to recognize it. The question of the originality becomes specially urgent, since the Gospel of Thomas has transmitted all parables without context.

(b) *Situations and Transitions Created by the Redactor.* A distinction must be made between the cases mentioned above, in which a parable has been inserted into an apparently appropriate setting, and those in which the details of a situation have been added to a parable or its interpretation by the tradition. Thus we repeatedly find situations in the Gospels, in which Jesus addresses a discourse to the public and subsequently reveals the deeper meaning of his words to the trusted circle of his disciples: Mark 4.1 ff., 10 ff.; 7.14 f., 17 ff.;

[25] See p. 45.
[26] See pp. 45, 176 ff.
[27] See pp. 39, 132 ff.
[28] Luke does not know the connection between 17.3 f. and the parable. Moreover, the διὰ τοῦτο (Matt. 18.23) indicating the link between Matt. 18.21 f. and the parable of the Unmerciful Servant, is a linguistic peculiarity of Matthew.
[29] See pp. 157 ff.

10.1 ff., 10 ff.; Matt. 13.24 ff., 36 ff.; John 6.22 ff., 60 ff. In an instructive article [30] D. Daube has shown that here we have to do
with a pattern which is to be found in rabbinical narratives from the
first century AD onwards,[31] and is especially employed in contro-
versies between Christians and Jews:[32] a scholar is questioned with
polemical intention by a Gentile or by the Minim, gives an answer,
and when his interlocutor has departed, reveals the deeper meaning
of the problem to his disciples. It would no doubt often have happened that, similarly, after a polemical utterance, Jesus would have
given deeper instruction to the narrower circle of the disciples. The
probability, however, that the above-mentioned passages imply this
pattern, and are not drawing on historical reminiscence, is enhanced
by the fact that the introductory verse of such instruction to the
disciples frequently exhibits the stylistic peculiarities of the evangelist,[33] and also by the fact that we have already recognized as secondary
the interpretations of the parable of the Sower (Mark 4.13 ff.) and of
the Tares (Matt. 13.36 ff.), which are introduced in this fashion.
In the Gospel of Thomas (20), too, a similar introduction to the
parable of the Mustard Seed: 'The disciples said to Jesus: Tell us
what the Kingdom of Heaven is like', is secondary by comparison
with Mark 4.30, where Jesus himself puts the question, since such
questions from the disciples are characteristic of the Gospel of
Thomas.[34]

Moreover, the introductions to the parables themselves also exhibit an unusual number of the stylistic peculiarities of the individual
evangelists.[35] We must, then, take into account the consideration that
much is due to editorial style. It is, for example, not accidental that
in the parables of the Tares (Matt. 13.24–30), the Two Sons (21.28–
32), and the Wedding Feast (22.1–14), which are inserted by
Matthew into a Marcan setting, it is precisely the introductions

[30] 'Public Pronouncement and Private Explanation in the Gospels', in *Exp. T.*,
57 (1945–46), pp. 175–177. Reproduced in D. Daube, *The New Testament and
Rabbinic Judaism*, London, 1956, pp. 141–50.

[31] j.Sanh. 1.19b; Pesiq. 40ab; b.Ḥull. 27b; Lev.r. 4 (on 4.1 f.).

[32] j.Ber. 9.12d–13a.

[33] Mark 7.17 f.: εἰς οἶκον (only found in Mark in the NT, and there always in
redactional introduction), ἐπερωτᾶν, καὶ λέγει (hist. pres.); 10.10 f.: πάλιν,
ἐπερωτᾶν, καὶ λέγει; on Matt. 13.36, see pp. 82 f.

[34] Cf., e.g., logion 18, 21a, 24, 37, 51, 53.

[35] Cf. the tables of the linguistic peculiarities of the first three evangelists in
Hawkins, pp. 4 ff. The fact that the linguistic and stylistic peculiarities of the
evangelists occur most frequently in the introductions to the parables, is to be
observed equally in each of the three Synoptists.

which betray the hand of Matthew.[36] In the Gospel of Thomas a
transition only occurs in Logion 21b, where the parable of the
Burglar is introduced by the phrase 'therefore I say unto you'.[37]

Hence the situation in which each parable is set must be tested to
see whether it shows signs of redactional activity. We may take
Luke 12.41 as an example. At the end of the parable of the House-
breaker it says in Luke: 'And Peter said, Lord, speakest thou this
parable unto us only,[38] or even unto all?'—a question which is
answered in the first sense by the parable of the Servant set in
Authority which immediately follows. Already the omission of the
verse by Matthew, who otherwise agrees with the Lucan parallel
(Matt. 24.43–51), raises the problem. But the decisive factor is that
this question of Peter's, and especially its answer, contradict the
original meaning of both parables; since, as we saw on pp. 48 ff.,
55 ff., neither of them was an exhortation to the narrow circle of
the apostles not to grow negligent in consequence of the delayed
Parousia, but an eschatological note of warning addressed to the
crowd (the parable of the Housebreaker), or to the scribes (the
parable of the Servant set in Authority). Thus in Luke 12.41, we are
confronted by a case of a created situation; the linguistic usage shows
that it was already in Luke's source;[39] the promotion of the servant
of Luke 12.42 ff. over his fellow servants has led to the limitation of
the meaning of the parable to the leaders of the community. Especially
in Luke do we find frequent examples of situations which have been
deduced from the content of the parables and which, on closer examination, are found to be secondary. We saw on pp. 58 ff. that the
parable of the Pounds is certainly not, as Luke 19.11 assumes, an
announcement of the delay of the *Parousia*, and it is no accident that
we find in this verse a strongly marked accumulation of Lucan stylistic
peculiarities.[40] We shall see, furthermore (pp. 156 f.), that the defini-

[36] Ἄλλην παραβολὴν παρέθηκεν and λέγων (Matt. 13.24), τί δὲ ὑμῖν δοκεῖ (21.28),
ἀποκριθεὶς εἶπεν and λέγων (22.1) are linguistic peculiarities of Matthew.

[37] See above, p. 87.

[38] See above, p. 39, n. 59.

[39] Κύριε (v. 41) and ὁ κύριος used of Jesus in the narrative (v. 42), are characteristic of the Lucan source.

[40] Lucan characteristics are, the skilful phrasing, ἀκουόντων δὲ αὐτῶν ταῦτα
(cf. Luke 20.45), προστιθέναι (Luke 7 times, Acts 6 times, elsewhere in the N.T. 5
times), διὰ τό with the infinitive (Matt. twice, Mark 3 times, John once, Luke and
Acts 8 times each), εἶναι after a preposition and article (never in Matthew and
Mark, Luke 7 times, Acts 3 times), Ἱερουσαλήμ (Luke and Acts 66 times, Matthew
twice, never in Mark), παραχρῆμα (in the N.T., except Matt. 21.19 f., only in Luke
and Acts 16 times), ἀναφαίνεσθαι (only in Acts 21.3 elsewhere in the N.T.).

tion of purpose prefixed to the parable of the Unjust Judge in Luke 18.1, Ἔλεγεν δὲ παραβολὴν αὐτοῖς πρὸς τὸ δεῖν πάντοτε προσεύχεσθαι αὐτοὺς καὶ μὴ ἐγκακεῖν (despair); can hardly be a correct indication of the aim of the parable.[41] Moreover, the dialogue which serves to introduce the parable of the Rich Fool (Luke 12.13–15) appears to have been linked with the parable secondarily, since it is preserved independently in the Gospel of Thomas (without v. 15) (see p. 165). Nevertheless cases may differ considerably: to the situation presented in Luke 15.1–2 neither factual nor linguistic objections can be raised,[42] and Luke 18.9, too, goes well with the parable that follows (see p. 139).

(c) *Introductory Formulae.* The parables of Jesus, like contemporary parables, have two basic forms.[43] We have (1) the parable beginning with a noun in the nominative (a simple narrative without any introductory formula): Mark 4.3 par.; 12.1 par.; Luke 7.41; 10.30; 12.16; 13.6; 14.16; 15.11; 16.1, 19; 18.2, 10; 19.12; Gospel of Thomas 9 (the Sower); 63 (the Rich Fool); 64 (the Great Supper); 65 (the Wicked Husbandmen); this is the form most commonly found in Luke; (2) the parable beginning with a dative (Aramaic *lᵉ*). Most of the rabbinical parables begin with the words: *mašal. lᵉ* (e.g. a very common form is *mašal. lᵉ melekh še . . .* 'a parable: like a king, who . . .').[44] This usage is an abbreviation of: *'emšol lᵉkha mašal. lᵉma haddabhar dome? lᵉ . . .* ('I will relate a parable to you. With what shall the matter be compared? It is the case with it as with . . .').[45] Hence, occasionally, all this may be replaced by the bare dative (*lᵉ*).[46]

---

[41] See p. 156 below. Lucan style in 18.1: see above, p. 93, n. 13.
[42] Luke 15.1–3 has been thoroughly worked over by Luke, though not all the comments made in this connection are apt. F. Hauck, *Das Evangelium des Lukas,* Leipzig, 1934, p. 195, has noted three Lucan peculiarities in 15.2, but wrongly: (a) διαγογγύζειν (in the N.T. only Luke 15.2 and 19.7) is a peculiarity of the Lucan source, not of Luke himself. (b) τε might be claimed as a Lucan characteristic because it occurs 140 times in Acts. The evidence in the gospel, however, calls for caution. There are only 8 instances of τε, 6 of them in the Lucan source, and only two (both 21.11) in a passage drawn from Mark. Apparently Luke was not in the habit of introducing τε into his *Vorlagen,* although he had plenty of opportunity to do so. (c) προσδέχεσθαι occurs 5 times in Luke (Mark once), but this is the only place where it means 'to receive (guests)'.
[43] P. Fiebig, *Rabbinische Gleichnisse,* Leipzig, 1929, p. 3, n. 4.
[44] Examples in Bill., II, p. 8, and in P. Fiebig, op. cit., p. 3, l. 4; p. 4, l. 12; p. 9, l. 7; p. 10, l. 15; p. 14, ll. 5 f.; p. 17, ll. 6, 20 f.; p. 21, l. 11; p. 22, l. 7; p. 23, l. 7 *et al.*
[45] Examples: Bill., II, pp. 8 f.; Fiebig, op. cit., p. 27, ll. 3 f.; p. 32, ll. 1 f.; p. 34, ll. 1 f., 13 f., *et al.*
[46] Bill., II, pp. 7 f.; Fiebig, op. cit., p. 20, l. 7; p. 38, ll. 6, 14, 17; p. 39, ll. 5, 8 *et al.*

In the parables of Jesus, corresponding to the introductory dative with a preceding question, we have in Mark 4.30 f., Πῶς ὁμοιώσωμεν τὴν βασιλείαν τοῦ θεοῦ; ἢ ἐν τίνι αὐτὴν παραβολῇ θῶμεν; ὡς . . .,[47] or in Luke 13.20 f., τίνι ὁμοιώσω τὴν βασιλείαν τοῦ θεοῦ; ὁμοία ἐστὶν . . .[48] Corresponding to the shortened form beginning with the dative we have: ὡς,[49] ὥσπερ,[50] or in better Greek, ὁμοιωθήσεται,[51] ὡμοιώθη,[52] ὅμοιός ἐστιν.[53] The equivalent Aramaic *l·* underlies all these five forms. This *l·* is, as we have seen, an abbreviation, and should not be translated 'It is like', but 'It is the case with . . . as with . . .'.[54] In many cases the content of the parable forces upon our attention the shifting of the real point of comparison which is caused by this ambiguity in the introductory formula.[55] In Matt. 13.45, the Kingdom of God is, of course, not 'like a merchant', but like a pearl; in Matt. 25.1, it is not 'like ten virgins', but like the wedding; in 22.2 it is not 'like a king', but like a marriage feast; in 20.1 it is not 'like a householder', but like a distribution of wages; in 13.24 it is not 'like a man who sowed good seed', but like the harvest; in 18.23 it is not 'like an earthly king', but like the settlement of accounts. In all these cases we shall avoid error by remembering that behind the Greek ὅμοιός ἐστιν lies an Aramaic *l·*, which we must translate, 'It is the case with . . . as with. . .'. The same holds for the remaining instances in which the ambiguity of the introductory formula is generally overlooked.[56] In Matt. 13.31 we should not, after what has been said,

[47] Also with par. membr. Luke 7.31 f.; 13.18 f.
[48] Also without par. membr. Matt. 11.16. (Luke 6.47 has an indirect question instead of a direct question.)
[49] Mark 13.34; cf. 4.31. With οὕτως ἐστίν prefixed, 4.26 (improvement of Greek).
[50] Matt. 25.14.
[51] Matt. 7.24, 26; 25.1.
[52] Matt. 13.24; 18.23; 22.2.
[53] Matt. 13.31, 33, 44, 45, 47, 52; 20.1; Luke 6.49; 12.36. Ὅμοιός ἐστιν is most grecized. For while ὁμοιωθήσεται, ὡμοιώθη refer to a previous subject which is about to be described, ὅμοιός ἐστιν often gives the erroneous impression of an identification.
[54] A rabbinical example is to be found in j. Ber. 2.5c (funeral oration at the grave of Rabbi Bun): 'To whom shall Rabbi Bun bar Rabbi Ḥijja be compared? *L·melekh* who hired many labourers. . . .' (Rabbi Bun being a specially industrious labourer, for which reason God allowed him to die young). This must not be translated, 'He is like a king who hired many labourers', but rather, 'His case is like that of a king who hired many labourers', see pp. 138 f.
[55] P. Fiebig, *Die Gleichnisreden Jesu*, Tübingen, 1912, p. 12, 131.
[56] This has already taken place in the Gospel of Thomas, where (except the parable of the Mustard Seed) the βασιλεία is always compared with a person, even in the parable of the Leaven (96, 'the Kingdom is like a woman, who . . .'), and

translate the introductory formula by 'The Kingdom of God is like a grain of mustard seed', but 'It is the case with the Kingdom of God as with a grain of mustard seed', i.e. the Kingdom of God is not compared to the grain of mustard seed, but to the tall shrub in whose boughs the birds make their nests. In the same way, in Matt. 13.33, the Kingdom of Heaven is not 'like leaven', but like the prepared, risen dough (cf. Rom. 11.16), and in Matt. 13.47 the Kingdom of Heaven is not compared to a seine-net, but the situation at its coming is compared to the sorting out of the fish caught in the seine-net.

In the parables the introductory dative occurs with varying frequency in the several Gospels. In Mark it occurs 3 times (4.26, 31; 13.34: always ὡς), in Luke 6 times (6.48, 49; 7.32; 12.36; 13.19, 21: always ὅμοιός ἐστιν, or, without the copula, ὑμεῖς ὅμοιοι), in Matthew 15 times (25.14: ὥσπερ; 11.16; 13.31, 33, 44, 45, 47, 52; 20.1: ὅμοιός ἐστιν; 7.24, 26; 25.1: ὁμοιώθησεται; 13.24; 18.23; 22.2: ὡμοιώθη), 9 times in the Gospel of Thomas.[57] While Luke predominantly uses the beginning with the nominative, Matthew shows an equal preference for the datival beginning. Thus the expression ὁμοία ἐστὶν (or ὡμοιώθη, ὁμοιωθήσεται) ἡ βασιλεία τῶν οὐρανῶν alone occurs no fewer than 10 times in Matthew: in the parables of the Tares, Grain of Mustard Seed, Leaven, Treasure Hid in the Field, Pearl, Seine-net, Wicked Servant, Labourers in the Vineyard, Wedding-feast, Ten Virgins; 8 examples occur in the Gospel of Thomas;[58] in Mark it only occurs twice (Seed growing secretly, Mustard Seed), and the same in Luke (Mustard Seed, Leaven); in Luke's special material it is not found at all. Thus we have to do with an introductory formula which Matthew and the Gospel of Thomas prefer, and we must admit the possibility that it has been inserted in various cases, e.g. Matt. 22.2 (otherwise in Luke 14.16 and the Gospel of Thomas 64),[59] also Gospel of Thomas 107 where the parable of the Lost

that of the Treasure in the Field (109, 'the Kingdom is like a man, who . . .'), and that of the Great Fish (8, 'the Kingdom [conjectural] is like a wise fisherman, who . . .'). Cf. H. W. Montefiore, 'A Comparison of the Parables of the Gospel According to Thomas and of the Synoptic Gospels', in *NTS*, 7 (1960–61), pp. 246 f.

[57] Mustard Seed (20); Little Children in the Field (21a); Tares (57); Pearl (76); Leaven (96); Careless Woman (97); Attacker (98); Lost Sheep (107); Hidden Treasure (109).

[58] See n. 57 with the exception of logion 21a.

[59] See pp. 65, 67 f. Similarly in rabbinical literature a king becomes the subject of secondary parables, e.g. in Sifr. Dt. §26 on 3.23; the king is missing from the

Sheep (Matt. 18.12–14; Luke 15.4–7) has become a parable of the βασιλεία, 'the Kingdom is like a shepherd . . .'

The parable or metaphor in the form of a question is a special case of the nominatival beginning: ἐάν . . .;[60] μή . . .;[61] μήτι . . .;[62] τίς . . .;[63] τίς ἐξ ὑμῶν.[64] The last-mentioned question τίς ἐξ ὑμῶν, by its direct address, seeks to force the hearer to take up a definite standpoint. Anyone to whom the question might be addressed, 'Can you imagine that a man whose son asks him for a piece of bread, will give him a stone?' (Matt. 7.9), would indignantly deny it. This τίς ἐξ ὑμῶν is noteworthy for the fact that it does not seem to have any contemporary parallels.[65] It only occurs in the Prophets (Isa. 42.23; 50.10; Hag. 2.3),[66] but not as the introduction to a parable. Hence we are here 'as close as possible to the *ipsissima verba Domini*'. [67] Jesus prefers to use these emphatic questions in disputes with opponents or in addressing the crowds.[68] This is expressly stated in Matt. 12.11 (par. Luke 14.5), Luke 15.4 (opponents) and 14.28 (crowd); it is a sound conjecture in Matt. 7.9 (par. Luke 11.11, see pp. 158 f.), and it may be regarded as a possibility in Matt. 6.27 (par. Luke 12.25, see p. 171) and Luke 17.7 (see p. 193).

(d) *The Conclusion of the Parables*. What do the parables mean? What message have they for the community? What practical directions, what consolation, what promises, has the Lord given us in his parables? Such were the questions which occupied the mind of the primitive Church when they related the parables of Jesus and meditated upon them. This enables us to understand how it is that the most important expansions and recastings of the parables occur where it is a question of the meaning and application of the stories, i.e. at the end. The parables have been transmitted to us with very varied

---

parallel passages in Yoma 86b; Num.r. 19 on 20.12. Cf. G. Kittel, *Sifre zu Deuteronomium*, Stuttgart, 1922, p. 36, n. 5. On pp. 138 f. it is interesting to observe that a N.T. parable dealing with a 'householder', in its Talmudic form has become a king-parable.

[60] Mark 9.50; Matt. 18.12.
[61] Mark 2.19 par.
[62] Mark 4.21; Luke 6.39.
[63] Matt. 24.45 (par. Luke 12.42); Luke 14.31; 15.8, cf. Matt. 17.25 (ἀπὸ τίνων).
[64] Matt. 6.27 (par. Luke 12.25); Matt. 7.9 (par. Luke 11.11); Matt. 12.11 (par. Luke 14.5); Luke 11.5; 14.28; 15.4; 17.7.
[65] H. Greeven, ' "Wer unter euch . . .?" ', in *Wort und Dienst, Jahrbuch der Theologischen Schule Bethel*, N.S., 3 (1952), p. 100.
[66] Op. cit., p. 100, n. 14.
[67] Op. cit., p. 101.
[68] The only exception might be Luke 11.5 (see pp. 158 f.).

endings. Some of them are limited to the symbolic material, some insert a brief comparison or a detailed interpretation, some end with an injunction, a question, or an instruction. In which of such cases is an expansion to be seen? In attempting an answer to this we shall do well to distinguish between expansions of the actual parable-material, and those which concern its application.

1. It is no accident, but agrees rather with what has been said above, that the cases are rare in which there had been an expansion of the parable material itself, the so-called symbolic part. In some of these cases the cause of the expansion is entirely external. To the little parable about the new wine which must not be put into old wine-skins (Luke 5.37 f.) the tradition has added the sentence: 'And no man having drunk old wine desireth new; for he saith: The old is better'[69] (Luke 5.39; the Gospel of Thomas 47b with the sentence prefixed). The addition is unfortunate, for, while the parable sets forth the incompatibility of the new wine with the old, the new wine being a symbol of the New Age, the addition emphasizes the superiority of the old. Evidently the addition is due to an entirely external cause, the catchword οἶνος νέος.[70] A similar case, only not so obvious, occurs in Luke 12.42–46, in the parable of the Servant entrusted with Authority. To this Luke has added a logion in antithetic parallelism setting forth the different degrees of punishment inflicted upon disobedient servants, according to whether they knew their lord's will or not (vv. 47–48a). The logion, which is missing in Matthew, ill consorts with the content of the parable, since the latter is not concerned with knowledge or ignorance of the lord's will, but with the use or abuse of the entrusted authority. The description of the punishment of the unfaithful servant (12.46) has attracted to itself the logion dealing with the varying degrees of punishment. Further examples of the secondary expansion of the conclusion of the symbolic part of a parable may be mentioned: Mark 2.19b–20 (see p. 52, n. 14); Matt. 21.41b (cf. Mark 12.9!); Matt. 22.11–13 (see pp. 65 f.); Luke 12.37b (see pp. 53 f.); Luke 19.27 (see p. 59); finally, Matthew has three times concluded a parable with his characteristic (Matt. 6 times, Luke once) closing formula: ἐκεῖ ἔσται ὁ κλαυθμὸς καὶ ὁ βρυγμὸς τῶν ὀδόντων (Matt. 22.13; 24.

---

[69] Χρηστός='better'. Semitic speech has no comparative.

[70] It is difficult to see how Luke intended v. 39 in its present context to be understood. A. T. Cadoux, *The Parables of Jesus*, New York, 1931, pp. 128 f., suggests that by the old wine Luke meant the Old Testament, and by the new wine the Halachah.

51c; 25.30); in two cases he has prefixed to this closing formula the expression, also characteristic of him, εἰς τὸ σκότος τὸ ἐξώτερον (only found in Matthew in the NT), 22.13, and 25.30. 'Wailing and gnashing of teeth' is there a symbol of despair, a despair caused by a salvation forfeited by one's own fault.

2. Far more numerous than such expanded conclusions of the symbolic part of the parable are the cases in which the expansion relates to the application of the parable, either by adding an application to a parable which has no interpretation, or by expanding an earlier application.

We shall deal first with the cases in which parables *without an interpretation* have been secondarily provided with an application. Eight parables end abruptly without an explicit application: Mark 4.26–29 (Patient Husbandman); 4.30–32 (Mustard Seed); Matt. 13.33 par. Luke 13.20 f. (Leaven); Matt. 13.44 (Treasure in the Field); 13.45 f. (Pearl); 24.45–51 par. Luke 12.42–46 (Faithful and Unfaithful Servant); Luke 13.6–9 (Barren Figtree); 15.11–32 (the Father's Love). Originally, however, the number of these parables in which Jesus left his hearers to draw their own conclusions was considerably greater. This can be seen from the Gospel of Thomas where all the parables except the Burglar (21b), the Great Supper (64), and the Pearl (76), end without an interpretation. It is easy to understand that a tendency to provide an application for parables which had no interpretation would arise at an early date. The clearest example is furnished by the three parables to which a detailed interpretation has been secondarily supplied: Mark 4.13–20 (see pp. 77 ff.); Matt. 13.36–43, 49–50 (see pp. 81 ff.). These three cases, however, do not stand alone.

The group of logia in Luke 11.9–13, preserved by Matthew as an independent unit (7.7–11), has been used by Luke as the application of the parable of the Importunate Friend (Luke 11.5–8); since the transition (11.9: κἀγὼ ὑμῖν λέγω with ὑμῖν preceding) is a peculiarity of the Lucan source,[71] and there is also the occurrence of the association of ideas ('knocking' in v. 5 and v. 9 f.), the linking of the two passages in Luke is secondary. The point of the parable has been distorted by this expansion. Originally, as we shall see on pp. 157 ff., the focus of the story was the helping friend (God helps as unconditionally as the friend did), but the Lucan interpretation places the praying friend in the centre of the picture (men ought always to pray and not to faint). The parable of the Labourers in

the Vineyard becomes intelligible if we discard the secondary concluding interpretation in Matt. 20.16 (see pp. 36 f.). The logion which
forms the interpretation of the parable of the Supper in Matthew:
πολλοὶ γὰρ κλητοί, ὀλίγοι δὲ ἐκλεκτοί (22.14), does not agree with
the story; since the truth that only a small number will be saved
is not inculcated either in Matt. 22.1–10 (the guest-room is full),
nor in 22.11–13 (only one unworthy guest is rejected). Similarly,
Luke 14.33 does not agree with the preceding parables of the Tower
Builder and the King Going to War (14.28–32), since in both
parables it is a question of self-testing, not of self-sacrifice. The
closing application in Matt. 12.45c: οὕτως ἔσται (a literary characteristic of Matthew, see p. 84, n. 74) καὶ τῇ γενεᾷ ταύτῃ τῇ πονηρᾷ
which applies the parable of the return of the expelled evil spirit to
the Jewish people, is missing from Luke; this is all the more remarkable, since Matt. 12.43–45 and Luke 11.24–26, with only slight verbal
differences, are in complete agreement. The exhortation to watchfulness (Matt. 25.13), which serves as the interpretation of the parable of the Ten Virgins, can easily be recognized as an expansion,
since it does not agree with the parable (see pp. 51 f.). The closing
sentence, too, of the parable of the Rich Fool: 'So (foolishly [72]
behaves the man) who heaps up treasure for himself and does not
gather wealth [73] toward God' (Luke 12.21), must be an addition; [74] it
is missing from the Gospel of Thomas (63), and gives a moralizing
meaning to the parable, which blunts the sharp edge of its warning.
The eschatological warning (Fool, obsessed by his possessions and
unconscious of the sword of Damocles hanging over his head, see
pp. 164 f.), has been transformed into a warning against the wrong
use of possessions (Fool, heaping up wealth, instead of entrusting it to
God). The maxim in Matt. 25.29, parallel Luke 19.26, has been preserved elsewhere as an independent logion (see p. 62, n. 60). Luke
12.47 f. is missing in Matthew. In the Gospel of Thomas the parable
of the Pearl ends with the following hortatory application: 'Do you
also seek for his treasure (the merchant's) which fails not, (but) which

[72] Cf. p. 46, n. 83.

[73] Πλουτεῖν has here the same active meaning as the parallel θησαυρίζειν, 'to
enrich oneself' (P. Joüon, *Recherches de science religieuse*, 29 (1939), p. 487). As
in Matt. 6.19–21, it is a question of where the treasure has been laid up; the fool
is he who has laid up treasure for himself on earth; the wise man, on the other
hand, has entrusted it to God.

[74] Cf. D. Buzy, 'Les sentences finales des paraboles évangéliques', in *Revue biblique*, 40 (1931), pp. 321–44; M. Dibelius, *Die Formgeschichte des Evangeliums*₂,
Tübingen, 1933, p. 258.

endures, there where no moth comes near to devour, and where no worm destroys'.[75]

A special problem is presented by the cases in which the same simile or parable has been transmitted with divergent applications. Thus the simile of the lamp under the bushel is applied in Matthew to Jesus' disciples (5.16), while in Mark and in the Gospel of Thomas (33b) it is apparently applied to the gospel (4.22), see p. 120. To the simile of the salt Matthew gives the interpretation at the beginning (5.13a: 'Ye are the salt of the earth'), while Mark gives a different application at the end (9.50b). In exactly the same way Luke has placed the application of the parable of the Supper at the beginning in the form of a logion (14.12-14), while in Matthew a different application comes at the end of the parable (22.14). Moreover, an application has been prefixed to the parable of the invited guests in the version found in the D-text of Matthew 20.28: 'But do you seek from little to become great, and from great to become less.'[76] In Luke 14.11, on the other hand, a related though different application comes at the end ('Everyone who exalts himself will be humbled by God, but he who humbles himself will be exalted by God'). In Luke 18.14b the interpretation just quoted recurs as the conclusion of the parable of the Pharisee and the Publican, while in Matt. 23.12 (cf. 18.4) it is found as an independent logion; and from this it might be inferred that in Luke 14.11 it is secondary. Such an inference would be mistaken—a warning to be cautious, since in Lev. r. 1.5 (to 1.1) we have a corresponding table-rule of Shim'on b. 'Azzai (c. AD 110), 'Stand two or three places below your (proper) place and wait, until they say to you, "Come up here", etc.', concluded by the following saying, closely related to Luke 14.11, 'And so has Hillel (20 BC) said: "My humiliation is my exaltation, and my exaltation is my humiliation".' (On the other hand it is not equally certain whether the sentence is also original in Luke 18.14b; it is quite appropriate so far as its content is concerned, but it has been objected that it gives the parable 'a suggestion of popular morality which is wholly out of keeping with its wording'.) [77] With regard to such cases of divergent applications it may often remain

---

[75] Cf. Matt. 6.19 f.; Luke 12.33.

[76] On this agraphon, cf. J. Jeremias, *Unknown Sayings of Jesus*[2], London, 1964, p. 39.

[77] Thus M. Dibelius, *Die Formgeschichte des Evangeliums*[2], Tübingen, 1933, p. 254, somewhat too dogmatically, and failing to observe the possibility that the future tenses refer to God's action at the Last Judgement (see p. 142).

uncertain whether Jesus himself used the same simile on different occasions with a different application, or whether only one of the applications is original, or whether the simile was transmitted without an interpretation and all the applications are secondary.

3. Very often *an existing interpretation* has been modified or expanded. The parable of the Unjust Steward provides a typical example of this; it may be recalled that in this case the old interpretation in Luke 16.8a has been enlarged by a whole series of further interpretations (16.8b–13, see pp. 45 ff.). In the parable of the Wicked Husbandmen (Mark 12.1–9 and parallels) three stages of the expansion may be observed: before Mark a secondary proof-text was added (vv. 10 f.); Matthew and Luke have added to this proof-text an expository comment in the form of a description of the destructive activity of the stone mentioned in the passage from the Old Testament (Matt. 21.44;[78] Luke 20.18), and Matthew has applied the parable to Israel and the Gentiles (Matt. 21.43) [79] which constitutes the third stage, and which disrupts the connection between the proof-text (v. 42) and its exposition (v. 44). Thus the three stages of the expansion are: (1) Mark 12.10 f.=Matt. 21.42; (2) Matt. 21.44 par. Luke 20.18; (3) Matt. 21.43. In Matt. 21.32 we can recognize Jesus' interpretation of the parable in 21.31b as secondarily applied to the Baptist (21.32, see pp. 80 f.). The concluding command in Mark 13.37 is missing in Luke 12.35–38; Matthew has prefixed the same command (γρηγορεῖτε) to the parable of the Burglar (24.42), thus he (but not Luke) has enclosed the parable in two identically similar warnings. In the Gospel of Thomas, as against Matthew and Luke, the concluding command in the parable of the Burglar is expanded by the warning, 'with loins girded' (21b). The parabolic saying about 'the sign of Jonah' is interpreted by Luke (11.30) as God's legitimation of his messenger through his deliverance from death; in Matt. 12.40 this interpretation is expanded and its emphasis shifted: the point of comparison is now the period of three days and three nights (Jonah 2.1).[80] Specially noteworthy is the way in which the simile of the two kinds of tree acquires a new and secondary interpretation: it is fused with the simile of the two kinds of treasure in such a way as to make the

[78] The fact that the verse is wanting in D it sy^sin in no way justifies its omission, cf. J. Jeremias, *The Eucharistic Words of Jesus*₂, London, 1966, pp. 145–52, on the shortened text in D it vet.-syr.
[79] See p. 77.
[80] Cf. *ThWBNT*, III, p. 412.32 ff., and in this book, p. 187, n. 65.

latter an interpretation of the former (Matt. 12.33–35).[81] The double
simile of the City on a Hill and the Lamp (Matt. 5.14b–15; Gospel
of Thomas 32), is interpreted by Thomas, through the insertion of
the logion about the Preaching from the Housetops (33a), as referring to preaching; in Matthew it has two interpretations, one at the
beginning (v. 14a) and one at the end (v. 16); the latter was,
perhaps, originally an independent simile. An example of the way
in which an existing interpretation can have its meaning altered
without a change in its wording is to be found in Matt. 18.35:
οὕτως καὶ ὁ πατήρ μου ὁ οὐράνιος ποιήσει ὑμῖν, ἐὰν μὴ ἀφῆτε ἕκαστος
τῷ ἀδελφῷ αὐτοῦ ἀπὸ τῶν καρδιῶν ὑμῶν. The words ἕκαστος τῷ
ἀδελφῷ αὐτοῦ are a literal translation of the Aramaic g·bhar
l·'ahuhi, by which the Targums in agreement with the Hebrew 'iš
l·'ahiw express the missing reciprocal pronoun; hence the expression
has entirely general sense (each other, one another), as is confirmed
by Matt. 6.15 (τοῖς ἀνθρώποις) and Mark 11.25 (τὶς). Matthew, however, has limited the word ἀδελφός in 18.35 to the Christian brother,
thus giving a Christian application to the parable; for he makes 18.35
the conclusion of the great community code in ch. 18.[82] The warning-
cry 'He that hath ears (to hear), let him hear', forms a special class
of parable-endings. In all three Synoptics it occurs only after the
parable of the Patient Husbandman (Mark 4.9; Matt. 13.9; Luke
8.8), after the simile of the Lamp, only in Mark (4.23), and after the
simile of the Salt, only in Luke (14.35); lastly, Matthew has it after

[81] See p. 94.
[82] This limitation of the meaning of ἀδελφός is characteristic of Matthew.
Following the well-established early Christian usage, he seems to use the word,
except when it refers to a blood-brother, entirely of a Christian brother. This usage
goes back to Jesus himself (Mark 3.33–35 par.). Yet in most cases it is clear that,
as in Matt. 18.35, the limitation of the wider implication of the word is due to a
secondary Christian interpretation: thus in Matt. 5.22; 18.15, 21 (Jesus in these
passages is referring to Lev. 19.17: 'Thou shalt not hate thy brother in thine heart:
thou shalt surely rebuke thy neighbour'); in 5.23 f. (where the parallel in Mark
11.25 has τὶς instead of ἀδελφός), 47 (where the second half of the verse says that the
Gentiles limit their affectionate greetings to their compatriots); in 7.3–5 (see p. 167,
n. 75); and in 25.40 (see p. 207). It would seem that in all these passages ἀδελφός
had originally the wider meaning of 'neighbour, compatriot'. Matthew's tendency
to Christianize the word is substantiated by the comparison of Matt. 12.49 (ἐπὶ τοὺς
μαθητὰς αὐτοῦ) with Mark 3.34 (τοὺς περὶ αὐτὸν κύκλῳ καθημένους). This secondary Christianization of ἀδελφός only occurs in Luke in two places (6.41 f.; 17.3 f.),
and never in Mark. The Gospel of the Nazarenes agrees with Mark in representing
Jesus as using the word 'brother', unless it means a blood-brother, in the broader
sense of 'neighbour' (J. Jeremias, Unknown Sayings of Jesus₂, London, 1964, pp.
44 ff., 94–96): a sign of ancient tradition.

the saying about Elijah (11.15), and as the conclusion of his inter-pretation of the parable of the Tares (13.43). On the other hand, the Gospel of Thomas gives the warning-cry as the conclusion of no less than five parables,[83] doubtless as an appeal to the Gnostics to give careful heed to the secret meaning of the parables. This survey shows that the warning-cry is in most cases secondary.[84]

4. The most important observation which results from the study of these secondary and expanded interpretations is that there was a strong tendency to add conclusions to the parables in the form of generalizing logia.[85] Where such generalizations are found, they are predominantly secondary in their present context; [86] we must em-phasize the point that it is their present place in the context which is secondary, and that we are not in any way calling in question the authenticity of the logia themselves, but only insisting that they were not originally uttered as the conclusion of a parable.[87] This is sup-ported by the fact that they are entirely missing from the Gospel of Thomas. By employing them in this way it was intended to give the parables the widest possible application. A typical example of this tendency may be seen in the fact that the parable of the Labourers in the Vineyard displays two successive expansions by a generalizing logion (Matt. 20.16a, 16b, see pp. 34 ff.) and also that the secondary parable of the Closed Door (Luke 13.22–30, see p. 96) has in v. 30 been provided with a generalizing conclusion. As the result of our discussion in pp. 105–10, the following parables and similes appear to have acquired a secondary generalizing conclusion: [88]

The Lamp (Mark 4.22): οὐ γάρ ἐστίν τι κρυπτόν,
ἐὰν μὴ ἵνα φανερωθῇ·
οὐδὲ ἐγένετο ἀπόκρυφον,
ἀλλ' ἵνα ἔλθῃ εἰς φανερόν.

The Measure (Mark 4.25): [89] ὃς γὰρ ἔχει, δοθήσεται αὐτῷ·
καὶ ὃς οὐκ ἔχει, καὶ ὃ ἔχει ἀρθή-
σεται ἀπ' αὐτοῦ.

[83] The Great Fish (8), the Rich Fool (63), the Wicked Husbandmen (65), the Leaven (96), and at the end of a parabolic conglomerate (21).
[84] Cf., for example, on Matt. 13.43, p. 84, n. 88.
[85] B. T. D. Smith, p. 179.
[86] Certainly not always. Cf. the conjectures concerning Luke 14.11, p. 107.
[87] This has also been widely recognized by Catholic exegesis, cf. D. Buzy, see above, p. 106, n. 74; M. Hermaniuk, *La Parabole évangélique*, Bruges-Paris-Louvain, 1947, *passim*.
[88] The generalizing expressions are italicized throughout the list.
[89] See p. 91.

The Doorkeeper (Mark 13.37):

ὁ δὲ ὑμῖν λέγω, πᾶσιν λέγω, γρηγορεῖτε.

The Labourers in the Vineyard (Matt. 20.16a, 16b):

(1) οὕτως ἔσονται οἱ ἔσχατοι πρῶτοι καὶ οἱ πρῶτοι ἔσχατοι·

(2) πολλοὶ γάρ εἰσιν κλητοί, ὀλίγοι δὲ ἐκλεκτοί.

The Wicked Husbandmen (Matt. 21.44;[90] Luke 20.18):

καὶ (Lk. πᾶς) ὁ πεσὼν ἐπὶ τὸν λίθον τοῦτον (Lk. ἐπ᾽ ἐκεῖνον τὸν λίθον), συνθλασθήσεται· ἐφ᾽ ὃν δ᾽ἂν πέσῃ, λικμήσει αὐτόν.

The Wedding Feast (Matt. 22.14):

πολλοὶ γάρ εἰσιν κλητοί, ὀλίγοι δὲ ἐκλεκτοί.

The Ten Virgins (Matt. 25.13):

γρηγορεῖτε οὖν, ὅτι οὐκ οἴδατε τὴν ἡμέραν οὐδὲ τὴν ὥραν.

The Talents (and the Pounds) (Matt. 25.29 par. Luke 19.26):

τῷ γὰρ ἔχοντι παντὶ δοθήσεται καὶ περισσευθήσεται. τοῦ δὲ μὴ ἔχοντος καὶ ὃ ἔχει ἀρθήσεται ἀπ᾽ αὐτοῦ.

The Friend Begging for Help (Luke 11.10):

πᾶς γὰρ ὁ αἰτῶν λαμβάνει . . .

The Rich Fool (Luke 12.21):

οὕτως ὁ θησαυρίζων αὐτῷ καὶ μὴ εἰς θεὸν πλουτῶν.

The Servant entrusted with Authority (Luke 12.48b):

παντὶ δὲ ᾧ ἐδόθη πολύ, πολὺ ζητηθήσεται παρ᾽ αὐτοῦ, καὶ ᾧ παρέθεντο πολύ, περισσότερον αἰτήσουσιν αὐτόν.

The Closed Door (Luke 13.30):

καὶ ἰδοὺ εἰσὶν ἔσχατοι, οἳ ἔσονται πρῶτοι, καὶ εἰσὶν πρῶτοι, οἳ ἔσονται ἔσχατοι.

The Unjust Steward (Luke 16.10):

ὁ πιστὸς ἐν ἐλαχίστῳ καὶ ἐν πολλῷ πιστός ἐστιν, καὶ ὁ ἐν ἐλαχίστῳ ἄδικος καὶ ἐν πολλῷ ἄδικός ἐστιν.

(16.13):

οὐδεὶς οἰκέτης δύναται δυσὶ κυρίοις δουλεύειν . . .

Pharisees and Publicans (Luke 18.14b):

ὅτι πᾶς ὁ ὑψῶν ἑαυτὸν ταπεινωθήσεται, ὁ δὲ ταπεινῶν ἑαυτὸν ὑψωθήσεται.[91]

[90] On the originality of the verse, see p. 108, n. 78.

A survey of these generalizing conclusions shows that they deal only sporadically with guidance for daily life, but that the majority consist of eschatological promises, threats, and warnings. The recognition of the fact that these generalizing conclusions occupy a secondary place in their context is of the greatest importance for the understanding of the parables concerned, since their emphasis, as the result of the new conclusion, has in nearly every case been shifted, often fundamentally. But even when the generalization agrees with the meaning of the parable (Luke 18.14b) or at least is not incompatible with it (so, for instance, Luke 12.21), the recognition of its secondary nature is significant, since, through the addition of such generalizations, the parables concerned have acquired a moralizing sense which obscures the original situation and blunts the sense of conflict, the sharp edge of the eschatological warning, the sternness of the threat. The parable of the Labourers in the Vineyard, which is intended to vindicate, in an actual situation, the good news in the face of its critics, to assert God's goodness, has been transformed, through a generalizing conclusion (the last shall be first and the first last), into a general instruction about degrees of importance in the Kingdom of Heaven, or about the unconditional nature of divine grace.[92] The parable of the Unjust Steward, which is a summons to those who hesitate to decide on a fresh start in view of the threatened crisis, has, by the insertion of the sentence, 'He that is faithful in that which is least is faithful also in much, and he that is unfaithful in that which is least is unfaithful also in much', been transformed into a general moral lesson. The recognition of the secondary character of these generalizing conclusions is also important for the total understanding of the parables. It is the voice of the Christian preacher or teacher, bent on interpreting the Lord's message,[93] which we hear in the insertion of generalizing conclusions. We see in them how early the tendency arose to make the parables of Jesus serviceable in this way for the Christian community, giving them thus a general instructional or hortatory meaning. This is the tendency which finally succeeded in transforming Jesus into a Teacher of Wisdom, and which, as we saw on p. 19, celebrated

[91] To these examples should be added Luke 14.33 (οὕτως οὖν πᾶς ἐξ ὑμῶν), if, as most commentators assume, the logion did not originally belong to the double parable of the Tower-builder and the King planning a Campaign. The double parable is an exhortation to self-examination, not to self-denial.

[92] See pp. 34–36.

[93] F. C. Grant, *Anglican Theological Review*, 30 (1948), p. 120.

its greatest triumph at the close of last century in Jülicher's exposition of the parables. This method of facilitating the application of
the parables to ecclesiastical exhortation was specially favoured by
Luke (or at least by his sources), while Matthew sought to attain
the same end by the method of allegorical interpretation. Hence we
can only hope to recover the original meaning of the parables of
Jesus by an interpretation which resolutely takes this tendency into
account and makes allowance for it.

Summing up, then, the results of our enquiry. The parables have
a two-fold historical setting. First, the original historical setting, not
only of the parables, but of all the sayings of Jesus, is their individual,
concrete situation in the activity of Jesus. Then, secondly, they went
on to live in the primitive Church. We only know the parables in the
form which they received from the primitive Church; hence we are
faced with the task of recovering their original form in so far as that
is possible for us. Observation of the following laws of transformation
will help us in this task.

1. The translation of the parables into Greek involved an inevitable change in their meaning.
2. For the same reason representational material is occasionally
   'translated'.
3. Pleasure in the embellishment of the parables is noticeable at
   an early date.
4. Occasionally passages of Scripture and folk-story themes have
   influenced the shaping of the material.
5. Parables which were originally addressed to opponents or to
   the crowd have in many cases been applied by the primitive
   Church to the Christian community.
6. This led to an increasing shift of emphasis to the hortatory
   aspect, especially from the eschatological to the hortatory.
7. The primitive Church related the parables to its own actual
   situation, whose chief features were the missionary motive and
   the delay of the *Parousia*; it interpreted and expanded them
   with these factors in view.
8. To an increasing degree the primitive Church interpreted the
   parables allegorically with a view to their hortatory use.
9. The primitive Church made collections of parables, and
   occasionally two parables were fused together.
10. The primitive Church provided the parables with a setting,

and this often produced a change in the meaning; in particular, by the addition of generalizing conclusions, many parables acquired a universal meaning.

The analysis of the parables with the help of these ten laws of transformation was, in the first five editions of this book, confined to the synoptic material. In the meantime the Gospel of Thomas has been discovered. The fact that this has confirmed the results of our analysis to a surprising degree proves that it has been conducted on the right lines.

These ten laws of transformation are ten aids to the recovery of the original meaning of the parables of Jesus. They will help us to lift in some measure here and there the veil, sometimes thin, sometimes almost impenetrable, which has fallen upon the parables of Jesus. Our task is a return to the actual living voice of Jesus. How great the gain if we succeed in rediscovering here and there behind the veil the features of the Son of Man! Everything depends on his Word. To meet with him can alone give power to our preaching.

III

THE MESSAGE OF
THE PARABLES OF JESUS

IF WE TAKE into account the laws of transformation set forth in the second chapter of this book, and with their help attempt to recover the original meaning of the parables of Jesus, we shall find that the total impression of the parables has been immensely simplified. We shall find that many parables express one and the same idea by means of varying symbols. Differences which are commonplaces to us, are now seen to be secondary. As a result, a few simple essential ideas stand out with increased importance. It becomes clear that Jesus was never tired of expressing the central ideas of his message in constantly changing images. The parables and similes seem to fall naturally into groups, and it may be suggested that ten groups emerge from our study of them. As a whole these groups present a comprehensive conception of the message of Jesus. But before embarking on their exposition, it must again be emphasized that throughout this enquiry the term parable will be understood in the broad sense of the Aramaic *mathla* (see p. 20).[1]

I. NOW IS THE DAY OF SALVATION

'Blind see,
Lame walk,
Lepers are cleansed,
Deaf hear,
Dead are raised,
Poor have the gospel preached to them',

this, according to Luke 7.22; Matt. 11.5, was the reply given by

[1] This broader conception of the subject greatly extends the range of material available for the study of the symbolic elements in the discourse of Jesus. Hence an exhaustive treatment is only aimed at for the formal parabolic stories.

Jesus to the question asked by the Baptist from his prison. But we are not intended to understand by it that all these miracles were performed before the eyes of the imprisoned Baptist's messengers so that they might relate to their master what they had themselves just witnessed (thus Luke 7.21 f.);[2] it is not the primary object of the passage to enumerate the miracles of Jesus,[3] but Jesus here takes up primeval prophetic images of the Messianic age:

'Then the eyes of the blind shall be opened,
And the ears of the deaf shall be unstopped.
Then shall the lame man leap as an hart,
And the tongue of the dumb shall sing:
For in the wilderness shall waters break out,
And streams in the desert.'

(Isa. 35.5–6.)[4]

The saying of Jesus is simply a free quotation of this passage combined with Isa. 61.1 (the preaching of good tidings to the poor); the fact that the mention of the lepers and the dead goes beyond Isa. 35.5 f. implies that the fulfilment exceeds all hopes, expectations, and promises.[5] It is his cry of exultation, 'the hour is come, the blind see and the lame walk, and living water flows through the thirsty land—salvation is here, the curse is gone, paradise has come again, the end of the Age is upon us, and manifests itself (as the Spirit usually does) in a twofold way, by act and by word. This is my message to John, and if you tell him, add "Blessed is he whosoever shall not be offended in me" (Matt. 11.6; Luke 7.23). Blessed is he who believes in spite of all present disappointing appearances.'[6]

There is another saying of Jesus closely related to this, taking up another passage from Isaiah (61.1 f.): 'The Spirit of the Lord is upon me, because he hath anointed me to preach good tidings to

[2] In the same way it was not by chance that Matthew had previously related the healing of a blind man (9.27–31), a lame man (9.1–8), a leper (8.1–4), a dumb man (9.32–34), and the raising of a dead person (9.18–26).

[3] Cf. M. Dibelius, *Jesus*, London, 1963, p. 71.

[4] Cf., too, the continuation 35.7–10, and further 29.18, *et al.*

[5] It should be observed that Jesus omits the announcement of God's vengeance (Isa. 35.4), see below, p. 218, n. 49.

[6] J. Jeremias, *Jesus als Weltvollender*, Gütersloh, 1930, pp. 19 ff. The question whether the Baptist's Messianic enquiry could have taken place before Peter's confession, is of no importance in our context, since we are only concerned with Jesus' logion.

the poor; he hath sent me to proclaim release to the captives, and recovering of sight to the blind, to set at liberty them that are bruised, to proclaim the acceptable year of the Lord' (Luke 4.18 f.).[7] The hour has come. Today is this Scripture fulfilled (Luke 4.21). The Creator Spirit whom the sins of the people had driven into exile with the last of the writing prophets,[8] now broods again over the thirsty land; new creation has begun. The wretched hear the good news, the prison-doors open, the oppressed breathe again the air of freedom, blind pilgrims see the light, the day of salvation is here.

'Realized eschatology'[9] is also the meaning of Mark 2.19. To the question why his disciples do not fast, Jesus replies: 'Can the bridal guests mourn during the bridal celebrations?'[10] In the symbolic language of the East the wedding is the symbol of the day of salvation, as the language of the Apocalypse bears witness: 'The marriage of the Lamb is come' (Apoc. 19.7, cf. v. 9; 21.2, 9; 22.17). The day is come, the wedding songs resound. Here is no place for mourning. This is the time for the bridal festivities, why then should my disciples fast?

The sayings which follow about the new garment and the new wine, may have been spoken on another occasion (Mark 2.21 f. par. Matt. 9.16 f.; Luke 5.36–38; Gospel of Thomas 47b); but in fact the three Synoptists have rightly connected them with the image of the wedding. They also describe foolish actions (using valuable new material to mend a tattered garment;[11] pouring fermenting new wine into worn-out damaged wine-skins), and use traditional metaphors for the New Age. It is unnecessary to draw on the abundant material furnished by the history of religion in which the cosmos is compared to the world-garment[12] in order to illustrate the meaning of the symbol of the garment; it will suffice to quote two New Testament

[7] Jesus again (see p. 116, n. 5) omits the announcement of God's vengeance (Isa. 61.2), see below, p. 218, n. 49.

[8] J. Jeremias, *Jesus als Weltvollender*, pp. 13 ff.; Bill., II, pp. 128 ff.; G. Friedrich in *ThWBNT*, VI, p. 841. 12 f.

[9] Dodd, p. 198.

[10] Mark 2.19 par. Matt. 9.15; Luke 5.34. The translation given above is established on p. 52, n. 14.

[11] See p. 29.

[12] R. Eisler, *Weltenmantel und Himmelszelt*, München, 1910; A. Jeremias, *Das Alte Testament im Lichte des Alten Orients*₄, Leipzig, 1930, subject index s. v. Weltenmantel; J. Jeremias, *Jesus als Weltvollender*, Gütersloh, 1930, pp. 25 ff.; H. Windisch in *ZNW*, 32 (1933), pp. 69 f.; W. Staerk, *Die Erlösererwartung in den östlichen Religionen*, Stuttgart, 1938, pp. 18 f.

examples. Heb. 1.10–12, following Ps. 102.26–28, describes how at
the *Parousia* Christ rolls up the cosmos like an old garment and un-
folds the new cosmos. Even more significant is the passage in Acts
10.11 ff.; 11.5 ff., where Peter, in the symbol of the sheet tied at the
four corners and containing every kind of living creature, beholds
the new cosmos, restored and declared clean by God. Tent, sheet,
and garment are common symbols of the cosmos. To this context
Mark 2.21 belongs: the old world's age has run out; it is compared
to the old garment which is no longer worth patching with new
cloth; the New Age has arrived.[13] If this interpretation should seem
too far-fetched, the numerous examples may be recalled in which
wine, the subject of the parallel verse in Mark 2.22, is used as a
symbol of the time of salvation. For this, too, it will suffice to quote
a few biblical examples; extra-biblical examples are legion. After the
Deluge Noah plants a vine in the restored earth (Gen. 9.20). The
deliverer binds his ass to the vine, he washes his garment in wine, his
eyes are bright with wine (Gen. 49.11–12). The spies bring a bunch
of grapes from the Promised Land (Num. 13.23 f.). In the story of
the miracle at Cana of Galilee in John 2.11, we are told that Jesus
manifested his glory, with the implication that the wine is the symbol
of the New Age: in the pouring out of the abundance of the wine
Jesus reveals himself as the one who brings in the time of salvation.
The old garment and the new wine tell us that the old is past, and
the New Age has been ushered in.[14]

The harvest, like the wedding and the wine, is a well-established
symbol of the New Age. Harvest is the great time of rejoicing:

> 'Thou has multiplied the exultation,
>   Thou hast increased the joy.
> They rejoice before thee
>   As men rejoice in harvest-time,
>   As they rejoice when they divide the spoil.'
>
> (Isa. 9.2.)

[13] The putting on of the new garment is a symbol of the New Age, see p. 130.
[14] Joh. Jeremias, *Das Evangelium nach Markus*₂, Chemnitz, 1928, p. 46; Joach.
Jeremias, *Jesus als Weltvollender*, Gütersloh, 1930, pp. 24 ff. The story of the
Canaanite woman should also find a place in this context (Mark 7.24–30; Matt.
15.21–28). As R. Hermann has seen, the key to the meaning of Jesus' words to
the woman who sought his help lies in the fact that she understood that Jesus
was speaking of the Messianic banquet. Her 'great faith' (Matt. 15.28) consisted
in her recognition, as shown by her words about the crumbs that the little dogs
might venture to eat, that Jesus was the giver of the Bread of Life. J. Jeremias,
*The Eucharistic Words of Jesus*₂, London, 1966, p. 234.

'Though a man may go forth in tears,
  At the sowing of the seed,
Yet he shall come again rejoicing,
  Bearing his sheaves with him.'

(Ps. 126.6.)

Harvest and vintage symbolize in particular the Last Judgement
with which the New Age begins. Joel (3.13) proclaims in view of the
judgement over all peoples, 'Thrust in the sickle for the harvest is
ripe: come, tread ye; for the wine-press is full, the fats overflow;
for their wickedness is great.' The Baptist depicts the Coming One
with the winnowing-fan in his hand, bringing in the harvest (Matt.
3.12; Luke 3.17). Paul compares the Last Judgement to the harvest
(Gal. 6.7 f.). In the last book of the Bible (Apoc. 14.15), the angel
cries from the Temple of God, 'Send forth thy sickle, and reap: for
the hour to reap is come; for the harvest of the earth is over-ripe.'
And the angel with the firebrand replies, 'Send forth thy sharp
sickle, and gather the clusters of the vine of the earth: for her grapes
are fully ripe.' The hour is come, says Jesus, as he sends out his
disciples, not to sow, but to reap.[15] The fields are white (John
4.35); sowing and reaping go on together (4.36). 'The harvest is
great, but the labourers are few. Pray ye therefore the Lord of the
harvest that he would send forth labourers into his harvest' (Matt.
9.37 f.; Luke 10.2; Gospel of Thomas 73). The little *parable of the
Fig-tree*, whose shoots and leaves herald the summer, is another
saying concerned with harvest-time: 'When her branch is now become tender, and putteth forth its leaves, ye know that the summer
is nigh; even so ye also, when ye see these things (ταῦτα) coming to
pass, know ye that he is nigh, even at the doors' (Mark 13.28 f. par.
Matt. 24.32 f.; Luke 21.29–31).[16] Who stands at the door? The
Messiah.[17] And what is the sign of the near approach of his coming?
In its present context the answer is: the dreadful portents which
herald the end. But it is doubtful whether this was the original
meaning, since the present context (the discourse about the signs of
the end) is a secondary composition, and the symbol of the fig-tree
points in another direction: the fig-tree putting out its leaves is a
sign of the coming blessing (Joel 2.22). The simile was intended by

[15] Dodd, p. 187. See above, p. 78.
[16] On the Lucan version, 'See the fig-tree and all the trees' (21.29), see above,
p. 29.
[17] Luke 21.31, the Kingdom of God.

Jesus to direct the minds of his disciples not towards the horrors of the end of the age, but towards the signs of the time of salvation. The fig-tree is distinguished from the other trees of Palestine, such as the olive, the ilex, or the carob, by the fact that it casts its leaves, so that the bare spiky twigs which give it an appearance of being utterly dead, make it possible to watch the return of the rising sap with special clearness.[18] Its shoots, bursting with life out of death, a symbol of the great mystery of death and life, herald the summer. In like fashion, says Jesus, the Messiah has his harbingers. Consider the signs: the dead fig-tree is clothed with green, the young shoots sprout, winter is over at last, summer is at the threshold, those destined for salvation awake to new life (Matt. 11.5), the hour is come, the final fulfilment has begun, the Messiah is knocking at the door (Rev. 3.20).

It is the day of salvation because the Saviour is already here. The light is kindled.

Unfortunately we do not know what meaning Jesus gave to the *simile of the Lamp whose Place is on the Lamp-stand* (Mark 4.21; Matt. 5.15; Luke 8.16; 11.33; Gospel of Thomas 33b). According to the context Mark (4.22) and Thomas relate it to the Gospel, Matthew to the disciples (cf. 5.16), Luke to the inner light (cf. 11.34–36, see below, pp. 162 f.). From the exegesis a conjecture may be hazarded as to what was the original meaning. What is the meaning of, 'neither do they place the lamp under a bushel'? If a bushel-measure[19] were placed over the small clay lamp, it would extinguish it.[20] In the little, windowless, one-roomed peasants' houses which have no chimney,[21] this might well have been the customary method of putting out the lamp; since blowing it out might cause unpleasant smoke and smell, as well as the risk of fire through sparks (cf. Shab. 3.6). A free rendering, then, would be: 'They do not light a lamp in order to put it out again immediately. No! Its place is on the lamp-stand, so that it may give light to all the inmates (all through the night, as is still customary among the Palestinian fellaheen)' (Matt.

---

[18] L. Fonck, *Die Parabeln des Herrn im Evangelium*₃, Innsbruck, 1909, p. 456; M. Meinertz, *Die Gleichnisse Jesu*₄, Münster, 1948, pp. 67, 73.

[19] Μόδιος = a bushel of 8.75 litres, then a measure in general (cf. S. Krauss, Talmudische Archäologie, II, Leipzig, 1911, p. 395 and n. 561), thus here.

[20] Shab. 16.7; Tam. 5.5; b. Betzah 22a. Cf. A. Schlatter, *Der Evangelist Matthäus*, Stuttgart, 1929, p. 149.

[21] Luther renders *'ªrubba* in Hos. 13.3 as 'chimney', but the correct meaning is 'hole' (in the wall or the roof).

5.15). The sharp contrast between kindling and extinguishing, which corresponds to the similar contrast in the metaphor of the Salt (seasoning—casting away) (Matt. 5.13), would be most intelligible if the saying had been uttered by Jesus in reference to his mission, possibly in circumstances in which he had been warned of danger and urged to protect himself (cf. Luke 13.31). But it was not for him to protect himself. The lamp has been lit, the light is shining, but not in order to be put out again! No, but in order to give light![22]

Jesus loved to speak of his mission in the various figures and symbols which traditionally depicted the deliverer.[23] A thread of eschatological meaning runs through all the figures belonging to this category. The shepherd[24] is sent to the unshepherded, oppressed flock, the 'lost sheep of the house of Israel' (Matt. 15.24 cf. 10.6; John 10.1 ff.); he seeks the lost sheep and bears it home (Luke 19.10);[25] he gathers the little flock around him (Luke 12.32); he gives his life for the flock (Mark 14.27; John 10.11 ff.); he separates the sheep from the goats (Matt. 25.32), and after the great crisis he will again go before his own as their shepherd (Mark 14.28).[26] The physician has come to the sick (Mark 2.17). The teacher instructs his scholars concerning the will of God (Matt. 10.24; Luke 6.40). The messenger brings the summons to the banquet of salvation (Mark 2.17).[27] The householder gathers the family of God around him (Matt. 10.25; Mark 3.35; Gospel of Thomas 99), and invites the guests to his table (Luke 22.29 f.), and as a servant offers them food and drink (Luke 22.27). The fisherman appoints fishers of men in his service (Mark 1.17). The architect builds the Temple of the New Age (Mark 14.58; Matt. 16.18). The king makes his triumphal entry amid shouts of joy (Mark 11.1-10 par.), and the stones will

[22] Cf. J. Jeremias, 'Die Lampe unter dem Scheffel', in *ZNW*, 39 (1940), pp. 237-240.

[23] J. Jeremias, *Jesus als Weltvollender*, Gütersloh, 1930, pp. 32 ff.

[24] The shepherd was already a symbol of the King in the ancient East, cf. *ThWBNT*, VI, p. 485. 12-35.

[25] That Luke 19.10 presupposes the figure of the shepherd (ζητῆσαι καὶ σῶσαι τὸ ἀπολωλός), may be inferred from the fact that Ezek. 34.16 is quoted.

[26] Προάγειν in Mark 14.28 is a technical term for the shepherd's work; thus, v. 28 continues the symbolism of v. 27 (see p. 220). The antiquity of Mark 14.27 follows from the fact (1) that the quotation from Zech. 13.7 follows the Hebrew text, and shows no trace of the influence of the LXX which is here completely different, and (2) from the mention of the flight of the disciples (*ThWBNT*, VI, p. 492).

[27] In Luke 5.32 the simile is changed by the addition of εἰς μετάνοιαν.

raise accusing voices [28] against those who would be silent (Luke 19.40). It should not, however, be overlooked that in all these metaphors the meaning is self-evident only for believers, while for the outsiders they keep the secret of the hidden Son of Man still unrevealed.[29]

God's gifts of salvation bear witness to the presence of the deliverer. Lepers are cleansed and death has lost its awful power so that it is now only a sleep (Mark 5.39). The gospel is proclaimed, with its pronouncement of the forgiveness of sins, the supreme gift of the Messianic Age:[30] 'God [31] forgives you your sins' (Mark 2.5). Among the manifold benefits of the New Age symbolically depicted, one stands out with special prominence, the conquest of Satan. Jesus sees Satan like lightning cast down [32] to earth from heaven (Luke 10.18);[33] unclean spirits yield to the Spirit of God (Matt. 12.28); those bound by Satan are set free (Luke 13.16). The strong man is bound, his plunder is wrested from him (Mark 3.27 par. Matt. 12.29; Gospel of Thomas 35), since he the Coming One is here who shall 'despoil the strong of their prey', the Servant of the Lord, the conqueror.[34] The binding of the strong man is evidently to be understood as referring to an actual experience, hence, clearly, to the temptation of Jesus. It appears from an analysis of the accounts of

[28] *ThWBNT*, IV, p. 273.31 ff. Cf. Hab. 2.11.

[29] E. Sjöberg, *Der verborgene Menschensohn in den Evangelien*, Lund, 1955, *passim*.

[30] J. Schniewind in *Das Neue Testament Deutsch*, I, on Mark 2.12.

[31] The passive in Mark 2.5 (ἀφίενται) is a circumlocution for the divine name. The recognition of this fact is of considerable importance, see p. 209, n. 96.

[32] Cf. Apoc. 12.9.

[33] An entirely different view of this passage is presented by M. van Rhijn, *Een blik in het onderwijs van Jezus₂*, Amsterdam, 1927 (according to A. M. Brouwer, *De Gelijkenissen*, Leiden, 1946, p. 232). He regards Luke 10.18 as an ironical saying of Jesus, and would interpret Luke 10.17–20 as follows: The disciples, full of joy, report that even the demons obey them when they are driven out by the power of Jesus (ἐν τῷ ὀνόματί σου), v. 17. But Jesus sees the danger that the disciples may set too high a value upon their successful attempts at exorcism: Satan is not to be so easily conquered. So he replies with cutting irony: 'I saw (in your enthusiastic report) Satan fallen like a lightning flash from heaven' (v. 18). He had certainly given the disciples power against all the might of the enemy (v. 19); but the reason for their joy should not lie in the subjection of the demons, but in something very different, namely, that God (the passive ἐγγέγραπται is a circumlocution for the divine name) has written their names in the book of life (v. 20). According to this view, v. 18 is thus intended to warn the disciples against overvaluing their conquest of the demons, just as v. 20 does. The objection to this interpretation lies in the fact that the bald statement of v. 18 does not suggest an ironic meaning.

[34] The Lucan version of our passage (11.22) is perhaps directly connected with Isa. 53.12 (thus W. Grundmann in *ThWBNT*, III, p. 402 ff.).

the temptation of Jesus (Mark 1.12 f.; Matt. 4.1–11; Luke 4.1–13), that the three temptation episodes in Matthew and Luke originally existed in a separate form, since Mark 1.12 f. shows that the temptation in the wilderness was originally transmitted separately, and the Gospel of the Hebrews makes a similar conjecture possible for the temptation on the mountain.[35] It is preferable, therefore, to speak of three versions of the account of the temptation, rather than of three temptations. The subject of all three (the wilderness, the gate of the Temple,[36] the mountain) is the overcoming of the temptation to entertain a false Messianic expectation.[37] Since this temptation has its *Sitz im Leben* in the period before Good Friday, and the political temptation did not exist for the primitive Church, it is not legitimate to attribute the substance of the temptation-stories to the poetic imagination of the primitive community. If that is so, in view of Luke 22.31 f., where Jesus tells his disciples about a conflict with Satan, it may be conjectured that underlying the different versions of the temptation-stories are words of Jesus in which, in the form of a *mašal*, he told his disciples about his victory over the temptation to present himself as a political Messiah—perhaps in order to warn them against a similar temptation.[38] Hence we may conclude that the different variants of the temptation-story should be closely associated with Mark 3.27; by them, in the form of a *mašal*, Jesus assures his disciples of the same experience as that which in Mark 3.27 he asserts against his opponents—now, at this very hour, Satan is conquered, Christ is greater than Satan![39]

When we examine the material we observe that all the sayings announcing that salvation is here are only similes. It is not an accident that none of the elaborate parables belongs in this category. Our next section will show that such parabolic stories were used by Jesus in the first place as weapons of controversy, and secondly to embody a threat or cry of warning, and to illustrate his instruction. Here, on

[35] Cf. E. Lohmeyer, *Ztschr. f. syst. Theologie*, 14 (1937), pp. 619–50.

[36] J. Jeremias, 'Die "Zinne" des Tempels (Mt. 4, 5; Lk. 4, 9)', in *ZDPV*, 59 (1936), pp. 206–208.

[37] J. Schniewind in *Das Neue Testament Deutsch*, 2, on Matt. 4.1–11; F. Hauck, *Das Evangelium des Lukas* (1934), pp. 60 f.; J. Jeremias, ibid.

[38] Cf. T. W. Manson, *The Servant-Messiah*, Cambridge, 1953, p. 55: the story of the Temptations is 'spiritual experience of Jesus thrown into parabolic narrative form for the instruction of his disciples'.

[39] It is simply a change in the metaphor, not in the fact, that Satan in Mark 3.27 is the one who is attacked, while in Matt. 4.1 ff. he is the attacker; in both instances it is a question of his overthrow.

the contrary, where his object was predominantly proclamation, we find Jesus, in agreement with the Old Testament prophets, especially Isaiah, preferring terse similes.

2. GOD'S MERCY FOR SINNERS

We now come to a second group of parables. They are those which contain the Good News itself. The gospel in the true sense of the word does not only say that God's day of salvation has dawned, that the New Age is here, and that the Redeemer has appeared, but also that salvation is sent to the poor, and that Jesus has come as a Saviour for sinners. The parables of this group, which are the most familiar and the most important, have without exception one special characteristic and one distinctive note which we shall recognize when we observe to whom they are addressed. The parables of the Lost Sheep and the Lost Piece of Money are addressed to the murmuring scribes and Pharisees (Luke 15.2); the parable of the Two Debtors is spoken to Simon the Pharisee (Luke 7.40): the saying about the sick is directed against the critics of Jesus among the group of theologians belonging to the Pharisaic party (Mark 2.16); the parable of the Pharisee and the Publican is likewise addressed to the Pharisees (Luke 18.9);[40] the parable of the Two Sons is spoken to members of the Sanhedrin (Matt. 21.23). The parables which have as their subject the gospel message in its narrower sense are, apparently without exception, addressed, not to the poor, but to opponents.[41] That is their distinctive note, their *Sitz im Leben*: their main object is not the presentation of the gospel, but defence and vindication of the gospel; they are controversial weapons against the critics and foes of the gospel who are indignant that Jesus should declare that God cares about sinners, and whose special attack is directed against Jesus' practice of eating with the despised. At the same time the parables are intended to win over the opponents. How does Jesus vindicate the gospel against its critics? He does it in three ways.

1. In the first place, in a series of parables he directs the attention of his critics to the poor to whom he is proclaiming the Good News. How vividly does the simile of the physician depict their position:

[40] On Luke 18.9, see p. 139.
[41] Thus the tendency, demonstrated on pp. 33 ff., to present as addressed to the disciples, parables which were addressed to the opponents of Jesus and to the crowds, has not affected the above-mentioned parables. This tells strongly in favour of the details which they give about the audience.

'It is the sick [42] who need a physician' (Mark 2.17). 'Do you not understand why I gather the despised into my company? They are sick, they need help!' The *parable of the Two Sons* (Matt. 21.28–31)[43] goes even further with its closing word,[44] 'Verily, I say unto you, publicans [45] and harlots [45] shall (at the Last Judgement) [46] enter the Kingdom of God rather than you.' The publicans, for whom you regard penitence as almost impossible,[47] are nearer to God than you! For they may have disobeyed the call of God, but they have shown sorrow and repentance. Therefore they are admitted into the Kingdom of God, not you.[48] But there is yet another reason why they are nearer to God than the pious who do not understand Jesus' love for

[42] The strange rendering 'the strong' (οἱ ἰσχύοντες Mark 2.17; Matt. 9.12) is a mistranslation of the Aram. *b⁽r'a*, which means (a) 'strong', (b) 'healthy'. Luke has correctly replaced it by 'healthy' (οἱ ὑγιαίνοντες), 5.31.

[43] The textual evidence is divergent; some witnesses put first (a) the son who refused (אCLZ...syr^cur Orig Eus Chrys), and some (b) the son who assented (BΘsa bo syr^pal). The situation described in the parable assumes that (a) is the right order: the refusal of the order by the first son makes it necessary for the father to turn to the second. Otherwise J. Schmid, 'Das textgeschichtliche Problem der Parabel von den zwei Söhnen', in *Vom Wort des Lebens* (Festschrift für M. Meinertz), Münster, 1951, pp. 68–84. He appeals to the actual situation which Jesus is describing: the leaders of the people refuse to believe. Hence it must be assumed that they are represented by the son who assented (pp. 83 f.). This view may also be supported by Matt. 22.1–14, where the invitation is first addressed to the leaders of the people. This, however, simply indicates the way of thinking which led to the secondary placing of the son first who assented: the assenter was interpreted as the Jews, the refuser as the Gentiles, and the parable was rearranged in the historical order.

[44] On v. 32, see pp. 80 f.

[45] The article has generic significance, and hence need not be translated. It is an Aramaism.

[46] Προάγουσιν renders an Aramaic participle, which has timeless force. Hence the situation in time must be determined by the context and the meaning. In this case the participle has a future significance, since all the sayings of Jesus concerning entry into the Kingdom of God have an eschatological meaning (H. Windisch, 'Die Sprüche vom Eingehen in das Reich Gottes', in *ZNW*, 27 (1928), pp. 163–92). Cf. W. Michaelis, *Täufer, Jesus, Urgemeinde*, Gütersloh, 1928, p. 66.

[47] On account of the difficulty of restitution, which was the pre-condition of repentance, and on account of the avarice of the tax-farmers (Bill., II, pp. 247 ff.).

[48] The meaning of προ in προάγουσιν is not temporal but exclusive. In reply to the objection of W. G. Kümmel, *Promise and Fulfilment*, London, 1957, p. 78, n. 198, that προάγειν is only used in a temporal not in an exclusive sense, it must be said that there is clear evidence that the Aramaic *'aqdem* (to precede) which underlies προάγειν occurs with an exclusive sense along with a temporal sense. Cf. for example, Targ. of Job 41.3 *man 'aqd⁽minnani bh⁽'obhadhe bh⁽reshith*, 'Who preceded me in the work of creation?' is obviously not temporal but exclusive. Or, j. Sanh.1. 18c. 43 *'aqd⁽mun leh ḥadh sabh b⁽'ibbur*, 'they preferred an old man to him at the session for intercalation'.

sinners, and this is set forth in the little *parable of the Two Debtors* (Luke 7.41–43).

In order to understand Luke 7.41–43 certain exegetical observations must be taken into account, from which the fact emerges that the episode related in Luke 7.36–50 has a previous history. (1) The meal to which the Pharisee invited Jesus is clearly a banquet (κατεκλίθη, v. 36);[49] it is in honour of Jesus, since Simon is allowing for the possibility that Jesus may be a prophet, and that with him the departed Spirit of God[50] has returned, bringing the New Age. Since it was a meritorious act to invite travelling teachers, especially if they had preached in the synagogue, to a sabbath meal (cf., e.g., Mark 1.29–31),[51] we may at all events infer that before the episode which the story relates took place, Jesus had preached a sermon which had impressed them all, the host, the guests, and an uninvited guest, the woman. (2) The designation of the woman as ἁμαρτωλός (v. 37) indicates that she was either a prostitute, or the wife of a man engaged in a dishonourable occupation.[52] In view of v. 49 the first mentioned meaning is to be preferred.[53] The question must remain undecided: we are not told the cause of the woman's tears.[54] All that is disclosed is a boundless gratitude; since to kiss a person's knee or foot (v. 38) is a sign of the most heartfelt gratitude, such as a man might show to one who had saved his life.[55] How completely the woman was overcome by gratitude towards her saviour is shown by the fact that unselfconsciously[56] she took off her head-covering and unbound her hair in order to wipe Jesus' feet, although it was the greatest disgrace for a woman to unbind her hair in the presence of men;[57] evidently she was so shocked at having bedewed Jesus with her tears, that she entirely forgot her surroundings. The fact that vv. 37 f. describes a gesture of profoundest gratitude (for pardon bestowed, as we see from vv. 41–43, 47), is confirmed by an im-

---

[49] At ordinary meals people were seated, cf. J. Jeremias, *The Eucharistic Words of Jesus*₂, London, 1966, pp. 48 f.

[50] See p. 117.

[51] F. Hauck, *Das Evangelium des Lukas*, Leipzig, 1934, p. 102.

[52] See p. 132.

[53] W. Michaelis, *Die Gleichnisse Jesu*, Hamburg, 1956, p. 262, n. 133.

[54] A. Schlatter, *Das Evangelium des Lukas*, Stuttgart, 1931, p. 259.

[55] b. Sanh. 27b: a man accused of murder kissed the feet of the lawyer to whom he owed his acquittal and deliverance from death.

[56] The aorist (ἐξέμαξεν, v. 38) in contrast with the imperfect expresses the impulsive nature of the action.

[57] According to Tos. Soṭa 5.9; j. Giṭ. 9.50d it was a reason for divorce.

portant linguistic observation: Hebrew, Aramaic, and Syriac have no word for 'thank' and 'thankfulness'.[58] This lack is supplied by the choice of a word which, in the context, can imply the emotion of gratitude, for example, *berekh*, 'to bless' (in gratitude); in this case ἀγαπᾶν. From this it follows that Jesus' question in v. 42 means: 'Which of them will feel the deepest thankfulness?' It also implies that Jesus interpreted (vv. 44–46) the woman's actions as signs of gratitude, and lastly, that in v. 47 ἀγαπᾶν may similarly bear the meaning of gratitude. Hence it is conclusively established that in the much-discussed phrase in v. 47a, forgiveness comes first, as is shown unequivocally by v. 47b and by the parable, and this implies that ὅτι in v. 47a indicates the evidence of forgiveness: 'Therefore I say to you that God [59] must have forgiven her sins, many as they are,[60] since she displays such deep thankfulness (grateful love);[61] he to whom God [59] forgives little, shows little thankfulness (thankful love).' The story therefore implies that Jesus in his sermon had offered forgiveness. It is against some such background as this that the parable of the Two Debtors must be understood. In it Jesus replied to Simon's unspoken criticism, and explained why he had allowed a woman who was a sinner to touch him. Why did he allow this to happen?

Thus he points the clear-cut contrast between the great debt and the small, the deep gratitude and the slight. Only the poor can fathom the full meaning of God's goodness. 'Do you not understand, Simon, that in spite of her sin-burdened life this woman is nearer to God than you? Do you not recognize that what she has, you lack, a deep gratitude? And that the gratitude which she has shown to me is directed toward God?' (See n. 59.)

2. Not only to the poor does Jesus direct the attention of the critics of the Good News, but also to themselves. In the parables of this group the vindication of the gospel is accompanied by the sternest rebuke. 'You,' he says, 'are like the son who promised to obey his father's command, but afterwards neglected to fulfil his promise (Matt. 21.28–31). You are like the husbandmen who refused year

[58] P. Joüon, 'Reconnaissance et action de grâces dans le Nouveau Testament', *Recherches de science religieuse*, 29 (1939), pp. 112–14.

[59] Ἀφέωνται, ἀφίεται (v. 47): the passive is a circumlocution for the divine action.

[60] Αἱ πολλαί is an inclusive πολύς, cf. J. Jeremias, *The Eucharistic Words of Jesus*₂, London, 1966, p. 180.

[61] The aorist ἠγάπησεν is here the equivalent of a semitic 'stative perfect' which is to be rendered by a present (M. Black, *An Aramaic Approach to the Gospels and Acts*₃, Oxford, 1967, p. 129).

after year to render to their Lord his due share of the produce of his land, heaping outrage upon outrage upon him (Mark 12.1–9, par.; Gospel of Thomas 65).[62] You are like the respectable guests who rudely declined the invitation to the banquet—what right have you to pour scorn and derision upon the wretched crowd that sit at my table? (Matt. 22.1–10; Luke 14.16–24; Gospel of Thomas 64, see pp. 176 ff.).

3. But we have not yet spoken of the third line of attack, by far the most decisive, with which Jesus vindicates the proclamation of the Good News to the despised and outcast. It appears most clearly in the *parable of the Prodigal Son*, which might more correctly be called the *parable of the Father's Love* [63] (Luke 15.11—32).[64]

The parable is not an allegory, but a story drawn from life, as is shown by vv. 18, 21, where, in a periphrastic way, God is named: 'Father, I have sinned against heaven (i.e. God) and against thee.' Thus the father is not God, but an earthly father; yet some of the expressions used are meant to reveal that in his love he is an image of God.[65] In v. 12 the younger son demands 'the portion that falls' to him, that is, according to Deut. 21.17 (the firstborn obtains twice as much as the rest of the sons), a third of the property. The legal position was as follows:[66] there were two ways in which property might pass from father to son, by a will, or by a gift during the life of the father. In the latter case the rule was that the beneficiary obtained possession of the capital immediately, but the interest on it only became available upon the death of the father.[67] That means: in the case of a gift during the father's life-time, (a) the son obtains the right of possession (the land in question, for example, cannot be sold by the father), (b) but he does not acquire the right of disposal (if the son sells the property the purchaser can take possession only upon the death of the father), and (c) he does not acquire the

[62] On the text, see pp. 70–77

[63] The father, and not the returning son, is the central figure. Elsewhere also inaccurate and even misleading designations of the parables of Jesus have sprung up (see p. 136, n. 16; 156, n. 17; 157, n. 19; 150, n. 81; 151, n. 89).

[64] Literature: K. Bornhäuser, *Studien zum Sondergut des Lukas*, Gütersloh, 1934, pp. 103–137; J. Schniewind, *Das Gleichnis vom verlorenen Sohn*, Göttingen, 1940, reprinted in *Die Freude der Busse*, Göttingen, 1956, pp. 34–87; J. Jeremias, 'Zum Gleichnis vom verlorenen Sohn', in *Th. Ztschr.*, 5 (1949), pp. 228–31 (a collection of the numerous Semitisms in view of the question of authenticity).

[65] Vv. 18, 21: ἐνώπιόν σου (cf. G. Dalman, *Die Worte Jesu*, I₂, Leipzig, 1930, p. 174); v. 20: ἐσπλαγχνίσθη; v. 29: ἐντολή.

[66] Bill., III, p. 550.

[67] b. B.B. 136a.

usufruct which remains in the father's unrestricted possession until his death. This legal position is correctly depicted in the parable when the elder brother is indicated as the sole future owner (v. 31), but nevertheless the father continues to enjoy the usufruct (vv. 22 f., 29). In v. 12 the younger son demands not only the right of possession, but also the right of disposal; he wants a settlement because he proposes to lead an independent life.[68] V. 13: Συναγαγὼν πάντα: after turning the property into cash.[69] Ἀπεδήμησεν εἰς χώραν μακράν = he emigrates. The size of the Diaspora which has been estimated at over four million, as against a Jewish Palestinian population of half a million at the most,[70] may give us some idea of the extent of the dispersion which was stimulated by the inducement of the more favourable living conditions in the great mercantile cities of the Levant, and by the frequent occurrence of famine in Palestine.[71] The younger son is evidently unmarried,[72] which allows us to draw conclusions about his age: the normal marriageable age for a man was eighteen to twenty.[73] V. 15: the non-indication of the change of subject is a semitism (ἐκολλήθη/ἔπεμψεν): he was forced to be in contact with unclean animals (Lev. 11.7), and could not have observed the Sabbath: hence he must have been reduced to the lowest depths of degradation and practically forced to renounce the regular practice of his religion.[74] V. 16 raises the question why he did not partake of the swine's food. The answer is supplied by rendering the verse: 'And he would have been only too glad [75] to fill his belly [76] with the carob-beans with which the swine were fed (sc. but he was too disgusted to do so), and no one gave him (sc. anything to eat)'.[77]

---

[68] That legal settlement took place in the talmudic period is attested by D. Daube, 'Inheritance in two Lucan pericopes', in: Zeitschr. der Savigny-Stiftung für Rechtsgeschichte, rom. Abt., 72 (1955), p. 334 with Tos. B.B. 2.5; b.B.B. 47a.

[69] W. Bauer, Wörterbuch zum NT₅, Berlin, 1958, col. 1549.

[70] A. v. Harnack, The Mission and Expansion of Christianity, I, London, 1908, p. 4; J. Jeremias, Jerusalem in the Time of Jesus, London, 1969, pp. 205 f.

[71] A synopsis in Jeremias, ibid., pp. 140 ff.

[72] K. Bornhäuser, p. 105.

[73] Bill., II, p. 374, n. a.

[74] b. B.Q. 82b: 'Cursed be the man who breeds swine.'

[75] Ἐπεθύμει with the inf. is a stylistic peculiarity of the Lucan source, in which the usage occurs four times (15.16; 16.21; 17.22; 22.15). In Matt. 13.17 and Luke 17.22 it expresses an unfulfilled wish, as also in the other three passages, cf. p. 184 and J. Jeremias, The Eucharistic Words of Jesus₂, London, 1966, p. 208.

[76] The coarse expression has been emended in many manuscripts.

[77] The additions follow a suggestion by A. Fridrichsen, Uppsala.

Hence he must have stolen what food he got.[78] V. 17: εἰς ἑαυτὸν δὲ ἐλθών: 'he came back to himself', 'he came into himself', is in Hebrew and Aramaic [79] an expression of repentance. V. 18: 'Αναστὰς πορεύσομαι =Aramaic '*qum w*'ezel, Targ. to II Sam. 3.21 = 'I will go at once.' V. 19: 'Ὡς ἕνα τῶν μισθίων σου: after the legal settlement he has no further claim, not even to food and clothing. He asks to be allowed to earn both. V. 20: δραμών: a most unusual and undignified procedure for an aged oriental even though he is in such haste.[80] Κατεφίλησεν αὐτόν: the kiss is (as in II Sam. 14.33) a sign of forgiveness. V. 21 = 18 f. except the final words ποίησόν με ὡς ἕνα τῶν μισθίων σου: the father does not allow him to utter them, and changes the words left unspoken to their opposite: he treats the returning one, not as a wage-earner, but as an honoured guest. In vv. 22 f. the father gives three orders with which Gen. 41.42 may be compared: when Joseph was appointed chief vizier he received from Pharaoh a ring, a robe of fine linen, and a golden chain: (1) First comes the ceremonial robe, which in the East is a mark of high distinction. There is no bestowal of orders, but when the king wishes to honour a deserving official, he presents him with a costly robe; investiture with a new garment is therefore a symbol of the New Age.[81] The returning son is treated as a guest of honour. (2) The ring and the shoes. Excavations have shown that the ring is to be regarded as a signet-ring; the gift of a ring signified the bestowal of authority (cf. I Macc. 6.15). Shoes are a luxury, worn by free men; here they mean that the son must no longer go about barefoot like a slave. (3) As a rule meat is only rarely eaten. For special occasions a fatted calf is prepared. Its killing means a feast for the family and the servants, and the festal reception of the returning son to the family table. The three orders given by the father are the manifest tokens of forgiveness and reinstatement, evident to all. In v. 24 we have two most vivid images in synonymous parallelism; both describe the change: resurrection from the dead, and the finding of the lost sheep. V. 25: After the feast comes music (loud singing and hand-clapping) and dancing by the men.[82] V. 28: παρεκάλει (the imperfect after the preceding aorists): 'he spoke kindly to him', 'addressed him in friendly fashion'. V. 29: The elder son omits the address, and

[78] J. Schniewind, p. 58.
[79] Bill., II, p. 215, cf. I, pp. 261 ff.
[80] L. Weatherhead, *In Quest of a Kingdom*, 1943, p. 90.
[81] See above, p. 118.
[82] Cf. the 'skipping' in Luke 6.23.

heaps reproaches upon his father. V. 30: He avoids giving the returned prodigal the name of brother; οὗτος is here used contemptuously, as in Matt. 20.12; Luke 18.11; Acts 17.18. V. 31: The father's address is specially affectionate, τέκνον, 'my dear child'. V. 32: ἔδει: The father is not speaking apologetically, 'I had to make a feast', but reproachfully, 'you ought to be glad and make merry, since it is *your* brother [83] who has come home'.

The parable describes with touching simplicity what God is like, his goodness, his grace, his boundless mercy, his abounding love. He rejoices over the return of the lost, like the father who prepared the feast of welcome. But this is only the content of the first half of the parable (vv. 11–24); for it has a double application: it describes not only the return of the younger son, but also the protest of the elder son; and the division is emphasized by the fact that each half of the parable ends with the same logion (vv. 24, 32). Since the first half is complete in itself, the second part appears at first sight superfluous. But it is erroneous to regard, for that reason, the second part as an addition. In language and content it fits the pattern of the story, without allegorizing or distorting it; it has a foundation in v. 11, and the contrast between the two sons finds an analogy in Matt. 21.28–31. Why did Jesus add it? There can be only one answer, because of the actual situation. The parable was addressed to men who were like the elder brother, men who were offended at the gospel. An appeal must be addressed to their conscience. To them Jesus says: 'Behold the greatness of God's love for his lost children, and contrast it with your own joyless, loveless, thankless and self-righteous lives. Cease then from your loveless ways, and be merciful. The spiritually dead are rising to new life, the lost are returning home, rejoice with him.' Hence we see that like the other three double-edged parables the emphasis falls on the second half. [84] The parable of the Prodigal Son is therefore not primarily a proclamation of the Good News to the poor, but a vindication of the Good News in reply to its critics. Jesus' justification lies in the boundless love of God. But Jesus does not remain on the defensive; the parable breaks off abruptly, and the issue is still open. No doubt this is a reflection of the situation which confronted Jesus. [85] His hearers were in the position of the elder son

[83] Οὗτος in v. 32 (otherwise in v. 30, see above) is a superfluous demonstrative pronoun, cf. p. 39, n. 61.
[84] On Matt. 20.1–15, see pp. 37 f.; on 22.1–14, see pp. 65 f.; on Luke 16.19–31, see p. 186.
[85] Th. Zahn, *Das Evangelium des Lucas*₃,₄, Leipzig-Erlangen, 1920, p. 564.

who had to decide whether he would accept his father's invitation and share his joy. So Jesus does not yet pronounce sentence; he still has hope of moving them to abandon their resistance to the gospel, he still hopes that they will recognize how their selfrighteousness and lovelessness separate them from God, and that they may come to experience the great joy which the Good News brings (v. 32a). The vindication of the Good News takes the form of a reproach and an appeal to the hearts of his critics.

The recognition that Luke 15.11–32 is primarily an apologetic parable, in which Jesus vindicates his table companionship with sinners against his critics (cf. vv. 1 f.), carries with it a very important consequence.[86] As we have seen, Jesus vindicates his revolutionary conduct by claiming in the parable, 'God's love to the returning sinner knows no bounds. What I do represents God's nature and will.' *Jesus thus claims that in his actions the love of God to the repentant sinner is made effectual.* Thus the parable, without making any kind of christological statement, reveals itself as a veiled assertion of authority: Jesus makes the claim for himself that he is acting in God's stead, that he is God's representative.

The *twin parables*[87] *of the Lost Sheep* (Luke 15.4–7; Matt. 18. 12–14), and *the Lost Drachma* (Luke 15.8–10)[88] are closely related to the parable of the Prodigal Son. In Luke 15.2, we are told that Jesus received (προσδέχεται)[89] publicans and 'sinners' and ate with them. The term 'sinners' means: (1) People who led an immoral life (e.g. adulterers, swindlers, Luke 18.11) and (2) people who followed a dishonourable calling (i.e. an occupation which notoriously involved immorality or dishonesty), and who were on that account deprived of civil rights, such as holding office, or bearing witness in legal proceedings. For example, excise-men, tax-collectors, shepherds, donkey-drivers, pedlars, and tanners.[90] When the Pharisees and scribes asked why Jesus accepted such people as table companions, they were not expressing surprise but disapproval; they were implying that he was an irreligious man, and warning his followers not to associate with him. Vv. 4–10: The twin parables,

[86] E. Fuchs, 'Die Frage nach dem historischen Jesus', in *Zeitschr. für Theol. und Kirche*, 53 (1956), pp. 210–29, here: p. 219.
[87] See p. 91.
[88] On the parable of the Lost Sheep, see pp. 38 ff.
[89] See p. 227, n. 92.
[90] J. Jeremias, *Jerusalem in the Time of Jesus*, London, 1969, pp. 303–12.

which contain Jesus' reply, play on the contrast between man and
woman, and perhaps between rich and poor. It is true that the owner
of the flock was not a very rich man. Among the Bedouin the size of
a flock varies from 20 to 200 head of small cattle;[91] in Jewish law
300 head is reckoned as an unusually large flock.[92] Hence, with 100
sheep the man possesses a medium-sized flock; he looks after it
himself (like the man in John 10.12), he cannot afford a watchman.
Although no Croesus, he is well off compared with the poor widow.
In the Gospel of Thomas (107) the parable of the Lost Sheep runs as
follows: 'The Kingdom is like a shepherd who has 100 sheep. One
of them went astray, which was the largest. He left behind the 99, he
sought for the one until he found it. Having tired himself out, he
said to the sheep, I love thee more than the 99.' In Luke the parable,
as far as v. 6, is a question. Verbal comparison between Luke 15.4–7
and Matt. 18.12–14 reveals a number of translational variants (e.g.
ἐν τῇ ἐρήμῳ in Luke 15.4 corresponds to ἐπὶ τὰ ὄρη in Matt. 18.12
as the translation of b‘ṭura, 'in the hill-country').[93] V. 4: τίς ἄνθρωπος
ἐξ ὑμῶν: shepherds are reckoned among the ἁμαρτωλοί, because
they are suspected of driving their flocks into foreign fields, and of
embezzling the produce of their flocks;[94] but this does not prevent
Jesus from using the shepherd as an image of God's activity of love.
Καὶ ἀπολέσας ἐξ αὐτῶν ἕν: A Palestinian shepherd counts his flock
before putting them in the fold at night, to make sure that none of
the animals is lost. The number 99 implies that the counting has just
been carried out.[95] Καταλείπει τὰ ἐνενήκοντα ἐννέα: Experts on
Palestinian life all agree that a shepherd cannot possibly leave his
flock to itself.[96] If he has to look for a lost animal he leaves the others
in the charge of the shepherds who share the fold with him (Luke
2.8; John 10.4 f.), or drives them into a cave. The young goatherd
Muhammad ed-Deeb, who discovered Qumran Cave 1, counted
his flock at the unusual hour of 11 a.m., because he had twice omitted
to count them in the evening; before he set off in search of his lost

[91] G. Dalman, *Arbeit und Sitte*, VI, Gütersloh, 1939, p. 246. Cf. Gen. 32.14: two
flocks of 220 goats and sheep respectively.
[92] Tos. B.Q. 6.20.
[93] For further remarks on the underlying Aramaic basis of the tradition, see
pp. 38 ff.
[94] J. Jeremias, *Jerusalem in the Time of Jesus*, London, 1969, p. 305.
[95] E. F. F. Bishop, 'The Parable of the Lost or Wandering Sheep', in: *Anglican
Theological Review*, 44 (1962), p. 50.
[96] Bishop, op. cit., pp. 50 f.; 52, n. 35; 57.

goat he asked his two companions to look after his flock (55 head).[97] 'Εν τῇ ἐρήμῳ: ἡ ἔρημος is here the pasture-ground in the desolate hill-country. Πορεύεται ἐπὶ τὸ ἀπολωλός: in the Gospel of Thomas the motive for the shepherd's laborious search is represented as being the loss of the largest and most valuable beast, which he loved more than all the rest. A comparison with Matthew and Luke, as well as with the general trend of Jesus' message, shows that this is a complete misunderstanding of the parable. For the expression used by Matthew (v. 14), 'one of the least' (see p. 207), and the setting of the parable in Luke, with v. 5, tend to show that it is more likely that the lost sheep was thought of as a specially weak one. It was not the high value of the animal that caused the shepherd to set out on his search, but simply the fact that it belonged to him, and without his help it could not find its way back to the flock. The statement in v. 5 (absent from Matthew) that the shepherd lays the sheep on his shoulders when he has found it should not lead us to attribute this simile to the influence upon Luke of the representations of Hermes Kriophoros, since this action is a daily occurrence in the East. When a sheep has strayed from the flock, it usually lies down helplessly, and will not move, stand up, or run. Hence there is nothing for the shepherd to do but to carry it, and over long distances this can only be done by putting it on his shoulders, i.e. round his neck;[98] he grasps its fore- and hind-legs with each hand, or if he needs one hand free for his shepherd's staff, he holds all four legs with one hand firmly against his breast.[99] V. 6: συγκαλεῖ (6, 9) suggests the preparation of a feast.[1] V. 8: In the parable of the Lost Drachma, which, as far as v. 9, is also to be read as a question, the 10 drachmas will remind every one who is familiar with Arab Palestine of the woman's head-dress bedecked with coins which is part of her dowry, and may not be laid aside, even in sleep;[2] the custom of wearing gold dinars is also attested by the Tosephta.[3] If the woman's

[97] W. H. Brownlee, 'Muhammad ed-Deeb's Own Story of His Scroll Discovery', in: *Journal of Near Eastern Studies*, 16 (1957), p. 236.

[98] A. M. Brouwer, *De Gelijkenissen*, Leiden, 1946, pp. 225 f., in part following van Koetsveld.

[99] Abundant material for the period from 1000 BC to AD 400 may be found in Th. Klauser, 'Studien zur Entstehungsgeschichte der christlichen Kunst I', in *Jahrbuch für Antike und Christentum*, I (1958), pp. 20–51 and Bildanhang; also G. Dalman, *Arbeit und Sitte*, VI, Gütersloh (1939), ill. 35.

[1] Cf. *qara* with accusative, e.g. I Kings 1.9 f.

[2] Brouwer, ibid., p. 226. E. F. F. Bishop, *Jesus of Palestine*, London, 1955, p. 191.

[3] Tos. M. Sh. 1.1.

10 drachmas were on her head-dress, she was indeed a very poor creature, considering that today many a woman prides herself on a head-dress of hundreds of gold and silver coins.[4] 'She lights a candle', not because it is night, but because the low door lets very little light into the miserable, windowless [5] dwelling, and she 'sweeps the house' with a palm-twig,[6] because in the dark the broom may make the coin tinkle on the stone floor. V. 9: if συγκαλεῖ here is to be understood as the preparation of a feast, it could, in the case of the poor woman, be interpreted as merely a modest entertainment of her friends and neighbours.

Both parables end with a sentence which contains a paraphrase for the divine name, since emotions might not be ascribed to God. Hence we must translate Luke 15.7: 'Thus God, at the Last Judgement, will rejoice more over one sinner [7] who has repented,[8] than over ninety-nine respectable persons (δίκαιοι), who have not committed any gross sin' [9] (according to Matt. 18.14: 'Thus is God pleased when one of the least important is saved'); [10] correspondingly Luke 15.10 should be translated: 'Thus I say to you, God [11] will [12] rejoice over one sinner who repents.' The *tertium comparationis* in Luke 15.4–7 is not the intimate bond between the shepherd and the flock (as in John 10, but this does not suit Luke 15.8–10), nor is it the unwearied search (as in Matt. 18.12–14, in the present context),[13] but simply and solely the joy. 'Finding creates boundless joy.'[14] As the shepherd rejoices over the lamb brought home, and the poor woman over her recovered drachma, so will God rejoice. The future tense in Luke 15.7, is to be understood in an eschatological sense: at

---

[4] G. Dalman, *Arbeit und Sitte in Palästina*, V, Gütersloh, 1937, p. 328, describes a specimen: 244 coins weighing, together with the cap itself, 2.130 kg.

[5] See p. 120.

[6] S. Krauss, *Talmudische Archäologie*, I, Leipzig, 1910, p. 77.

[7] The alliteration should be noticed: ḥedhwa (joy), ḥadh (one), ḥaṭʲja (sinner), cf. M. Black, *An Aramaic Approach to the Gospels and Acts*₃, Oxford, 1967, p. 184.

[8] The semitic ptcp. is atemporal and takes its tense from the governing verb. In this case the (eschatological) ἔσται requires the ptcp. μετανοοῦντι to be translated by a preterite.

[9] This is the meaning of οἵτινες οὐ χρείαν ἔχουσιν μετανοίας.

[10] For the grounds on which these translations rest, see p. 39.

[11] A fusion of two circumlocutions for the divine name has taken place in the expression γίνεται χαρὰ ἐνώπιον τῶν ἀγγέλων τοῦ θεοῦ, namely (1) ἄγγελοι, (2) ἐνώπιον τοῦ θεοῦ (the angels stand 'before' God).

[12] An Aramaic imperfect underlies γίνεται, which, as in the case of ἔσται in Luke 15.7, should be translated by a future.

[13] On which see pp. 39 f.

[14] E. Linnemann, *Parables of Jesus*, London, 1966, p. 66.

the final judgement God will rejoice when among the many righteous he finds a despised sinner upon whom he may pronounce absolution, nay more, it will give him even greater joy. Such is the character of God; it is his good pleasure that the lost should be redeemed, because they are his; their wanderings have caused him pain, and he rejoices over their return home. It is the 'redemptive joy' of God,[15] of which Jesus speaks, the joy in forgiving. This is Jesus' defence of the gospel: 'since God's mercy is so infinite that his supreme joy is in forgiving, my mission as Saviour is to wrest his prey from Satan and to bring home the lost.' Once again, Jesus—as God's representative (see p. 132).

As we have already seen on pp. 33 ff., the *parable of the Good Employer* (Matt. 20.1–15)[16] is also concerned with the vindication of the gospel against its critics. V. 1: We have a parable with a datival opening: 'Thus it is with the Kingdom of God.' [17] The Kingdom here is not compared to the master of the house, nor to the labourers or the vineyard, but, as so often, its arrival is compared to a reckoning.[18] Hence in Matt. 20.1, as throughout the preaching of Jesus, the Kingdom of God is to be understood in an eschatological sense. Ἅμα πρωΐ: 'at dawn.' V. 2: A denarius [19] is the usual day's wage for a labourer.[20] V. 3: 'About the third hour', i.e. between 8 and 9 a.m.[21] Ἑστῶτας ἐν τῇ ἀγορᾷ: ἑστῶτας has here the weakened sense of being present as in John 1.26; 18.18; Matt. 13.2. No oriental will *stand* for hours in the market-place.[22] Hence they sit about idly gossiping in the market-place. V. 4: Δίκαιον = 'what is right and fair': they would understand by this that their pay would be a fraction of a denarius. V. 6: The fact that between 4 and 5 p.m. the master of the house was still looking for more labour, shows that the work was unusually urgent. The vintage and the pressing had to be finished before the onset of the rainy season; with a heavy yield the race against time became serious. The question in v. 6b does not

---

[15] E. G. Gulin, *Die Freude im Neuen Testament*, I, Helsinki, 1932, p. 99.

[16] The employer is the central figure; the usual designation ('The Labourers in the Vineyard') obscures that fact (cf. p. 128, n. 63).

[17] See pp. 100 ff.

[18] Matt. 25.14 ff. par. Luke 19.12 ff.; Luke 16.2; cf. Matt. 6.2, 5, 16; 24.45 ff. par. Luke 12.42 ff.; Matt. 18.23 ff.; cf. pp. 210 ff.

[19] As in Matt. 27.7; Acts 1.18, ἐκ is a paraphrase for the genitive of price.

[20] Bill., I, p. 831.

[21] Although the day begins at sunset (cf. the 'hallowing' of the Sabbath on Friday evening), nevertheless the hours of the day are reckoned from sunrise. Obviously, because they had no clocks. The night, on the other hand, was not divided into hours, but into three (Luke 12.38) nightwatches (cf. p. 27).

[22] P. Joüon, *L'Évangile de Notre-Seigneur Jésus-Christ*, Paris, 1930, p. 122.

express surprise, but reproach. V. 7: The poor excuse conceals their characteristic oriental indifference.[23] V. 8: The paying of wages in the evening is such an obvious occurrence (Lev. 19.13; Deut. 24.14 f.), that the issuing of a special order suggests some definite purpose in the mind of the owner. This special intention was certainly not, as it might have seemed at first, that the last should be the first to receive their wages, but that all, without exception, should receive the full day's wages.[24] Ἀπόδος τὸν μισθόν therefore means: 'Pay the (full day's) wages', and ἀρξάμενος ἀπό has perhaps the weakened meaning 'including'.[25] V. 11: Κατὰ τοῦ οἰκοδεσπότου: The master of the house is hardly likely to be present; hence their noisy complaints must be directed towards his house.[26] V. 12: Οὗτοι: They force their unduly privileged fellow labourers to come with them.[27] In their indignation they omit the address (cf. Luke 15.29). They have suffered a double injustice: (1) They have been obliged to toil for twelve hours, while the others have only [28] worked one hour; (2) they have worked in the burning midday heat, the others in the cool of the evening. Hence they consider that the duration and hardship of their work entitle them to a higher rate of pay. V. 13: 'Ενί = ḥaḍh = τινί (see pp. 199 f.): he picks out the chief objector.[29] Ἑταῖρε: They had omitted the address: the master of the house puts them to shame by his mode of addressing them (cf. Luke 15.31, p. 131). The word ἑταῖρε is a mode of addressing someone whose name is unknown:[30] it implies an attitude that is both friendly and reproachful: 'my dear fellow', 'comrade'. In all three places in the New Testament where the term occurs (Matt. 20.13; 22.12; 26.50), the person addressed is in the wrong.[31] Οὐκ ἀδικῶ σε (cf. Luke 18.11 where ἄδικοι means 'defrauders'): 'I am not cheating you.' V. 14: Καὶ ὕπαγε: 'You have no more business here'. Θέλω: 'It is my firm intention'. V. 15: 'Εν τοῖς ἐμοῖς is usually rendered, 'with what is my own' (ἐν = b· instrumentale): in that case ἐκ τῶν ἐμῶν would have been expected.[32] The

[23] See p. 37.
[24] Cf. Jülicher, II, p. 462. See above, pp. 35 f.
[25] See p. 35, n. 41.
[26] Jülicher, II, p. 463.
[27] Ibid.
[28] On the omission of 'only', see p. 39, n. 59.
[29] W. Michaelis, *Die Gleichnisse Jesu*, Hamburg, 1956, p. 176.
[30] W. Bauer, *Wörterbuch zum N.T.*₅, Berlin, 1958, col. 622. Thus Matt. 20.13; 22.12.
[31] K. H. Rengstorf in *ThWBNT*, II, p. 698.
[32] P. Joüon, *L'Évangile de Notre-Seigneur Jésus-Christ*, Paris, 1930, p. 124.

meaning is, 'on my own estate' (ἐν = *b·* locale).[33] Ὀφθαλμὸς πονηρός means 'envy' (Mark 7.22). V. 16: On this verse, see pp. 36 f. On the historic present in vv. 6, 7 (twice), 8, see p. 199, n. 34.

The clearness and simplicity with which our parable presents the Good News is thrown into sharp relief by comparison with a rabbinical parallel which has been preserved in the Jerusalem Talmud. A distinguished scholar, Rabbi Bun bar Ḥijja, died at an early age *c.* AD 325, on the same day on which his son and namesake, subsequently known as Rabbi Bun II, was born. His former teachers, who had become his colleagues, assembled to pay him the last honours, and one of them, R. Zᶜera, pronounced his funeral oration in the form of a parable. He began by saying that the situation was like that of a king who had hired a great number of labourers. Two hours after the work began, the king inspected the labourers. He saw that one of them surpassed the others in industry and skill. He took him by the hand and walked up and down with him till the evening. When the labourers came to receive their wages, each of them received the same amount as all the others. Then they murmured and said: 'We have worked the whole day, and this man only two hours, yet you have paid him the full day's wages.' The king replied: 'I have not wronged you; this labourer has done more in two hours than you have done during the whole day.' So likewise, concluded the funeral oration, has Rabbi Bun bar Ḥijja accomplished more in his short life of twenty-eight years than many a grey-haired scholar in a hundred years (*sc.* therefore, after so brief a span of labour, God has taken him by the hand and gathered him to himself).[34] The resemblance between the New Testament and the Talmudic version of the parable is so striking that it can hardly be attributed to chance. It raises the question whether Jesus had made use of a Jewish parable and recast it, or whether R. Zᶜera used a parable of Jesus, perhaps without being aware of its source. We can assert with a probability bordering on certainty that the priority belongs to Jesus, altogether apart from the fact that Zᶜera lived 300 years after Jesus. The reasons are that the rabbinical version shows secondary traits (e.g. the owner of the vineyard has become a king),[35] and is artificial in character (the king walks with the industrious

---

[33] W. H. P. Hatch, 'A Note on Matthew 20.15', in *Angl. Theol. Rev.*; 26 (1944), pp. 250–3.

[34] j. Ber. 2.3c (par. Qoh. r. 5.11; Cant. r. 6.2), free paraphrase.

[35] See p. 102, n. 59.

labourer from 8 a.m. till 6 p.m., that is, for ten hours); but most significant is the feature that only by Jesus is the murmuring of the discontented labourers made to arise naturally out of the actual situation which the parable depicts. Hence the transformation which the parable has undergone in the mouth of the rabbinical scholar is all the more instructive. While in other respects the course of the story in both versions is substantially the same, in one point they differ essentially. In the rabbinical version the labourer who has only worked a short time has done more than all the rest; he is represented as having fully earned his wages, and the purpose of the parable is to extol his excellence. In the parable of Jesus, the labourers who were engaged last show nothing to warrant a claim to a full day's wages; that they receive it is entirely due to the goodness of their employer. Thus in this apparently trivial detail lies the difference between two worlds: the world of merit, and the world of grace; the law contrasted with the gospel.

Our parable is set in a period over which broods the spectre of unemployment.[36] Originally, as we have seen,[37] the parable, spoken to men who resembled the murmuring labourers, ended with the reproachful question (v. 15): 'Are you envious because I am good?' God is depicted as acting like an employer who has compassion for the unemployed and their families. He gives to publicans and sinners a share, all undeserved, in his Kingdom. So will he deal with them on the Last Day. That, says Jesus, is what he is like; and because he is like that, so am I; since I am acting under his orders and in his stead. Will you then murmur against God's goodness? That is the core of Jesus' vindication of the gospel: Look what God is like—all goodness.

There still remain a number of parables devoted to this central thought, to which Jesus never wearied of recurring. The *parable of the Pharisee and the Publican* (Luke 18.9–14) is, according to v. 9, addressed to 'those who trusted in themselves (instead of in God), because they were righteous, and looked upon others with contempt',[38] i.e. to the Pharisees. That the parable was addressed to them is confirmed by its content.

---

[36] As an illustration—after the completion of the enlargements to the Temple, relief works were instituted in Jerusalem which employed 18,000 men out of work (Jos., *Ant.*, 20.219 ff.). Cf. Luke 16.3.

[37] P. 38.

[38] Πρός τινας τοὺς πεποιθότας ἐφ' ἑαυτοῖς ὅτι εἰσὶν δίκαιοι καὶ ἐξουθενοῦντας τοὺς λοιπούς does not mean merely: 'who trusted in themselves, that they were righteous, and looked upon others with contempt', but is much more severe.

The Semitizing asyndeta (vv. 11, 12, 13) occur in such profusion in no other Lucan parable;[39] moreover, other details of language and content reveal the parable as belonging to an early Palestinian tradition. V. 10: The two men go up to the Temple at the hour of prayer, i.e. about 9 a.m., or 3 p.m. V. 11: πρὸς ἑαυτόν: the order of the words is not certain; they have been connected, either with προσ-ηύχετο (B Θ λ), or with σταθείς (AD [καθ'] Wφ). Of these two, only the second arrangement (σταθεὶς πρὸς ἑαυτὸν ταῦτα προσηύχετο) corresponds to the semitic style of speech.[40] Πρὸς ἑαυτόν renders an Aramaic reflexive (leh), which lays a definite emphasis on the action. Thus it would mean somewhat as follows: 'he took up a prominent position and uttered this prayer'. In v. 11b the prayer enumerates the sins from which the Pharisee had refrained, and in v. 12 his good deeds. Ἅρπαξ in distinction from λῃστής, means 'a rogue', ἄδικος (as in I Cor. 6.9) means 'a swindler'. V. 12 is grammatically an independent sentence, but it depends logically upon εὐχαριστῶ σοι,[41] hence we should render 'I thank thee that . . .' following which he mentions two works of supererogation: (1) While the law prescribed only one annual fast, namely, that on the Day of Atonement, he fasted voluntarily twice a week, on Monday and Thursday, probably in intercession for the sins of the people.[42] Anyone who is familiar with the East is aware that on account of the heat abstinence from drinking is the severest element in a fast. (2) He gave tithes of everything he bought, thereby insuring that he used nothing that had not been tithed, although corn, new wine, and oil should already have been tithed by the producer.[43] Hence this was a signal act of voluntary self-denial: to his personal offering he added

As may be seen from a comparison with II Cor. 1.9, τοὺς πεποιθότας ἐφ' ἑαυτοῖς designates those who trusted in themselves in contrast with those who trusted in God; hence ὅτι must be translated 'because': 'who trusted in themselves (instead of God), because they were "righteous" '. The Pharisees were not only charged with having too good an opinion of themselves, but they were condemned for allowing the self-confidence which rested on their piety to take the place of trust in God (T. W. Manson, *Sayings*, p. 309).

[39] M. Black, *An Aramaic Approach to the Gospels and Acts*₃, Oxford, 1967, pp. 59 f.
[40] Fr. Targ. to Exod. 20.15; j. R. H. 2.58b. 9.
[41] Jülicher, II, p. 603.
[42] Bill., II, pp. 243 f.
[43] Less probably (with the emphasis on πάντα): he went beyond what was prescribed and tithed everything, even garden-herbs such as mint, dill, cummin (Matt. 23.23) and rue (Luke 11.42). Or: he gave 10 per cent of his income for charitable purposes. G. Dalman, *Arbeit und Sitte*, I, Gütersloh, 1928, p. 587, also regards the explanation given in the text as the correct one.

the agricultural tithe. V. 13: While the taxes, such as poll-tax and land-tax, were collected by state-officials, the customs of a district were farmed out, apparently to the highest bidder. Hence the collectors of customs made private profit out of the transaction. Tariffs were, no doubt, fixed by the state, but the collectors had no lack of devices for defrauding the public. In the general estimation they stood on a level with robbers; they possessed no civic rights,[44] and were shunned by all respectable persons. Μακρόθεν ἑστώς: in contrast to the Pharisee (v. 11) he remained standing at a distance. Οὐκ ἤθελεν: 'he did not venture'.[45] Smiting the breast, or more accurately the heart, as the seat of sin,[46] is an expression of the deepest contrition. V. 14a: He went home (lit. 'down', because the Temple lies on a hill surrounded by valleys except in the North) δεδικαιωμένος: δικαιοῦσθαι (passive) means in late Judaism, 'to obtain justice, to be acquitted, to find justice, favour, grace.'[47] A particularly instructive parallel to Luke 18.14a is afforded by IV Ezra 12.7 (Latin) where it is said in a prayer: *Dominator domine, si inveni gratiam ante oculos tuos et si iustificatus sum apud te prae multis et si certum ascendit deprecatio mea ante faciem tuam.* . . . Here the parallelism of *inveni gratiam* and *iustificatus sum* makes it certain that *iustificari* means, 'to find favour'. With the passive used as a circumlocution for the divine name, δεδικαιωμένος should thus be rendered, '(he went home) as one to whom God had extended his favours.' Our passage is the only one in the Gospels in which the verb δικαιοῦν is used in a sense similar to that in which Paul generally uses it. Nevertheless Pauline influence is not to be assumed here, since it is excluded by the un-pauline semitizing construction of δικαιοῦν with παρά or ἤ, which we shall proceed to discuss. Our passage shows, on the other hand, that the Pauline doctrine of justification has its roots in the teaching of Jesus.[48] Παρ' ἐκεῖνον (א B L) or ἤ ἐκεῖνος (W Θ) are attempts to translate an Aramaic *min* (Semitic grammar has neither comparative nor superlative, but represents both by the preposition *min*),[49] hence we might translate

[44] J. Jeremias, *Jerusalem in the Time of Jesus*, London, 1969, pp. 304 f. (b.Sanh. 25b Bar.).

[45] Cf. Mark 6.26; Luke 18.4; John 7.1. Semitic has no word for 'to venture', cf. P. Joüon, *L'Évangile de Notre-Seigneur Jésus-Christ*, Paris, 1930, p. 216.

[46] Midr. Qoh. 7.2.

[47] See the evidence in G. Schrenk, δικαιόω B 2a, *ThWBNT*, II, p. 217.18–47. Cf. also p. 142, n. 51.

[48] For a similar observation on τὴν πίστιν in Luke 18.8b see p. 155, n. 13.

[49] The comparative *min* is rendered by ἤ in Mark 9.43, 45, 47; Luke 15.7 *et al.*; by παρά with the accus. in Luke 13.2, 4 *et al.*

'more justified than the other'. This comparative *min*, however, is very often used with an exclusive sense (e.g. II Sam. 19.44: *bdwd* [read: *b·khor*] *'ani mimm·kha*=LXX πρωτότοκος ἐγὼ ἢ σύ=‘I am the firstborn and not thou’; Ps. 45 [LXX 44]. 8: *m·šaḥ·kha . . . šemen meḥ·bherekha* =LXX ἔχρισέν σε . . . ἔλαιον . . . παρὰ τοὺς μετόχους σου =‘he hath anointed *thee* with oil and not thy companions’; Rom. 1.25: ‘They worshipped the creature, instead of (παρά) the Creator’, *et al.*);[50] notice especially the locution δικαιοῦσθαι ἤ, cf. LXX Gen. 38.26: δεδικαίωται Θάμαρ ἢ ἐγώ (‘Tamar is righteous and I am not’).[51] The frequent exclusive sense is to be assumed for Luke 18.14a, too: ‘God had extended his favours to him, not to the other.’[52] Thus there is a severe judgement implied in παρ’ ἐκεῖνον: God did not accept the Pharisee’s prayer. V. 14b contains a generalizing conclusion which affirms a favourite gospel theme, the eschatological reversal of existing conditions.[53] It is in the form of an antithetic parallelism, describing God’s dealings at the Last Judgement:[54] he will humble the proud, and exalt the humble.

To its first hearers the parable must have seemed shocking and inconceivable. A prayer very similar to the prayer of the Pharisee has come down to us from the first century AD in the Talmud: ‘I thank thee, O Lord, my God, that thou hast given me my lot with those who sit in the seat of learning, and not with those who sit at the street-corners; for I am early to work, and they are early to work; I am early to work on the words of the Torah, and they are early to work on things of no moment. I weary myself, and they weary themselves; I weary myself and profit thereby, while they weary themselves to no profit. I run and they run; I run towards the life of the Age to Come, and they run towards the pit of destruction’ (b.Ber. 28b).[55] Hence we can see that the prayer of the Pharisee

---

[50] I have given numerous examples of the exclusive *min* and its various renderings in the LXX in: *Unknown Sayings of Jesus*, London, 1957, p. 78, n. 1.

[51] Furthermore, Origen, *In Jer. hom.* 8.7 (E. Klostermann, *Apocrypha, III, Kleine Texte* 11₂, Bonn, 1911, p. 11, no. 53b): ἐδικαιώθη, γάρ φησι [Ez. 16.52], Σόδομα ἐκ σοῦ (‘Sodom found favour rather than you’, ‘not you’); *Const. Ap.*, II 60.1 (ibid., no. 53a): πῶς δὲ οὐχὶ καὶ νῦν ἐρεῖ τῷ τοιούτῳ ὁ κύριος [God]· ἐδικαιώθη τὰ ἔθνη ὑπὲρ ὑμᾶς (‘the heathen found favour, not you’), ὥσπερ καὶ τὴν Ἰερουσαλὴμ ὀνειδίζων ἔλεγεν [Ez. 16.52]· ἐδικαιώθη Σόδομα ἐκ σοῦ (‘not you’).

[52] Similarly G. Schrenk in *ThWBNT*, II, p. 219, n. 16.

[53] J. Jeremias, *Jesus als Weltvollender*, Gütersloh, 1930, p. 73.

[54] Ταπεινωθήσεται, ὑψωθήσεται: the passive is a circumlocution for the divine name, and the future is eschatological.

[55] Cf. also 1QH 7.34: ‘I praise thee, O Lord, that thou hast not allowed my lot to fall among the worthless community, nor assigned me a part in the circle of the secret ones.’

in Luke 18.11 f. is taken from life, indeed we have in the prayer in b.Ber. 28b a commentary on the εὐχαριστῶ in Luke 18.11. He gives thanks, actually, for God's guidance. He knows that he owes his other self, his better self, to 'his God', who has given him 'his lot' with those who take their religious duties seriously. He would not at any price change places with the other man, even if the latter were better off than he; since his way, wearisome as it is, holds the promise of 'the life of the Age to Come'. Has he not manifold cause for thanksgiving? And be it observed that his prayer contains no petition, only thanksgiving [56]—he has been granted 'the greatest blessing man can desire, a foretaste of the world to come'.[57] What fault can be found with his prayer? The publican, too, must be viewed from the standpoint of his own time. He dared not, so it says, 'so much as lift up his eyes to heaven', to say nothing of his hands (so we must complete the description), for the uplifted hands were part of usual gesture in prayer; but his head was bowed and his hands were crossed upon his breast.[58] What follows is no part of the usual attitude in prayer; [59] it is an expression of despair.[60] The man smites upon his heart,[61] wholly forgetting where he is, overwhelmed by the bitter sense of his distance from God. He and his family are in a hopeless position, since for him repentance involves, not only the abandonment of his sinful way of life, i.e. of his calling, but also the restitution of his fraudulent gains plus an added fifth. How can he know everyone with whom he has had dealings? Not only is his situation hopeless, but even his cry for mercy. And then comes the concluding sentence: 'I say unto you that when this man went home, God had justified him rather than the other' (Luke 18.14a). God has bestowed

[56] V. 12 also belongs to the thanksgiving (see above).

[57] Jülicher, II, p. 604.

[58] On the two attitudes for prayer (hands and eyes uplifted—bowed head and crossed hands), cf. illus. 11 and 8 in my book, *Die Passahfeier der Samaritaner*, BZAW, 59, Giessen-Berlin, 1932.

[59] This inference is drawn from the very rare occurrences of τύπτειν the breast. In distinction from the frequently mentioned κόπτεσθαι the breast, performed by women in mourning (see p. 161), the different gesture of τύπτειν the breast, so far as I know, only occurs in Luke 18.13; 23.48; *Joseph and Aseneth* 10 (ed. P. Batiffol, *Le livre de la prière d'Aseneth*, Studia Patristica, I, Paris, 1889, p. 50.22, about the utterly desperate Aseneth: κλαίουσα καὶ πατάσσουσα τῇ χειρὶ τὸ στῆθος αὐτῆς πυκνῶς; 52.21: καὶ ἐπάτασσε τὸ στῆθος αὐτῆς πυκνῶς ταῖς χερσὶν αὐτῆς) and in Midr. Qoh. 7.2 (ed. princ. Pesaro, 1519: koth'sin 'al ha-lebh='they smote their hearts for sorrow').

[60] Cf. *Joseph and Aseneth* 10 (see previous note).

[61] Cf. Midr. Qoh. 7.2 (see n. 59).

his favour on him, and not on the other! Such a conclusion must have come as a complete surprise to its hearers. It was beyond the capacity of any of them to imagine. What fault had the Pharisee committed, and what had the publican done by way of reparation? Leaving v. 14b out of consideration,[62] Jesus does not go into this question. He simply says: That is God's decision. He does, however, give us an indirect explanation of God's apparent injustice. The prayer of the publican is a quotation: he uses the opening words of Ps. 51,[63] only adding (with an adversative sense) τῷ ἁμαρτωλῷ, 'My[64] God, have mercy on me, although I am such a sinner' (v. 13). But we find in the same psalm: 'The sacrifices of God are a broken spirit: a broken and a contrite heart, O God, thou wilt not despise' (v. 19). The character of God, says Jesus, is such as is described in Ps. 51. He welcomes the despairing, hopeless sinner, and rejects the self-righteous. He is the God of the despairing, and for the broken heart his mercy is boundless. That is what God is like, and that is how he is now acting through me.

It is also possible that the *simile of the Father and the Child* (Matt. 7.9–11; Luke 11.11–13) is concerned with the vindication of the gospel. A. T. Cadoux [65] has pointed out that (a) Jesus addressed the condemnation πονηροὶ ὄντες elsewhere not to his disciples but to the Pharisees (Matt. 12.34), and that (b) in Matt. 7.11b the change from the 2nd to the 3rd person is striking (it does not say, as might have been expected from its present connection, 'he will give you', but 'he will give to those who ask him'). Hence those who ask God are contrasted with ὑμεῖς πονηροὶ ὄντες. From this Cadoux concludes that we have here a polemical utterance of Jesus. He expresses himself in favour of the priority of the Lucan form of the saying (11.13: δώσει πνεῦμα ἅγιον), upon which he bases his suggestion that the Beelzebul controversy is the situation which gave occasion ior the logion. It says, in effect: 'Just as you give good gifts to your children, so God gives to those who ask him, that Spirit through whom I am casting out demons.' The conjecture that in Matt 7.9–11 par. we have a polemical utterance of Jesus receives an obvious confirmation from Matt. 12.34 and from the change from the 2nd to

---

[62] See p. 107. It is not possible to decide with certainty whether v. 14b is part of the original tradition.

[63] Cf. the translation of the end of Luke 18.13 in the Peshitta: '*elaha ḥunnen* with Ps. 51.3: *ḥonneni. 'elohim*.

[64] Ὁ θεός, Aram. *'ᵉlahi*, 'my God'.

[65] *The Parables of Jesus*, New York, 1931, pp. 76 f.

the 3rd person in Matt. 7.11. To this must be added the fact that the question: τίς ἐξ ὑμῶν generally introduces sayings of Jesus addressed to opponents (Matt. 12.11, cf. par. Luke 14.5; 15.4; see above, p. 103). But Cadoux's preference for the Lucan version of the saying is unnecessary. Ἀγαθά (Matt. 7.11) has the same eschatological significance as πνεῦμα ἅγιον (Luke 11.13), since τὰ ἀγαθά (Semitic speech lacks the superlative) frequently designates the gifts of the Messianic Age (Rom. 3.8; 10.15 cited from Isa. 52.7; [66] Heb. 9.11; 10.1, cf. Luke 1.53). Hence we may well regard Matt. 7.9–11 par. as a saying of Jesus directed against the misinterpretation of his words and acts. The usual attack of the opponents of Jesus on his proclamation of the gospel to the despised may most naturally be suggested as its occasion. Publicans pray to God (Luke 18.13 f.), and he listens to them—shocking! But Jesus replies: 'Your eyes are closed against the fatherly goodness of God. Consider how you behave towards your children. If, although you are evil you know how to give good gifts to your children, why are you unwilling to believe that God will give the gifts of the New Age to those who ask him?'

Finally let us recall the *parable of the Two Debtors*, one owing much and one owing little, but both forgiven by their creditor (Luke 7.41–43). Surely a *rara avis* [67] among creditors! Where may such a one be found? Clearly Jesus was speaking about God, of his inconceivable goodness. 'Do you not understand, Simon? This woman's love, which you despise, is the expression of her boundless gratitude for God's inconceivable goodness. Wronging both her and me, you are missing God's best gift!'

All the Gospel parables are a defence of the Good News. The actual proclamation of the Good News to sinners took a different form: in the offer of forgiveness, in Jesus' invitation of the guilty to taste his hospitality, in his call to follow him. It was not to sinners that he addressed the Gospel parables, but to his critics: to those who rejected him because he gathered the despised around him. His opponents were disappointed because they were expecting a Day of Wrath; they had closed their hearts to the Good News because they had made up their minds to walk in God's way, to serve him with unfaltering piety, and in so doing had achieved too good an opinion of themselves. To these men the gospel was an offence, and it should be noticed that through-

---

[66] For the rabbinic application of Isa. 52.7 to the Messianic Age, cf. Bill., III, pp. 282 f.

[67] E. Klostermann, *Das Lukasevangelium*₂, Tübingen, 1929, in loc.

out it was not the offence of the Cross (I Cor. 1.23), but a cause of
offence which antedates the Cross: the humble appearance of the
Messianic community—a point of some importance in connection with
the question of authenticity. Again and again they ask: 'Why do you
associate with this riff-raff, shunned by all respectable people?' And
he replies: 'Because they are sick and need me, because they are truly
repentant, and because they feel the gratitude of children forgiven by
God. Because, on the other hand, you, with your loveless, self-
righteous, disobedient hearts, have rejected the gospel. But, above all,
because I know what God is like, so good to the poor, so glad when the
lost are found, so overflowing with a father's love for the returning
child, so merciful to the despairing, the helpless, and the needy. That
is why!'

3. THE GREAT ASSURANCE

This group of parables to which belong on the one hand the four
contrasting parables (the Mustard Seed, the Leaven, the Sower, and
the Patient Husbandman), and on the other hand the parables of
the Unjust Judge, and the Man asking for Help by Night, contains
one of the central elements of the preaching of Jesus.

The *parables of the Mustard Seed* (Mark 4.30–32; Matt. 13.31 f.;
Luke 13.18 f.; Gospel of Thomas 20) and *the Leaven* (Matt. 13.33;
Luke 13.20 f.; Gospel of Thomas 96) are so closely connected by their
content that it seems necessary to discuss them together, although
they may have been spoken on separate occasions (see above p. 92).
In the Gospel of Thomas the two parables appear as follows: 'The
disciples said to Jesus: Tell us what the Kingdom of Heaven is like. He
said to them: It is like a mustard-seed smaller than all seeds. But when
it falls on the tilled earth, it produces a large branch and becomes
shelter for the birds of heaven' (Gospel of Thomas 20)—'Jesus said:
The Kingdom of the Father is like a woman. She took a little leaven,
hid it in dough and made large loaves of it. He that has ears, let him
hear' (Gospel of Thomas 96). Both parables show a strongly marked
Palestinian colouring.[68] In order to understand them aright it is

[68] When it is translated back into Aramaic, the parable of the Mustard seed, as
M. Black has shown in *An Aramaic Approach to the Gospels and Acts*₃, Oxford, 1967,
pp. 165 f., exhibits alliteration and play on words: Mark 4.31: *di kadh zᵉriʿ* (sown)
ʿal ʾarʿa (earth) *zᵉʿer* (little) *hu min kullhᵉhon zarʿin* (seeds) *dibhᵉʾarʿa* (32) *wᵉkhadh zᵉriʿ*
rᵉbha (grows) *wahᵃwa rabba* (great) . . . *ʿanpin* (boughs) *rabhrᵉbhin* (great) . . . *ʿophin*
(birds). The parable of the Leaven: σάτον (= 13.13 litres) is a Palestinian measure.

essential to recognize that the translation, 'The Kingdom of Heaven is like a grain of mustard seed', or 'like a morsel of leaven', is misleading: in reality we have here two parables with a datival introduction, corresponding to an Aramaic *l* (see pp. 100 ff.), which should be rendered, 'It is the case with the Kingdom of God as with a grain of mustard seed', or 'as with a morsel of leaven'. The purpose of the parable is to compare the Kingdom of God with the final stage of the process there described (see p. 102), with the tall shrub affording shelter to the birds, and with the mass of dough wholly permeated by the leaven: the tree which shelters the birds is a common metaphor for a mighty kingdom which protects its vassals,[69] and the dough in Rom. 11.16 is a metaphor for the people of God.

The eschatological character of the metaphor of the tree or the shrub is established by the fact that κατασκηνοῦν (Mark 4.32; Matt. 13.32; Luke 13.19) is actually an eschatological technical term for the incorporation of the Gentiles into the people of God, cf. *Joseph and Aseneth* 15:[70] Καὶ οὐκέτι ἀπὸ τοῦ νῦν κληθήσῃ Ἀσενέθ, ἀλλ' ἔσται τὸ ὄνομά σου πόλις καταφυγῆς, διότι ἐν σοὶ καταφεύξονται ἔθνη πολλὰ καὶ ὑπὸ τὰς πτέρυγάς σου κατασκηνώσουσι, καὶ σκεπασθήσονται διὰ σοῦ ἔθνη πολλά, καὶ ἐπὶ τὰ τείχη σου διαφυλαχθήσονται οἱ προσκείμενοι τῷ θεῷ τῷ ὑψίστῳ διὰ μετανοίας. Moreover, Matthew and Luke have added touches of eschatological colour in both parables. In the parable of the Mustard Seed they made the mustard plant (Mark 4.32; Gospel of Thomas 20) a tree (see p. 31); in the parable of the Leaven they drastically pictured the overflowing mass of dough by borrowing from Gen. 18.6 (see pp. 31 f.) the number of 3 *se'a* (39.4 litres)—3 *se'a* are something like 50 pounds of flour, and the bread baked from this amount would provide a meal for more than 100 persons.[71] The features of the parables which transcend the bounds of actuality, δένδρον Matt. 13.32; Luke 13.19 (mustard is not a tree), σάτα τρία (no housewife would bake so vast a quantity of meal), are meant to tell us that we have to do with divine realities.

Both parables picture a sharp contrast. This agreement in pattern was the reason why both Matthew (13.31–33) and Luke (13.18–21)

---

[69] Dodd, p. 190, refers to Ezek. 17.23; 31.6; Dan. 4.9, 11, 18; T. W. Manson, *Teaching*, p. 133, n. 1, shows by examples from apocalyptic (Eth. En. 90.30, 33, 37) and rabbinic (Midr. to Ps. 104.12) literature, that the birds symbolize the Gentiles seeking refuge with Israel.

[70] Ed. P. Batiffol, *Le livre de la prière d'Aseneth*, Studia patristica, I, Paris, 1889, p. 61.9 ff.

[71] Pe'a 8.7: A loaf of bread containing 0.675 litres of flour, enough for two meals.

preserved them as a double parable. Thus we are shown the mustard seed, the very smallest thing the human eye can perceive,[72] 'the least of all the seeds which are on the earth' (Mark 4.31)—every word emphasizes its smallness—and when it is grown, it is 'the greatest among all the herbs, and puts forth great branches, so that the birds of heaven make their nests in its shadow' (v. 32)—every word depicts the size of the shrub, which, by the Lake of Gennesaret, attains a height of about 8 to 10 feet.[73] Again we are shown a tiny morsel of leaven (cf. I Cor. 5.6; Gal. 5.9), absurdly small in comparison with the great mass of more than a bushel of meal. The housewife mixes it, covers it with a cloth, leaves the mass to stand overnight, and when she returns to it in the morning the whole mass of dough is leavened.[74] It is not the purpose of either parable merely to describe a process: that would be the way of the western mind. The oriental mind includes both beginning and end in its purview,[75] seizing the paradoxical element in both cases, the two successive, yet fundamentally differing, situations.[76] It is no mere coincidence that in the Talmud (b. Sanh. 90b), in Paul (I Cor. 15.35–38), in John (12.24), in I Clement (24.4–5), the seed is the image of the resurrection, the symbol of mystery of life out of death. The oriental mind sees two wholly different situations: on the one hand the dead seed, on the other, the waving corn-field, here death, there, through the divine creative power, life. 'Let us take the crops: how and in what way does the sowing take place? The sower went forth and cast each of the seeds into the ground, and they fall on to the ground, parched and bare, and suffer decay: then from their

[72] Lev. r. 31 on 24.2.
[73] G. Dalman, *Arbeit und Sitte in Palästina*, II, Gütersloh, 1932, p. 293; K.-E. Wilken, *Biblisches Erleben im Heiligen Land*, I, Lahr-Dinglingen, 1953, p. 108. The birds are attracted by the shade and the seed; ibid., p. 109.
[74] When the Gospel of Thomas contrasts the small piece of leaven with the large loaves, the parabolic contrast may be preserved, but the original point is missed; the emphasis no longer rests on the moment when the leavened dough is uncovered (cf. B. Gärtner, *The Theology of the Gospel According to Thomas*, New York, 1961, p. 231).
[75] Cf. the characteristic Semitic way of only dwelling on the beginning and end of a story without reference to what happens between: e.g. in Matt. 27.8 (*sc.* 'and bears this name'); 28.15 (*sc.* 'and has persisted'); Luke 4.14 ('Jesus returned', *sc.* 'and worked. . . .'); John 12.24 (see p.220, n. 59); Acts 7.44 f. ('and let it stand' should be supplied before ἕως); Rev. 12.5 (birth and taking up are regarded as two consecutive events, and the earthly life of Jesus is passed over, cf. M. Rissi, *Zeit und Geschichte in der Offb. d. Joh.*, Zurich, 1952, p. 44). Similarly in Matt. 13.33; Luke 13.21 ('and allowed the dough to rest' should be supplied before ἕως).
[76] Cf. A. Schweitzer, *Geschichte der Leben-Jesu-Forschung₂*, Tübingen, 1913, pp. 402 f.

decay the greatness of the providence of the Master raises them up, and from one grain more grow and bring forth fruit' (I Clem. 24.4–5). The modern man, passing through the ploughed field, thinks of what is going on beneath the soil, and envisages a biological development. The people of the Bible, passing through the same plough-land, look up and see miracle upon miracle, nothing less than resurrection from the dead. Thus did Jesus' audience understand the parables of the Mustard seed and the Leaven as parables of contrast. Their meaning is that out of the most insignificant beginnings, invisible to human eye, God creates his mighty Kingdom, which embraces all the peoples of the world.[77]

If that is right, the occasion of the utterance of the two parables may be taken to be some expression of doubt concerning the mission of Jesus.[78] How differently the beginnings of the Messianic Age announced by Jesus appeared than was commonly expected! Could this wretched band, comprising so many disreputable characters, be the wedding-guests of God's redeemed community? 'Yes', says Jesus, 'it is. With the same compelling certainty that causes a tall shrub to grow out of a minute grain of mustard-seed, or a small piece of leaven to produce a vast mass of dough, will God's miraculous power cause my small band to swell into the mighty host of the people of God in the Messianic Age, embracing the Gentiles.' 'Not knowing the power of God' (Mark 12.25), 'Ye do greatly err' (v. 27).

In order to understand the impact of this statement of Jesus, attention must be drawn to one final point. Jesus' audience knew the simile of the high tree from the Scripture (Ezek. 31; Dan. 4) where it symbolizes the world-power, and the tiny piece of leaven which leavens a mass of dough was familiar to them from the Passover *haggadah* as a symbol of malice and wickedness.[79] Jesus is bold enough to employ both similes in the opposite sense. They apply—not to the powers of Evil, but to God's royal majesty.

In order to understand the *parable of the Sower* (Mark 4.3–8; Matt. 13.3–8; Luke 8.5–8; Gospel of Thomas 9, see above, p. 28)[80]

[77] J. Jeremias, *Jesus' Promise to the Nations*₂ (Studies in Biblical Theology 24), London, 1967, pp. 68 f.; see above p. 147, n. 69.
[78] N. A. Dahl, 'The Parables of Growth', in *Studia Theologica*, 5 (1951), p. 140.
[79] I Cor. 5.6, cf. J. Jeremias, *The Eucharistic Words of Jesus*₂, London, 1966, p. 60.
[80] It has a Palestinian character: cf. the numerous semitisms (examples on p. 11, n. 2; in Mark 4.8, 20 the thrice repeated εἰς or ἐν [as it should be read, not εἰς or ἐν] is a mistranslation of the Aram. repetitive sign *ḥadh*), and the Palestinian sowing technique (see pp. 11 f.).

in what is probably its original meaning, we must reject the interpretation which misses its eschatological point, shifts its emphasis from the eschatological to the psychological and hortatory aspect, and turns it into a warning to the converted against a failure to stand fast in time of persecution and against worldliness (see pp. 78 f.).[81] The understanding of the parable depends on the recognition of the fact that its beginning describes a different point of time from its conclusion. First we have a general description of the sowing, but in the last verse it is already harvest-time. The breaking-in of the Kingdom of God is compared, as so often, to the harvest (see pp. 118 f.). Again we are presented with a contrast-parable. On the one hand we have a description of the manifold frustrations to which the sower's labour is liable: [82] that is the only reason why the as yet unploughed fallow land (see pp. 11 f.) is described; Jesus could have gone on to depict weeds, drought, scorching wind (sirocco), locusts, and other enemies of the seed among which the Gospel of Thomas (9) even mentions the worm.[83] A hopeless prospect! But now a miracle happens. From the dreary fallow land grows a field of waving corn, with a yield that surpasses all prayer and understanding. As so often (see pp. 118 ff.) the dawn of the Kingdom of God is compared to the harvest. The abnormal [84] tripling, presented in true oriental fashion,[85] of the harvest's yield (thirty, sixty, a hundredfold) symbolizes the eschatological overflowing of the divine fullness, surpassing all human measure [86] (v. 8). To human eyes much of the labour seems futile and fruitless, resulting apparently in repeated failure, but Jesus is full of joyful confidence: he knows that God has made a beginning, bringing with it a harvest of reward beyond all asking or conceiving. In spite of every failure and opposition, from hopeless beginnings, God brings forth the triumphant end which he had promised.[87] Once again it

[81] The title, arising from its interpretation, 'the Fourfold Field', is misleading, cf. p. 128, n. 63.

[82] Dodd, pp. 19, 24, 182.

[83] 'And other seeds fell on the thorns: they choked the seeds and the worm ate them' (see above, p. 28).

[84] G. Dalman, *Arbeit und Sitte*, III, Gütersloh, 1933, pp. 153–65: *Der Ertrag*. Dalman's abundant statistics show that a tenfold yield counts as a good harvest, and a yield of seven and a half as an average one.

[85] Cf. Sir. 41.4: 'Mayest thou now live 1,000 years, or 100, or 10.'

[86] The abnormal yield of the soil in the Messianic Age is already depicted in eschatological metaphors both in the OT and in the rabbinic and pseudepigraphical literature (Dahl [p. 149, n. 78], p. 153; J. Jeremias, *Unknown Sayings of Jesus2*, London, 1964, pp. 33 f.).

[87] That this is the correct interpretation of the intention of the parable is con-

is easy to visualize the situation which caused Jesus to utter the parable;[88] it is closely related to that which called forth the parables of the Mustard-seed and the Leaven: doubts. They were not, however, occasioned, as there, by the meagreness of Jesus' following, but by the apparently ineffectual preaching (Mark 6.5 f.), the bitter hostility (Mark 3.6), and the increasing desertions (John 6.60). Did not all this contradict the claims of his mission? Consider the husbandman, says Jesus; he might well despair in view of the many adverse factors which destroy and threaten his seed. Nevertheless he remains unshaken in his confidence that a rich harvest will reward his labours. O ye of little faith! 'How is it that ye have no faith?' (Mark 4.40).

Finally, to the parables of contrast belongs the *parable of the Seed growing secretly*, which might more accurately be called the *parable of the Patient Husbandman*[89] (Mark 4.26–29). Once more the advent of the Kingdom of God is compared to the harvest.[90] Again we are confronted with a sharp contrast; the inactivity of the farmer after sowing is vividly depicted: his life follows its ordered round of sleeping and waking, night and day:[91] without his taking anxious thought (ὡς οὐκ οἶδεν αὐτός) or any active steps (αὐτομάτη), the seed grows from stalk to ear, and from ear to ripened corn— the naming of each stage of the process describes the unceasing process of growth. Then, suddenly, the moment arrives which rewards the patient waiting. The corn is ripe, the sickle is thrust in, the joyful cry rings out, 'the harvest has come' (v. 29: cf. Joel 3.13). Thus it is with the Kingdom of God; thus with the same certainty as the harvest comes for the husbandman after his long waiting, does God when his hour has come, when the eschatological term is

---

firmed by the earliest exegesis: Justin Martyr and the author of the Pseudo-Clementine Recognitions do not understand the parable of the Sower as a challenge to self-examination on the part of the audience, but as an encouragement to the Christian preacher not to be faint-hearted in his labours (Justin, *Dial.*, 125; *Clem. Rec.*, 3.14. Cf. M. F. Wiles, 'Early Exegesis of the Parables', in *Scottish Journal of Theology*, 11 (1958), p. 293). This interpretation is the more noteworthy in that it goes beyond the allegorical exposition which Justin and the author of the Recognitions found in all three Synoptics. It must go back to an early tradition.

[88] Dahl, op. cit., pp. 148 ff.

[89] B. T. D. Smith, pp. 129 ff.; Dahl, op. cit., p. 149. For other erroneous titles of the parables of Jesus see p. 128, n. 63.

[90] Not with the seed! Cf. the reference contained in Mark 4.29b,c to Joel 3.13, and above p. 78.

[91] Notice the two present tenses καθεύδῃ καὶ ἐγείρηται following the aorist βάλῃ, which emphasize the inactivity.

complete,[92] bring in the Last Judgement and the Kingdom.[93] Man can do nothing with regard to it; he can only wait with the patience of the husbandman (James 5.7). It has often been conjectured that this parable was intended as a contrast to the efforts of the Zealots to bring in the Messianic deliverance by a forcible throwing off of the Roman yoke:[94] and here it must be remembered that ex-Zealots too belonged to the circle of the disciples.[95] Why did Jesus not act when action was what the hour demanded? Why did he not take vigorous steps to purge out the sinners and establish the purified community (Matt. 13.24-30, see pp. 226 f.)? Why did he not give the signal for the liberation of Israel from the Gentile yoke (Mark 12.14 par.; [John] 8.5 f.)?[96] Was not this refusal of Jesus a denial of the claim of his mission? Once again it is a contrast-parable by which Jesus replied to the doubts about his mission, and to frustrated hopes. Consider the husbandman, says Jesus, who patiently awaits the time of the harvest. So, too, God's hour comes irresistibly. He has made the decisive beginning, the seed has been sown. He leaves nothing undone (cf. Phil. 1.6). His beginning ripens to its fulfilment. Till then it behoves man to wait in patience and not to try and anticipate God, but in full confidence to leave everything to him.

The feature common to all four parables is that they contrast the beginning with the end, and what a contrast! The insignificance of the beginning and the triumph of the end! But the contrast is not the whole truth.[97] The fruit is the *result* of the seed; the end is *implicit* in the beginning. The infinitely great is already active in the infinitely small. In the present, and indeed in secret, the event is already in motion. This undisclosed nature of the Basileia is a matter

[92] The conception of the eschatological measure of time, which is prominent in the N.T. calls for further study. We hear of the fullness of time (Gal. 4.4), of the Gentiles (Rom. 11.25), of the martyrs (Apoc. 6.11), of sufferings (Col. 1.24), of the period for repentance (Apoc. 11.3, 7), of sins (Matt. 23.32; I Thess. 2.16).

[93] With Mark 4.26-29 may be compared IV Ezra where a pregnant woman is depicted as symbolizing the end which will come with absolute certainty although, perhaps, after long waiting (4.33): 'When is this to happen? . . . (40) Go and ask the pregnant whether her womb will be able to keep her child after her nine months have passed?'

[94] Especially C. A. Bugge, *Die Hauptparabeln Jesu,* I, Giessen, 1903, pp. 157 ff., illustrates this point of view.

[95] It is not perhaps accidental that in Mark 3.18 f. par. Matt. 10.4 Simon the Zealot and (probably) Judas Iscariot are named together as a couple (cf. Mark 6.7).

[96] On [John] 7.53-8.11 see *ZNW,* 43 (1950-51), pp. 148 f.

[97] Cf. E. Lohse, 'Die Gottesherrschaft in den Gleichnissen Jesu', in *Evangelische Theologie,* 18 (1958), p. 157.

of faith in a world to which nothing is yet known. Those to whom it has been given to understand the mystery of the Kingdom (Mark 4.11) see already in its hidden and insignificant beginnings the coming glory of God.

This unwavering assurance that God's hour approaches is an essential element in the preaching of Jesus. God's hour is coming: nay more, it has already begun. In his beginning the end is already implicit. No doubts with regard to his mission, no scorn, no lack of faith, no impatience, can make Jesus waver in his certainty that out of nothing, ignoring all failure, God is carrying on his beginnings to completion. All that is necessary is to take God seriously, to take him into account in spite of all outward appearance.

On what grounds does this confidence rest?

The answer to this question is to be found in two closely related parables. First, the *parable of the Unjust Judge* (Luke 18.2–8).

On v. 1 see pp. 156 f. V.2: For the description ὁ κριτὴς τῆς ἀδικίας (v. 6) see p. 46, n. 86. Ἄνθρωπον μὴ ἐντρεπόμενος: He does not care what people say about him. V. 3: The widow need not be regarded as an old woman. The result of the early marriageable age (between 13 and 14 for girls) [98] was that widows were frequently quite young.[99] Since the widow brings her case to a single judge, and not before a tribunal, it would appear to be a money-matter:[1] a debt, a pledge, or a portion of an inheritance, is being withheld from her. She is too poor to bribe the judge [2] (in the Old Testament widows and orphans are already standing types of the helpless and defenceless); her opponent in the case is to be thought of as a rich and influential man;[3] hence persistence is her only weapon.[4] Ἐκδίκησόν με ἀπὸ τοῦ ἀντιδίκου μου: 'Help me to obtain justice in my suit'. V. 4: οὐκ ἤθελεν: 'he refused', as in Mark 6.26 and Luke 18.13 with the nuance, 'He did not dare'.[5] V. 5: Finally he yields, διά γε τὸ παρέχειν μοι κόπον τὴν χήραν ταύτην, 'because this widow (ταύτην carries a depreciatory overtone as οὗτος in 15.30) gets on my nerves'. Ἵνα μὴ εἰς τέλος ἐρχομένη ὑπωπιάζῃ με should not be translated as Luther

[98] Bill., II, p. 374.
[99] Cf. E. F. F. Bishop, *Jesus of Palestine*, London, 1955, p. 229.
[1] b. Sanh. 4b (Bar.): 'An authorized scholar may decide money cases sitting alone' (Bill., I, p. 289), cf. Matt. 5.25.
[2] T. W. Manson, *Sayings*, p. 306.
[3] K. Bornhäuser, *Studien zum Sondergut des Lukas*, Gütersloh, 1934, pp. 162 f.
[4] Ἤρχετο is an iterative imperfect: 'repeatedly'.
[5] On Luke 18.13, see p. 141.

has done: 'So that she may not finally deafen me'; ὑπωπιάζειν, 'to
hit under the eye (in boxing)', is rather to be understood figuratively,
as in Syr ^{cur pal pesh}, Georg, etc., and the majority of modern commentators (cf. I Cor. 9.27): 'So that she may not finish me off
(ὑπωπιάζῃ με) completely (εἰς τέλος) by her obstinacy (ἐρχομένη).'⁶
It is not the fear of an outburst of rage on the part of the woman that
makes him give way, but her persistence. He is tired of her perpetual
nagging and wants to be left in peace.⁷ This, as we shall see, is the
only rendering which makes the application in vv. 7–8a intelligible.
V. 7: ὁ δὲ θεὸς οὐ μὴ ποιήσῃ τὴν ἐκδίκησιν τῶν ἐκλεκτῶν αὐτοῦ τῶν
βοώντων αὐτῷ ἡμέρας καὶ νυκτός, καὶ μακροθυμεῖ ἐπ' αὐτοῖς: The verse
presents a difficulty because of the change from the subjunctive
(ποιήσῃ) to the indicative (μακροθυμεῖ); this change of mood makes
v. 7b an independent sentence. Literally rendered it reads: 'And will
not God hasten to the rescue ⁸ of his elect, who cry to him day and
night? and he has patience with them.' To understand the change of
mood it is necessary to note, first, that in this passage μακροθυμεῖν
has the same meaning as in Sir. 32 (35).22 f. LXX,⁹ the content of
which is closely connected with this passage: 'hesitate, be composed,
keep waiting'.¹⁰ As far as sentence construction is concerned, the
main clause καὶ μακροθυμεῖ ἐπ' αὐτοῖς reproduces a finite Semitic

⁶ Ἐρχομένη is iterative as in v. 3, cf. Luke 16.21. On ἔρχεσθαι, 'to return'
(Semitism), see below, pp. 198 f., esp. n. 32. For ὑπωπιάζῃ see F. Blass – A.
Debrunner, *A Greek Grammar of the New Testament*, Cambridge, 1961, §207.3: 'in
order that she may not gradually (pres. ὑπωπιάζῃ!) wear me out completely by her
continued coming (pres.!)'. *The New English Bible*, Oxford–Cambridge, 1961, has:
'before she wears me out with her persistence'.

⁷ H. B. Tristram, *Eastern Customs in Bible Lands*, London, 1894, p. 228 (cited by
B. T. D. Smith, p. 150), gives a very vivid description of the judicial court at
Nisibis (Mesopotamia). Opposite the entrance sat the Cadi, half buried in
cushions, and surrounded by secretaries. The front of the hall was crowded with
people, each demanding that his case should be heard first. The wise ones whis-
pered to the secretaries and slipped over bribes, and had their business quickly
despatched. In the meanwhile, a poor woman broke through the orderly proceedings with loud cries for justice. She was sternly bidden to be quiet, and
reproachfully told that she came every day. 'And so I will do,' she loudly exclaimed,
'until the Cadi hears my case.' At length, at the end of the session, the Cadi im-
patiently asked, 'What does the woman want?' Her story was soon told. The
tax-collector was demanding payment from her, although her only son was on
military service. The case was quickly decided and her patience was rewarded.
If she had had money to pay a clerk she would have obtained justice much
sooner. It is an exact modern analogy to Luke 18.2 ff.!

⁸ That is what τὴν ἐκδίκησιν ποιεῖν means in Test. Sol. 22.4, probably also Acts
7.24. Cf. ἐκδικεῖν in our parable vv. 3, 5, 'to give judgement in favour of a person'.

⁹ The analogy was recognized by H. Riesenfeld, 'Zu μακροθυμεῖν (Lk. 18.7)',
in: *Neutestamentliche Aufsätze. Festschrift für J. Schmid*, Regensburg, 1963, pp. 214–17.

¹⁰ Cf. H. Riesenfeld, ibid., pp. 216 f.; H. Ljungvik, 'Zur Erklärung einer
Lukasstelle (Lk XVIII 7)', in: *NTS*, 10 (1963–4), pp. 289–94, here p. 290;
A. Wifstrand, 'Lukas XVIII 7', in: *NTS*, 11 (1964–5), pp. 72–4.

circumstantial clause [11] which has a concessive nuance: [12] 'And will not God hasten to the help of his elect who cry to him day and night, even if he puts their patience to the test?' [13] It is also possible to understand καὶ μακροθυμεῖ ἐπ' αὐτοῖς as an independent question; in that case the introductory καί would reproduce an interrogative wᵉ: 'Would he put their patience to the test?' V.8a: ᾽Εν τάχει here means 'before they realize it' (cf. LXX Deut. 11.17; Josh. 8.18 f.; Ps. 2.12; Ezek. 29.5; Sir. 27.3) [14] he will deliver them. V. 8b: The parable closes on an unexpected note of profound gravity: 'The question is (πλήν), when the Son of Man comes, will he find faith on the earth?' The conjecture advanced in the earlier editions that v. 8b was inserted by Luke as the conclusion of the parable is untenable. [15]

Bultmann has concisely summed up the doubts brought forward by many scholars concerning the genuineness of vv. 6–8: 'the application in vv. 6–8 is certainly secondary (cf. Jülicher); it is separated from what precedes by εἶπεν δὲ ὁ κύριος and is missing from the parallel in 11.5–8. In addition, it has received a secondary addition in v. 8b.' [16] Now the reference to Jülicher should be rejected, for he bases his opinion on the observation that vv. 6–8 betray 'a frame of mind' which was 'as unlikely with Jesus as it was current in the primitive Church'. [17] That is a psychological argument drawn from the idea of revenge which Jülicher wrongly feels is expressed by τὴν ἐκδίκησιν ποιεῖν

[11] K. Beyer, *Semitische Syntax im NT*, I, 1, Göttingen, 1962, p. 268, n. 1; A. Wilstrand, ibid., pp. 73 f.

[12] H. Riesenfeld, ibid., pp. 216 f., following K. H. Rengstorf and C. F. D. Moule.

[13] H. Riesenfeld, ibid., p. 217. For the concessive nuance see Apoc. 2.2, 9; 3.9; often in the LXX, e.g. Jer. 14.15.

[14] C. Spicq, 'La parabole de la veuve obstinée et du juge inerte, aux decisions impromptues (Lc. XVIII, 1–8)', *RB*, 68 (1961), pp. 68–90, here pp. 81–5.

[15] There is no question of a special Lucan usage: πλήν with the sense 'although', 'however' does occur in Luke 14 times, but not in Acts; it is also absent from the Marcan material worked over by Luke, and is therefore characteristic of the Lucan source, not of Luke's own style. Without πλήν, ἄρα cannot be claimed as Lucan (in the N.T. it only occurs in Luke 18.8; Acts 8.30; Gal. 2.17; perhaps Rom. 7.25). Moreover, the emphasis on faith can hardly be attributed to Pauline influence, since the presence of the article (τὴν πίστιν) is probably an Aramaism; in Aramaic *hemanutha* is always used in the determined state (cf. C. C. Torrey, *The Four Gospels*, London, 1933, p. 312; also in Deut. 32.20 the determined state is used in Targum Yerushalmi I, the undetermined state only in the Targum of Onkelos). Finally, ὁ υἱὸς τοῦ ἀνθρώπου points to a pre-Lucan tradition, since Luke never uses the expression (25 times in the Gospel) independently. Hence we have in Luke 18.8b an early Son of Man saying.

[16] R. Bultmann, *The History of the Synoptic Tradition₂*, Oxford, 1968, p. 175.

[17] Jülicher, II, p. 286.

(vv. 7 f.). To be consistent he should have claimed the whole parable to be unauthentic because he finds that same desire for revenge also in ἐκδικεῖν (vv. 3, 5) (again wrongly). Nevertheless Bultmann is right in pointing out that in Luke 11.5–8, a parable closely related to the Unjust Judge, an analogous application is lacking. It should be remembered, however, that Luke 11.5–8 could be applied to God without difficulty whereas Jesus' choice of this brutal judge to illustrate God's helpfulness must have shocked his audience to a degree which simply made an interpretation indispensable. At any rate, as we have seen, vv. 6–8 (including v. 8b) are shown to be pre-Lucan and Palestinian on linguistic grounds.

Luke clearly links this parable with that of the Pharisee and the Publican as intended to furnish guidance concerning the right way to pray (cf. 18.1): prayer should be persistent and humble. But the parable of the Pharisee and the Publican is very far from being a lesson on how to pray, and the same may be said about the parable under discussion, in spite of its introductory verse (18.1) which exhibits Lucan peculiarities (see p. 93, n. 13). On this interpretation the widow is the central figure in the parable, while Jesus' interpretation (vv. 6–8a) shows that he intended to direct attention to the figure of the judge.[18] Why did Jesus tell the story? He gives the answer himself in vv. 7–8a: he expected his hearers to draw the conclusion from the Judge to God. If this inconsiderate man, who had refused to hear the widow's case, finally gives heed to her distress, and that after long delay, only in order to rid himself of the incessant pestering of the plaintiff, how much more will God! God listens to the cry of the poor with unwearied patience, they are his elect, he is moved with compassion for their need, and suddenly (ἐν τάχει) he intervenes for their deliverance. If the parable, as v. 8b assumes, is addressed to the disciples,[19] it was clearly called forth by the grief and

---

[18] Hence the usual designation of the parable as the parable of the Importunate Widow is clearly inappropriate.

[19] G. Delling, 'Das Gleichnis vom gottlosen Richter', in *ZNW*, 53 (1962), pp. 1–25, thinks that Jesus told the parable to 'certain pious circles' (p. 22). This would be to say that there were, in Jesus' time, certain groups who considered themselves 'elect' (v. 7), waited for the Son of Man (v. 8), and even cried in agony and despair to make him come (v. 7). All this would in fact apply to the community who produced the Parabolic Discourses of the Ethiopic book of Enoch (chs. 37–71). These people call themselves 'the elect', wait for the Son of Man, and suffer from persecution (cf. En. 46.8 which reads, according to the superior text: 'and they persecuted the houses of his congregations and the faithful who cling to the name of the Lord

THE GREAT ASSURANCE

anxiety of the disciples in view of the time of tribulation which
Jesus had depicted for them with unmitigated clarity: persecutions,
injuries, denunciations, trials, martyrdoms, a final failure of faith
at the revelation of Satan. Who can endure to the end? Have no
anxiety in the face of persecution, says Jesus. You are God's elect.
He will hear your cry. By the intervention of his holy will he will
even shorten the time of tribulation (Mark 13.20). Let there be no
doubting his power, goodness, and help. That is the final certainty.
Your concern should be with a different matter: when the Son of Man
comes, will he find faith on the earth?

Almost a doublet of the parable of the Unjust Judge is the *parable
of the Friend who was aroused in the Night by a Request for Help* (Luke
11.5–8).[20]

The parable gives a vivid description of conditions in a Palestinian village. V. 5: There are no shops, and before sunrise the
housewife bakes the day's supply of bread for the family; but it is
generally known in the village who has still got some bread left in
the evening.[21] Even today three loaves are regarded as a meal for
one person. He only intends to borrow it and return it at once. V. 6:
It is an imperative duty in the East to entertain a guest. V. 7: The
annoyance of the neighbour at being disturbed already finds expression in his omission of the address (otherwise in v. 5).[22] Ἤδη
means 'long ago' (as also, for example, in John 19.28): the oriental
goes to sleep early. In the evening the house is dark; the little oil-lamp
which burns during the night, only gives a faint light. 'The door
was shut long ago', that is, bolted and locked. The bolt is a wooden
or iron bar thrust through rings in the doorpanels;[23] drawing the
bolt is a tiresome business and makes a lot of noise. 'And the children,
as well as myself (μετ' ἐμοῦ), are in bed': we are to imagine a single-
roomed peasant's house,[24] in which the whole family slept on a mat

---

of Spirits'; 47.1–4: bloody persecutions). May we assume that this group did still
exist in Jesus' days and was still being persecuted? Or was the book of Enoch which
is a composite work compiled precisely at this time? But where in the Palestine of
those days ought this group to be sought? And who could be supposed to be their
persecutors?

[20] The usual description of the parable as the parable of the Importunate
Friend is misleading, see p. 128, n. 63.

[21] A. M. Brouwer, *De Gelijkenissen*, Leiden, 1946, p. 211.

[22] T. W. Manson, *Sayings*, p. 267.

[23] G. Dalman, *Arbeit und Sitte in Palästina*, VII, Gütersloh, 1942, p. 70–2.

[24] Thus also in Matt. 5.15.

in the raised part of the room. Hence all would be disturbed if the father had to get up and draw the bolt.[25] Οὐ δύναμαι: 'I can't,' means, as it so often does, 'I won't'.[26] V. 8: 'Surely (λέγω ὑμῖν)[27] even if he will not rise and give him what he asks for friendship's sake, διά γε τὴν ἀναίδειαν αὐτοῦ (i.e. either: because of the importunity of his asking, or: because of his [own] shamelessness, that is to say, so that he may not lose face in the matter)[28] he will rise and give him as much as he needs.'[29]

Luke has transmitted the parable in the context of the instruction about prayer in 11.1–13, and therefore understood it to be an exhortation to unwearied prayer, as 11.9–13 plainly shows; but this context is, as we saw on p. 105, secondary, and should not therefore be taken as a starting-point for an attempt to set forth the original meaning of the parable. The meaning of the parable should rather be sought in the recognition that τίς ἐξ ὑμῶν (11.5) in the New Testament regularly introduces questions which expect the emphatic answer 'No one! Impossible!' or 'Everyone, of course!'[29] In English this τίς ἐξ ὑμῶν would best be rendered by 'Can you imagine that any of you would . . .' (Matt. 6.27 par. Luke 12.25; Matt. 7.9 par. Luke 11.11; Matt. 12.11 par. Luke 14.5; Luke 14.28; 15.4; 17.7). But, in that case, the question cannot possibly end with v. 6, since v. 6 only describes the situation, and does not insistently demand a reply. Hence vv. 5–7 should rather be regarded as one continuous rhetorical question:[30] 'Can you imagine that, if one of you had a friend who came to you at midnight and said to you, "My friend, lend me three loaves, because a friend has come to me on a journey, and I have nothing to set before him", you would call out, "Don't disturb me . . ."'? Can you imagine such a thing?' The answer would be—'Unthinkable!' Under no circumstances would he leave his friend's request unanswered. Hence it is only if we understand v.7 as describing not a refusal of the request, but rather the utter impossibility of such a refusal, that the parable truly depicts the custom

25 K. H. Rengstorf, in *Das Neue Testament Deutsch*, 3, Göttingen, 1962, in loc.
26 T. W. Manson, *Sayings*, p. 267.
27 Jülicher, II, p. 269.
28 Thus A. Fridrichsen, *Symbolae Osloenses*, XIII (1934), pp. 40 ff. A striking example of the possibility of this rendering occurs in b. Ta'an. 25a, *miššum kissupha*, i.e. 'on account of shame', 'so as not to lose face'.
29 See p. 103.
30 A. Fridrichsen, op. cit.

of oriental hospitality, and its real point becomes clear.[31] For the result of taking vv. 5–7 as a single connected question is that v. 8 is seen to be no longer concerned with the neighbour's reiterated request, but solely with the motive that actuates the friend to whom he is applying for help: if he will not grant the request for friendship's sake, he will at least do it to rid himself of his importunity.[32] Hence v. 8 simply emphasizes afresh the unthinkable nature of the suggestion, so that the central figure is not the petitioner (as in the Lucan context), but the friend who is roused from sleep. The parable is not concerned with the importunity of the petitioner, but with the certainty that the petition will be granted. It becomes clear, then, that the parable, like that of the Unjust Judge, expects the hearers to draw a conclusion from the lesser to the greater. If the friend, roused from his sleep in the middle of the night, without a moment's delay hastens to fulfil the request of a neighbour in distress, even though the whole family must be disturbed by the drawing of the bolt, how much more will God! He is a God who hearkens to the cry of the needy and comes to their help. He does more than they ask. Hence you may in all confidence leave everything to him.

With these two parables of the Judge, and the Friend asking for help by night, both of which express the confidence that God will hear the appeal of his own when they cry to him in their need, we should connect the short logion, πᾶς γὰρ ὁ αἰτῶν λαμβάνει (Matt. 7.8 = Luke 11.10). This short gnomic sentence[33] evidently springs from the experience of the *beggar*:[34] he has only to persist, to take no refusal, be unscared by abuse, and he will receive a gift. Every visitor to the East can tell stories of the persistence of oriental beggars.[35] Jesus applies the beggar's wisdom[36] to the disciples. If the beggar,

[31] Ibid.
[32] Or (see n. 25 above, on v. 8): 'so as not to appear disobliging'.
[33] J. Schniewind in *NTD* 2, Göttingen, 1956, on the passage.
[34] K. H. Rengstorf, 'Geben ist seliger denn Nehmen' in *Die Leibhaftigkeit des Wortes*, Festgabe für A. Köberle, Hamburg, 1958, pp. 23–33, here pp. 28 f.
[35] Incidentally, this pertinacity is not mere greed, but springs from deeper grounds: on the one hand the poor are specially protected by divine law, and have therefore a divinely guaranteed right to the gift, hence the beggar's 'calling' [sic] is by no means to be despised; on the other hand, the beggar is so pertinacious because he needs the gift in order that he himself also may have the power to do good: 'Even a poor man who lives by alms may be charitable' (b. Giṭ. 7b; cf. Mark 12.41 ff. par. Luke 21.1 ff. and cf. John 13.29 with Luke 8.3). Cf. K. H. Rengstorf, op. cit., pp. 29, 32.
[36] Ibid., p. 29.

although harshly repulsed at first, knows that persistent appeals will open the hands of his hard-hearted fellow men, how much more certain should you be that your persistence in prayer will open the hands of your heavenly Father.

The four contrast-parables and the two with which we have just been occupied were, if our interpretation be accepted, called forth by different occasions. While the contrast-parables express the confidence of Jesus in the face of doubt concerning his mission, the parables of the Judge and the Friend are intended to imbue the disciples with the certainty that God will deliver them from the coming tribulation. Nonetheless, the two groups of parables are very closely related. In both the same unwavering trust is expressed; in both we hear Jesus saying, Take God seriously: he works wonders, and nothing is more certain than his mercy for his own.

4. THE IMMINENCE OF CATASTROPHE

The message of Jesus is not only the proclamation of salvation, but also the announcement of judgement, a cry of warning, and a call to repentance in view of the terrible urgency of the crisis. The number of parables in this category is nothing less than awe-inspiring. Over and over again did Jesus raise his voice in warning, striving to open the eyes of a blinded people.

That the little *parable of the Children in the Market-Place* (Matt. 11.16 f. par. Luke 7.31 f.) belongs to the early stage of the tradition is shown already by the excessively hostile estimate of Jesus which it contains in v. 19a. The denigration of Jesus as ἄνθρωπος φάγος καὶ οἰνοπότης is derived from Deut. 21.20 and stigmatizes him on the strength of this connection as 'a refractory and rebellious son', who deserved to be stoned.[37] In reply Jesus says, You are like the children

[37] Linguistically the translation variants indicated by a comparison of Matthew and Luke are noteworthy indications of age (e.g. Matthew has ἐκόψασθε, 'You smote upon your breasts', where Luke has ἐκλαύσατε, 'You raised the funeral lament', both of which represent *'arqedhtun*); note further the rhyming word-play (*raqqedhtun*, 'you danced', corresponding to *'arqedhtun*, 'you lamented'), exhibited by the Syriac versions, and the two antithetic parallelisms (Matt. 11.17a with 17b and 18 with 19a). The content of the saying, apart from the criticism of Jesus, shows its early date, since Jesus places himself on an equality with John, whereas the primitive Church always emphasized the subordination of John. In spite of its public use, the expression 'Son of Man' does not militate against the early date of v. 19a, since it is not used here as an apocalyptic term, but in the same sense as the ἄνθρωπος which immediately follows it, representing the Aram. *bar naš*.

THE IMMINENCE OF CATASTROPHE
161

in the streets, shouting at their companions: 'Spoilsports! spoilsports!
We played the flute, but you would not dance! We sang the funeral
dirge, but you would not beat your breasts!' (Matt. 11.17; Luke
7.32). 'We wanted to play at weddings', shout the boys to their
playmates (the round dance at a wedding is the men's dance),[38] 'but
you wouldn't.' 'We wanted to play at funerals' (cf. b. Yeb. 121b:
children play at burying a grasshopper), but, 'you wouldn't play',
cry the girls to their playfellows (the mourners' dirge is the women's
business).[39] And so their noisy quarrels put an end to play. Vivid
as is the description of this everyday street-scene, its application to
the taunts which the people levelled at the Baptist and Jesus has
nevertheless been the cause of much perplexity (Matt. 11.18 f.;
Luke 7.33 f.). For the metaphor is ambiguous. Are the children
whose words Jesus repeats quarrelling with each other because some
of them want to play a merry game, while the others prefer a sad
one (so, evidently Luke 7.32, ἀλλήλοις), or, are they angry with the
other children because they do not wish to join in the games (so,
evidently Matt. 11.16, τοῖς ἑτέροις)? The question is not irrelevant,
since the application of the metaphor varies according to the way it
is answered. A glance at the commentaries will show that numerous
attempts at an answer have been made, without yielding a completely satisfactory result. In my opinion, everything becomes clear
if we listen to the suggestion of one who is familiar with Palestinian
customs, that attention should be paid to the word καθημένοις (Matt.
11.16; Luke 7.32): from which it may be inferred that the children
described by Jesus have cast themselves in the role of passive spec-
tators, and prefer the less strenuous guise of flute-players and dirge-
singers, leaving to their playmates 'the more strenuous exercises'.[40]
But the latter will not comply, and are consequently assailed with
reproaches (προσφωνεῖν, Matt. 11.16; Luke 7.32). Thus the dispute
is not between the boys and the girls as to what game they should
play (so, clearly, Luke 7.32, ἀλλήλοις) but the boys and girls sitting
by the side of the street blame the other children for not falling in
with their suggestion (so, correctly, Matt. 11.16, τοῖς ἑτέροις). 'And
you', says Jesus, 'are exactly like these domineering and disagreeable
children, who blame their companions for being spoilsports because

[38] Bill., I, p. 514r, 1040; E. Baumann, 'Zur Hochzeit geladen', in *Palästina-
Jahrbuch*, 4 (1908), pp. 69–71 (with the notes of the dance-tunes); cf. G. Dalman,
Palästinischer Diwan, Leipzig, 1901, Melodienanhang, pp. 354–63.
[39] Bill., I, pp. 521–3.
[40] E. F. F. Bishop, *Jesus of Palestine*, London, 1955, p. 104.

they will not dance to their piping. God sends you his messengers, the last messengers, to the last generation before the catastrophe. But all you do is to give orders and criticize. For you the Baptist is a madman because he fasts, while you want to make merry; me you reproach because I eat with publicans, while you insist on strict separation from sinners. You hate the preaching of repentance, and you hate the proclamation of the gospel. So you play your childish game with God's messengers while Rome burns![41] Can you not see that God (ἡ σοφία) is vindicated[42] by[43] his works[44] (Matt. 11.19), that is, that the ἔργα, signs that the decisive moment has arrived, are God's vindication?[45] That the call to repentance and the preaching of the good news are God's very last and final warnings?'

'How blind you are! You can read the signs of the weather, but you cannot recognize the signs of the time' (Luke 12.54–56). 'Where the carcase is, the vultures are gathered together' (Matt. 24.28 par. Luke 17.37).[46] They do not circle over empty space.[47] They scent the prey. Do you not see there is something in the air? No, you are like a house whose rooms are dark because their source of light has failed. You are blind, you are hardened (Matt. 6.22 f.; Luke 11.34–36).

The *simile of the Eye as the Lamp of the Body* is in Matthew (6. 22f.) addressed to the disciples; in Luke (11.34–36) it is a rebuke to the crowd. Moreover, Matthew understood it as an allegory, as his context shows; having said in 6.19–21: 'Give! Lay up treasures with God!', he goes on to add: 'Give gladly! Give without jealousy' (ὀφθαλμὸς πονηρός = envy, jealousy[48]). But this allegorical interpretation spoils the application 6.23b, which is preserved only if the simile in 6.22–23a is taken as referring to a simple everyday experience:

[41] Dodd, p. 29.

[42] Ἐδικαιώθη is a timeless aorist (translation Greek).

[43] Ἀπό=min qᵒdham='in view of', cf. J. Wellhausen, *Das Evangelium Matthaei*, Berlin, 1904, p. 55.

[44] It has often been suggested that ἀπὸ τῶν ἔργων αὐτῆς (Matt. 11.19) and ἀπὸ τῶν τέκνων αὐτῆς (Luke 7.35) are variant translations going back to one Aramaic expression. Τὰ ἔργα αὐτῆς is in Aramaic ᵒbhadhaih; the pre-Lucan tradition, mistakenly hearing 'abhdhaih, would have translated this by οἱ παῖδες αὐτῆς and later on emended to τὰ τέκνα αὐτῆς—a conceivable though complicated process.

[45] Dodd, p. 115, on Matt. 11.19: 'The actual facts of the present situation . . . are the manifestation of his "Kingdom".'

[46] Instead of ἀετοί (eagles) we must understand γῦπες (vultures). Only vultures feed on carcases, eagles hunt living prey. It is a question of mistranslation; the Aram. nišra can mean either 'eagle' or 'vulture'.

[47] Bishop Lilje in a sermon.

[48] An established turn of phrase. Examples in Bill., I, pp. 833–35.

'The eye is the lamp of the body.
When your eye is sound,[49] your whole body is light.
When your eye is diseased,[50] your whole body is dark.'

6.23b then follows as the application of the simile (this is confirmed by the imperative σκόπει οὖν Luke 11.35):

'Now, if your inner light is dark (σκότος),
how dense will the darkness (σκότος) [51] be!'

If bodily blindness is terrible, what, then, must inner blindness be! (Concerning the idea of the 'inner light' which shines from within a man,[52] cf. Gospel of Thomas 24: 'Within a man of light there is light and it [or: he] lights the whole world.' Incidentally, the same idea is behind the rabbinical rule not to look at the priests while they pronounced the priestly blessing; in doing so they had to hold their hands before their eyes with the fingers spread out like a screen, because, as it was said, the divine glory 'glanced through the lattice [Cant. 2.9]' [53].) If Matt. 6.22 f. par. Luke 11.34–36 is not a warning against covetousness, but against inner blindness, then Luke is right in recording the saying as addressed to the crowd and with reference to Jesus' opponents.[54] To be blind means to be hardened.[55] You are hardened. What a fearful darkness (τὸ σκότος πόσον, Matt. 6.23)!

You are feasting and dancing—on the volcano which may erupt at any moment. The terrible catastrophe of Sodom and Gomorrha will occur once again (Luke 17.28 f.). The Deluge is at hand (Matt. 24.37–39; Luke 17.26 f.).[56]

The coupling of the deluge of fire with that of water also lies behind the double metaphor in Luke 12.49 f.: 'I have come to kindle[57] a fire on earth, and how I wish it were already burning! I have a baptism to be baptized with, and I am torn between conflicting feelings until

---

[49] 'Ἁπλοῦς=Aram. šᵉlim='perfect', 'healthy', cf. E. Sjöberg, 'Das Licht in dir. Zur Deutung von Matth. 6, 22 f. Par.', in *Studia Theologica*, 5 (1951), pp. 89–105, see pp. 91 f.

[50] Πονηρός=Aram. biš='sick', 'ill'.

[51] The double σκότος can be explained from Aramaic-Aram. ḥᵃšakh=1. adj. 'dark' (= σκότος 1°); 2. subst. 'darkness' (= σκότος 2°). The first σκότος in Matt. 6.23b is thus a mistranslation: σκοτεινόν would be correct.

[52] Dr C. Burchard drew my attention to this conception.

[53] Examples in Bill., IV, pp. 239, 245 f.

[54] Thus, too, C. Edlund, *Das Auge der Einfalt*, Copenhagen-Lund, 1952, p. 117.

[55] Isa. 6.10; Matt. 15.14; 23.16 f., 19, 26; Oxyrh. Pap. 1 and 840, and on that J. Jeremias, *Unknown Sayings of Jesus*₂, London, 1964, pp. 47 ff., 106 ff.

[56] Cf. also Matt. 7.24–27 par. Luke 6.47–49.

[57] Πῦρ βαλεῖν is a Semitism and does not mean 'to cast fire', but 'to kindle fire'.

it be completed!'[58] In this double metaphor we have an echo of that tragic conflict whose intensity finds no parallel elsewhere in the Bible except in the self-revelations of the prophet Jeremiah, the conflict between the imperative call of his mission, and the reluctance of natural affections.[59] Jesus is the bringer-in of the New Age. But he knows—and this troubles him deeply—that the way to New Creation lies through disaster and destruction, through purging and judgement, through the deluge of fire and water.[60] 'He who is near me is near the fire; he who is far from me, is far from the Kingdom.'[61]

God's curse lies upon the unfruitful fig-tree (Luke 13.7). The tree that did not bear fruit will be cut down (Matt. 7.19). The fate of the dry tree will be more terrible than that of the green tree (Luke 23.31). Calamity will overtake you as unexpectedly as the snare catches the unwary bird (Luke 21.34 f.). The simile of the traveller offers the warning that there are only twelve hours in the day. There is only a little daylight left before the coming of night, when the traveller stumbles on the stony path and loses his way in the dark (John 12.35, cf. 11.9 f.). Take warning from the householder who lay sunk in sleep while his house was broken into (Matt. 24.43 f.; Luke 12.39 f.; Gospel of Thomas 21b) (see pp. 48–51). Hear the *story of the Rich Fool* (Luke 12.16–20; Gospel of Thomas 63 [62]), who, after a rich harvest, makes his preparations for a still heavier one, and whose security God shatters in a night.

In Luke an introductory dialogue (vv. 13–15) provides the occasion for the parable.[63] The situation which it depicts is necessary for the understanding of the parable. The younger of two brothers complains that the elder refuses to give him his share of the inheritance:[64] the fact that he appealed to Jesus, although the latter

---

[58] Συνέχομαι is used as in Phil. 1.23 of conflicting emotions.

[59] T. W. Manson, *Sayings*, p. 120.

[60] The parallelism militates against the usual limitation of v. 50 to Jesus' own fate.

[61] An agraphon (Gospel of Thomas 82; Origen, *In Jerem. hom. lat.*, 3.3), cf. J. Jeremias, *Unknown Sayings of Jesus₂*, London, 1964, pp. 66–68.

[62] Jesus said: There was a rich man who had much property. He said: I will use my property that I may sow and reap and plant and fill my storehouses with fruit, so that I lack nothing. This was what he thought in his heart. And that night he died. Whoever has ears let him hear.

[63] T. W. Manson, *Sayings*, p. 271.

[64] The elder brother would rather leave the inheritance undivided. Such a jointly held inheritance is praised by the Psalmist (Ps. 133.1, 'Behold how good and pleasant it is for brethren to dwell together in unity'), and is presupposed, e.g., in Matt. 6.24 (see p. 194, n. 1).

was a layman, shows the great prestige which Jesus enjoyed among the people (v. 13). Jesus does not base his refusal to give a decision merely on the fact that he has no authority to do so (v. 14), but primarily on the ground that the possession of property is irrelevant to the life of the Age to come (v. 15). The parable explains why Jesus regards earthly wealth as wholly negligible. This dialogue (vv. 13–14, although without the logion in v. 15) is preserved in the Gospel of Thomas 72 as an independent fragment; hence it will not originally have belonged to the parable. V. 16: Ἀνθρώπου τινός: a large land-holder. V. 18: τὰς ἀποθήκας 'does not mean barns where the corn can be kept till it is threshed, but warehouses or stores in which later on the grain can be laid up'.[65] V. 20: Εἶπεν δὲ αὐτῷ ὁ θεός: God sent him a message (e.g. in a dream through the angel of death). Τὴν ψυχήν σου ἀπαιτοῦσιν (the 3rd pers. pl. means God) ἀπὸ σοῦ: life is a loan, God gave it, and declares that its return will be demanded that very night. Ἃ δὲ ἡτοίμασας, 'what you have acquired', cf. Herm. Sim. 1.1,2,6. On v. 21 see p. 106. In the Gospel of Thomas the parable is much shortened (see p. 164, n. 62).

This rich farmer, who thinks that he need not fear bad harvests for many a year (v. 19), is a fool (v. 20), that is, according to the biblical meaning of the term, a man who in practice denies the existence of God (Ps. 14.1). He does not take God into account, and fails to see the sword of Damocles, the threat of death, hanging over his head. Here it is necessary to avoid a too obvious conclusion. We are not to think that Jesus intended to impress upon his audience the ancient maxim, 'Death comes suddenly upon man'. Rather do all the appeals and parables of warning taken together show that Jesus is not thinking of the inevitable death of the individual as the impending danger, but of the approaching eschatological catastrophe, and the coming Judgement. Thus here too in Luke 12.16–20 we have an eschatological parable. Jesus expected his hearers to apply its conclusion to their own situation: we are just as foolish as the rich fool under the threat of death if we heap up property and possessions when the Deluge is threatening.

What is coming? The jackal, who feeds on corpses, will attack the Son of Man as he attacked the Baptist (Luke 13.32).[66] That will be the prelude. Then will come the great hour of temptation, the final

[65] W. Michaelis, *Die Gleichnisse Jesu*, Hamburg, 1956, p. 264, n. 154.
[66] A. M. Brouwer, *De Gelijkenissen*, Leiden, 1946, pp. 221 f. Aram. *ta'ala* means both 'jackal' and 'fox'; it remains permissible to interpret ἀλώπηξ of the vulpine cunning (cf. Bill., II, pp. 200 f.) of Herod Antipas.

assault of the Evil One, destruction of the Temple, and unspeakable calamity (Luke 23.29), and thereafter the judgement of God. The hour of separation is coming. The distinction between wise and foolish virgins, between faithful and unfaithful stewards, will become apparent; the division between hearers and doers of the word will take place, the sheep will be separated from the goats; there will be two in the field, two at the mill, men there, women here, outwardly alike, to human eyes indistinguishable; but the moment of separation will reveal the terrible difference between the two classes: the one a child of God, the other a child of destruction (Matt. 24.40 f.).

It is a characteristic of the numerous parables which are concerned with the coming judgement, that many of them address a warning to quite definite groups of persons. Against the opponents of Jesus is directed the parable of the claimant to the throne[67] which may be inferred from Luke 19.12, 14 f., 17, 19, 27. The parables of the Servant entrusted with Authority (Matt. 24.45–51a; Luke 12.42–46),[68] of the Pounds and the Talents (Matt. 25.14–30; Luke 19.12–27),[69] and of the Doorkeeper (Mark 13.33–37; Luke 12.35–38) [70] are addressed, as we have seen, apparently to the leaders of the people, especially to the scribes. God has entrusted them with much: the spiritual leadership of the nation, the knowledge of his will, the key of the Kingdom of God.[71] Now the judgement of God is about to be revealed; now it will be decided whether the theologians have justified or abused God's great trust; whether they have made good use of God's gift, or have turned it to their own advantage and to the imposition of burdens upon their fellow men; whether they have opened the door of the Kingdom of God, or closed it. Their judgement will be specially severe. In the simile of the two servants (Luke 12.47–48a) Jesus tells them that he who knows the will of God will be more severely punished than the common people who know not the Law. The evangelists tell us that the parable of the Wicked Husbandmen (Mark 12.1 ff. par.)[72] was addressed to the members of the Sanhedrin (11.27 par.). This must be correct. In the Song of the Vineyard (Isa. 5. 1 ff.) to which Jesus refers, the people of God are

[67] See p. 59.
[68] See pp. 55 ff.
[69] See pp. 58 ff.
[70] See p. 53 ff.
[71] Cf. *ThWBNT*, III, p. 747. 12 ff.
[72] See above, pp. 70 ff.

compared to the vineyard, since when the vineyard had been the usual symbol of Israel,[73] and it may be assumed that since Jesus is not speaking about the vineyard, but about its tenants, he is not talking of the people as a whole, but of their leaders. Moreover, it is very possible that the parable was spoken in connection with the cleansing of the Temple, as the present context says. In that case it would be the Temple authorities, especially the priestly members of the Sanhedrin,[74] to whom the parable's terrible threat refers. The House of God has become a den of thieves. God, who has waited with such inconceivable patience, is now about to demand his dues, and the last generation must expiate the accumulated guilt. According to Matt. 15.12 the saying about the blind leaders of the blind, who fall into the ditch together with those whom they guide, applies to the Pharisees (Matt. 15.14; Luke 6.39; Gospel of Thomas 34). Moreover, the related metaphor of the Mote and the Beam (Matt. 7.3–5; Luke 6.41 f.; Gospel of Thomas 26) was originally addressed to them,[75] and according to Matt. 12.33 the saying about the good and evil trees (par. Matt. 7.16–20; Luke 6.43–44), to which the metaphor of the good and evil treasure (Matt. 12.35; Luke 6.45; Gospel of Thomas 45b) provides a similarly contrasting pendant, was also directed at them: 'Your acts and words show that you are essentially evil, and lie under the judgement of God.'[76] Similarly, according to John 9.40 (cf. 10.6, 19–21), the parable of the Shepherd was addressed to the Pharisees.[77] It charges the leaders of the people with destroying God's flock like thieves and robbers; the coming of the Good Shepherd has exposed their destructive activities. Finally, it is over the capital that the lament in Matt. 23.37 par. Luke 13.34, the saying about the hen and her chickens, is uttered. The reference is to Isa. 31.5: 'Like

[73] Isa. 27.2–6; Jer. 12.10; Ps. 80.9–18.

[74] E. Lohmeyer, *Kultus und Evangelium*, Göttingen, 1942, pp. 52 ff. On the college of high priests as a section of the Sanhedrin, cf. J. Jeremias, *Jerusalem in the Time of Jesus*, London, 1969, pp. 178 ff.

[75] The word ὑποκριτής (Matt. 7.5 par. Luke 6.42; absent from the Gospel of Thomas) is never applied elsewhere in the Gospels to the disciples. Cf. A. Schlatter, *Der Evangelist Matthäus*, Stuttgart, 1929, p. 243: 'This (saying) bitterly offended the Pharisees.'

[76] A linguistic point to notice in Luke 6.44a (ἕκαστον γὰρ δένδρον ἐκ τοῦ ἰδίου καρποῦ γινώσκεται), is that ἕκαστος here does not mean 'every' (in which case 6.44a would be a universal statement), but represents ἑκάτερος *uterque* (thus: 'In the case of a good or a bad tree, each of them is known by its fruit'), cf. H. Sahlin, *Symbolae Biblicae Upsalienses*, 4, Uppsala, 1945, p. 5.

[77] Strongly emphasized by J. A. T. Robinson, 'The Parable of the Shepherd (John 10.1–5)', *Twelve New Testament Studies*, London, 1962, pp. 67 ff.

fluttering birds, so will Yahweh of Hosts overshadow Jerusalem, he will overshadow and deliver her, spare and protect her.' In vivid metaphor God is here compared to fluttering birds protecting their young. Jesus transfers the simile to himself, as God's appointed representative. Before the oncoming destruction which threatened Jerusalem like the swoop of an attacking bird of prey upon a clutch of chickens, Jesus had watched, longing 'to overshadow, deliver, spare and protect'. 'But ye would not.' Now God has forsaken the Temple which you have desecrated, and abandoned it and you to judgement (Matt. 23.38; Luke 13.35).

The parable of the Fig-tree (Luke 13.6–9), and the threat implied in the *saying about the Salt which has become useless and which is cast into the street and trodden under foot* (Matt. 5.13; Luke 14.34 f.; Mark 9.50a) are directed against Israel as a whole. To belong to the people of God will not serve as a protection against the judgement of God. The strange locution: 'If the salt becomes foolish' (Matt. 5.13; Luke 14.34 f.), rests on a faulty translation. In Hebrew (and, according to the evidence of our logion, in Aramaic as well), *tpl* has a double meaning: (1) to be ἄναλος (Aquila Ezek. 13.10, 15; 22.28); (2) 'to talk foolishly'. The underlying word-play, *'in taphel milḥa, bᵉma yᵉthabbᵉlun*,[78] makes it certain that the Aramaic original actually had *taphel*. Mark has translated it correctly: 'If salt loses its salinity (ἄναλος γένηται)' (9.50); Matthew and Luke, translating 'if the salt becomes foolish', have clearly anticipated the interpretation of the saying as referring to the foolish disciples, or foolish Israel. It is to be assumed that Jesus in using the expression 'salt that has become saltless', is making use of a popular saying, indicating something useless, or meaningless.[79] Ἐν τίνι ἁλισθήσεται (Matt. 5.13): probably not: 'how shall it (the salt) regain its salinity' (so Mark 9.50), but 'with what shall (food) be salted' (so Luke 14.34). Εἰ μή (Matt. 5.13) does not express an exception, but is rather used adversatively ('but', cf. Luke 4.26, 27; Matt. 12.4; Gal. 1.19): Salt that has become saltless is of no further use, but will be cast out into the street. To the question under what circumstances in the daily life of Jesus' audience might salt become saltless and be cast out into the street, the usual answer is given that Arab bakers sometimes cover the floor of their ovens with slabs of salt whose catalytic effect on the poorly burning fuel (e.g. dried camel dung) might promote combustion; after about fifteen years the cataly-

78 M. Black, *An Aramaic Approach to the Gospels and Acts*₃, Oxford, 1967, pp. 166 f.
79 M. Black, ibid.

tic effect of the salt wears out and it is thrown into the street.[80] But
this explanation overlooks the fact that the saying is clearly concerned
with salt used as food (see above). Hence we must abide by the simpler explanation, based on everyday experience, which recalls the
fact that salt was not artificially prepared, but obtained from eva-
porated pools by the shore of the Dead Sea, or from the small lakes
on the edge of the Syrian desert which dry up in the summer.[81] This
salt crust, dug up from the surface of the soil, is never pure, but contains impurities (magnesia, lime, vegetable remains) which, when
the salt is dissolved by moisture, remain as useless refuse.[82] While
Matthew and Mark take the saying about salt as addressed to the
disciples, Luke regards it as a threat addressed to the crowd (14.25).
He is right, since according to b.Bech. 8b Judaism understood the
saying about salt as a warning addressed to Israel.[83]

The last generation of the chosen people, Messiah's generation,
is the generation upon which will fall the fateful decision; it will
either bear the burden of the common guilt (Matt. 23.35; Luke
11.50, cf. Mark 12.9), or become the recipient of complete forgiveness (Luke 19.42). But Jesus' sternest warning of disaster was addressed to the Messianic community, among whom also the final
separation was to be effected. Two followers of Jesus build themselves
a house; no outward difference is apparent. But the Flood of the
final tribulation reveals that one had built his house on the rock, the
other on the sand (Matt. 7.24–27; Luke 6.47–49).

The parables which deal with the impending crisis were each
uttered in a particular concrete situation, a fact which is essential
for their understanding. It is not their purpose to propound moral
precepts, but to shock into realization of its danger a nation rushing
upon its own destruction, and more especially its leaders, the theologians and priests. But above all they are a call to repentance.

5. IT MAY BE TOO LATE

It is the last hour. The Deluge is impending (Matt. 24.37–39, cf.

---

[80] This explanation was first offered by F. Scholten, *Palästina. Bibel, Talmud,
Koran*, II, Stuttgart, 1931, in connection with ill. 114–7. He was followed by
L. Köhler in *ZDPV*, 59 (1936), pp. 133 f.; by the same author in *Kleine Lichter:
50 Bibelstellen erklärt*, Zurich, 1945, pp. 73–76; S. Bender-F. A. Paneth, 'Das Salz
der Erde', in *Deutsches Pfarrerblatt*, 53 (1953), pp. 31 f.
[81] A. Schlatter, *Der Evangelist Matthäus*, Stuttgart, 1929, p. 147. I recall from
my childhood in the manse at Jerusalem that Beduins used to offer us salt of this
kind from the Dead Sea for sale.
[82] Cf. W. Bauer, *Wörterbuch zum N.T.*₅, Berlin, 1958, col. 114.
[83] Bill., I, p. 236.

7.24–27), the axe lies at the root of the unfruitful fig-tree. But God, marvellously suspending the fulfilment of his holy will, has allowed yet one more respite for repentance (*the parable of the Fig-tree*, Luke 13.6–9), even as he can again, in the last extremity, suspend the fulfilment of his holy will and shorten for the sake of his elect the time of Antichrist's power (Mark 13.20).

Luke 13.6: Ἐν τῷ ἀμπελῶνι: In Palestine vineyards and vegetable-gardens are generally planted with fruit-trees. V. 7: Τρία ἔτη: The first three years of a fig-tree's growth were allowed to elapse before its fruit became clean (Lev. 19.23), hence six years had already passed since it was planted. It is thus hopelessly barren. Καταργεῖ: A fig-tree absorbs a specially large amount of nourishment and hence deprives the surrounding vines of their needed sustenance. V. 8: Λέγει: On the historic present in Luke as an indication of early tradition see pp. 182 f. Καὶ βάλω κόπρια: manuring a vineyard is not mentioned in any passage of the OT;[84] moreover, as a matter of duty, the undemanding fig-tree does not need such care. Hence the gardener proposes to do something unusual, to take the last possible measures. V. 9: Εἰς τὸ μέλλον (*sc.* ἔτος): this one year is the ultimate limit. In the story of Aḥiqar (earlier than the fifth century BC) the words occur: 'My son, you are like a tree which yielded no fruit, although it stood by the water, and its owner was forced to cut it down. And it said to him, Transplant me, and if even then I bear no fruit, cut me down. But its owner said to it, When you stood by the water you bore no fruit, how then will you bear fruit·if you stand in another place?'[85] Jesus makes use of this folk-tale, which was probably current in various versions, but gives it another ending: the request is not refused but granted; an announcement of judgement becomes a call to repentance. God's mercy goes so far as to grant a reprieve from the sentence already pronounced. The intercessory figure of the ἀμπελουργός is a new element which Jesus added to the story. Is the introduction of this figure to be ascribed merely to the desire to add vividness to the picture? Or is there a deeper meaning behind it? Does the figure of the gardener, pleading for the reprieve from the judgement pronounced, conceal the figure of Jesus himself? In this connection it must be remembered that the parable must have been understood by the disciples in a different

---

[84] G. Dalman, *Arbeit und Sitte*, IV, Gütersloh, 1935, p. 325.
[85] Arab. 8.30 (A. S. Lewis in: R. H. Charles, *The Apocrypha and Pseudepigrapha of the Old Testament*, II, Oxford, 1913, p. 775).

manner from the crowd or the opponents. As to the way in which the disciples understood it, the second alternative—cf. Luke 22.31 f.—may very well be right. But the stay of execution granted by mercy is the irrevocable final limit. His patience is exhausted when the final *dies poenitentiae* passes unheeded. When the limit granted by God for repentance has run out, no human power can prolong it (Luke 13.9).

This must also have been the original meaning of Matt. 6.27 (par. Luke 12.25): τίς δὲ ἐξ ὑμῶν μεριμνῶν δύναται προσθεῖναι ἐπὶ τὴν ἡλικίαν αὐτοῦ πῆχυν ἕνα; This logion has found its way into its present context through the catchword μεριμνῶν. Originally it will have been an independent saying, and it may possibly be conjectured from the introductory τίς δὲ ἐξ ὑμῶν that it was addressed to the public (see p. 103). Πῆχυς cannot mean a bodily measure for it is much too big (an ell=0.52 m.). But if a minimal measure of time is intended, then the logion may have an eschatological reference. In the hour of catastrophe the utmost care (on μεριμνᾶν see p. 214) will not avail to prolong the span of life.

Then will the door of the festal hall be closed, and the word will be heard: Too late! Two closely related parables describe what it means to be too late: they both deal with the closed door of the festal hall filled with guests. They are the parable of the Ten Virgins (Matt. 25.1–12 cf. Luke 13.25–27) and the parable of the Great Supper (Luke 14.15–24 par. Matt. 22.1–10).

The *parable of the Ten Virgins* calls for a preliminary remark. We have seen on pp. 51–53 that there are weighty grounds for the view that the parable was not originally an allegory, but the description of an actual wedding with which Jesus intended to startle the crowd in view of the impending eschatological crisis. But against the genuineness of the parable the objection has been advanced that it contains a number of details to which the rabbinical sources offer no parallels; for example, the placing of the beginning of the wedding feast in the night, the reception of the bridegroom with lamps, and the delay of his coming till midnight.[86] Hence, since these features, which are said not to 'belong to the picture of an ordinary wedding',[87] show a connection with the primitive Church's expectation of the *Parousia*, the parable should be regarded as an allegory subsequently

[86] G. Bornkamm, 'Die Verzögerung der Parusie' in *In memoriam E. Lohmeyer*, Stuttgart, 1951, pp. 119–26.
[87] Ibid., p. 122.

attributed to Jesus by the early Church, and intended to exhort the community, in spite of the delay of the *Parousia*, not to be negligent in preparation for the End.[88] With regard to this objection it must be said that the assumption is unwarranted that the wedding customs to which allusion has been made are not to be found in rabbinic literature. The mistaken idea has arisen because we possess no connected description of a wedding-feast from the time of Jesus, but only modern collections of material which attempt to construct a connected mosaic out of the scattered allusions to be found in the rabbinic literature.[89] There is evidence that these collections of material are incomplete. This is not surprising in view of the situation with regard to the sources; the material is unlimited and widely scattered, and the picture is extraordinarily varied: then as now, wedding customs differed in different districts; moreover, after the destruction of the Temple, under the repeated impact of national disasters, they underwent far-reaching restrictions;[90] but above all the occasional reports which we possess are widely distributed in space and time: in space they come from Palestine and Babylonia, while in time they are spread over many centuries. This is why numerous details have hitherto remained unrecorded. Among those wedding customs hitherto unnoticed are the reception of the bridegroom with lamps, and the occasional delay of his arrival. That the torch-light entrance of the Bridegroom at night was not unknown to late Judaism is shown by Mech. Ex. 19.17, where Deut. 33.2 'Yahweh came from Sinai (on his right was burning fire)', is interpreted with the words: 'like a bridegroom who goes to meet the bride'. Similarly the case might occur, though obviously exceptional, that the coming of the bridegroom might be delayed till midnight, if there was a lengthy dispute over the marriage settlement before it was signed.[91]

The conclusion that both the reception of the bridegroom with lamps and the delay of his arrival till the night are not mere fictions of the imagination, but are drawn from life, is confirmed by modern Palestinian bridal customs. In this connection the reports from

[88] Ibid., pp. 125 f.
[89] The best collection is in Bill., I, pp. 504–17; also S. Krauss, *Talmudische Archäologie*, II, Leipzig, 1911, pp. 37–43.
[90] Soṭa 9.14: after AD 70: prohibition of the bridegroom's garland, and the drum; after AD 117: prohibition of the bridal wreath; after AD 135: prohibition of the bride's litter.
[91] I am indebted for this reference to my colleague C.-H. Hunzinger.

different parts of the country [92] give us a very varied picture,[93] differing in details from village to village; but the feature common to almost all [94] is that the climax and conclusion of the wedding celebrations consists in the subsequent nocturnal entry of the bridegroom into the paternal house.[95] Here are two examples. Village conditions, agreeing in all essentials, are described by two authorities of long acquaintance with Palestine, F. A. Klein (1883) and L. Bauer (1903).[96] After the day has been spent in dancing and other entertainments, the wedding-feast takes place at nightfall. The bride is then accompanied with torches to the bridegroom's house. Finally a messenger announces the coming of the bridegroom, who had to keep outside the house; the women leave the bride alone and go with torches to meet the bridegroom who appears at the head of his friends. A description of a Jerusalem wedding (1906) under city (Christian) conditions has been given by my late father, published in 1909.[97] In the late evening the guests were entertained in the bride's house. After hours of waiting for the bridegroom, whose coming was repeatedly announced by messengers, at last he came, half an hour before midnight, to fetch the bride; he was accompanied by his friends, floodlit by burning candles, and received by the guests who had come out to meet him. The wedding assembly then moved off, again in a flood of light, in festal procession to the house of the bridegroom's father, where the marriage ceremony and fresh entertainment took place. Both the reception of the bridegroom with lights and the hour-long waiting for the bridegroom's arrival, are frequently mentioned in modern reports of Arab weddings in Palestine. Even today the usual reason for delay is that agreement cannot be

---

[92] F. A. Klein, 'Mitteilungen über Leben, Sitten und Gebräuche der Fellachen in Palästina' in: *ZDPV*, 6 (1883), pp. 81–101; L. Schneller, *Kennst du das Land?*[16], Jerusalem, 1899; G. Dalman, *Palästinischer Diwan*, Leipzig, 1901; L. Bauer, *Volksleben im Lande der Bibel*, Leipzig, 1903; E. Baumann, 'Zur Hochzeit geladen' in: *Palästina-Jahrbuch*, 4 (1908), pp. 67–76; F. Jeremias, 'Eine Hochzeit in Jerusalem' in: *Kirchl. Monatsblatt d. Limbach-Rabensteiner Pastorenkonferenz*, IV. Jahrg. Nr. 4, Juli, 1909; G. Rothstein, 'Moslemische Hochzeitsgebräuche in Lifta bei Jerusalem' in: *Palästina-Jahrbuch*, 6 (1910), pp. 102–36; H. Granqvist, *Marriage Conditions in a Palestinian Village*, II, Helsingfors, 1935.

[93] The fundamental work of H. Granqvist (see above note) furnishes accurate evidence of this.

[94] Otherwise: Bethlehem and surroundings (L. Schneller, p. 140).

[95] F. A. Klein, p. 98; L. Schneller, p. 140; G. Dalman, p. 193 (a Mohammedan wedding); L. Bauer, p. 94; E. Baumann, p. 76; F. Jeremias, pp. 3 f.; G. Rothstein, p. 122; H. Granqvist, p. 115.

[96] See n. 92.

[97] Ibid.

reached about the presents due to the relatives of the bride.[98] To neglect this often lively bargaining might be taken to imply an insufficient regard for the relatives of the bride; on the other hand, it must be interpreted as a compliment to the bridegroom if his future relations show in this way that they give away the bride only with the greatest reluctance.[99]

We see, then, that it can in no wise be said that the parable of the Ten Virgins 'describes a situation which is incompatible with the events of everyday life'.[1] Moreover, considering that the comparison of the Messianic community to the wise virgins lies within the scope of Jesus' imagery, while in an early Christian allegory a comparison with the bride might be expected,[2] we should hesitate to see in the parable 'a later product of the church, interspersed with allegorical features'.[3] The early Church has certainly often interpreted parables allegorically; but it is utterly incredible that she should have produced an artistic picture of a wedding corresponding in every detail to the reality as a mere fiction.

V. 1 f.: Ὁμοιωθήσεται: The parable of the Ten Virgins is one of those which begin with a dative; the Kingdom of God is not compared to the virgins, but to the wedding (see p. 101). Δέκα is a round figure, as is πέντε in v. 2. Εἰς ὑπάντησιν: We have seen that in modern Palestine the wedding ceremony reaches its climax and conclusion with the nocturnal entry of the bridegroom into his paternal house. The λαμπάδες with which the young women go to meet the procession are certainly not clay lamps (λύχνοι, Mark 4.21, etc.), nor are they lanterns (φανοί, John 18.3), but torches (sticks wrapped round with oil-soaked rags or tow [4]). Thus: 'The arrival of the Kingdom of God is as it is when young women go out with torches to

[98] K.-E. Wilken, *Biblisches Erleben im Heiligen Land*, I, Lahr-Dinglingen, 1953, pp. 243 f.
[99] H. Granqvist (see above, n. 92), p. 73.
[1] G. Bornkamm (see p. 171, n. 86), p. 125.
[2] The bride is never mentioned (in Matt. 25.1 the words καὶ τῆς νύμφης, only found in DΘλ it vg syr, are an addition, as vv. 5 and 6 show, cf. *ThWBNT*, IV, p. 1093. 8 ff.). Just as the comparison of the redeemed community to the bride is frequent in early Christian literature (II Cor. 11.2; Eph. 5.31 f. [in connection with the *Parousia*: Christ leaves the heavenly sphere to unite himself with the Church]; Rev. 19.7 f.; 21.2, 9; 22.17 ⸴cf. John 3.29), so the same comparison is unknown in the whole of Jesus' teaching. It is rather Jesus' custom to compare the Messianic community with the wedding guests (Mark 2.19a; Matt. 22.1 ff., 11 ff.). Similarly Matt. 25.1–12: thus we are to see here Jesus' customary manner of speaking, not that of the early Church.
[3] G. Bornkamm, p. 125, following R. Bultmann, *The History of the Synoptic Tradition₂*, Oxford, 1968, pp. 176 ff.
[4] J. Jeremias, 'ΛΑΜΠΑΔΕΣ', in: *ZNW*, 56 (1965), pp. 196–201.

meet the bridegroom. V. 3: Οὐκ ἔλαβον μεθ' ἑαυτῶν ἔλαιον: in their hasty exodus had they forgotten their ἀγγεῖα (see v. 4)? The epithet 'foolish' applied to them suggests another explanation: they were so shortsighted as to overlook the possibility of the bridegroom's delay, and forgot that they would need oil to replenish the torches. V. 4: Τὰ ἀγγεῖα: small jugs with handles. V. 5: Χρονίζοντος τοῦ νυμφίου: for the reason for the delay see pp. 172 ff. Ἐνύσταξαν (ingressive aor.) πᾶσαι καὶ ἐκάθευδον (durative impf.): 'they all fell into a light twilight sleep' (cf. b. Pes. 120).[6] V. 7: They wait with burning torches (cf. v. 8: σβέννυνται), since if the bridegroom comes unexpectedly it is not easy to kindle the flame in a hurry.[7] Ἐκόσμησαν τὰς λαμπάδας ἑαυτῶν: they take the charred remnants of the rags away and dip the torches in oil again, to make them burn more brightly. V. 10: Εἰς τοὺς γάμους: to the wedding house, where they dance with the torches until these go out.[8] V. 11: On the use of the historic present ἔρχονται as an evidence of early tradition, see p. 199, n. 34. V. 12: Οὐκ οἶδα ὑμᾶς is the formula of nᵉzipha (the teacher's order, forbidding his scholar access to him for seven days),[9] hence the phrase means: 'I will have nothing to do with you.' On v. 13 see above.[10]

The parable is one of the crisis-parables.[11] The wedding-day has come, the banquet is ready. 'The Lord our God, sovereign over all, has entered upon his reign. Let us exult and shout for joy and do him homage, for the wedding has come. . . . Happy are those who are invited to the wedding-supper' (Rev. 19.6 f., 9). Only he who pays attention to the note of joy on which the parable starts (v. 1) is able to grasp the stern warning it conveys: all the more let it be your concern to prepare yourself for the hour of trial and judgement that will precede the fulfilment. This hour comes as suddenly as the bridegroom. Alas for those who are like the foolish virgins, whose lamps had gone out and who then found the door of the wedding house closed against them. For them it is too late. For, as the *parable of the Closed Door* (Luke 13.24–30) adds, a parallel to the conclusion of Matt. 25.1–12: their appeal to the fact that they have enjoyed companionship with Jesus avails them nothing if their deeds have been evil (Luke 13.27).[12]

[6] Bill., I, p. 970.
[7] G. Dalman, *Arbeit und Sitte*, IV, Gütersloh, 1935, p. 25.
[8] Schneller (op. cit. p. 173, no. 92), p. 188.
[9] Bill., I, p. 469; IV, p. 293.
[10] Pp. 51, 106, 111.
[11] See above, p. 53.
[12] Similar ideas are reflected in the parable of the woman who carried a leaking jar of flour and arrived home with an empty jar (Gospel of Thomas 97); it is worth considering whether it goes back to Jesus. It is a warning against false security.

'It may be too late', is also the message of the *parable of the Great Supper* (Matt. 22.1–10; Luke 14.15–24). In the Gospel of Thomas (64) it reads: 'Jesus said: A man had guests, and when he had prepared the meal, he sent his servant that he might invite the guests. He (the servant) went to the first and told him: "My lord invites you." He said: "I have money (to collect) from merchants. They are coming to see me tonight, and I shall go and give them instructions. I beg to be excused from the meal." He went to another one and told him: "My lord has invited you." He said to him: "I bought a house, and it requires a day's attention. I shall have no time." He came to another one and told him: "My lord invites you." He said to him: "My friend will marry, and I shall take care of the feast. I shall not be able to come; I beg to be excused from the meal." He went to another one and told him: "My lord invites you." He said to him: "I bought a village and am going out to collect the rent. I shall not be able to come; I beg to be excused." The servant returned and told his master: "Those whom you invited to dinner, have given excuses." The master told his servant: "Go out into the streets and bring in whom you will find, that they take part in my banquet." The buyers and the merchants will not enter the places of my father.'

We have already seen that the parable of the Great Supper has been so drastically edited by Matthew that it has been transformed into nothing less than an allegory of the plan of salvation.[13] On the other hand, in Luke and the Gospel of Thomas (apart from a few expansions such as the doubling of the invitation to the uninvited in Luke,[14] and the expansion of the excuses in the Gospel of Thomas [15]), the original form of the parable has remained essentially unchanged. V. 16: the private person, who has only one servant, is earlier than the ἄνθρωπος βασιλεύς (Matt. 22.2), see pp. 28, 67 f., 101. The invited guests are well-to-do people, large landowners (see on v. 19). V. 17: the banquet is ἤδη, 'long ago' (as in Luke 11.7, see p. 157) ready. The repetition of the invitation at the time of the banquet is a special courtesy, practised by upper circles in Jerusalem.[16] V. 18: the hapaxlegomenon ἀπὸ μιᾶς is a literal translation of the Pal.-Syr. *min ḥᵃdha*, 'all at once'.[17] V. 19: Ζεύγη βοῶν—among the Palestinian

[13] See pp. 63 ff., 67 ff. [14] See p. 64.
[15] See above. [16] Lam.rabba 4.2 (Bill., I, p. 881). Cf. Est. 6.14.
[17] M. Black, *An Aramaic Approach to the Gospels and Acts₃*, Oxford, 1967, p. 113 (in agreement with J. Wellhausen, *Einleitung in die drei ersten Evangelien₂*, Berlin, 1911, p. 20). For instance, ἐφάπαξ (I Cor. 15.6) 'at once' is translated in Pal.-Syr. by *min ḥᵃdha*.

Arabs the *feddān* is the commonest unit of land measurement; this is
usually taken to be the amount of land which can be ploughed in a
day by a yoke of oxen. Besides this there is the legal *feddān* which corresponds to a year's work of a yoke of oxen, averaging, for good land,
from 9 to 9.45 hectares.[18] In general a farmer owns as much land as
1–2 yoke of oxen can plough,[19] that is, about 10–20 hectares. The
Letter of Aristeas (*c.* 145–127 BC) places the average extent of a holding somewhat higher, and states that at the time of the settlement in
Palestine, every Israelite received 100 *arurae* (=27.56 hectares,
116). The man in the parable had just bought 5 yoke of oxen. He
therefore possessed at least 45 hectares, and probably much more,
and was consequently a large landowner. V. 20: Γυναῖκα ἔγημα:
The semitic perfect underlying the aorist ἔγημα describes a recently
completed transaction, 'I have just been married'. Only men were
invited to a banquet, and the newly married man does not wish to
leave his young wife alone.[20] V. 21: 'the lame, the blind, and the
halt' are *ipso facto* beggars in the East. They are not invited out of
compassion, or from a religious motive (as in v. 13), but out of
vexation. V. 23: in addition to the beggars the servant is to fetch
in the homeless from 'the streets and the hedges of the vineyards'.[21]
Ἀνάγκασον: even the poorest, with oriental courtesy, modestly
resist the invitation to the entertainment until they are taken by the
hand and gently forced to enter the house.[22] Γεμισθῇ: it is of the utmost importance to the host that even the last place shall be filled.
V. 24: Who is meant by the 'I' in Luke 14.24 ('I say unto you', 'my
supper') is a disputed question. The plural in λέγω γὰρ ὑμῖν does
not agree with what has previously been said by the host, who in
v. 23 addresses only *one* servant. Hence it appears, as in 11.8; 15.7,
10; 16.9; 18.8, 14; 19.26, to be the introduction to Jesus' final
judgement, and by the words μου τοῦ δείπνου, 'my supper', he
will have been referring to the Messianic banquet (cf. Luke 22.30).
So Luke may have understood it, and may have seen in the parable
an allegory of the Messianic banquet. Also in the Gospel of Thomas
64 the final sentence is understood as a word of Jesus and connected
with the heavenly banquet: 'Buyers and merchants shall not enter

[18] G. Dalman, *Arbeit und Sitte*, II, Gütersloh, 1932, pp. 47 f.
[19] Ibid., p. 40.
[20] W. Michaelis, *Die Gleichnisse Jesu*, Hamburg, 1956, p. 156.
[21] See p. 64.
[22] Cf. A. M. Rihbany, *Morgenländischen Sitten im Leben Jesu₅*, Basel n.d. (1962),
pp. 90 f.

the places of my Father.' Originally, however, v. 24 will have been spoken by the host, since (1) γάρ refers back to the order in v. 23, and (2) μου τοῦ δείπνου (v. 24) corresponds to μου ὁ οἶκος (v. 23). But even if v. 24 be taken as spoken by the host it breaks through the pattern of the story: it is only a real threat if it refers to the Messianic banquet.[23]

If this story were not so familiar, its unreality would strike us more forcibly. There are two features in particular which would appear absurd in real life: (1) the invited guests, one and all, as if by agreement, 'all at once' decline the invitation, and (2) in their place the host deliberately invites the beggars and the homeless.[24] The conclusion that the whole is an allegory seems unavoidable; but such a conclusion would be erroneous. A recent study [25] has shown convincingly that Jesus was making use of some well-known story material,[26] namely, the story of the rich tax-gatherer Bar Ma'jan and a poor scholar, which occurs in Aramaic in the Palestinian Talmud.[27] That Jesus knew this story is confirmed by the fact that he used it again: in the parable of the Rich Man and the poor Lazarus he made use of its conclusion, as we shall see later.[28] We are told that the rich tax-gatherer Ma'jan died and was given a splendid funeral; work stopped throughout the city, since the whole population wished to escort him to his last resting-place. At the same time a poor scholar died, and no one took any notice of his burial. How could God be so unjust as to allow this? The answer is as follows: although Bar Ma'jan had by no means lived a pious life, yet

[23] A guest who has no intention of coming will not be impressed by the threat that he will not be admitted. E. Linnemann, *Parables of Jesus*, London, 1966, p. 89, has tried to fit v. 24 into the story by suggesting that those invited did not mean by their replies in vv. 18 f. to decline the invitation, but merely to announce that they would be late. In that case v. 24 would indeed make sense as a real threat: guests arriving late will find all seats occupied. Yet Miss Linnemann can hardly be right. When read by themselves, vv. 18 f. do not convey the meaning she would like to give them; v. 20 is definitely a refusal (which Linnemann is bound to interpret as an addition); and, above all, the Gospel of Thomas, Matthew (22.6), and the rabbinical parallel which will be quoted presently all take the replies to mean definite refusals.

[24] To entertain a needy person at a meal in one's house on a holiday counts as a good work (Tob. 2.2, cf. Pes. 9.11). But in our story an entire banquet-hall is filled with beggars.

[25] W. Salm, *Beiträge zur Gleichnisforschung*, Diss., Göttingen, 1953, pp. 144–46.

[26] For further examples of such connections, see p. 200.

[27] j. Sanh. 6.23c par. j. Ḥagh. 2.77d; critical edition of the text in G. Dalman, *Aram. Dialektproben*, Leipzig, 1927, pp. 33 f.

[28] See p. 183.

he had once done a single good deed, and had been surprised by death in the act. Since the moment of his death had ensured that his good deed could not be cancelled by any further evil deeds, it was necessary that it should be rewarded by God, and this was effected by his splendid funeral. What then was the good deed of Bar Ma'jan? 'He had arranged a banquet (*'*riston=ἄριστον) for the city councillors (*bulbuṭayya*=βουλευταί), but they did not come. So he gave orders that the poor (*miskene*) should come and eat it, so that the food should not be wasted.'[29] The flood-light of this story now reveals to us the meaning of the mysterious behaviour of the invited guests in Luke 14.18-20.[30] The host is to be understood as a tax-gatherer who has become wealthy, and has sent out invitations in the hope that he may in this way be fully accepted in the highest circles. But they all, as if by agreement, show him the cold shoulder, and decline his invitation with the flimsiest of excuses. Then in his rage he invites the beggars to his house, in order to show the city magnates that he cares nothing for them and will have nothing more to do with them. Just as Jesus does not hesitate to illustrate from the behaviour of the deceitful steward the need for decisive action (pp. 47, 182), or from the conduct of the unscrupulous judge (pp. 156 f.), the despised shepherd (pp. 132-6), and the poor woman (ibid.), the boundless mercy of God, so he has not the slightest hesitation, in this case, in choosing the behaviour of a tax-gatherer to illustrate both the wrath and the mercy of God. That the man's motive was just as selfish and ignoble as that of the judge who yielded to the importunate plaintiff simply in order to be left in peace (p. 154), has not in any way disturbed Jesus, but has rather induced him to choose just these persons as examples. The incredible seriousness of the conclusion (v. 24) could not be better expressed.[31] We must picture to ourselves how Jesus' audience would smile at the description of the insolence with which the parvenu was treated, and of his consequent rage; we must imagine them breaking out into audible laughter at the depiction of the upper ten with scornful glances watching from their windows the curious stream of seedy guests moving toward the gaily bedecked custom-house. How shocked they must have been when Jesus, the master of the house, sharply declared, 'The house

---

[29] Dalman, op. cit., p. 34.6 f. The continuation of the story is given on p. 183.
[30] For what follows cf. W. Salm, op. cit., pp. 144-46.
[31] Rightly understood by W. Salm, ibid. What follows is to some extent in close agreement with Salm's excellent treatment.

is full, the number is complete, the last place is occupied; close the doors, none henceforth may be admitted.'

This parable, too, is not fully understood until attention is paid to the note of joy which rings through the summons: 'everything is ready' (v. 17). 'Behold, now is the accepted time; behold, now is the day of salvation' (II Cor. 6.2). God fulfils his promises and finally comes out of concealment.[32] But if the 'children of the kingdom', the theologians and the pious circles, pay no heed to his call, the despised and ungodly will take their place; the others will receive nothing but a 'Too late' from behind the closed doors of the banquet hall.

6. THE CHALLENGE OF THE HOUR

'It may be too late': the threat implied in these words tells what the hour demands. It calls for resolute action. That is the message of the *parable of the Debtor* (Matt. 5.25 f.; Luke 12.58 f.).[33] Matt. 5.25: Τῷ ἀντιδίκῳ: who has gone to court to recover a debt. Μήποτέ (σε παραδῷ ὁ ἀντίδικος τῷ κριτῇ) must not be rendered, 'lest some day' (Luther), thus implying that the action may happen some time in the future, but, 'lest (before you know what happens)'. Καὶ εἰς φυλακὴν βληθήσῃ: imprisonment for debt is unknown to Jewish law. Hence we must conclude that Jesus is deliberately referring to non-Jewish legal practice which his audience considered inhuman (the same is true of the καταποντισμός, Mark 9.42, selling one's wife, Matt. 18.25, torture, Matt. 18.34) to stress the fearfulness of the judgement. V. 26: Οὐ μὴ ἐξέλθῃς: 'you will not be released' (semitic avoidance of the passive). Τὸν ἔσχατον κοδράντην: the quarter of an as (in Palestine 1/100 denarius, Bill., I, p. 291) was the smallest denomination of Roman currency. Not a farthing will be remitted: the accuracy employed in accounting serves to illustrate how rigidly the sentence will be executed. You, says Jesus, are in the position of the defendant who must shortly appear before the Judge, and at any moment may be arrested, and who meets his opponent on his way to court. Carried away by the situation he depicts, Jesus imploringly cries:[34] Make a settlement while there is still time! Acknowledge your debts! Ask your opponent for indulgence and patience (cf. Matt. 18.26, 29)! If you do not succeed in doing so, the worst may happen to you!

[32] A point rightly made by E. Linnemann, op. cit., pp. 90–92.
[33] See pp. 43 f.
[34] W. Salm, op. cit., p. 107.

This parable is closely connected with the *parable of the Unjust Steward* (Luke 16.1–8).

V. 1: Ἄνθρωπος πλούσιος: Apparently Galilean conditions are presupposed; the πλούσιος is probably to be regarded as the owner of a large estate who lives abroad and is represented by a steward.[35] διεβλήθη: The East knows nothing of book-keeping or audit. V. 3: Εἶπεν δὲ ἐν ἑαυτῷ, he considered (Semitic has no word for 'think', 'ponder', 'consider'). Σκάπτειν: he is not accustomed to 'work in the field'. V. 4: Ἔγνων: (Aor.) 'it has occurred to me'. Vv. 5–7: He tries to cover up his embezzlements (v. 1) by falsifying the accounts. The debtors (χρεοφειλέτης) are either tenants who have to deliver a specified portion (a half, a third, or a quarter) of the yield of their land in lieu of rent, or wholesale merchants, who have given promissory notes for goods received. 100 baths (=c. 800 gals.) of oil corresponds to the yield of 146 olive-trees,[36] and a debt of about 1,000 denarii; 100 cors (=c. 120 quarters)[37] of wheat equals 550 cwt. and corresponds to the yield of about 100 acres,[38] and a debt of about 2,500 denarii. Hence heavy obligations were involved. The remission (400 gals. of the oil and 24 quarters of the wheat) is approximately equal in the two cases, since oil is much dearer than wheat;[39] its value in currency would be about 500 denarii.[40] In our parable Jesus betrays the oriental story-teller's love for large numbers.[41] V. 6 f.: Δέξαι σου τὰ γράμματα: 'There is your bill.' The steward has the promissory notes in his own keeping. He lets the debtors make their own alterations, hoping that the fraud, being in the same hand-writing, will pass unnoticed; or he lets them make out fresh notes. V. 7: Λέγει: On the historic present see pp. 182 f. The steward dealt in similar fashion with the rest of the debtors (ἕνα ἕκαστον, v. 5). V. 8:

[35] W. Grundmann, *Die Geschichte Jesu Christi*, Berlin, 1956, p. 171. See above, pp. 74 f.

[36] The average yield of an olive-tree in Palestine amounted to 120 kilos of olives or 25 litres of oil, cf. J. Herz, 'Grossgrundbesitz in Palästina zur Zeit Jesu', in *Palästina-Jahrbuch*, 24 (1928), p. 100; G. Dalman, *Arbeit und Sitte in Palästina*, IV, Gütersloh, 1935, p. 192. Up to 30 l.: K.-E. Wilken, *Biblisches Erleben im Heiligen Land*, II, Lahr-Dinglingen, 1954, p. 89.

[37] G. Dalman, ibid., III (1933), p. 152.

[38] G. Dalman, ibid., p. 155, 159 according to L. Pinner, *Wheat Culture in Palestine* (1930), p. 68: in modern Palestine the average yield of a hectare over an eight-year period amounted to 652.4 kilos of wheat.

[39] K. H. Rengstorf in *Das Neue Testament Deutsch*, 3₉, Göttingen, 1962, in loc.

[40] According to B.M. 5. 1, the regular price for 1 cor of wheat is 1 gold dinar or 25 silver dinars. Hence the value of 20 cors is 500 dinars. On wheat prices, cf. also J. Jeremias, *Jerusalem in the Time of Jesus*, London, 1969, p. 122.

[41] For further examples, see pp. 27 f.

Καὶ ἐπῄνεσεν ὁ κύριος τὸν οἰκονόμον τῆς ἀδικίας: apparently κύριος originally referred to Jesus, see above, pp. 45 f.

The shock, much discussed, naturally produced by a parable which seems to present a criminal as a pattern,[42] disappears when we consider the parable in its original form (vv. 1–8), and disregard the expansions (vv. 9–13).[43] As in the parable of the House broken into by Night,[44] Jesus is apparently dealing with an actual case which had been indignantly related to him. He deliberately took it as an example, knowing that it would secure redoubled attention, so far as his hearers did not know the incident. They would expect that Jesus would end the story with an expression of strong disapproval, instead of which, to their surprise, Jesus praises the criminal. 'It is very well for you to be indignant, but you should apply the lesson to yourselves. You are in the same position as this steward who saw the imminent disaster threatening him with ruin, but the crisis which threatens you, in which, indeed, you are already involved, is incomparably more terrible. This man was φρόνιμος (v. 8a), i.e. he recognized the critical nature of the situation.[45] He did not let things take their course, he acted, unscrupulously no doubt (τῆς ἀδικίας v. 8), Jesus did not excuse his action, though we are not concerned with that here, but boldly, resolutely, and prudently, with the purpose of making a new life for himself. For you, too, the challenge of the hour demands prudence, everything is at stake!'

In the face of this challenge of the hour, evasion is impossible. That is the message of the *parable of the Rich Man and Lazarus* (Luke 16.19–31).

Very noteworthy from the linguistic point of view is the occurrence in Luke of the twice repeated historic present (v. 23: ὁρᾷ; v. 29: λέγει). Of the 90 examples of the historic present occurring in the Marcan material which he has taken over,[46] he has only retained one (Luke 8.49: ἔρχεται), the other 89 he has rejected. From

[42] The various attempts to whitewash the Unjust Steward have all been unsuccessful.
[43] On the expansions of the text, see pp. 45 ff.
[44] See pp. 48 f.
[45] See p. 46, n. 83.
[46] Luke has inserted the Marcan material in blocks into Proto-Luke: (1) Mark 1.21–39; (2) Mark 1.40–3.11; (3) Mark 4.1–25; 3.31–35; 4.35–6.44; 8.27–9.40; (4) Mark 10.13–52; (5) Mark 11.1–14.16. In his composition of Acts Luke has used the same method of inserting his material in blocks into his source, cf. J. Jeremias, 'Untersuchungen zum Quellenproblem der Apostelgeschichte,' in *ZNW*, 36 (1937), pp. 205–21, esp. 219.

which it results that the six historic presents which occur in the Lucan parables (13.8; 16.7, 23, 29; 19.22) and in the introduction to a parable (7.40), are clear evidence of the existence of an underlying pre-Lucan tradition. In order to understand the parable in detail and as a whole, it is essential to recognize that the first part derives from well-known folk-material concerned with the reversal of fortune in the after life. This is the Egyptian folk-tale of the journey of Si-Osiris, the son of Setme Chamoïs to the under-world, which concludes with the words: 'He who has been good on earth, will be blessed in the kingdom of the dead, and he who has been evil on earth, will suffer in the kingdom of the dead.'[47] Alexandrian Jews brought this story to Palestine, where it became very popular as the story of the poor scholar and the rich publican Bar Ma'jan. That Jesus was familiar with this story is proved by the fact that he has used it in the parable of the Great Supper (see pp. 178 ff.). There we have already related the beginning of the story: how the scholar's funeral was unattended, while the publican was buried with great pomp. Here is the end of the story. One of the poor scholar's colleagues was allowed to see in a dream the fate of the two men in the next world: 'A few days later that scholar saw his colleague in gardens of paradisal beauty, watered by flowing streams. He also saw Bar Ma'jan the publican standing on the bank of a stream and trying to reach the water, but unable to do so.'[48] V. 19: The rich man, who had no need to work, feasted every day, arrayed in a costly mantle of purple wool, with underwear of fine Egyptian linen.[49] The lack of emphasis on his guilt, although, as his fate shows, he is represented as an impious reveller, is explained by the fact that Jesus was drawing on material which was well known to his hearers. V. 20: Lazarus is the only figure in the parables who is given a name; the name (God helps) thus has a special significance. Lazarus is a cripple (ἐβέβλητο = r^eme = 'thrown down, lying'), suffering from a skin-disease (v. 21b). As a beggar (πτωχός cf. John 13.29) he has his pitch in the street, at the gate of the rich man's mansion where he begs for a gift from the

[47] H. Gressmann, *Vom reichen Mann und armen Lazarus*, Abh. d. preuss. Akad. d. Wiss., 1918, phil.—hist. Klasse, no. 7. The MS. dates from about AD 50–100; the story itself is older than 331 BC (see Morenz in *ThLZ*, 78, 1953, col. 188).
[48] j. Sanh. 6.23c par. j. Hagh. 2.27d, critical edition of the text by G. Dalman, *Aramäische Dialektproben*₂, Leipzig, 1927, pp. 33 f. The above quotation is from Dalman, pp. 34, ll. 9–11.
[49] R. Delbrueck in *ZNW*, 41 (1942), p. 128. Purple mantles were very costly; similarly, linen garments were regarded as a special luxury.

184   THE MESSAGE OF THE PARABLES OF JESUS

passers-by. V. 21: ἐπιθυμεῖν with the infinitive, in Luke always ⁵⁰ indicates an unfulfilled desire: 'he would gladly (if he could) have filled
himself'.⁵¹ Ἀπὸ τῶν πιπτόντων ἀπὸ τῆς τραπέζης τοῦ πλουσίου: πίπτειν
= nᵉphal, semitic avoidance of the passive: 'to be thrown'.⁵² Hence it
should be translated: 'what was thrown on the ground by those who
sat at the rich man's table'. We are not to think of 'that which fell
from the rich man's table' as 'crumbs', but as pieces of bread which
the guests dipped in the dish, wiped their hands with and then
threw under the table.⁵³ How gladly would Lazarus have satisfied his
hunger with them. The dogs are wild, roaming street-dogs who cannot refrain from nosing the helpless, scantily-clad cripple. According
to the outlook of late Judaism, his miserable condition would have
indicated that he was a sinner being punished by God. Hence the
sequel must have been wholly unexpected by the audience. V. 22:
Εἰς τὸν κόλπον Ἀβραάμ is a designation of the place of honour at the
heavenly banquet at the right hand of Father Abraham (cf. John
13.23); this place of honour, the highest that could be hoped for,
indicates that Lazarus occupies the highest place in the assembly of
the righteous. He has experienced a complete reversal of fortune:
on earth he saw the rich man seated at his table, now he himself is
entitled to sit at the festal board; on earth he was despised, now he
enjoys the highest honour. He has discovered that God is the God
of the poorest and most destitute. Ἀπέθανεν δὲ καὶ ὁ πλούσιος καὶ
ἐτάφη: The funeral of the rich man was, as the folk-material mentioned above shows, a magnificent affair. Vv. 22–31 are not concerned with the final fate, but with the state immediately after death.⁵⁴

⁵⁰ Luke 15.16; 16.21; 17.22; 22.15; similarly Matt. 13.17; I Pet. 1.12; Rev.
9.6. Otherwise only in Heb. 6.11.
⁵¹ Cf. p. 129 n. 75, on ἐπεθύμει Luke 15.16. This is the meaning of the variant
reading καὶ οὐδεὶς ἐδίδου αὐτῷ φλ vgᶜˡ.
⁵² Cf. Luke 10.18 πεσόντα (Satan) with John 12.31 ἐκβληθήσεται and with
Rev. 12.9 ἐβλήθη; further, John 12.24 πεσών (the corn of wheat), 'being sown'.
⁵³ After the meal the remains of bread lying on the floor should be gathered
up; he who neglects this duty, falls into the hands of the Prince of the poor (on
account of his waste of bread) (b. Ḥul. 105b). Hence the proverb, 'Waste of
bread in a house brings in poverty' (b. Pes. 111b). In the houses of scholars they
were specially careful. 'If a scholar is serving at table, he gathers up fragments as
small as an olive' (Tos. Ber. 6.4; b.Ber. 52b [Bar.]). But in general people were very
careless. 'One should not bite a piece of bread (which has been dipped in the dish)
and then dip it in again, on account of danger to life' (from infectious disease)
(Tos. Ber. 5.8)—sc. but the rest of it should be thrown under the table (S. Krauss,
Talmudische Archäologie, III, Leipzig, 1912, pp. 51 f.)
⁵⁴ Cf. ThWBNT, V, p. 767, n. 37, s.v. παράδεισος; W. Michaelis, Versöhnung des
Alls, Gümlingen, 1950, pp. 65 f.

That is apparent from a comparison with the folk-tale on which Jesus was drawing, and is confirmed by the use of the word ᾅδης (v. 23); since the New Testament draws a sharp distinction between the intermediate state of ᾅδης and the final γέεννα.[55] Hence it is the intermediate state which is in question here.[56] V. 23: It is a common late-Jewish conception that the righteous and the wicked can see one another in the intermediate state.[57] V. 24: The rich man appeals to his kinship with Abraham, that is, to his share (by right of descent) in the vicarious merit of Abraham. His modest request shows how terrible was his torture: a single drop of water on his tongue from the springs which flow through the abode of the righteous would be an alleviation of his suffering. V. 25: His kinship with Abraham was acknowledged (τέκνον),[58] but not as entitling him to salvation.[59] According to the wording of v. 25 it might appear as though the doctrine of retribution which is here expounded is of purely external application (on earth, wealth, in the life beyond, torment; on earth, poverty, in the next life, refreshment). But, quite apart from the contradiction in the context (vv. 14 f.), where has Jesus ever suggested that wealth in itself merits hell, and that poverty in itself is rewarded by paradise? What v. 25 really says is that impiety and lovelessness are punished, and that piety and humility are rewarded; this is clearly shown by comparison with the folk-material made use of by Jesus. Since the material was well known, Jesus only suggests, without elaborating the picture, the condition of the two men, on the one hand by the use of the name 'Lazarus' which means 'God helps', see on v. 20, and on the other hand by the prayer in vv. 27 ff., in which the rich man reveals his impenitent state.[60] V. 26: The

---

[55] ThWBNT, I, pp. 148 f., 655 f.

[56] The physical torments do not militate against this. They belong to the material of the tradition, and were used by Judaism to describe the intermediate state, although this is disembodied.

[57] In the intermediate state: IV Ezra 7.85, 93; Syr. Bar. 51.5 f.; rabbinical examples: Bill., II, p. 228; IV, p. 1040. In the final state: Luke 13.28; Bill., IV, pp. 1114 f.

[58] K. Bornhäuser, Studien zum Sondergut des Lukas, Gütersloh, 1934, p. 155.

[59] Cf. Matt. 3.9 par.; John 8.37 ff.

[60] No conclusions should be drawn from the verb ἀπέλαβες (16.25) about the behaviour of the two in their earthly life (that the rich man had selfishly accumulated his wealth, and that Lazarus had humbly accepted his hard lot, cf. W. Michaelis, Die Gleichnisse Jesu, Hamburg, 1956, p. 217). The word ὁμοίως is clearly against this view. It is much more a question of the aramaizing avoidance of the passive (ἀπολαμβάνειν='to receive from God', as in Gal. 4.5; Col. 3.24; II John 8).

'gulf' expresses the irrevocability of God's judgement; hence Jesus knows no doctrine of purgatory. V. 27: Πέμψῃς suggests an appearance of the dead Lazarus 'perhaps in a dream or in a vision'.[61] V. 28: Διαμαρτύρεσθαι meaning 'to adjure' (viz. with reference to retribution after death). V. 31: 'Αναστῇ introduces the climax. Hitherto it was only a question of an appearance of the dead Lazarus, 'perhaps in a dream or a vision', now the idea actually emerges of his bodily resurrection. Even so great a marvel, transcending all the daily evidences of God's power, leaves men unimpressed who will not 'hear Moses and the Prophets', i.e. who will not obey them. The reference to 'Moses and the Prophets' as the substance of revelation (vv. 29, 31) is pre-resurrection (this also holds good for Luke 13.28); the expression does not exclude obedience toward Messianic revelation, but rather, as is shown by Luke 24.27, 44, includes it, since this brings the revelation in the Law and the Prophets to its fulfilment (Matt. 5.17).

The parable is one of the four double-edged parables.[62] The first point is concerned with the reversal of fortune in the after-life (vv. 19–26), the second (vv. 27–31) with the petition of the rich man that Abraham may send Lazarus to his five brethren. Since the first part is drawn from well-known folk-material, the emphasis lies on the new 'epilogue'[63] which Jesus added to the first part. Like all the other double-edged parables, this one also has its stress on the second point. That means that Jesus does not want to comment on a social problem, nor does he intend to give teaching about the after-life, but he relates the parable to warn men who resemble the brothers of the rich man of the impending danger. Hence the poor Lazarus is only a secondary figure, introduced by way of contrast. The parable is about the five brothers, and it should not be styled the parable of the Rich Man and Lazarus, but the parable of the Six Brothers. The surviving brothers, who have their counterpart in the men of the Flood generation, living a careless life, heedless of the rumble of the approaching flood (Matt. 24.37–39 par.), are men of this world, like their dead brother. Like him they live in selfish luxury, deaf to God's word, in the belief that death ends all (v. 28). Scornfully, Jesus was asked by these sceptical worldlings for a valid proof of a life after death, if they were to be paying heed

[61] W. Michaelis, op. cit., p. 264, n. 151.
[62] See pp. 37 f.
[63] T. W. Manson, *Sayings*, p. 298.

to his warning. Jesus wanted to open their eyes, but to grant their demand would not be the right way to do so. Why did Jesus refuse it? Because its fulfilment would have been meaningless; even the greatest wonder, a resurrection, would be in vain.[64] He who will not submit to the Word of God, will not be converted by a miracle. *Auditu salvamur, non apparitionibus* (Bengel). The demand for a sign is an evasion and a sign of impenitence. Hence the sentence is pronounced: 'God will never give a sign to this generation' (Mark 8.12).[65]

What is to be done? Jesus replied in ever new similes: Be on the watch (Mark 13.35), gird up your loins,[66] let your lamps be burning (Luke 12.35), put on the wedding-garment (Matt. 22.11–13). The meaning of these and similar metaphors is best illustrated by the little *parable of the Guest without a Wedding Garment* (Matt. 22.11–13).[67] V. 11: Εἰσελθὼν δὲ ὁ βασιλεὺς θεάσασθαι τοὺς ἀνακειμένους: At formal banquets it is a mark of special courtesy that the host should not partake of the meal (see, e.g., Lev. r. 28 on 23.10); he leaves the guests by themselves and only appears during the meal. Ἔνδυμα γάμου: the missing 'wedding-garment' (v. 11) is not to be understood as a special garment, worn on festive occasions, but a newly washed garment (cf. Apoc. 22.14; 19.8).[68] The soiled garment is an insult to the host. V. 12: For the mode of address ἑταῖρε see on Matt. 20.13 (p. 137). Πῶς εἰσῆλθες means 'By what right (not "by what means") did you enter here?' 'But he was silent', and so we are not told how he came to be without the proper attire. Did he slip in uninvited, and was ashamed because he had been detected? Or was

---

[64] Cf. John 11.46 ff.: the raising of Lazarus served to complete the hardening of the Jews.

[65] In any case, that is also the meaning of the logion of the sign of Jonah (the Matthaean form is secondary, see p. 108). Luke 11.30 ('as Jonah was a sign to the men of Nineveh, so shall the Son of Man be to this generation') is the older form, according to which the return of God's messenger from the dead is the subject of comparison. The *Parousia* is the only sign that God will give, too late, however, for repentance; he gives no other sign. Cf. *ThWBNT*, III, p. 413; A. Vögtle, 'Der Spruch vom Jonaszeichen', in *Festschr. f. A. Wikenhauser*, Munich, 1954, pp. 230–77.

[66] Girding consisted in tucking the end of the long loose garment into the girdle, so that the garment did not hinder work or become soiled (G. Dalman, *Arbeit und Sitte*, V, Gütersloh, 1937, pp. 232–40).

[67] On the context, see above, pp. 63 ff. On v. 14 see p. 106.

[68] I. K. Madsen, 'Zur Erklärung der evangelischen Parabeln', in *ThStKr*, 101 (1929), p. 301, n. 2. Cf. Ta'an. 4.8 (on the dancing festival of the virgins of Jerusalem): 'all garments must be newly washed'.

his unauthorized intrusion a deliberate insult to the host and his silence a gesture of defiance? The rabbinic parallel cited below suggests another answer: he was invited, but he was a fool; the summons to the wedding-feast came earlier than he had expected, and found him unprepared. Hence the parable is one of the numerous crisis-parables.[69] The summons may come at any moment. Woe to the unprepared!

What exactly did Jesus mean by the clean garment which was the necessary condition for admission to the wedding-feast? Here we must choose between the rabbinic answer and the Gospel's. The rabbinic answer will be found in b. Shab. 153a, as follows: A Palestinian theologian of the end of the first century AD, R. Eliezer said: 'Repent one day before your death. His scholars asked him: How can a man know the day of his death? He answered them: Since he may die tomorrow, it is all the more necessary to repent today; thus all through his life he will be found in a state of penitence. Moreover, Solomon in his wisdom has said: Let thy garments be always white; and let not thy head lack ointment' (Eccles. 9.8). In explanation of this saying there follows a parable of Rabban Johanan ben Zakkai (c. AD 80)[70] about a king who issued invitations to a banquet, without specifying the hour. The wise attired themselves, while the foolish went on with their work. Suddenly the summons came, and those who were not dressed in clean clothes were not admitted to the banquet. Here the implication is unmistakable: the festal garment is repentance.[71] Put it on the day before your death, the day before the Deluge breaks, put it on today! The demand of the crisis is conversion. But there is another interpretation of the metaphor of the Wedding-Garment which stems from the Old Testament, and it is clear from the general tenor of Jesus' teaching that he had the second interpretation in mind. We read in Isa. 61.10 (a chapter to which Jesus attached special importance: Matt. 5.3 f.; 11.5 par. Luke 7.22, see pp. 115 f.; Luke 4.18 f. see pp. 116 f., 218, n. 49):

---

[69] See pp. 48–63.

[70] The parallel in Midr. Qoh. 9.8 ascribes the parable to R. Jehuda I (died, 217). But, as W. Bacher, *Agada der Tannaiten*, I₂, Strassburg, 1903, p. 36, n. 1, rightly insists, R. Meir (c. 150) was already familiar with it; so R. Johanan ben Zakkai as indicated in b. Shab. 153a is to be preferred as the author.

[71] The parallel in Midr. Qoh. 9.8 interprets the white garment as the fulfilment of the commandments, good works, and the study of the Torah. This does not differ materially, but is the rabbinical commentary on the word 'repentance'.

'He hath clothed me with the garments of salvation,
he hath covered me with the robe of righteousness,
as a bridegroom decketh himself with a garland,
and as a bride adorneth herself with her jewels.'

God clothes the redeemed with the wedding-garment of salvation. The Apocalyptic literature frequently speaks of this apparel. Eth. En. 62.15 f. describes the 'Glorious Robe' with which 'the Righteous and the Elect' shall be invested, as follows:

'And this shall be your clothing:
a garment of Life from the Lord of Spirits.
Your clothing shall not grow old,
and your dominion shall not pass away from before the Lord of
Spirits.'[72]

Repeatedly does the Apocalypse speak of the eschatological clothing as the white garment (3.4, 5, 18), the royal robe of fine linen (19.8), which God will give. *Pistis Sophia* 8[73] says: 'Rejoice and exult and let joy be added to joy, for the times are fulfilled for me to put on my garment (ἔνδυμα) which was prepared for me from the beginning.'

In all these passages the white robe, or the garment of Life and Glory, is a symbol of the righteousness awarded by God (cf. esp. Isa. 61.10), and to be clothed with this garment is a symbol of membership of the redeemed community. It may be remembered that Jesus spoke of the Messianic Age as a new garment (Mark 2.21 par. see pp. 117 f.), and that he compared forgiveness with the best robe with which the father clothed the prodigal son (Luke 15.22, see p. 130); hence we cannot doubt that it is this comparison that underlies Matt. 22.11–13. God offers you the clean garment of forgiveness and imputed righteousness. Put it on, one day before the Flood arrives, one day before the inspection of the wedding-guests— today!

What Jesus meant by conversion has been emphasized for us repeatedly by J. Schniewind,[74] it is the trimmed lamp and the wedding-garment (Matt. 5.16), it is the face anointed with oil (6.17),

[72] Cf. also Slav.En. 9 (ed. A. Vaillant, *Le Livre des Secrets d'Hénoch*, Paris, 1952, p. 24.15 ff.): 'And the Lord said to Michael: take Enoch and remove from him his earthly clothing, and anoint him with the best oil, and put on him glorious garments.'

[73] Ed. C. Schmidt, *Koptisch-gnostische Schriften*, I, Leipzig, 1905, p. 9, 27–29.

[74] E.g., *Das Gleichnis vom verlorenen Sohn*, Göttingen, 1940, pp. 8 f., reprinted in *Die Freude der Busse*, Göttingen, 1956, pp. 40 f.

it is music and dancing (Luke 15.25), because it means joy—the joy of the child returning home, the joy of God rejoicing over the returning one more than over the ninety-nine righteous persons. But the return home is only genuine when it brings about a renewal of life. The first step on the homeward journey is *'to become again* [75] *like little children'* (Matt. 18.3). [76] The point of comparison for 'like little children' is a well-known problem, and many interpretations have been offered. But in any case it must be regarded as certain that by 'children' we are to understand 'little' children; this is how the Gospel of Thomas 22 takes it: 'These little (children) who are being suckled are like those who enter the Kingdom.' We must disregard such interpretations as spring from Western ways of thinking, and are unsupported by oriental, and especially by Biblical, usage. For example, the child is ready to receive, the child is naturally humble, [77] and so forth. This leaves us with three possible interpretations. First, it is a well-established usage in Jewish baptismal terminology to compare the proselyte to a 'new-born child', because in baptism God has forgiven him his sins. [78] Here the child, that is, the very young child, is a type of purity. In Matt. 18.3, then, the comparison would have the meaning: 'If you do not become clean (through God's forgiveness) like (new-born) children, you will not be allowed to enter [79] the Kingdom of God.' A second, more probable interpretation, is put forward by Matthew in the context. He explains the phrase 'to become again like a child' by: ταπεινοῦν ἑαυτόν (Matt. 18.4); 'to humble oneself' is the act of confession of guilt, [80] self-abasement before God; thus we

---

[75] Ἐὰν μὴ στραφῆτε καὶ γένησθε ὡς τὰ παιδία ... Στρέφεσθαι can hardly mean here 'to be converted', since the word only rarely has this meaning (in the N.T. only in John 12.40). The more usual word for 'to be converted' is ἐπιστρέφειν. Hence it may be assumed that στρέφεσθαι in our passage is a rendering of the Aram. *tubh*, *ḥᵃzar*, with the meaning 'again'. (Cf. P. Joüon in *Recherches de science religieuse*, 18 (1928), pp. 347 f.)

[76] Matt. 18.3 is more strongly coloured by Semitic linguistic usage than the parallels in Mark 10.15; Luke 18.17; John 3.3, 5 (cf. J. Jeremias, *Infant Baptism in the First Four Centuries*, London, 1960, p. 52, n. 1) and therefore to be regarded as the most ancient version of the logion.

[77] T. W. Manson, *Sayings*, p. 207: 'There is no parallel in rabbinical literature to the idea that the child is the type of humility.'

[78] Examples in J. Jeremias, ibid., pp. 32 ff.; E. Sjöberg, 'Wiedergeburt und Neuschöpfung im palästinischen Judentum', in *Studia Theologica*, 4 (1950), pp. 44–85.

[79] Εἰσέλθητε: the underlying Aramaic imperfect has a modal force ('can'), and avoids the passive (literally: 'you will not be entering').

[80] Ταπεινοῦν ἑαυτόν=Heb. *hišpil 'aṣmo*=Aram. *'ašpel garmeh*='to confess one's guilt' (A. Schlatter, *Der Evangelist Matthäus*, Stuttgart, 1929, p. 545).

find in Matt. 18.4: 'Whoso humbles himself (before God), (so as to become) like this child.'[81] In this interpretation the force of the comparison with the child lies in the littleness of the child, and 'to become again like a child' means 'to become little again', that is, before God. But comparison of Matt. 18.3 with the Marcan and Lucan parallels shows that the logion was originally transmitted in isolation; only in a later stage of the tradition was v. 4 (perhaps an altered form of Matt. 23.12b) set in its present context. Hence we must attempt a third interpretation of 'to become again like a child'. Jesus' use of the word *Abba* (Mark 14.36) in addressing God is unparalleled in the whole of Jewish literature.[82] The explanation of this striking fact is to be found in the fact that it was an everyday family word, which no one had ventured to use in addressing God. Jesus did so. He spoke to his heavenly Father in as childlike, trustful, and intimate a way as a little child to its father.[83] Here probably we have the key to Matt. 18.3:[84] children can say *Abba*. 'If you do not learn to say Abba, you cannot enter the Kingdom of God.' In favour of this interpretation of 'to become again like a child' are its simplicity, and the fact that it is rooted in the heart of the gospel. Thus the first step in conversion and the new life is learning how to call God *Abba* with child-like confidence, safe under his protection, and conscious of his boundless love.

But it is surely necessary to recognize that to become again like a little child, as we find it in Matt. 18.4, involves the confession of guilt (cf. Luke 15.18), humiliation, self-abasement, and becoming little again before God. That is what Jesus had in mind in the παραβολή *about the Choice of Places at the Table* (Luke 14.7–11 par. Matt. 20.28 D it syᶜ). In Aramaic this logion, transmitted in two versions, has the form of a 'rhythmic couplet' in antithetic parallelism.[85] Both versions, exhibiting agreement in content and structure, together

---

[81] With ὡς τὸ παιδίον τοῦτο (Matt. 18.4) compare ὡς παιδίον (Mark 10.15; Luke 18.17), 'as if he were a child'.

[82] J. Jeremias, 'Characteristics of the *ipsissima vox Jesu*', in: *The Prayers of Jesus*, London, 1967, pp. 108–12. Cf. Bill., I, pp. 393 f., 410; II, pp. 49 f.; among the material there collected concerning the modes of address to God as Father, Abba is not to be found. This surely represents an original utterance of Jesus.

[83] The central significance of *Abba* as a title for God and an address to God is described in detail in: J. Jeremias, 'Abba', in *The Prayers of Jesus*, London, 1967, pp. 11–65.

[84] T. W. Manson, *Teaching*, p. 331.

[85] M. Black, *An Aramaic Approach to the Gospels and Acts₃*, Oxford, 1967, p. 174.

with completely different wording, provide a classical example of translation variants in the NT (see above, pp. 25 f.). Γάμοι (Luke 14.8) corresponding to δειπνῆσαι (Matt. 20.28 D), has the general meaning of 'banquet'.[86] The most important guests, who are distinguished by reason of age or social standing,[87] usually arrive last. The humiliated guest is obliged to take the lowest place, since all the intermediate places have already been occupied. The exhortation to take the lowest place voluntarily has its Old Testament equivalent in Prov. 25.6 f.: 'Glorify not thyself in the presence of the king, and stand not in the place of great men: for better it is that it be said unto thee, Come up hither; than that thou shouldest be put lower in the presence of the prince'; in rabbinical literature a similar saying is attributed to R. Simeon ben Azzai (c. AD 110);[88] its closest parallel occurs in Mark 12.39 par. Luke 20.46, where Jesus sternly rebukes the scribes for the greedy way in which they choose the most honourable places at table. Jesus therefore is actually giving a direction for table-manners, and the word παραβολή should be so translated.[89] With regard to the question of what the concluding sentence in v. 11 (ὅτι πᾶς ὁ ὑψῶν ἑαυτὸν ταπεινωθήσεται, καὶ ὁ ταπεινῶν ἑαυτὸν ὑψωθήσεται) implies, it may first of all be conjectured that we have here a secondary generalizing conclusion (see above, pp. 110 f.). But of decisive weight against this conjecture is that the rabbinic parallel just mentioned concludes with a saying of Hillel's (c. 20 BC) of quite similar content: 'My abasement is my exaltation, and my exaltation is my abasement.' From this we may infer that v. 11 is an ancient proverb which Jesus found already in use, and which was also in rabbinical literature associated with a direction concerning table-manners. The question is only whether the concluding sentence had the same meaning for Jesus as for Hillel. For the latter it is a piece of practical wisdom: 'Pride will have a fall; humility will be rewarded.' Is Luke 14.11 similarly intended to be a piece of practical wisdom, a rule of social etiquette? Surely not! The comparison with 14.11, as well as with Luke 14.14b,[90] with 18.14, and with Matt. 23.12 shows that Luke 14.11 is speaking of God's eschatological activity, the humbling of the

---

[86] See p. 26.
[87] T. W. Manson, *Sayings*, p. 278.
[88] Lev. r. 1.5 (see p. 107).
[89] See p. 20.
[90] Both Luke 14.8-11 and 12-14 are arranged in antithetic parallelism with an eschatological conclusion.

proud and the exaltation of the humble in the Last Day.[91] Hence the direction in Luke 14.11 about the desirability of modest behaviour in a guest becomes the introduction to an 'eschatological warning',[92] which looks forward to the heavenly banquet, and is a call to renounce self-righteous pretensions and to self-abasement before God.

In the same way the *simile of the Servant's Reward* in Luke 17.7–10 is a demand for renunciation of all Pharisaic self-righteousness. It is not certain whether the saying was originally addressed to the disciples (as its present context suggests, but which is marked by strong Lucan colouring):[93] since it is doubtful whether the company of the ἀπόστολοι (17.5) included farmers who possessed fields, cattle, and slaves, as is presupposed by Jesus in the case of those whom he is addressing even the farmer who is the subject of the simile could only afford one slave to whom it fell to do both the fieldwork and the housework. Hence, since the use of the expression τίς ἐξ ὑμῶν (17.7) generally introduces sayings addressed to the opponents or to the crowd,[94] it may be assumed that the same holds good for this parable. 'Can you imagine',[95] says Jesus, 'that any of you would say to his slave when the latter came in from ploughing or tending the cattle, "Be quick, and sit down to your supper"? Would he not be more likely to say, "Get my supper ready, gird yourself (see p. 187, n. 66) and wait on me till I have finished my meal; afterwards you can have your own supper"? Will he thank his slave when he has carried out his orders? So should you, when you have done all that God commanded you,[96] think,[97] "We are just poor[98] slaves, we have only[99] done our duty".' We have done nothing to merit God's approbation, and all our good works give us no claim upon him.

But conversion goes further; it is expressed in acts, renunciation of sins, refusal to serve two masters (Matt. 6.24; Luke 16.13; Gospel

[91] The passives in Luke 14.11 are thus a circumlocution for the divine name, and the future tenses refer to the Last Judgement.
[92] M. Dibelius, *Die Formgeschichte des Evangeliums*₂, Tübingen, 1933, p. 249.
[93] Luke 17.5: οἱ ἀπόστολοι, προστιθέναι; 17.6: εἶπεν δέ.
[94] See p. 103.
[95] See above, p. 158.
[96] Πάντα τὰ διαταχθέντα: the passive is a periphrasis for the divine name, cf. W. Pesch, *Der Lohngedanke in der Lehre Jesu*, München, 1955, p. 21, n. 59.
[97] λέγειν='to think' (cf. Matt. 9.3 par.; 14.26). Semitic has no exact equivalent for our word 'think'.
[98] Ἀχρεῖος here does not mean 'useless', but 'miserable'. The servants do not say that the fulfilment of their duty is worthless, nor that they themselves are lazy and negligent, but ἀχρεῖος is an expression of modesty.
[99] See p. 39, n. 59.

of Thomas 47a),[1] obedience to God's command (Luke 16.29–31), obedience to the word of Jesus. Just as the man who carries a load places the yoke upon his neck and shoulders, so that the load may be taken by the chains or cords at each end of the yoke,[2] so should Jesus' disciples take their Master's yoke upon their shoulders to lighten the load;[3] Jesus' burden is lighter than that which formerly lay upon their shoulders (Matt. 11.28–30). Everything depends on action; that is the message of the *parable of the Two Houses* (Matt. 7.24–27; Luke 6.47–49). As the torrential autumn rains,[4] accompanied by a storm,[5] test the foundation of the houses, so will the sudden irruption of the Deluge put your lives to the test. The Sermon on the Mount closes with the Final Judgement! Who will survive it? The φρόνιμος, i.e. the man who has recognized the eschatological situation.[6] The scripture said that only the house built upon the sure foundation-stone laid in Zion, will abide the onset of the Flood (Isa. 28.15): 'He who believeth will not flee' (Isa. 28.16). The contemporaries of Jesus taught that the man who knows the Torah and obeys it, cannot be moved.[7] Jesus takes them back to the Scriptures, but he gives a new answer to the question, drawn from his own profound consciousness of authority: 'Whosoever hears my words and obeys them.' Merely hearing the word of Jesus may lead to perdition,[8] everything depends on obedience.

But the obedience required must be complete. The door of the festal chamber which is to be the scene of the banquet of salvation, is a narrow one; he who wishes to gain admittance must strive for it while there is still time; many will seek to enter, but will not put

---

[1] It was not unusual that a slave should have to serve two masters (e.g., Acts 16.16, 19), especially when brothers left an estate undivided after their father's death.

[2] For this interpretation of ζυγός (Matt. 11.29) I am indebted to K. Bornhäuser. Cf. Isa. 10.27: 'His burden shall depart from off thy shoulder, and his yoke from off thy neck'; 14.25.

[3] To take up the yoke of Jesus means actually becoming one of his followers.

[4] Thus Matthew. Luke changes the simile and thinks of a river overflowing its banks, an unlikely occurrence in Palestine.

[5] G. Dalman, *Arbeit und Sitte in Palästina*, I, Gütersloh, 1928, p. 188; in Palestine heavy rain is always accompanied by a storm.

[6] See p. 46, n. 83.

[7] Bill., I, pp. 469 f.

[8] Ἦν ἡ πτῶσις αὐτοῦ μεγάλη (Matt. 7.27) is a proverbial expression, cf. μέγα πτῶμα πίπτειν (Philo, *mut. nom.* 7.55; *ebriet.* 38.156; *migr. Abr.* 13.80). It means a complete collapse (L. Haefeli, *Sprichwörter und Redensarten aus der Zeit Christi*, Lucerne (1934), p. 40).

forth the necessary effort (Luke 13.23 f.).[9] It is particularly hard for the rich, the brutal rich of the East, of whom Jesus is thinking when he says that it is easier for a camel (the largest animal known in Palestine)[10] to go through the eye of a needle than for a rich man to enter the Kingdom of God (Mark 10.25 par.).[11] For Jesus assumes on the part of his followers a readiness to make a complete surrender. The eschatological crisis demands a complete break with the past, even, if necessary, from one's nearest relations (Luke 14.26 f. par.). This is the implication of the metaphor of dead left to bury their own dead (Matt. 8.21 f.; Luke 9.59 f.), and of the ploughman who must only look straight ahead of him.

The very light Palestinian plough is guided with one hand.[12] This one hand, generally the left,[13] must at the same time keep the plough upright, regulate its depth by pressure, and lift it over the rocks and stones in its path.[14] The ploughman uses the other hand to drive the unruly oxen [15] with a goad about two yards long, fitted with an iron spike.[16] At the same time he must continually look between the hindquarters of the oxen, keeping the furrow in sight. This primitive kind of plough needs dexterity and concentrated attention. If the ploughman looks round, the new furrow becomes crooked. Thus, whoever wishes to follow Jesus must be resolved to break every link with the past, and fix his eye only on the coming Kingdom of God.

[9] In this logion Matthew lays the emphasis on the point that if the disciples wish to be saved they must have the courage to cut themselves off from the mass of their people, and tread the *via dolorosa* of the little flock (7.13 f.). Luke has preserved the setting of the logion. Some nameless person asked the question: 'Lord, are there only (see p. 39, n. 59) a few who will be saved?' Jesus replied with the exhortation to strive earnestly, because many will lack perseverance (13.23 f.). It is a summons to become a follower, where the emphasis is laid wholly on the high stake demanded.

[10] Cf. Matt. 23.24, where, in the contrasted pair, camel and gnat, the contrast is drawn between the largest and the smallest creature of the Palestinian environment.

[11] The poorly supported reading κάμιλος, 'ship's cable' (instead of κάμηλος, 'camel') would be appropriate to the simile of the needle's eye. But against it is the rabbinically attested proverb: 'You clearly come from Pumbeditha, where an elephant (the largest animal known in Mesopotamia) can go through the eye of a needle' (b.B.M. 38b).

[12] E. F. F. Bishop, *Jesus of Palestine*, London, 1955, pp. 93 f.

[13] G. Dalman, *Arbeit und Sitte*, II, Gütersloh, 1932, ill. 25, 28, 31, 34, 35, 36, 38, 39.

[14] Ibid., p. 78.

[15] Oxen were generally used to draw the plough, cf. Luke 14.19 and on this see p. 177.

[16] Acts 26.14.

Jesus repeatedly discourages the enthusiast by reminding him of the
difficulties of discipleship: this is the object of the saying in Matt.
10.37 f. par. Luke 14.26 f., of the simile which illustrates the home-
lessness of the Son of Man (Matt. 8.19 f.; Luke 9.57; Gospel of Thomas
86, here without introduction), and of the agraphon about Fire
preserved in the Gospel of Thomas (82), and in Origen:[17]

> 'He who is near me,
>   Is near the fire;
> He who is far from me,
>   Is far from the Kingdom.'

To be near Jesus is dangerous. It offers no prospect of earthly happi-
ness, but involves the fire of tribulation and the test of suffering. But
it must indeed be borne in upon every one who, yielding to fear,
turns away from the call of Jesus, that he excludes himself from the
Kingdom of God. Only through fire may the Kingdom be at-
tained.[18] In the same way as these discouraging sayings, the *parable
of the 'Tower'-builder*, and *of the King contemplating a Campaign*,
is a call to self-testing (Luke 14.28–32). By the lesser example of the
farmer whose unfinished farm buildings[19] make him an object of
ridicule, and the more important case of the king who, in planning
a campaign, has underestimated the strength of his enemy, and must
therefore submit to his terms of peace,[20] Jesus drives home the exhortation: Do not act without mature consideration,[21] for a thing
half-done is worse than a thing never begun.

Included with these two parables in virtue of its content is the
parable of the Assassin in the Gospel of Thomas 98, a parable which
draws upon the stern reality of the Zealot movement:[22] 'Jesus said:
The Kingdom of the Father is like a man who wished to kill a powerful
man. He drew the sword in his house and stuck it into the wall, in

[17] Origen, *In Jerem. hom. lat.* 3.3. Origen only quotes the first half in *In lib.
Jesu Nave hom.*, 4.3.
[18] J. Jeremias, *Unknown Sayings of Jesus*₂, London, 1964, pp. 66–68.
[19] Πύργος means (1) 'tower' (2) 'farm buildings'. The emphasis on the high cost
of the foundation suggests a larger building (B. T. D. Smith, p. 220).
[20] Ἐρωτᾷ τὰ πρὸς εἰρήνην=Heb. *ša'al b°šalom*=Aram. *š°'el biš°lam* 'to greet the
opponent, do him homage, surrender unconditionally' (cf. W. Foerster in
ThWBNT, II, p. 410. 22 ff.).
[21] See p. 112, n. 91.
[22] See above, pp. 74 f.

order to know whether his hand would carry through: then he slew the powerful man.' Just as this political assassin first makes trial of his strength before he embarks on his dangerous venture, so should you test yourselves to see whether you have strength to carry the adventure through.[23]

The *parable of the Return of the Unclean Spirit* (Matt. 12.43–45b;[24] Luke 11.24–26) contains the same warning. Both the language and the content of the parable are unmistakably Palestinian. V. 43: An 'unclean spirit' is a Jewish synonym for 'demon';[25] ἐξέλθῃ is an Aramaism (avoidance of the passive), and should be rendered: 'when a demon has been driven out'. In the desert, the natural abode of demons,[26] he finds no rest since he can only be satisfied where he can wreak destruction. V. 44: The comparison of a possessed person to the 'house' of a demon is still common in the East.[27] The house is 'empty, swept, and garnished', i.e. prepared for the ceremonious reception of a guest. V. 45: 'He taketh with him seven other demons': his victim is an easy prey! Seven is the number of totality; the seven evil spirits represent every form of demonic seduction and wickedness.

The parable presents one great difficulty: it seems to depict the relapse, without reservation, as a universal fact of experience. But in that case Jesus' expulsion of demons would have been meaningless! The difficulty disappears if we recognize [28] that v. 44b is really,

---

[23] C.-H. Hunzinger, 'Unbekannte Gleichnisse Jesu aus dem Thomas-Evangelium' in *BZNW*, 26, Berlin, 1960, pp. 209-20, points out that the four parables introduced by τίς ἐξ ὑμῶν (Luke 15.4 ff., 8 ff. [the second time only τίς is repeated]; 11.5 ff., 11 ff.), appeal to the audience to draw a conclusion concerning God's way of acting. Since Luke 14.28–30, 31 f. also begin with τίς ἐξ ὑμῶν (the second time only τίς is repeated), he suggests that the two parables of the tower-builder and the king planning a campaign, as well as the parable of the Assassin, are to be interpreted accordingly: as an appeal to be confident. If men so carefully test their preparedness, how much more does God do so. He leaves nothing half prepared. 'What God has begun, he carries through' (p. 216). But in the parable it is not a question of successfully carrying to completion a plan that was not left half prepared, but an assertion that the assassin, before putting his intention into execution, assures himself that his hand is strong enough. This cannot apply to God (cf. E. Haenchen, *Die Botschaft des Thomas-Evangeliums*, Berlin, 1961, p. 60, n. 85).

[24] On Matt. 12.45c, see p. 106.

[25] T. W. Manson, *Sayings*, p. 87.

[26] Tob. 8.3; Matt. 4.1 ff. par.; Mark 5.1 ff.

[27] P. Joüon, *L'Évangile de Notre-Seigneur Jésus-Christ*, Paris, 1930, p. 83.

[28] H. S. Nyberg, 'Zum grammatischen Verständnis von Matt. 12.44 f.', in *Arbeiten und Mitteilungen aus dem neutestamentlichen Seminar zu Uppsala*, IV (1936), pp. 22–35, and A. Fridrichsen, 'Nachträge', ibid., pp. 44 f.

in Semitic grammatical construction, a conditional sentence,[29] and should be translated: 'If he (the demon) on his return finds the house empty, swept, and garnished, then he takes with him seven other spirits, more wicked than himself, and they enter in and dwell there, and the last state of that man is worse than the first' (Matt. 12.44b–45a). Hence the relapse is not something predetermined and inevitable, but something for which the man himself is responsible. The house must not remain empty when the spirit hostile to God has been expelled. A new master must reign there, the word of Jesus must be its rule of life, and the joy of the Kingdom of God must pervade it. It must become a κατοικητήριον τοῦ θεοῦ ἐν πνεύματι (Eph. 2.22).[30]

7. REALIZED DISCIPLESHIP

This part of our subject must be introduced by the *twin parables of the Treasure in the Field* (Matt. 13.44; Gospel of Thomas 109) and *the Pearl* (Matt. 13.45 f.; Gospel of Thomas 76). They are closely connected, but will have been spoken on different occasions (see above, p. 90).

The completely distorted version of the parable of the Treasure in the Field in the Gospel of Thomas is given on p. 32. V. 44: A parable with a datival introduction (see above, pp. 100 ff.): 'This is the case with the Kingdom of God.' Θησαυρῷ κεκρυμμένῳ: Jesus will have thought of a jar containing silver coins or jewels. The many invasions which had swept over Palestine in the course of centuries as the result of her position between Mesopotamia and Egypt, had repeatedly caused the burial of valuables in view of the threat of danger.[31] Hidden treasure is a favourite theme in oriental folklore; one is reminded of the copper scroll from Qumran. Ἐν τῷ ἀγρῷ: on the article see p. 11, n. 2. Ὃν εὑρὼν ἄνθρωπος: The man is evidently a poor day-labourer; his ox (as in j. Hor. 3.48a) sinks into a hole while ploughing. Ἔκρυψεν: Semitic speech has no compounds, and hence does not express the repeating of an action where we should feel it

---

[29] The Gospels furnish abundant examples of such a substitution of parataxis for a conditional sentence. Closest to our passage are Matt. 8.9b; Mark 4.13. For good examples see Beyer, op. cit. (above, p. 154, n. 9), pp. 259–86.

[30] T. W. Manson, *Sayings*, p. 88.

[31] S. H. Hooke, *Alpha and Omega*, London, 1961, p. 178.

necessary,[32] hence we should render, 'he hid it again' (sc. 'and said nothing about it to anyone'). By so doing he achieved a double purpose: the treasure remained part of the field, and its safety was secured (burying was considered one of the best forms of security against theft, see p. 61, n. 51). The morality of his action is not under consideration. Nevertheless it is worth noting that his action was formally legitimate, as he had first bought the field.[33] The historical present tenses, ὑπάγει, πωλεῖ, ἀγοράζει, show that the traditional form of the parable is earlier than Matthew.[34]

In the Gospel of Thomas 76 the parable of the Pearl runs as follows: 'Jesus said: the Kingdom of the Father is like a man, a merchant, who possessed merchandise and found a pearl. That merchant was prudent. He sold the merchandise, he bought the one pearl for himself.' Matt. 13.45: Πάλιν ὁμοία ἐστίν: another parable with a datival introduction (see above, pp. 100 ff.), but this time with an aorist. Ἐμπόρῳ: the ἔμπορος is (in contrast with the κάπηλος, 'a shopkeeper') a wholesale trader, a big businessman. Ζητοῦντι καλοὺς μαργαρίτας: the Gospel of Thomas has instead: 'who possessed merchandise' (φορτίον), leaving open the question of what his merchandise was (Acts 27.10 uses φορτίον merely to denote the ship's cargo). If Matthew makes the merchant a dealer in pearls, that is surely a secondary feature, since it anticipates the element of surprise. Pearls were highly prized throughout the whole period of antiquity. They were fished for especially in the Red Sea, the Persian Gulf, and the Indian Ocean, by divers, and used for adornment, especially as necklaces.[35] We hear of pearls worth millions. Caesar presented the mother of his subsequent murderer Brutus with a pearl worth 6 million sesterces (=£150,000 to £200,000).[36] Cleopatra is said to have possessed a pearl worth 100 million sesterces (=£2½ million).[37] V. 46: Ἔνα (πολύτιμον μαργαρίτην) is, as so often, a literal rendering of the Aramaic ḥadh, which should be properly be rendered by τινά; hence

[32] Cf. Matt. 21.3 (ἀποστελεῖ, 'he will send them back at once'); Luke 13.27 (ἐρεῖ λέγων, 'he will repeat'); 18.5 (ἐρχομένη='returning', see p. 154); 19.13 (ἐν ᾧ ἔρχομαι, 'until I return'). See also ἡ παρουσία (Matt. 24.37, 39) = 'the return'. he

[33] The clearest instance is Midr. Cant. 4.12 (see above, p. 32); similarly Mek. Ex. on 14.5 (treasure which is found by the purchaser of a piece of land when he is digging on it belongs to him). The decisive legal ruling is to be found in Kidd. 1.5: movable effects are included in the purchase of property. Cf. J. Dauvillier, 'Le parabole du trésor et les droits orientaux', in: Revue Internationale des Droits de l'Antiquité, 3ᵉ série, 4 (1957), pp. 1071–5.

[34] Matthew tries to avoid the historic present; in the Marcan material taken over by him, he has removed it in 88 instances out of 110 (J. C. Hawkins, Horae Synopticae₂, Oxford, 1909, pp. 144–149). Luke has gone even further in this direction (see pp. 182 f.). [35] F. Hauck in ThWBNT, IV, pp. 475 f.

[36] Suetonius, De vita Caesarum, 50. [37] Plinius, Hist. nat., IX, 119 ff.

it is not: 'the one precious pearl', but, 'a specially valuable pearl;[38] thus it is understood by the Gospel of Thomas ('he found a pearl'). Πέπρακεν πάντα ὅσα εἶχεν: again the Gospel of Thomas has the original: 'he sold the merchandise'. This is the only way in which it fits the situation. Matthew has heightened the meaning under the influence of 13.44.[39]

The difference between the method of discovery in each case (v. 44 the labourer comes upon the treasure in the field unexpectedly, while in v. 45 the pearl is found after long and toilsome search) is irrelevant, since the merchant was not an expert in pearls. In both parables the discovery is a surprise; the doubling of the parable is not concerned with the manner of the discovery, but with the contrast between poor and rich.

Both parables make use of a favourite theme in oriental story-telling.[40] The audience expected that the story of the treasure in the field would be about a splendid palace which the finder built, or a train of slaves with whom he promenades through the bazaar (see p. 32), or about the decision of a wise judge that the son of the finder should marry the daughter of the owner of the field.[41] In the story of the pearl it would expect to hear that its discovery was the reward of special piety, or that the pearl would save the life of a merchant who had fallen into the hands of robbers.[42] Jesus, as always, surprises his audience by treating the well-known stories (pp. 178 ff., 183, 188) in such a way as to emphasize an aspect quite unexpected by his hearers. The question is, what aspect?

The double parable is generally understood as expressing the demand of Jesus for complete self-surrender. In reality, it is 'completely misunderstood if it is interpreted as an imperious call to heroic action.'[43] The key-words are rather ἀπὸ τῆς χαρᾶς (v. 44; they are not expressly repeated in the case of the merchant, but they

<hr/>

[38] Cf. Matt. 6.27 (not, 'one single cubit', but, as par. Luke 12.25 shows, 'as much as a cubit', cf. p.171); 19.16 (εἷς par. Luke 18.18 τὶς); 26.69 (μία par. Luke 22.56 τὶς); 27.48 (εἷς par. Mark 15.36 τὶς). Additional examples: Matt. 5.18; 8.19; 9.18; 12.11; 16.14 (par. Luke 9.19 τὶς); 18.6, 24, 28; 20.13; 21.19, 24; 22.35; 23.15; 25.40, 45; 26.51; 27.15; Mark 5.22; 6.15 (cf. Luke 9.8); 8.28 (cf. Luke 9.19); 9.17, 42; 10.17 (cf. Luke 18.18); 11.29; 12.28, 42 (cf. Luke 21.2); 13.1; 14.66; 15.6; Luke 5.3; 15.4, 15; 16.17; 17.2, 15. In most of these passages, εἷς, μία, ἕν render an Aramaic ḥadh used as an indefinite article.
[39] C.-H. Hunzinger, op. cit., p. 220.
[40] E. Hirsch, Frühgeschichte des Evangeliums, II, Tübingen, 1941, p. 315.
[41] Bill., I, p. 674.
[42] Ibid., p. 675.
[43] E. G. Gulin, Die Freude im N.T., I, Helsinki, 1932, p. 37.

apply to him as well). When that great joy, surpassing all measure, seizes a man, it carries him away, penetrates his inmost being, subjugates his mind. All else seems valueless compared with that surpassing worth. No price is too great to pay. The unreserved surrender of what is most valuable becomes a matter of course. The decisive thing in the twin parable is not what the two men give up, but the reason for their doing so; the overwhelming experience of the splendour of their discovery. Thus it is with the Kingdom of God. The effect of the joyful news is overpowering; it fills the heart with gladness; it makes life's whole aim the consummation of the divine community and produces the most whole-hearted self-sacrifice.[44]

The same thought [45] also finds expression in the *parable of the Great Fish*, preserved in the Gospel of Thomas 8: 'And he said: The Kingdom [46] is like a wise fisherman who cast his net into the sea and drew it up from the sea: (it was) full of small fish. Among them he found a large (and) good fish, that wise fisherman. He threw all the small fish (back) down into the sea and chose the large fish without hesitation. Whoever has ears to hear let him hear.'

The catch varies. When the fisherman throws his casting-net into the shallow water by the bank, weighted with lead round the edge, it falls into the water like a bell. The net often remains empty several times running. A modern observer counted twenty to twenty-five fish in one catch.[47] In the parable, when the fisherman drew his net to the shore (cf. p. 225) he found a great number of small fish in it, but among them one fine large fish. Although he might have hesitated about keeping a few of the small fish in his bag, yet in his joy over the καλλιχθύς [48] he cast aside all such hesitations and threw all the small fish back into the lake. Thus it is when a man is overwhelmed with joy over the glad Good News; all else becomes valueless compared with this surpassing value.[49]

What is the quality of a life which has been overmastered by this great joy? It is to follow Jesus. Its characteristic is the love whose pattern is to be found in the Lord who has become a servant (Luke

[44] Gulin, ibid., pp. 37–40. Cf. Luke 7.36 ff.; 19.1 ff.
[45] C.-H. Hunzinger, op. cit., pp. 217–20.
[46] See above, p. 101, n. 56.
[47] K.-E. Wilken, *Biblisches Erleben im Heiligen Land*, I, Lahr-Dinglingen (Baden), 1953, p. 192.
[48] Thus Clem. Alex., *Strom.*, I, 16.3 with reference to our parable.
[49] Cf. J. Jeremias, *Unknown Sayings of Jesus*₂, London, 1964, pp. 88–90.

22.27; Mark 10.45; John 13.15 f.). Such a love finds its expression in silent giving with no sounding of a trumpet (Matt. 6.2); it does not lay up treasure on earth, but it entrusts its possessions to God's faithful hands.[50] It is a boundless love, such as is depicted by the *parable of the Good Samaritan* (Luke 10.25-37).

Vv. 25-28: The usual view that the introductory verses 25-28 are simply a parallel to the question about the greatest commandment (Mark 12.28-34 par. Matt. 22.34-40) has recently been challenged on weighty grounds.[51] In fact, the only connection is the doubled command to love; all the rest is completely different, and it is quite probable that Jesus often uttered so important a thought as that contained in the double command. We have already seen (p. 115) that the statement 'great teachers constantly repeat themselves'[52] is true of Jesus. If the conjecture be accepted that the scribe, in repeating the double command to love, was quoting a saying of Jesus, his θέλων δικαιῶσαι ἑαυτόν (v. 29) becomes intelligible; he is excusing himself for asking Jesus, although he knows what Jesus thinks.

V. 25: That a learned theologian should ask a layman about the way to eternal life, was just as unusual then as it would be today. The probable explanation is that the man had been disturbed in conscience by Jesus' preaching. V. 28: When Jesus surprisingly tells him that action was the way to life (τοῦτο ποίει καὶ ζήσῃ), his direction must be understood as arising out of the actual situation: the enquirer's theological knowledge is of no avail if his life is not governed by love to God and his 'friend'.[53] V. 29: The counter-question as to what the scripture meant by the term 'friend' was justifiable, since the answer was in dispute. It was generally agreed that the term connoted fellow-countrymen, including full proselytes, but there was disagreement about the exceptions: the Pharisees were inclined to exclude non-Pharisees ('*am ha'areṣ*);[54] the Essenes required that a man 'should hate all the sons of darkness';[55] a rabbinical saying ruled that heretics, informers, and renegades 'should be

---

[50] Matt. 6.19-21; Luke 12.33 f. It is not a question of contrasting earthly with heavenly treasure, but of the place where the treasure is stored.

[51] T. W. Manson, *Sayings*, pp. 259 f.

[52] Ibid., p. 260.

[53] The import of the story is obscured if πλησίον (=*reaʿ*) in Luke 10.29 is translated 'neighbour'. The Christian conception of the 'neighbour' is not the starting-point of the story, but that which the story was intended to create.

[54] Bill., II, pp. 515 ff.

[55] IQS 1.10, cf. 9.16, 21 f.; 10.21.

pushed (into the ditch) and not pulled out',[56] and a wide-spread popular saying excepted personal enemies ('You have heard that God[57] said: You shall love your fellow-countryman; but[58] you need[59] not love[60] your enemy',[61] Matt. 5.43). Hence Jesus was not being asked for a definition of the term 'friend', but for an indication as to where, within the community, the limits of the duty of loving were to be drawn. How far does my responsibility extend? That is the meaning of the question. V. 30: The story embodying the answer has, at least in its local setting, probably arisen out of an actual occurrence.[62] Λῃσταῖς περιέπεσεν: the lonely descent from Jerusalem to Jericho, seventeen miles long, is still notorious for robberies.[63] Πληγὰς ἐπιθέντες: the wounds (v. 34) suggest that the victim had defended himself.[64] Vv. 31 f.: the question has been raised whether Jesus really intended to describe the priest and the Levite as callous and cowardly, and whether it is not more probable that he had in mind the Sadducean prescription which strictly forbade a priest to defile himself with 'a dead man by the way' (meth miṣwa).[65] It must then be supposed that the priest and the Levite regarded the unconscious man (10.30: ἡμιθανῆ) as dead, and avoided contact with him on Levitical grounds. This interpretation deserves careful consideration. It must however be recognized that it involves difficulties. Although, according to the text of Lev. 21.1 ff., the priest, even in everyday life, was forbidden to touch a corpse (with the exception of his nearest blood-relations), the Levite was only required to observe ritual cleanliness in the course of his cultic activities. If the Levite, like the priest in Luke 10.31, was journeying from Jerusalem

[56] b. 'A.Z. 26a (Bar.), cf. Abh.R.Nathan 16.7.
[57] Ἐρρέθη is the passive used as a circumlocution for the divine name.
[58] See p. 39, n. 59.
[59] In Aramaic the imperfect generally has a modal force; here it is permissive, cf. Matt. 7.4 (πῶς ἐρεῖς='how can you say?').
[60] Μισεῖν as the antithesis of ἀγαπᾶν in Semitic very often means 'to love less' (Matt. 6.24; further, compare Luke 14.26 with Matt. 10.37), or 'not to love' (Rom. 9.13), thus too Matt. 5.43.
[61] Luke 6.27 f. shows that ἐχθρός means a personal enemy.
[62] M. Meinertz, Die Gleichnisse Jesu₄, Münster, 1948, p. 64; E. F. F. Bishop, Jesus of Palestine, London, 1955, p. 173.
[63] K. Dannenbauer has given an account of a dramatic and alarming experience on the road between 'Ain Fara and Jerusalem in Der Bote aus Zion, 70 (1955), pp. 15–21.
[64] K. H. Rengstorf, Das Evangelium nach Lukas (NTD 3)₉, Göttingen, 1962, p. 140.
[65] J. Mann, 'Jesus and the Sadducean Priests, Luke 10.25–37', in Jewish Quarterly Review, N.S. 6 (1915–16), pp. 415–22. The Pharisees held otherwise.

to Jericho, there would be nothing to prevent him from touching 'a dead body by the road'. It must thus be assumed that if he were actuated by ritual considerations he was on his way to Jerusalem to perform his official duties. The passage (v. 32) does not exclude this assumption. But another difficulty then arises: the weekly detachments of priests, levites, and laymen who ran the temple service, used to travel up to Jerusalem in closed groups. Had the levite in the parable been delayed? Was he one of the head levites who served permanently in the temple? In short, it is difficult to regard the levite as governed by ritual considerations. V. 33: According to the triadic form of popular stories,[66] the audience would now have expected a third character, namely, after the priest and the Levite, an Israelite layman; they would hence have expected the parable to have an anti-clerical point.[67] It would have been completely unexpected and disconcerting for them to hear that the third character, who fulfilled the duty of love, was a Samaritan. The relations between the Jews and the mixed peoples, which had undergone considerable fluctuations, had become very much worse in the time of Jesus, after the Samaritans, between AD 6 and 9 at midnight, during a Passover, had defiled the Temple court by strewing dead men's bones;[68] as a result irreconcilable hostility existed between the two parties.[69] Hence it is clear that Jesus had intentionally chosen an extreme example; by comparing the failure of the ministers of God with the unselfishness of the hated Samaritan, his hearers should be able to measure the absolute and unlimited nature of the duty of love. V. 34: Κατέδησεν τὰ τραύματα αὐτοῦ: he would hardly have had a bandage with him, and would probably have used his head-cloth,[70] or torn up his linen undergarment. Ἔλαιον καὶ οἶνον: the oil would mollify (Isa. 1.6), the wine would disinfect [71] (one would expect the reverse order). Ἐπὶ τὸ ἴδιον κτῆνος: if the word ἴδιον does not simply represent the possess. pro. ἑαυτοῦ, it would have to be assumed that the man was a merchant who carried his wares on an ass or mule, and rode a second beast himself.[72] That the man was a merchant who often travelled on that

---

[66] Matt. 25.14–30 par.; Luke 14.18–20; 20.10–12.
[67] B. T. D. Smith, p. 180.
[68] Josephus, *Ant.*, 18.30.
[69] J. Jeremias, *Jerusalem in the Time of Jesus*, London, 1969, pp. 352–8.
[70] Thus E. F. F. Bishop, *Jesus of Palestine*, London, 1955, p. 172.
[71] Ibid.
[72] Ibid.

road is borne out by his acquaintance with the πανδοχεύς and by his promise of a speedy return. V. 35: Δύο δηνάρια: the cost of a day's board would be about one-twelfth of a denarius.[73] Ἐγὼ ἀποδώσω σοι is a binding formula for taking over debts.[74] V. 36: A much-debated subject is the form which Jesus' question took—Which of these three, thinkest thou, proved neighbour to him that fell among the robbers? While the scribe's question (v. 29) concerned the object of the love (Whom must I treat as a friend?), Jesus in v. 36, asks about the subject of the love (Who acted as a friend?). The scribe is thinking of himself, when he asks: What is the limit of my responsibility? (v. 29). Jesus says to him: Think of the sufferer, put yourself in his place, consider, Who needs help from me? (v. 36). Then you will see that love's demand knows no limit. Yet it is necessary here to be on one's guard against eisegesis. The alteration in the form of the question hardly conceals a deeper meaning. It is simply a formal inconsistency in which there is nothing surprising when once the philological facts are realized: the word *reaʿ* implies a reciprocal relation, like our word 'comrade'. When a man calls anyone his comrade, he assumes the responsibility to treat him as a comrade.[75] Thus both Jesus and the scribe are after the same thing: they are not seeking a definition, but the extent of the conception *reaʿ*: the only difference between them is that the scribe is looking at the matter from a theoretical point of view, while Jesus illuminates the question with a practical example. V. 37a: Ὁ ποιήσας τὸ ἔλεος μετʼ αὐτοῦ: he avoids using the hateful term Samaritan (*kuthi*). V. 37b repeats v. 28 with emphasis.

In this parable Jesus tells his questioner that while the 'friend' is certainly, in the first place, his fellow-countryman, yet the meaning of the term is not limited to that. The example of the despised half-breed was intended to teach him that no human being was beyond the range of his charity. The law of love called him to be ready at any time to give his life for another's need.

The boundless nature of love also finds expression in the fact that, following Jesus' example, it turns towards the very people who are

[73] J. Jeremias, *Jerusalem in the Time of Jesus*, London, 1969, p. 122.
[74] b.B.B. 174a, cf. J. D. M. Derrett, 'Law in the New Testament', in: *NTS*, 11 (1964/65), pp. 22–37, here pp. 29 f.
[75] B. Gerhardsson, 'The Good Samaritan—the Good Shepherd?', in *Coniectanea Neotestamentica*, XVI, Lund-Copenhagen, 1958, p. 7, in agreement with J. Lindblom and R. Gyllenberg.

206   THE MESSAGE OF THE PARABLES OF JESUS

significant (Matt. 18.10). The value which Jesus sets upon love to the
needy and afflicted, comes out in the *description of the Sentence pronounced at the Last Judgement* (Matt. 25.31–46).[77]

V. 31: Δόξα, ἄγγελοι αὐτοῦ, θρόνος δόξης αὐτοῦ (without article =
construct) are attributes of the Son of Man (Eth. En.). The Messianic royal throne stands in Zion. (The striking alternation between ὁ υἱὸς τοῦ ἀνθρώπου v. 31 and ὁ βασιλεύς [vv. 34 and 40] may
be due to the stylization of the introduction by Matthew, since it is
closely connected with Matt. 16.27, and the session of the Son of
Man on the royal throne only occurs in Matt. 25.31; 19.28.) V. 32:
Συναχθήσονται: συνάγειν is a shepherd's technical term;[78] the passive
use implies the divine action, which is here carried out by the
angels (cf. Mark 13.27; Matt. 24.31). The gathering of the scattered
flock is a feature of the Messianic Age (cf. John 10.16; 11.52).
Πάντα τὰ ἔθνη: that the passage which follows describes the judgement of the nations of the world is clearly shown by the word πάντα
and is confirmed by the description of an analogous situation in
'A.Z. 2a.[79] Ἀφορίσει: this is also a shepherd's technical term.
The Redeemer is the Shepherd (see p. 121). Ὥσπερ ὁ ποιμὴν ἀφορίζει
τὰ πρόβατα ἀπὸ τῶν ἐρίφων: the Palestinian shepherd does not separate sheep from rams (i.e. the females from the males), but sheep
from goats. In Palestine mixed flocks are customary; in the evening
the shepherd separates the sheep from the goats,[80] since the goats
need to be kept warm at night, for cold harms them, while the sheep
prefer open air at night.[81] V. 33: Ἐκ δεξιῶν: the sheep are the more
valuable animals;[82] moreover their white colour (in distinction from
the black of the goats) makes them a symbol of the righteous. The
separation constitutes the final judgement. All that comes after v. 34
describes the promulgation of the sentence. V. 34: The pre-existence
of the Kingdom emphasizes the certainty of the promise. Vv. 35 f.:
poor and despised (Luke 14.12–14),[76] helpless (Mark 9.37), and in-

---

[76] The exact opposite of the proverb quoted by Philo (*De spec. leg.*, I, 12.242):
'the rank of the guests reflects distinction on the host', meaning that one should
invite distinguished guests by preference.
[77] The whole pericope is a *mašal*, 'an apocalyptic revelation' (like the *mᵉšalim*
[Eth. *mesal*] of the Eth. Enoch, erroneously called 'Similitudes', see p. 16, n. 22);
mašal = 'comparison' is only the simile of the separation of the flock, vv. 32 f.
[78] J. Jeremias, *Jesus' Promise to the Nations*₂, London, 1967, p. 64.
[79] Bill., IV, pp. 1203 f.
[80] The present ἀφορίζει (v. 32b) shows that we have to do with a regular customary procedure.
[81] G. Dalman, *Arbeit und Sitte in Palästina*, VI, Gütersloh, 1939, p. 99.
[82] Ibid., pp. 99, 217.

Concerning the works of love in the New Testament, cf. *ZNW*, 35 (1936), pp. 77 f.; a list of six are given as examples, not intended to be exhaustive. With regard to the third work: Συνάγειν (absolute), meaning 'to entertain hospitably', is translation Greek; it is a rendering of the Aramaic *k·nas*, which means (1) to gather, (2) to show hospitality.[83] With regard to the fifth work of love: the sick are poor people, neglected, for whom no one cares. The sixth work to be mentioned, the visitation of prisoners, does not occur in Jewish lists of good works. Vv. 37–39: the passage is, like 7.22, a protest against the sentence which has been pronounced; they cannot understand it; they do not know when they can have shown love to the king. V. 40 gives them the explanation. It is a question of the acts of love which they have shown, not to Jesus personally,[84] but to his brethren, and through them to himself. Cf. Mid. Tan. on Deut. 15.9, where God says to Israel: 'My children, when you gave food to the poor I counted it as though you had given it to me'; in Matt. 25.31 ff. Jesus is God's representative. Ἐνὶ (=τινὶ[85]) τούτων τῶν ἀδελφῶν μου τῶν ἐλαχίστων = any one (not one particular one) of the least of my brethren: comparison with v. 45 shows that the 'brethren' in this passage are not the disciples, but all the afflicted and needy. The τούτων (vv. 40, 45) seemingly suggesting the contrary, is in fact a superfluous demonstrative.[86] Moreover, to limit the ἀδελφοί to the disciples in view of v. 32 (πάντα τὰ ἔθνη) would be to assume a world-wide mission to the remotest nations, a conception which does not correspond with the outlook of Jesus.[87] For the early occurrence, especially in Matthew, of the Christianizing of the word ἀδελφός, see p. 109, n. 82. V. 41: Τὸ πῦρ τὸ αἰώνιον is the Gehenna in the Hinnom Valley below the Temple mountain. V. 44 is (like vv. 37–39) an objection to the sentence. They have never seen the king in distress so that their help was called for. V. 45: Ἐνὶ τούτων: see on v. 40. Their guilt does not lie in the commission of gross sins, but in the omission of good deeds (cf. Luke 16.19–31). With regard to the question of authenticity, certain late features emerge: (1) The representation of Christ as Judge (v. 32) does not belong to the oldest stratum of tradition (according to this he is a witness at the Last Judgement, cf. Matt. 10.32 f.; Mark 8.38; Luke 9.26; 12.8 f.). But is Christ actually thought of as Judge? It is not a trial that is described, but only the

[83] C. C. Torrey, *The Four Gospels*, London, 1933, p. 296.
[84] E. Klostermann, *Das Matthäusevangelium₂*, Tübingen, 1927, in loc.
[85] See p. 200, n. 38.
[86] On this Semitism, cf. p. 39, n. 61.
[87] See pp. 64 f.

pronouncement of a sentence, and according to v. 34 (οἱ εὐλογημένοι τοῦ πατρός μου) Christ announces the judgement of the Father.[88] (2) Nowhere else in the Synoptic Gospels does Jesus designate himself as king (vv. 34–40); nevertheless we should compare Mark 15.2 par.; John 18.37; moreover, it should be noticed that the Messianic consciousness of Jesus included awareness of his kingship. It may be conjectured that the twice repeated ὁ βασιλεύς is a pre-Matthaean interpretation of the Messiahship for non-Jews, cf. Acts 17.7. (3) Διάβολος belongs to a later stratum of tradition than σατανᾶς.[89] None of these remarks, however, affects the substance of Matt. 25.31–46; they only indicate editorial working-over of the material in the course of transmission, as is proved also by the presence of certain Matthaean linguistic characteristics (τότε vv. 31, 34, 37, 41, 44 f.; ἐπὶ θρόνου δόξης αὐτοῦ v. 31; τοῦ πατρός μου v. 34 et al.).[90] But (4) there are Egyptian [91] and rabbinic [92] parallels which must be considered in relation to the substance of our passage. These similarly lay down the principle that works of mercy will be the decisive factor in the Judgement. But what a difference! Both in the Egyptian Book of the Dead and in the Midrash the dead man boasts self-confidently of his good deeds ('I have given satisfaction to God by doing that in which he delights: I have given bread to the hungry, water to the thirsty, clothed the naked . . .'; thus speaks the Egyptian Book of the Dead).[93] How differently sounds the surprised question of the righteous in vv. 37–39 of our passage, who are unconscious of having rendered any service, to say nothing of the conception that in the persons of the poor and wretched, men are confronted by the hidden Messiah. But it is this very conception which is attested as a characteristic of Jesus' preaching and as belonging to the early tradition by such sayings as we find in Mark 9.37, 41.[94] Our pericope, although

[88] Cf. T. W. Manson, *Sayings*, p. 250.
[89] See p. 81, n. 49.
[90] Further comment in J. A. T. Robinson, 'The "Parable" of the Sheep and the Goats' in *Twelve New Testament Studies*, London, 1962, pp. 76 ff.
[91] E. Klostermann, *Das Matthäusevangelium₂*, Tübingen, 1927, pp. 205 f., acc. to H. Gressmann, *Altorientalische Texte und Bilder*, I₂, Berlin, 1926, p. 188.
[92] Midr. Ps. 118, §17 (Bill., IV, p. 1212).
[93] See above, n. 91.
[94] Mark 9.41: ἐν ὀνόματί μου='for my sake'; the subsequent words: ὅτι Χριστοῦ (anarthrous, therefore late) ἐστε are an explanation, for Greek speaking people, of the Semitism ἐν ὀνόματί μου. The recipient of the cup of cold water was originally designated as 'one of the little ones', as is shown both by the parallel in Matt. 10.42 and by Mark 9.42 (in a catchword-connection), just as in Matt. 25.40, 45 and similarly with the redundant demonstrative τούτων (see above, p. 39, n. 61).

it may not be authentic in every detail, contains, in fact, 'features of such startling originality that it is difficult to credit them to anyone but the Master himself'.[95]

Matt. 25.31–46 is concerned with a wholly concrete question, namely, by what criterion will the heathen (v. 32) be judged? Jesus had always clearly distinguished between present and eschatological justification. In the present time he mediates[96] God's forgiveness and release from the great debt to home-coming sinners, to the lost and despairing, to 'God's beggars' (Matt. 5.3). On the other hand, he promises God's justification at the Last Judgement to the company of disciples when they should have been proved worthy by open confession of him (Matt. 10.32 f. par.) and obedience (Matt. 7.21, 22 f. par.), by readiness to forgive (Matt. 6.14 f.) and merciful love (Matt. 5.7)[97] and by endurance to the end (Mark 13.13 par.); at the Last Judgement God will look for faith that has been lived out. But even this justification for such faith remains simply an act of God's free grace, and has nothing to do with desert; the guilt is too great for that. Perhaps, as the result of such a saying as that in Matt. 10.32 f., where Jesus says that he will intercede at the Last Judgement for those of his disciples who have confessed him before men, the question might have been asked, 'By what criterion, then, will the heathen who have never known you be judged? Are they lost?' (for such was the general contemporary opinion). The gist of Jesus' reply is: 'The heathen have met me in my brethren; for the needy[98] are my brethren; he who has shown love to them has shown it to me, the Saviour of the poor. Therefore, at the Last Judgement, the heathen will be examined concerning the acts of love which they have shown to me in the form of the afflicted, and they will be granted the grace of a share in the Kingdom, if they have fulfilled Messiah's law (James 2.8), the duty of love'.[99] Thus for them justification is available on the ground of love, since for them also the ransom

[95] T. W. Manson, *Sayings*, p. 249.

[96] Jesus is the intermediary of the forgiveness; in the same way, for instance, in Mark 2.5 it is ultimately God who forgives. Hence Jesus says (the passive being used as a circumlocution for the divine name): 'My son, God forgives your sins.'

[97] Ἐλεηθήσονται: the future is eschatological, and the passive represents the divine name: 'God will be merciful to them (at the Last Judgement).'

[98] See above on v. 40.

[99] Cf. b.B.B. 10b (Bar.): 'Rabban Joḥanan ben Zakkai (contemporary with the Apostles) said to them: As the sin-offering atones for Israel, so almsgiving (sᵉdhaqa) atones for the Gentiles.'

has been paid (Mark 10.45: ἀντὶ πολλῶν, see p. 220, n. 62).[1]

But the deepest secret of this love which characterizes realized discipleship is that they have learnt how to forgive. They extend to others the divine forgiveness which they have experienced, a forgiveness which passes all understanding. The *parable of the Unmerciful Servant* is concerned with this (Matt. 18.23–35).

On the context, see p. 97. V. 23: We have here a parable with datival introduction ('it is the case with the (coming of the) Kingdom of God');[2] the breaking in of the Kingdom of God is again compared to an accounting.[3] Βασιλεύς: see p. 28, n. 17. Μετὰ τῶν δούλων αὐτοῦ: In the Bible and in the East 'the king's servants' is the term for his higher officials.[4] V. 24: 'There was brought to him one (εἷς = ḥadh = τὶς)[5] who owed him 10,000 talents', i.e. 100 million denarii.[6] The magnitude of the sum shows that the 'servant' is to be thought of as a satrap who was responsible for the revenue from his province (cf. below on v. 31); we know, for example, that in Ptolemaic Egypt the treasury officials were personally responsible for the whole revenue of their province;[7] but even so, the sum exceeds any actual situation;[8] it can only be explained if we realize that both μύρια and τάλαντα are the highest magnitudes in use (10,000 is the highest number used in reckoning,[9] and the talent is the largest currency unit in the whole of the Near East). The magnitude of a debt beyond conception

---

[1] It is striking to observe how Jesus' 'doctrine of justification' corresponds with Pauline doctrine even in details. Paul also distinguishes between the justification bestowed in baptism (I Cor. 6.11; Rom. 6.7), by faith alone (Rome. 3.28, cf. p. 39, n. 59), and the justification at the Last Judgement by faith working through love (Gal. 5.6). And Paul also knows of a justification of the Gentiles at the Last Judgement, if they have fulfilled the νόμος ἄγραφος (Rom. 2.12–16).

[2] See pp. 100 ff.

[3] Cf. p. 136, n. 18. Strictly speaking, the pardon in v. 27 corresponds to the present phase which leads up to the Kingdom, and only the judgement pronounced in v. 34 applies to the Last Judgement.

[4] J. Wellhausen, *Das Evangelium Matthaei*, Berlin, 1904, p. 95.

[5] See pp. 199 f.

[6] The value of the talent fluctuated. We have taken the valuation of Josephus as a basis; he estimates the value of 1 talent at 10,000 denarii. (Cf. *Ant.*, 17.323 with 190.)

[7] R. Sugranyes de Franch, *Études sur le droit palestinien a l'époque évangélique*, Fribourg, 1946, pp. 39 ff., provides an excellent analysis of the legal conditions implied in Matt. 18.23–35. He points out that analogies are not to be sought in Palestine, but in the Mediterranean lands, especially in Egypt; but he goes on to conjecture, which is the weakness of his book, that these conditions may also hold good in Palestine.

[8] For a comparative estimate, see pp. 27 f.

[9] Luke 12.1; I Cor. 4.15; 14.19.

was intended to heighten the impression made upon the audience by its contrast with the trifling debt of 100 denarii (v. 28). The interpretation is implicit in the parable: behind the king we see God, behind the debtor, the man who was allowed to hear the message of forgiveness. Προσηνέχθη: the passive indicates that the debtor is brought out of prison.[10] V. 25: 'Εκέλευσεν . . . πραθῆναι: first his lands and house property are to be sold. Αὐτόν . . . καὶ τὴν γυναῖκα: Jewish law only permitted the sale of an Israelite in case of theft, if the thief could not restore what he had stolen; the sale of a wife was absolutely forbidden under Jewish jurisdiction;[11] hence the king and his 'servants' are represented as Gentiles. Καὶ τὰ τέκνα: a rabbinical parable describes how the king caused the sons and daughters of his debtor to be sold, 'hence it was clear that nothing more remained in his possession';[12] which means that children are the last thing that a man has to sell. Does the sale of the family make sense? Since the average value of a slave was about 500 to 2,000 denarii,[13] the amount realized from the sale of the family bore no relation whatever to the monstrous debt of 100 million denarii. Hence the king's order in v. 25 must be understood in the main as an expression of his wrath. V. 26: Πεσὼν οὖν ὁ δοῦλος προσεκύνει αὐτῷ λέγων: His prostration, by which he indicates that he throws himself wholly on his lord's mercy, is the most urgent form of plea there is. 'Αποδώσω: he promises to work off the debt. V. 27: Τὸ δάνειον: ='the loan'. That does not make sense here. The Syriac versions (sy[sin cur pal pesh]) render τὸ δάνειον by *ḥwbt'* ='the debt'. We may suppose that this word was used in the Aramaic form of our parable and then too narrowly translated by τὸ δάνειον. 'The King's mercy far exceeds the plea of his servant.'[14] V. 28: Εὗρεν, *sc.* 'in the street'. "Ενα (=τινὰ [15]) τῶν συνδούλων αὐτοῦ: one of his subordinate officials (see on v. 31). 'Εκατὸν δηνάρια, *sc.* 'only'[16] (a Semitism). "Επνιγεν: cf. B.B. 10.8: 'If any one seizes another (who

---

[10] Both προσηνέχθη and the *v.l.* προσήχθη (BD) indicate the compulsory nature of his appearance (cf. W. Bauer, *Wörterbuch zum N.T.*₅, Berlin, 1958, col. 1427, 1410). Cf. also v. 27: 'He set him free.'

[11] Soṭa 3.8; Tos. Soṭa 2.9 (Bill., I, p. 798).

[12] Sifr. Dt. 26 on 3.23 (P. Fiebig, *Rabbinische Gleichnisse*, Leipzig, 1929, p. 10; Bill., I, p. 798).

[13] b. Qid. 18a (Bar.): 500–1000 denarii; B.Q. 4.5 gives 10,000 as the highest price; Jos., *Ant.*, 2.33 gives 20 minas=2,000 denarii as the price of Joseph (Gen. 37.28). Cf. J. Jeremias, *Jerusalem in the Time of Jesus*, London, 1969, p. 347.

[14] M. Doerne, *Er kommt auch noch heute*₄, Berlin, 1955, p. 149.

[15] See pp. 199 f.

[16] See p. 39, n. 59.

owes him money) by the throat on the street.' 'Ἀπόδος εἴ τι ὀφείλεις: of course εἴ τι does not imply a doubt ('if'); it is a translation of *ma dh*•='what'. The purpose of *manus iniectio* is to render impossible any attempt of the debtor to escape.[17] If he does not pay on the spot, he will be thrown into prison, or an order issued for his arrest (cf. Matt. 5.25 f.). V. 29: he is a minor official for whom the payment of even a small sum will be difficult. His plea for remission of the debt is literally identical (except for πάντα, v. 26) with that of the debtor himself; there is, however, this difference between the two: the promise in v. 26 is impossible of fulfilment, while that in v. 29 can be fulfilled. V. 30: Εἰς φυλακήν: the sale of the debtor (as in v. 25) does not come into question in this case, since (at least according to Jewish law,[18] which certainly held good elsewhere) it was only permissible when the debt exceeded the amount which would accrue from the sale of the debtor, and this would not be the case where the debt was not more than 100 dinars. In such a case, therefore, in Levantine countries,[19] a writ of attachment was enforced, in order that the debtor should work off the debt, or that his relations should set him free by paying his debt. In Jewish law such a personal attachment of the debtor was unknown (see p. 180). V. 31: οἱ σύνδουλοι: the expression only occurs in the LXX in II Esdr.=Ezra 4.7, 9, 17, 23; 5.3, 6; 6.6, 13 and there denotes high officials under the governors of Palestine and Syria. Thus the idea is confirmed that the 'servants' are not common slaves. Ἐλυπήθησαν as in LXX Neh. 5.6; Jonah 4.4, 9: 'they were shocked'.[20] Διεσάφησαν: this is the usual term for the report of an inferior to a superior, 'to report'. V. 32: for the historic pres. (λέγει), see p. 199, n. 34. V. 34: τοῖς βασανισταῖς: The punishment of torture was not allowed in Israel. It is again evident (see v. 25, 30) that non-Palestinian conditions are described here, unless the parable is referring to Herod the Great, who made abundant use of torture, heedless of Jewish law—but could he have been credited with the generosity of v. 27? Torture was regularly employed in the East against a disloyal governor, or one who was tardy in his delivery of the taxes, in order to discover where they had hidden the money, or to extort the amount from their relations or friends.[21] The non-Jewish practice in

[17] Jülicher, II, p. 307.
[18] Mech. Exod. 22.2, cf. Bill., IV, pp. 700 f.
[19] R. Sugranyes de Franch (see p. 210, n. 7), pp. 113 ff. §18: *La prison pour dettes*.
[20] T. W. Manson, *Sayings*, p. 214.
[21] J. Wellhausen, *Das Evangelium Matthaei*, Berlin, 1904, p. 95. On the 'Great Commandment' to set the prisoners free, cf. Bill., IV, pp. 568, 572 f.

legal proceedings, regarded by the Jews as inhumane (see p. 180 on Matt. 5.25), is drawn upon to intensify the frightfulness of the punishment. Ἕως οὗ ἀποδῷ πᾶν τὸ ὀφειλόμενον, in view of the magnitude of the debt, can only mean that the punishment would be endless; once more (see on v. 24) the parable implies its interpretation. V. 35: 'So likewise will your heavenly Father do to you, if ye forgive not one another [22] ἀπὸ τῶν καρδιῶν ὑμῶν'. Forgiveness from the heart is here contrasted with a forgiveness that is only with the lips (cf. Matt. 15.8 =Isa. 29.13). Everything depends on the genuineness of the forgiveness.

This is a parable about the Last Judgement; it combines an exhortation with a warning: 'God has extended to you in the gospel, through the offer of forgiveness, a merciful gift beyond conceiving,[23] but God will revoke the forgiveness of sin if you do not wholeheartedly share the forgiveness you have experienced, but harden your heart against your brother.[24] Everything is here at stake. Woe unto you if you try to stand on your rights; God will then stand on his and see that his sentence is executed rigorously.' As elsewhere,[25] Jesus makes use of the Jewish doctrine of the two measures,[26] but he completely transforms it. (It is not fortuitous that there are no Jewish parallels to our parable.) Jewish apocalyptic taught that God rules the world by the two measures of Mercy and Judgement; but at the last Judgement he only makes use of the measure of Judgement. 'And the Most High shall be revealed upon the throne of Judgement: and then cometh the End, and compassion shall pass away, and pity be far off, and long-suffering withdrawn; but Judgement alone shall remain.'[27] On the other hand, Jesus taught that the measure of Mercy is in force at the Last Judgement also. The decisive question is: When does God at the

---

[22] See p. 109.

[23] E. Linnemann, *Parables of Jesus*, London, 1966, p. 78 says: 'The idea of the bestowal of forgiveness on the disciples by Jesus is a belief of the early church, but cannot be assumed for Jesus.' Misconceptions such as these are bound to arise if one sticks to the concordance (*s.v.* ἀφιέναι) and disregards the fact that Jesus, unlike Paul, prefers to express himself, not in the language of theology, but by similes, parables, parabolic actions, in short, in the established language of symbols.

[24] See p. 109.

[25] Matt. 7.1–2 par. Luke 6.37 f.; Matt. 6.14 f.; James 2.12 f.; cf. Matt. 5.7; 25.31 ff.

[26] For the doctrine of the two measures, cf. K. Bornhäuser, *Die Bergpredigt*, Gütersloh, 1923, pp. 161 ff.; Bill., IV, p. 1247, index, s.v. Mass.

[27] IV Ezra 7.33, cf. 7.74, 105; Sib. 5.353, 510; Syr. Bar. 48.27, 29; 85.8–15. Eth. En. 38.6: 'thenceforward (after the last term of repentance has elapsed) none

Last Judgement use the measure of Mercy, and when the measure of Judgement? Jesus answers: 'Where God's forgiveness produces a readiness to forgive, there God's Mercy grants forgiveness of debts again at the Last Judgement; but he who abuses [28] God's gift, faces the full severity of Judgement, as if he had never received forgiveness' (Mt. 6.14 f.).

A second characteristic of the little flock, which is most strongly emphasized in Jesus' metaphors, is the absolute security of his disciples in God's hands. The simile of the slave and the son in John 8.35 assures them of their inalienable [29] possession of the privileges of sonship in God's family; they now belong to the family of God (Mark 3.31, 35; Gospel of Thomas 99). No more are they like underlings but like the sons of a king (Matt. 17.24 f.). They are clean like one who has been bathed (John 13.10). Their utter security in their Father's care is depicted by Jesus in the incomparable *images of the Birds of Heaven* (Matt. 6.26; Luke 12.24) and *the Flowers of the Field* (Matt. 6.28–30; Luke 12.27 f.). The full measure of the security of which these images speak can only be estimated by realizing their context. Jesus forbids μεριμνᾶν. The word means: (1) to take anxious thought, (2) to put forth an effort. That in Matt. 6.25–34 par. only the second meaning is intended is shown by the interchange of μεριμνᾶν with ζητεῖν[30] and ἐπιζητεῖν,[31] and by Matt. 6.27 par. Luke 12.25, where the meaning 'to take anxious thought' does not make sense; but most of all, it is proved unequivocally by our two metaphors, which do not speak of anxiety, but of effort.[32] Jesus thus forbids his disciples to expend their efforts in pursuit of

---

shall seek for themselves mercy from the Lord of Spirits'; 50.5: 'from henceforth (after the last term of repentance has elapsed) I will have no (more) mercy on them'; 60.5 f.: 'until this day lasted the day of His mercy; and He hath been merciful and long-suffering towards those who dwell on the earth. And when the day, and the power, and the punishment, and the judgement come . . .', then all this will stop (translation according to R. H. Charles, *The Apocrypha and Pseudepigrapha of the Old Testament*, II, Oxford, 1913).

[28] S. H. Hooke, *The Kingdom of God in the Experience of Jesus*, London, 1949, p. 115.

[29] Εἰς τὸν αἰῶνα see p. 86.

[30] Luke 12.29 (cf. with par. Matt. 6.31); Luke 12.31; Matt. 6.33.

[31] Matt. 6.32; Luke 12.30.

[32] As Bornhäuser has rightly seen (see above, n. 26), pp. 150 ff. A. Schlatter agrees with him, *Der Evangelist Matthäus*, Stuttgart, 1929, pp. 225 ff.

food and clothing. How can a prohibition of work be possible? The words with which Jesus forbids his disciples to work, find their true parallel in Mark 6.8, where they form part of his charge as he sends them out on a mission. The field is vast, and the time is short since the testing hour of the final crisis is at hand. The commission demands their utmost from the disciples; hence they must allow nothing to hinder them, not even the exchange of greetings by the way (Luke 10.4b),[33] much less the expenditure of effort for food and clothing. God will give them what they need. Hence what Jesus deprecates is not work, but its duplication. But that, surely, involves the possibility of having no food and nothing to wear, of starving and freezing! Such anxieties find their answer in the two similes of the birds and the flowers, touched by Jesus with a gleam of humour. 'Consider', says he, 'you men of little faith, Brother Raven:[34] does he plough, sow, and reap, and gather his harvest into his barn? and yet God gives him in abundance all that he needs. Consider, too, you men of little faith, Sister Anemone:[35] does she spin or weave?[36] and yet the royal purple pales before the splendour of her attire! You are God's children (Matt. 6.32; Luke 12.30). The Father knows what you need. He will not let you starve!'

They have, he says, a Father who cares for them and, moreover, they have a Master who calls them by name as a shepherd does his sheep (John 10.3),[37] and who prays for them. The great crisis is

---

[33] The Oriental has plenty of leisure, and dislikes haste. For him greetings entailed long conversations. In II Kings 4.29 we have a description of instructions forbidding all customary polite greeting: 'If thou meet any man, salute him not; and if any salute thee, answer him not again'; the utmost haste is enjoined. Jesus has in mind in his prohibition 'the temptation to join a caravan (and so waste time)' (E. F. F. Bishop, *Jesus of Palestine*, London, 1955, p. 170).

[34] In Aramaic birds are masculine, the anemones are feminine. The raven, only mentioned in Luke 12.24, is an unclean bird (Lev. 11.15; Deut. 14.14), yet God cares for 'the young ravens, when they cry unto him' (Ps. 147.9; Job 38.41).

[35] See the previous note.

[36] Probably an Aramaic word-play underlies Matt. 6.28: οὐ κοπιῶσιν ('ᵃmal) οὐδὲ νήθουσιν ('ᵃzal), cf. T. W. Manson, *Sayings*, p. 112.

[37] G. Dalman, *Arbeit und Sitte in Palästina*, VI, Gütersloh, 1939, pp. 250 f., gives numerous examples from modern Palestine. The names are assigned according to shape, colour, and peculiarities, and the names given to the lamb or kid are still borne by the grown animal, being familiar to it from its youth. As far as the owner is concerned, the name is not only a device to call the animal by, but also a sign of ownership.

imminent, to be ushered in by the Passion of Jesus. The power of darkness is about to be revealed in the last horror of the tribulation, from which there is only one way of escape—'Flee, and save your lives' (Mark 13.14 ff.). Even Jesus' disciples will not be spared. Satan, the accuser and destroyer of God's people, has asked permission from God to sift them in the tempest of tribulation as a man separates the chaff from the wheat in a sieve (Luke 22.31 f.).[38] And God has allowed it, it is his will. But Jesus has prayed for Peter, that his faith may hold fast, and that, in the eschatological time of sifting that is at hand, he may again [39] strengthen his brethren. Peter is the leader. In praying for him, Jesus has prayed for them all. His intercession will bring them through, since Christ is stronger than Satan.

A third characteristic of discipleship is that the gift of God and the call of Jesus impel to action. Just as Jesus loves to depict his saving mission under the figure of some special calling,[40] so he does with regard to the task of his disciples. In the story of Peter's call in Mark 1.17, Jesus, using a metaphor drawn from the fisherman's craft, designates him as a future fisher of men. If a scribe becomes a disciple of the Kingdom of God, Jesus compares him to a householder, who brings out of his store (θησαυρός) things old and new, the things he had previously learnt, and his newly acquired knowledge (Matt. 13.52). The harvest is great, but the number of labourers is small (Matt. 9.37; Gospel of Thomas 73).[41] The disciples are sent to the lost sheep of the house of Israel (Matt. 10.6)—presumably as shepherds, for so at least Matt. 18.12–14 understood their function. As the steward appointed by Jesus himself, Peter holds the keys of the Kingdom of God (Matt. 16.19). As proclaimers of the gospel, he and his fellow-disciples have full authority to bind and loose, that is, the authority to proclaim forgiveness, and where the message is rejected,

---

[38] Separation of chaff and wheat symbolizes the Judgement (Matt. 3.12; cf. pp. 224 f.).

[39] Ἐπιστρέψας (here=tubh, haphakh), meaning 'to repeat an action', see above, p. 190, n. 75. The ποτέ which occurs only here in the Synoptics, and which is never elsewhere in the NT related to the future, may be an addition by the Greek translator. It can hardly have been an Aramaic equivalent.

[40] See pp. 121 f.

[41] See p. 119. Cf. P. Abh. 2.15 'Rabbi Tarphon (c. AD 100) said: The day is short, and the task is great, and the labourers are idle, and the wage is abundant, and the master of the house is urgent.'

to announce judgement; hence, as the messengers of Jesus, they have judicial authority (Matt. 18.18; 16.19).[42] The responsibility is immeasurable. The time is short. Weal or woe, salvation or damnation, are at stake for innumerable souls (Matt. 10.12–15; Luke 10.5 f., 10–12). The great and perilous task demands, together with total surrender (see pp. 193 ff.), sincerity and divine-given wisdom. Jesus expresses this in two similes closely related in content: 'Be prudent (φρόνιμοι see p. 46, n. 83) as serpents and without guile as doves' (Matt. 10.16; Gospel of Thomas 39); and 'Have salt (=prudence) in yourselves, and be at peace with one another' (Mark 9.50b).[43] Prudence includes spiritual sobriety, to which the much-quoted agraphon 'Be wise money-changers'[44] is an exhortation. Just as the wise money-changer recognizes a false coin at a glance, so should the disciples of Jesus not be misled by the false prophets in whom the crowd delights.[45] Will they measure up to their task? It is in order that they may do so, that Jesus will not allow his disciples to be depressed in the face of opposition, nor by the consciousness of their own inability. The simile of the city set on a hill (Matt. 5.14b) reads in the Oxyrhynchus Papyrus 1.7 = Gospel of Thomas 32: 'Jesus said: a city which is set on the summit of a high hill, and on a firm foundation, cannot be brought low, nor can it be hidden.' The saying is meant to encourage Jesus' disciples, and preserve them from despondency. They are citizens of the lofty, eschatological city of God (Isa. 2.2–4; Micah 4.1–3),[46] a city which no earthquake, nor hostile onslaught, nor even the Powers of Hell (Matt. 16.18),[47] can shake, and whose light streams through the night, needing no human efforts. Having the gospel, they have all

[42] Credit must be given to A. Schlatter, *Der Evangelist Matthäus*, Stuttgart, 1929, pp. 511 f., for the recognition that 'binding and loosing' applies neither to scholars' authoritative decisions, nor to disciplinary powers (as it might seem to in the light of rabbinical language), but to juridical authority to pronounce acquittal or condemnation. The best illustration is to be seen in Matt. 10.12–15, where Jesus' disciples bring peace and announce judgement.

[43] That salt means prudence is clear (as W. Nauck, 'Salt as a Metaphor' in *Studia Theologica*, 6, 1952, pp. 165–78, has seen) from the comparison with the extracanonical tractate *Derekh 'ereṣ zuta* (A. Tawrogi, *Der talmudische Traktat Derech Erez Sutta*, Königsberg, 1885, p. 1). There it says in the very first words: 'The character of a scholar is humble, gentle, laborious, *salty* (*mᵉmullaḥ*), patient under wrong, beloved by all . . .'. Also cf. above, p. 168: 'saltless' means 'foolish'.

[44] Hom. Clem. 2.51; 3.50; 18.20; Apelles ap. Epiphanium, *Haer.*, 44.2 *et al.*

[45] J. Jeremias, *Unknown Sayings of Jesus₂*, London, 1964, pp. 100–104.

[46] G. v. Rad, 'The City on the Hill', *The Problem of the Hexateuch and other Essays*, London, 1966, pp. 232–42.

[47] Cf. on this passage, *ThWBNT*, VI, pp. 926 f.

they need. If they have faith, even as little as a grain of mustard, the smallest of seeds,[48] nothing will be impossible to them (Matt. 17.20; Luke 17.6).

Of one thing, however, they may be certain. They will not be spared the hate which Jesus has encountered. Jesus has experienced the truth that a prophet has no honour in his own country (Mark 6.4; Matt. 13.57; Luke 4.24; John 4.44; Gospel of Thomas 31a), since the gospel is a cause of offence.[49] The scholar can expect no better fate than this teacher, nor the slave than his master (Matt. 10.24 f.; Luke 6.40; John 15.20). Their mission entails the risk of life itself: Jesus sends them out defenceless, like sheep among wolves (Matt. 10.16; Luke 10.3). Some at least of the disciples must drain the cup of suffering together with Jesus [50] (Mark 10.38 f. cf. Mark 9.1!); for discipleship involves a readiness to lay down one's life,[51] and to bear the cross (Mark 8.34 par.). With regard to the expression 'bear his cross', we generally think of a cross-bearer as one who patiently accepts whatever God sends; but there is no instance of this meaning of αἴρειν τὸν σταυρόν. The word does not even carry the meaning of readiness for martyrdom. Rather does the expression envisage a concrete situation, namely, the moment when the man

---

[48] See p. 148.

[49] Ἐσκανδαλίζοντο in Mark 6.3 implies that the gospel is a stumbling-block, which is confirmed by Luke 4.16–30: there ἐμαρτύρουν αὐτῷ (4.22) must be taken as a dative of disadvantage ('against him'), and the words ἐθαύμαζον ἐπὶ τοῖς λόγοις τῆς χάριτος (4.22) must be understood, with K. Bornhäuser, *Das Wirken des Christus*, Gütersloh, 1921, p. 59, as meaning that the people of Nazareth were surprised that when Jesus read Isa. 61.1–2, he confined himself to the words of mercy, and broke off immediately before the words about the day of vengeance Isa. 61.2. G. Bornkamm has pointed out to me that in Luke 7.22; Matt. 11.5, where Jesus is quoting freely from Isa. 35.5 f. with a suggestion of Isa. 29.18 f. and an insertion from Isa. 61.1 (see above, p. 115 f.) he also omits the announcement of the vengeance of God (35.4); moreover, in Isa. 29 the punishment of the oppressors (v. 20) follows on the opening of the eyes of the blind, and of the ears of the deaf (v. 18) as well as on the joy of the poor (v. 19), just as in Isa. 61 the vengeance of God follows on the good news to the poor (v. 1). This implies that Luke 4.22 is not describing a sudden revulsion of feeling against Jesus on the part of his audience, but rather that they were opposed to Jesus from the start, because his message contradicted their nationalistic expectations. Cf. J. Jeremias, *Jesus' Promise to the Nations*₂, London, 1967, pp. 44–46.

[50] To partake of the cup with anyone means to share their fate, whether good or bad (T. W. Manson in: *Studies in the Gospels* (Lightfoot Festschrift), Oxford, 1955, p. 219, n. 1).

[51] A. Fridrichsen in *Coniectanea Neotestamentica*, II, Uppsala, 1936, pp. 1 ff., 37, has convincingly shown that ἀπαρνεῖσθαι ἑαυτόν in the NT does not mean 'self-denial', but actual 'self-surrender'. It is not a question of self-discipline by 'self-denial', but of an unreserved surrender of one's person.

who has been condemned to crucifixion, with the cross-piece (*patibulum*) laid on his shoulders, must run the gauntlet of the howling, shouting crowd, as it greets him with insults and curses. The anguish of this road lies in the realization of being an unpitied outcast from the community, and exposed defenceless to shame and scorn. Anyone who follows me, says Jesus, must expect a life as hard as the *via dolorosa* of one on the way to the place of execution.[52] But even in death they may be assured that they are in his hand, without whose will not even a sparrow [53] falls to the ground (Matt. 10.29; Luke 12.6). And they may learn from the example of the mother, how the bliss that awaits them will wipe out all memory of suffering (John 16.21 f.).

But however great their sacrifice and their success may be, the greatness of God's gift will keep them humble and guard them from Pharisaic self-righteousness (Luke 17.7–10).

8. THE VIA DOLOROSA AND EXALTATION OF THE SON OF MAN

The confession of Peter marks the great division in the activity of Jesus. After the period of public proclamation followed the period of private teaching concerning the passion and triumph of the Son of Man.[54] Already in his public ministry Jesus had used similes in speaking of his *via dolorosa*. He had no place where to lay his head; homeless, he must forgo even the shelter which birds and foxes enjoy (Matt. 8.20; Luke 9.58; Gospel of Thomas 86)—a simile for his being rejected almost everywhere. From Caesarea Philippi onwards the imminence of the Passion is fully disclosed to the disciples. In this esoteric self-revelation, too, Jesus often made use of metaphors.

[52] A. Fridrichsen, *Gamle spor og nye veier*, Christiania, 1922, p. 30.

[53] A proverbially worthless creature (Bill., I, p. 582). According to Matt. 10.29 two sparrows are worth one farthing; according to the par. in Luke 12.6 five sparrows are worth two farthings; they are cheaper 'by the dozen'. It may be remarked that the negative goes with the verb: ἐν ἐξ αὐτῶν οὐ πεσεῖται ἐπὶ τὴν γῆν. The Semitic idiom does not negate the pronoun; similarly in Matt. 5.18, 36; 24.22; Mark 13.20; Luke 1.37; 11.46.

[54] On the question of the historicity of Jesus' predictions of his passion, cf. W. Zimmerli and J. Jeremias, *The Servant of God*, London, 1957, pp. 58–104. While certain features may certainly have received their formulation after the event, on the other hand, in my judgement, a greater historical probability attaches to the view that Jesus expected a violent death, and that he found the necessity of his passion prefigured in Isa. 53.

He spoke of the cup which he must drink (Mark 10.38; 14.36), and of the baptism which he must undergo (10.38). By dying he would create the redeemed community, for the shepherd must lay down his life for the sheep;[55] he must be smitten with the sword (Mark 14.27; Zech. 13.7), in order that he may bring home the purified flock (Mark 14.28);[56] the stone must be rejected (Mark 8.31: ἀποδο-κιμασθῆναι, cf. 12.10 = Ps.118.22), in order that it may become the top-stone [57] of God's temple, the corn of wheat must die and (we must add)—be raised again by God,[58] in order that it may bring forth the full harvest of God's blessings (John 12.24).[59] Such is the efficacy of the death of Jesus, for it is the vicarious death of the sinless for a sinful, a ransom (Mark 10.45; Matt. 20.28)[60] and a sacrifice (Mark 14.24)[61] for the innumerable host [62] of the lost ones.

But this passion of the Son of Man, which represents the beginning of the final tribulation, is only the prelude to the last great victory of God (see p. 51). After three days Jesus will complete the new Temple, whose foundation and erection were initiated through his earthly ministry (Matt. 16.18), and of which he is himself the chief corner-

[55] K.-E. Wilken, *Biblisches Erleben im Heiligen Land*, II, Lahr-Dinglingen, 1954, p. 162, reports having heard from a shepherd the account of a nocturnal attack of more than thirty hyenas, giving the names of friends who had been killed in the fight.

[56] Mark 14.28 continues the simile of the shepherd (see p. 121, n. 26) and takes up the prediction in Zech. 13.8 f. that after the death of the shepherd the purified flock will reappear.

[57] See p. 73, n. 91.

[58] As frequently happens in oriental usage, John 12.24, in the figure of the grain of wheat, turns our attention only to the initial and final stages of the process when it says: 'if it die, it bringeth forth much fruit'. The important intermediate stage (the resurrection) must be supplied. Further examples of this Semitism may be found on p. 148, n. 75.

[59] John 12.24 is derived from an early pre-Johannine tradition (N. A. Dahl, 'The Parables of Growth' in *Studia Theologica*, 5 (1951), p. 155); evidence for this is to be found in the style (antithetic parallelism; also see n. 60) and the language (ὁ κόκκος with the article, see p. 11, n. 2; πεσώνis a Semitic avoidance of the passive, see p. 140, n. 52; on καρπὸν φέρειν cf. LXX Joel 2.22; Hos. 9.16). Hence no objection can be raised to the genuineness of the saying (cf. Dahl, ibid.). The logion does not merely announce the mystery of Life through Death, but it speaks of the eschatological fulfilment wrought by the dying of the corn of wheat (Dahl, ibid.).

[60] On the questions of authenticity and interpretation of Mark 10.45, see J. Jeremias, 'Das Lösegeld für Viele' in *Judaica*, 3 (1947), pp. 249–64. The figurative use of the symbol of the ransom-price is specifically late-Jewish.

[61] In the words spoken at the Last Supper, Jesus compares himself to the Pass-over lamb, see J. Jeremias, *The Eucharistic Words of Jesus₂*, London, 1966, pp. 222 ff.

[62] On the inclusive significance of πολλοί (=Aramaic *saggi'in*) in Mark 10.45 par.; 14.24 par. cf. *ThWBNT*, VI, pp. 536 ff.

stone (Mark 14.58 par.). As the lightning transforms the darkness into the clear light of day, so will be the *Parousia* of the Son of Man; suddenly and unexpectedly all will be illumined (Matt. 24.27 par. Luke 17.24).[63]

9. THE CONSUMMATION[64]

When Jesus speaks of the consummation he always uses symbols.

God is King, and will be worshipped in a new Temple (Mark 14.58). At his right hand on the throne sits the Son of Man (Mark 14.62), surrounded by the holy angels (Mark 8.38). Homage will be paid to him (Matt. 23.39). As the Good Shepherd he feeds the purified flock (Mark 14.28;[65] Matt. 25.32 f.).

Evil is banished: for the profaned Temple has been destroyed (Mark 13.2), the sinful world has passed away (Matt. 19.28; Luke 17.26-30), the judgement of the dead and the living (Matt. 12.41 f.) has taken place, and the final separation is completed (Matt. 13.30, 48). Satan has been cast out of heaven (Luke 10.18), and together with his angels thrown into eternal fire (Matt. 25.41). Death reigns no longer (Luke 20.36), there is an end of suffering (Matt. 11.5), and sorrow has ceased (cf. Mark 2.19).

Conditions are reversed; what is hidden becomes manifest (Matt. 6.4, 16, 18; 10.26 par.),[66] poor become rich (Luke 6.20), the last are

---

[63] On the Last Judgement see pp. 51-53, 55-63, 166-80, 187-9, 206-214.

[64] Cf. J. Jeremias, *Jesus als Weltvollender*, Gütersloh, 1930, pp. 69 ff.

[65] See p. 121, n. 26.

[66] The logion in Matt. 10.26 which has reached us by a fourfold transmission in the NT has been very differently interpreted by the Evangelists: by Mark (4.22) it is seen as a statement about the preaching of Jesus (the secret of the Kingdom, in 4.11, will become manifest to all); by Luke (12.2) it is regarded either as a warning against the hypocrisy of the Pharisees (cf. 12.1: their hypocrisy will avail them nothing, since what is secret will become manifest), or as a promise relating to the preaching of the disciples (cf. 12.3, also Luke 8.17); in Matthew (10.26) it is the basis for an exhortation to fearlessness (no hostility will be able to frustrate the preaching). Hence the evangelists no longer knew the original meaning of the logion; the same holds good for the two quotations in the Gospel of Thomas (5 and 6). It is only clear that already at an early date (in Matthew, and perhaps also in Luke 12.12) what was originally a prophetic saying had become a word of exhortation. Perhaps it is originally a proverb—everything comes to light. It may be assumed that for Jesus it had an eschatological meaning; the future tense, and the antithetic form of the saying, and the version in Oxyrh. Pap. 2, no. 5 (where there is an added parallel sentence: 'there is nothing buried which shall not be raised'), support this view. Above all it is clear from Matt. 6.4, 6, 18, that Jesus also declared elsewhere that on the Last Day what was hidden would be revealed. Hence, whatever was the particular application, the logion speaks of the eschatological reversal of the situation.

first (Mark 10.31), the small become great (Matt. 18.4), the hungry
are filled (Luke 6.21), the weary find rest (Matt. 11.28), those who
weep laugh (Luke 6.21), the mourners are comforted (Matt. 5.4), the
sick are healed, blind receive their sight, lame walk, lepers are
cleansed, deaf hear (Matt. 11.5), prisoners are freed, the oppressed
relieved (Luke 4.18), the lowly are exalted (Matt. 23.12; Luke 14.11;
18.14), the humble bear rule (Matt. 5.5), the members of the little
flock become kings (Luke 12.32), and the dead live (Matt. 11.5).

Sinners are forgiven (Matt. 6.14), the Servant of the Lord has
paid the ransom for the peoples (Mark 10.45 par.), the pure in heart
see God (Matt. 5.8), the new name is bestowed (v. 9), the heavenly
angelic garb of glory (δόξα) is conferred (Mark 12.25). They have
eternal life (Mark 9.43), they live to God (Luke 20.38).

God recompenses (Luke 14.14), and his great reward is paid
(Matt. 5.12), in measure pressed down, shaken together, and overflowing, it is poured into one's lap [67] (Luke 6.38), the inheritance is
distributed (Matt. 19.29), the treasure laid up in heaven is handed
out (6.20), thrones and positions of authority are bestowed (19.28).

The glorified community stands before the throne of God. Like
Noah and Lot it has been delivered out of destruction (Luke
17.27, 29). The harvest is gathered into everlasting garners (Matt.
13.30), the new Temple is built (Mark 14.58), the scattered elect are
gathered together (Mark 13.27), God's children are at home in their
Father's house (Matt. 5.9), the marriage is celebrated (Mark 2.19).
Fullness of joy after tribulation has begun (John 16.21). They dwell
in everlasting tabernacles (Luke 16.9), the Gentiles pour into the city
on the hill, and feast with the patriarchs (Matt. 8.11) at the table of
the Son of Man (Luke 22.29 f.). For them he breaks the bread of
salvation (Matt. 6.11), hands to them the cup of the wine of the New

[67] Each of these four qualities has its own distinctive character. Even today the
corn merchant tries to attract customers by broadcasting how completely his
measure is filled (T. W. Manson, *Sayings*, p. 56). The measuring of the corn is a
process which is carried out according to an established pattern. The seller
crouches on the ground with the measure between his legs. First of all he fills the
measure three-quarters full and gives it a good shake with a rotatory motion to
make the grains settle down. Then he fills the measure to the top and gives it
another shake. Next he presses the corn together strongly with both hands.
Finally he heaps it into a cone, tapping it carefully to press the grains together;
from time to time he bores a hole in the cone and pours a few more grains into it,
until there is literally no more room for a single grain. In this way the purchaser
is guaranteed an absolutely full measure; it cannot hold more (C. T. Wilson,
Peasant Life in the Holy Land, New York, 1906, p. 212, quoted by E. F. F. Bishop,
Jesus of Palestine, London, 1955, p. 80). Thus, says Jesus, will God's measure be.

Age (Mark 14.25), hunger and thirst are satisfied and the joyous laughter of the Messianic Age resounds (Luke 6.21). The communion between God and man, broken by sin, is restored.

We do not know who the pious enthusiasts were who asked Jesus, presumably by way of a challenge, why he did not establish the pure Messianic community by separation from sinners. It should never have been maintained that the question only became a burning one for the later community;[68] far otherwise.[69] Everywhere in the time of Jesus we meet with attempts to set up the Messianic community. We should first call to mind the Pharisaic movement. The word *pᵉriša*, 'separatist', from which their name is derived, is a synonym for *qaddiša*, 'holy one'. The Pharisees clearly claimed to represent the holy community, the true people of God, as distinct from the mass of the people which, through ignorance of the Law (John 7.49),[70] lay under God's curse. They are waiting for the Messiah who, being himself 'pure from sin', will 'do away with sinners through his powerful word' (Ps. Sol. 17.36 [41]). Then mention must be made of the Essenes (now known to us through their own evidence in the Qumran texts) who even exceeded the Pharisaic attempt to establish the pure community, and endeavoured to form the 'Community of the New Covenant', who emigrated from the city of the 'polluted sanctuary' (CD 4.18), and whose self-designation already indicates that they aspired to be the embodiment of the people of God in the Messianic Age. Finally, reference must be made to John the Baptist, whose entire activity was directed to the gathering of the saved community, and who proclaimed the Messiah as the one who would purge the threshing-floor and separate the chaff from the wheat (Matt. 3.12).

What Jesus actually did was the opposite of all these attempts. He roused the wrath of the religious leaders by declaring war on the Pharisaic community of the holy remnant, and by gathering around him the very people who were cursed because 'they know not the Law' (John 7.49). Among his followers were to be found people who, not only by Pharisaic standards, but by his own admission, had no standing before God. Why, they asked, did he allow this? Why did

[68] E.g. H. J. Holtzmann, *Hand-Commentar zum N.T.*, I, 1, Tübingen-Leipzig 1901, pp. 248 f.
[69] J. Jeremias, 'Der Gedanke des "Heiligen Restes" im Spätjudentum und in der Verkündigung Jesu' in *ZNW*, 42 (1949), pp. 184–94.
[70] J. Jeremias, *Jerusalem in the Time of Jesus*, London, 1969, pp. 266 ff.

he not demand the separation of the pure community from Israel? The indignation roused by Jesus' behaviour was once more the occasion of parabolic teaching. Jesus' reply is contained in the two *parables of the Tares among the Wheat* (Matt. 13.24–30) and *of the Seine-net* (13.47 f.).

These two parables could hardly have been spoken as a pair (see pp. 90 f.), but they are closely linked in content. The secondary [71] representation of the setting in v. 36 should not lead us to regard the parable of the Tares as addressed to the crowd (indicating that separation must await the End), while the parable of the Seine-net is an exhortation to the disciples (Throw out the net, you fishers of men!). For this second interpretation is refuted by the dative introduction (see below on v. 47). The parable of the Tares among the Wheat is given in the Gospel of Thomas 57 as follows: 'Jesus said: The Kingdom of the Father is like a man who had good seed. His enemy came by night and sowed a weed among the good seed. The man did not permit them (= his servants) to pull up the weed. He said to them: Lest perhaps you go to pull up the weed and pull up the wheat with it. For on the day of harvest the weeds will appear (or, come to light). They will pull them and burn them.' It will be seen that the ending is shorter than in Matthew, who, anticipating his allegorical interpretation, may (see pp. 81 ff.) have somewhat over-elaborated the separation of wheat from tares (v. 30). V. 24: Ὡμοιώθη ἡ βασιλεία τῶν οὐρανῶν ἀνθρώπῳ: 'It is with the Kingdom of God as with a man.' The comparison is not with the man, but with the harvest (see pp. 101 f.). Since a similar occurrence is reported from modern Palestine,[72] the parable of the Tares among the Wheat may spring from an actual event. V. 25: ὁ ἐχθρός: the definite article is a Semitism,[73] hence it should be rendered 'an enemy of his' (cf. the absence of the article in v. 28). Ζιζάνια: the poisonous darnel (*lolium temulentum*) is a weed which, botanically, is closely related to bearded wheat, and in the early stages of growth is hard to distinguish from it.[74] V. 26: The darnel shoots up in quantities which far exceed what might normally have been expected. V. 28: 'An enemy must have done this'. Hitherto, then, the whole of the introductory vv. 24–28a are intended simply

[71] See pp. 82 f.
[72] H. Schmidt-P. Kahle, *Volkserzählungen aus Palästina*, I, Göttingen, 1918, p. 32, with a correction by G. Dalman in *Arbeit und Sitte in Palästina*, II, Gütersloh, 1932, p. 308 f.
[73] See p. 11, n. 2.
[74] Dalman, op. cit., p. 249, and illus. 56.

to make it clear that the owner is not to blame for the quantity of tares.[75] The real problem is first stated in the question of the servants (v. 28b), whether they should root out the tares. This second question is by no means a foolish one; it is customary to weed out darnel,[76] even repeatedly.[77] V. 29: The master of the house is of the opinion that the darnel must be left alone,[78] evidently on account of the unusual quantity of it (for the historic present in vv. 28 and 29, see p. 199, n. 34). As a result of the profusion of the tares, their roots have become intertwined with the roots of the wheat. V. 30: τοῖς θερισταῖς: in the time of harvest the reapers are introduced in addition to the previously mentioned servants.[79] Συλλέξατε πρῶτον τὰ ζιζάνια: by the gathering out of the darnel we are not to understand that it was rooted up immediately before the reaping of the grain, but that, as the reaper cut the grain with his sickle, he let the darnel fall, so that it was not gathered into the sheaves.[80] Δήσατε αὐτὰ εἰς δέσμας: The binding of the darnel into bundles is not an unnecessary process; it was evidently dried and used for fuel; Palestine is lacking in forests, so that fuel is scarce (cf. Matt. 6.30).[81] On the application of the parable vv. 36–43 see above, pp. 81 ff.

In order to understand the parable of the Seine-net (Matt. 13.47 f.) it is essential to recognize that we have here another of the parables with a datival introduction (l·); the Kingdom of God is therefore not compared to a net, which catches good and bad fish and preserves them, but the opening formula (v. 47) must be translated: 'It is the case with the coming of the Kingdom of God'—to wit, as with the sorting out of the fish.[82] Σαγήνη is the seine-net, which is either dragged between two boats, or is laid out by a single boat and drawn to land with long ropes.[83] Ἐκ παντὸς γένους merely explains the necessity for the selection described in v. 48; the net contained fish 'of every kind', eatable and uneatable (hence there is no allegorical reference to the Gentile mission). In the lake of

[75] N. A. Dahl in *Studia Theologica*, 5 (1951), p. 151.
[76] Numerous examples based on observations in Palestine and statements by Palestinian experts are given in Sprenger, 'Jesu Säe- und Erntegleichnisse', in *Palästina-Jahrbuch*, 9 (1913), p. 92, and in Dalman, op. cit., pp. 324 f.
[77] Sprenger, ibid.
[78] It also happens in Palestine, cf. Dalman, ibid., p. 325 and p. 250.
[79] W. Michaelis, *Die Gleichnisse Jesu*, Hamburg, 1956, p. 43.
[80] Dalman, ibid., pp. 324–6.
[81] The grain is used as chicken-feed (Dalman, op. cit., pp. 250, 325).
[82] See p. 102.
[83] G. Dalman, *Orte und Wege Jesu*₃, Gütersloh, 1924, p. 145.

Gennesaret twenty-four different species of fish have been counted.[84]
V. 48: Τὰ σαπρά are (a) unclean fish (Lev. 11.10 f.: all fish without
scales such as the barbūṭ (clarias' macracanthus), which has almost the
appearance of a snake (cf. Matt. 7.10; Luke 11.11), and all fish
without fins); and (b) non-edible marine creatures, such as crabs,
which were regarded as worthless.[85] Ἔξω ἔβαλον does not necessarily
mean that they threw the useless fish back into the sea, but only in
contrast to εἰς τὰ ἄγγη, that they threw them away.[86] For the
interpretation of vv. 49 f. see p. 85.

Both parables are eschatological in character, since both are concerned with the Final Judgement which ushers in the Kingdom of
God; it is compared to a separation: in the former parable between
wheat and weeds, and in the latter between eatable and useless fish.
Prior to the separation, good and bad are mixed. In the parable of
the Tares, the idea of a premature separation is expressly rejected,
and patience until the harvest is enjoined. Why is such patience
necessary? Jesus gives two reasons. First, men are not capable of
carrying out the separation effectively (Matt. 13.29). As, in the early
stages of growth, darnel and wheat resemble each other, so are the
people of God to the hidden Messiah concealed among the false
believers. Men cannot discern the heart; if they attempt to make an
effective separation, they will inevitably commit errors of judgement
and root up good wheat with the tares.[87] Secondly, and more important, God has fixed the moment of separation. The measure of
time assigned by him must be fulfilled (Matt. 13.48: ἐπληρώθη),[88]
the seed must be allowed to ripen. Then comes the end,[89] and
with it the separation between tares and wheat, the sorting out of the
fish, with the dividing of good fish from bad. Then, no longer in a
servant's form, will the holy community of God, purged from all
evil men, from false believers, and from feigned confessors, be revealed at last. But that moment has not yet arrived. The last opportunity for repentance has not yet run out (Luke 13.6-9). Till then,

[84] G. Dalman, Arbeit und Sitte, VI, Gütersloh, 1939, p. 351 (acc. to Boden-
heimer).
[85] B. T. D. Smith, p. 201; A. M. Brouwer, De Gelijkenissen, Leiden, 1946, p. 154;
K.-E. Wilken, Biblisches Erleben im Heiligen Land, I, Lahr-Dinglingen, 1953,
pp. 127 f.
[86] W. Michaelis, Die Gleichnisse Jesu, Hamburg, 1956, p. 68, n. 30.
[87] Cf. I Cor. 4.5: 'Judge nothing before the time.'
[88] On the conception of the eschatological measure, see p. 152, n. 92.
[89] See pp. 118 f.

all false zeal must be checked, the field must be left to ripen in patience, the net must be cast widely, and everything else left to God in faith, until his hour comes.[90]

10. PARABOLIC ACTIONS

This aspect of our subject can only be treated briefly here by way of an appendix. Jesus did not confine himself to spoken parables, but also performed parabolic actions.[91] His most significant parabolic action was his extension of hospitality to the outcasts (Luke 19.5 f.) and their reception into his house (Luke 15.1–2)[92] and even into the circle of his disciples (Mark 2.14 par.; Matt. 10.3). These feasts for publicans are prophetic signs, more significant than words, silent proclamations that the Messianic Age is here, the Age of forgiveness.[93] On the night before his death he took the opportunity of the common meal to perform the last symbolic act of his life, by offering to his own a share in the atoning efficacy of the death that awaited him.[94] Jesus found ever new ways of proclaiming by his acts the advent of the Messianic Age: by the healings, by the rejection of fasting (Mark 2.19 f. par.), by bestowing on Simon bar Jona the new name of *Kepha*, thus designating him as the foundation stone of the eschatological Temple of God, of which the building had now begun (Matt. 16.17 f.). He expressed his sovereignty as Lord of the eschatological people of God (including the nine and a half lost tribes)[95] in the symbolic number of his disciples; he gave symbolic expression to his royal authority by his kingly entry into Jerusalem

[90] This attitude of Jesus is firmly embedded in the tradition. He repeatedly emphasizes the warning that the company of the disciples is not a purified community, and that at the end their ranks must undergo the process of separation (Matt. 7.21–23, 24–27; 22.11–14). He also summons to patience (Mark 4.26–29).

[91] G. Stählin, 'Die Gleichnishandlungen Jesu' in *Kosmos und Ekklesia, Festschrift für W. Stählin*, Kassel, 1953, pp. 9–22, traces out the sources and meaning of the symbolic actions of Jesus.

[92] Reception into Jesus' house is probably also the original meaning in Mark 2.15; the verse is linked to the preceding by a catch-word connection (the word τελώνης), and hence may originally have introduced an independent story. Moreover, if the αὐτόν (2.15) relates to Levi the publican, the name of Jesus would have been clumsily added in v. 15b (E. Lohmeyer, *Das Evangelium des Markus*, Göttingen, 1937, p. 55).

[93] J. Schniewind in *Das Neue Testament Deutsch*, I, on Mark 2.5.

[94] J. Jeremias, *The Eucharistic Words of Jesus*₂, London, 1966, pp. 231 ff., 261.

[95] Cf. Jeremias, *Jesus' Promise to the Nations*₂, London, 1967, p. 21.

and his cleansing of the Temple, both of which acts are inseparably connected as a symbol of the coming of the New Age;[96] he symbolized the peaceful purpose of his mission by his choice of an ass on which to make his entry (cf. Zech. 9.9). He rebuked his ambitious disciples by setting a child in their midst;[97] he washed their feet as an example of the love that stooped to serve (John 13.1 ff.). If we may assume that the *pericope de adultera* ([John] 7.53 ff.)[98] rests on early tradition, then the writing in the sand is another example of parabolic action; it would have reminded her accusers, without openly putting them to shame, of the scripture which said: 'They that depart from me shall be written in the earth' (Jer. 17.13),[99] and his action would have said to them, 'You are those of whom that scripture speaks'—a silent call to repentance.[1] The weeping of Jesus over Jerusalem can also be included among the symbolic actions, as a prophetic demonstration of sorrow over its approaching fate.[2] 'The overwhelming number of Jesus' symbolic actions serve to proclaim the fulfilment of the ἔσχατα.'[3] The Messianic Age has arrived. That means that the symbolic actions

---

[96] Numerous examples in *Jesus als Weltvollender*, Gütersloh, 1930, p. 35 ff. Matthew (21.12 ff.) and Luke (19.45 ff.) are therefore correct in placing the cleansing of the Temple immediately after the entry, cf. *The Eucharistic Words of Jesus*, London, 1966, ch. II.

[97] M. Black, *An Aramaic Approach to the Gospels and Acts*₃, Oxford, 1967, pp. 218–22, has convincingly proved that the key to Mark 9.33–36 lies in the ambiguity of the word *ṭalja*. Jesus teaches the ambitious disciples that he who wishes to be the greatest must become like a *ṭalja* (διάκονος), and adds to the parabolic saying a symbolic action by setting before the disciples a *ṭalja* (παιδίον, *servulus*).

[98] On this pericope cf. J. Jeremias in *ZNW*, 43 (1950–51), pp. 148 f. (the scene does not take place on the way to the court, but after leaving it); J. Blinzler in *NTS*, 4 (1957–58), pp. 32–47 (probably it is not, as has often been assumed, a question of a betrothed maiden, but of an espoused wife).

[99] R. Eisler in *ZNW*, 22 (1923), pp. 306 f.

[1] The writing of the name in the sand so that the wind may carry it away indicates a warning and a threat of destruction. Another interpretation of the writing in the sand is that Jesus was acting like a Roman judge who wrote down his sentence before reading it out. Jesus' sentence was—Acquittal (T. W. Manson in *ZNW*, 44 (1952–3), pp. 255 f.).

[2] W. Salm, *Beiträge zur Gleichnisforschung*, Diss., Göttingen, 1953, p. 93. It is questionable whether the cursing of the fig-tree should be considered in this context. H. W. Bartsch, 'Die "Verfluchung" des Feigenbaumes', in *ZNW*, 53 (1962), pp. 256–60, plausibly argued that Mark 11.14 par. Matt. 21.19b was originally an eschatological saying illustrating the nearness of the end. 'Nobody will eat of your fruit.' The erroneous rendering of an Aramaic imperfect by an optative (Mark 11.14), he thinks, then caused the saying to be interpreted as a curse and combined with an appropriate setting.

[3] Stählin, op. cit., p. 20.

are kerygmatic actions; they show that Jesus not only proclaimed the message of the parables, but that he lived it and embodied it in his own person. 'Jesus not only utters the message of the Kingdom of God, he himself is the message.' [4]

[4] C. Maurer, *Judaica*, 4 (1948), p. 147.

IV

CONCLUSION

IN ATTEMPTING TO recover the original significance of the parables, one thing above all becomes evident: it is that all the parables of Jesus compel his hearers to come to a decision about his person and mission.[1] For they are all full of 'the secret of the Kingdom of God' (Mark 4.11),[2] that is to say, the recognition of 'an eschatology that is in process of realization.'[3] The hour of fulfilment is come, that is the urgent note that sounds through them all. The strong man is disarmed, the forces of evil are in retreat, the physician comes to the sick, the lepers are cleansed, the great debt is wiped out, the lost sheep is brought home, the door of the father's house stands open, the poor and the beggars are summoned to the banquet, a master whose kindness is undeserved pays his wages in full, a great joy fills all hearts. God's acceptable year has come. For he has been manifested whose veiled glory shines through every word and through every parable—the Saviour.

[1] E. Fuchs, 'Bemerkungen zur Gleichnisauslegung' in *ThLZ*, 79 (1954), col. 345–8, emphasizes the point that the parables imply a christological self-attestation. When a parable depicts the goodness of God, that goodness is actualized in Jesus. When a parable speaks about the Kingdom, Jesus 'hides himself' behind the word Kingdom as its 'secret content'. I can only agree whole-heartedly with the decisive way in which Fuchs finds in the parables the veiled christological self-attestation of the historical Jesus.

[2] See pp. 13–18, further E. Hoskyns and R. N. Davey, *The Riddle of the New Testament*, London, 1931, pp. 126–35.

[3] Dodd, on p. 198, as a result of his general survey (see above, p. 21), speaks of 'realized eschatology'. The above form of expression (in German: 'sich realisierende Eschatologie') was communicated to me by Ernst Haenchen in a letter. C. H. Dodd has, to my joy, agreed with it (*The Interpretation of the Fourth Gospel*, Cambridge, 1953, p. 447, n. 1).

INDEX OF AUTHORS

INDEX OF BIBLICAL AND APOCRYPHAL PASSAGES

INDEX OF SYNOPTIC PARABLES

(main references only, metaphors and similes excluded)

* = literal quotation of the version of the Gospel of Thomas